The Mercenary Mediterranean

The Mercenary Mediterranean

Sovereignty, Religion, and Violence in the Medieval Crown of Aragon

HUSSEIN FANCY

THE UNIVERSITY OF CHICAGO PRESS   CHICAGO AND LONDON

HUSSEIN FANCY is assistant professor of history at the University of Michigan, Ann Arbor.

The University of Chicago Press, Chicago 60637
The University of Chicago Press, Ltd., London

Printed in the United States of America
25 24 23 22 21 20 19 18 17 16 1 2 3 4 5

ISBN-13: 978-0-226-32964-2 (cloth)
ISBN-13: 978-0-226-32978-9 (e-book)
DOI: 10.7208/chicago/9780226329789.001.0001

The University of Chicago Press gratefully acknowledges the generous support of the University of Michigan toward the publication of this book.

Library of Congress Cataloging-in-Publication Data

Fancy, Hussein Anwar, 1974– author.
The mercenary Mediterranean : sovereignty, religion, and violence in the medieval crown of Aragon / Hussein Fancy.
pages : illustrations, maps ; cm
Includes bibliographical references and index.
ISBN 978-0-226-32964-2 (cloth : alk. paper) — ISBN 978-0-226-32978-9 (e-book)
1. Soldiers of fortune—Spain—Aragon—History—13th century. 2. Soldiers of fortune—Spain—Aragon—History—14th century. 3. Foreign enlistment—Spain—Aragon—History. 4. Mudéjares—Spain—Aragon—History. 5. Muslims—Spain—Aragon—History—13th century. 6. Muslims—Spain—Aragon—History—14th century. 7. Muslims—Africa, North—History—13th century. 8. Muslims—Africa, North—History—14th century. 9. Aragon (Spain)—History, Military—13th century. 10. Aragon (Spain)—History, Military—14th century. I. Title.
DP302.A7F36 2016
355.3'540946550902—dc23

2015028774

♾ This paper meets the requirements of ANSI/NISO Z39.48-1992 (Permanence of Paper).

For J and z

ginete, *n*. Diego de Urrea dize que ginete, se pudo dezir de Cinete, que en terminacion Arabiga, es Cinetum, y sinífica ornamento del verbo Ceyene, hermosear, o ser hermoso, por la gallardia de los ginetes quando salen de fiesta con sus turbantes y plumas, sus marlotas, y borceguíes, y los jaezes de los cavallos ricos.

[Diego de Urrea said that *ginete* could have come from *Cinete*, which in Arabic is *Cinetum*, and means ornament, from the verb, *Ceyene*, to embellish, or to be beautiful, on account of the gallantry of the *ginetes* when they parade in celebrations with their turbans and feathers, their adorned boots, their robes and the trappings of sumptuous horses.]

SEBASTIÁN DE COVARRUBIAS, *Tesoro de la lengua castellana o española* (1611)

Contents

Illustrations

MAPS

FIGURES

TABLE

Acknowledgments

In the course of researching and writing this book, I have accrued more debts than I can repay or keep account of. First of all, I would like to thank my teachers. Without their guidance and generosity, I would have had neither the confidence nor the courage to follow this path. The inspiring María Rosa Menocal first introduced me to medieval Iberia as an undergraduate. She remained a friend and mentor long after. William Chester Jordan and Michael Cook not only introduced me to the study of medieval Europe and the Islamic world but also modeled a standard of scholarly rigor and intellectual honesty to which I continue to aspire.

I conducted the research for this book over the course of four years in Spain and North Africa. Brian Catlos accompanied me on my first day of research in Barcelona and gave me my first "taste of the archive." In person and on paper, he taught me how to navigate and think about these historical records. Ramón Pujades and Jaume Riera shared their archival expertise on numerous occasions. A paleography seminar in Cairo with Emad Abou Ghazi was extremely valuable. Ana Echevarría and Maribel Fierro read, commented on, and provided invaluable suggestions on early drafts of this manuscript. I also deeply appreciated conversations with and advice from María Teresa Ferrer i Mallol, Mercedes García-Arenal, Linda Gale Jones, Tomàs de Montagut, Lawrence Mott, Vincens Pons, Cristina de la Puente, Roser Salicrú, Delfina Serrano, and Max Turull. I would like to thank Gerard Wiegers, P. S. van Koningsveld, and Umar Ryad for sharing a copy of an unpublished manuscript from North Africa with me. I would also like to extend my thanks to the patient and gracious staff at the Arxiu de la Corona d'Aragó, Arxiu Capitular de la Catedral de Valencia, Archivo del Reino de Valencia, Archivo Histórico Nacional, Biblioteca Nacional de España, Real Biblioteca del Monasterio de San Lorenzo de El Escorial, British Library, Beinecke Rare Book and Manuscript Library, al-Maktaba al-Waṭaniyya al-Tūnisiyya, al-Maktaba al-Waṭaniyya li'l-Mamlaka al-Maghribiyya, Qarawīyīn Library, and Dār al-Kutub al-Miṣriyya.

At the University of Michigan, I found a community of extraordinary, warm, and welcoming scholars across disciplines. The argument and shape of this book developed first at the Michigan Society of Fellows, where I had the good fortune to share work with Donald Lopez, Deirdre de la Cruz, Miranda Johnson, Jeremy Mumford, Benjamin Paloff, and Christopher Skeaff, among many others. Tomoko Masuzawa and Paul Johnson led an inspiring faculty seminar on religion and the secular. Valerie Kivelson and Paolo Squatriti read the whole manuscript multiple times and at various stages. They saw me through the woods. Kathryn Babayan, Katherine French, Enrique García Santo-Tomás, Gottfried Hagen, and Rebecca Scott provided detailed and valuable comments and corrections. Stephen Berrey and Elise Lipkowitz were unflagging in their support. Saeed Al Alaslaa and John Posch provided assistance with copy editing. I also benefited from rich and enthusiastic conversations with Michael Bonner, Howard Brick, Pär Cassel, Sueann Caufield, Juan Cole, Alison Cornish, Will Glover, Mayte Green, George Hoffman, Diane Owen Hughes, Sue Juster, Webb Keane, Victor Lieberman, Rudi Lindner, Karla Mallette, Peggy McCracken, Farina Mir, Ian Moyer, Christian de Pee, Helmut Puff, Cathy Sanok, Jean-Frédéric Schaub, Lee Schlesinger, Scott Spector, Andrew Shryock, Ryan Szpiech, and Butch Ware.

I am also indebted to numerous other colleagues who read and commented on this work. David Nirenberg has been a constant source of encouragement and intellectual inspiration. Thomas Burman, Olivia Remie Constable, Adnan Husain, and Teofilo Ruiz read and provided detailed responses that fundamentally shifted this work. Many others commented, shared ideas, and gave encouragement: David Abulafia, Fred Astren, Abigail Krasner Balbale, Simon Barton, Adam Beaver, Stephen Bensch, Amira Bennison, Ross Brann, Sonja Brentjes, Philippe Buc, Richard Bulliet, Andrew Devreaux, Nahyan Fancy, Paul Freedman, Camilo Gómez-Rivas, Jocelyn Hendrickson, Daniel Hershenzon, Peregrine Horden, Nikolas Jaspert, Nancy Khalek, Sharon Kinoshita, Tamer El-Leithy, Anne Lester, Yuen-Gen Liang, Christopher MacEvitt, Kathryn Miller, Mark Pegg, Jonathan Ray, Jürgen Renn, Jarbel Rodriguez, Marina Rustow, Jonathan Sheehan, Daniel Smail, Gabrielle Spiegel, Justin Stearns, Devin Stewart, Sarah Stroumsa, Francesca Trivellato, and Kenneth Baxter Wolff.

I am grateful to Randy Petilos and Michael Koplow at the University of Chicago Press and for the incisive comments of the anonymous readers. I wish also to thank the Social Science Research Council, Fulbright-Hays Program, Medieval Academy of America, Program for Cultural Cooperation with Spain's Ministry of Culture, Charlotte Newcombe Foundation, Harry Frank Guggenheim Foundation, the National Endowment for the Humanities, Carnegie Scholars Program, and American Council of Learned Societies for their generous support for the research and writing of this book.

I am grateful for my wonderful family, scattered in New England, New York, England, and Pakistan. I owe my deepest debt to Jane Lynch, who endured countless conversations about medieval kingship, law, and theology and still wanted to read and did read every word of this book with care and love. Jane, this book is for you, just as it would not be but for you.

On Names, Places, Dates, and Transcriptions

Although they used both Catalan and Aragonese spellings for their names, throughout this book, I refer to and number the kings of the Crown of Aragon according to the Catalan tradition, e.g., Pere II rather than Pedro III, to avoid confusion with the names of the Castilian kings. Similarly, for the sake of simplicity, place names of towns are rendered according to the standard modern forms. Countries and regions are given in their modern English usage.

Records from the chancery registers of the Archive of the Crown of Aragon are dated according the Incarnation calendar. I have regularized these dates to the Common Era calendar. In the case that the year remains ambiguous, I have noted the less likely date in brackets, e.g., 1283 [1284]. Similarly, dates according to the Islamic calendar have been converted to the Common Era calendar. In notes, both Islamic and Common Era dates are given when relevant, e.g., 681/1283.

All Arabic, Latin, and Romance documents were consulted directly, and all transcriptions are my own unless otherwise specified. Wherever possible, I have tried to acknowledge existing transcriptions or editions of documents, particularly when they led me to additional sources. In transcribing Latin, Catalan, Castilian, and Aragonese, the original capitalization, spelling, and punctuation have been preserved. Ligatures and macrons have been silently expanded. The transliteration of Arabic follows the standards of the *International Journal of Middle Eastern Studies.* The following notations are used: [. . .] = illegible; <text> = uncertain reading; [text] = interpolation; \text/ = superscript; /text\ = subscript; //text// = redacted. In the case of illegible text, the periods indicate the estimated number of illegible characters.

INTRODUCTION

A Mercenary Logic

A handful of documents, scattered about the chancery registers of the Archive of the Crown of Aragon, tell of a remarkable journey: Sometime around April 1285, five Muslim horsemen crossed from the Islamic kingdom of Granada into the realms of the Christian Crown of Aragon. Their arrival should have raised an alarm. Bands of Muslim cavalry—whom the Aragonese called *jenets*—crossed this frontier in times of war and peace, wreaking havoc.[1] Their incursions were violent and swift. Raiders would arrive suddenly, driving panicked villagers into town walls, ransacking homes, taking captives for ransom, and burning fields. For two decades, these same soldiers had supported massive rebellions among the Crown's Muslim population—the Mudéjares.[2] On this occasion, however, they did not inspire terror. The five *jenets*—famous for their prowess on horses—rode mules that they had borrowed from a Jew in Granada. When they reached the border of Valencia, they produced letters of safe conduct, Latin documents coupled with Arabic translations that they presented to local officials, who then seized their swords, making them the least likely of marauders.[3]

Riding mules, unarmed, and from here confined to public roads, the *jenets* found themselves under the laws of the Crown of Aragon and the watchful eyes of royal officials, but they carried on, riding northeast (map 1).[4] The soldiers next appeared in the city of Valencia, where they met with the local Mudéjar leader who had facilitated their recruitment.[5] Some days after, the *jenets* stayed in the town of Vilafranca, north of Valencia, where a local Christian official would later write a letter to the king, grumbling that these Muslim travelers had borrowed fifteen *solidi* from him and failed to settle their tabs before leaving town, an incident that foreshadowed many more moments of tension to come.[6] Finally, they arrived at the base of the Pyrenees, at a mountain pass called Coll de

Panissars near the border with France. These five horsemen had traveled some two hundred miles, tracing the hypotenuse of the realms of the Crown of Aragon. But where were they going, and why? A few lines, haphazardly copied by a royal scribe into the chancery registers, tell us that the *jenets* were given an audience with the Aragonese king, Pere II (r. 1276–1285). They record that Pere showered these soldiers with gifts, including sumptuous cloth and decorative saddles. What inspired this gift giving? In his own words, in a letter addressed to his ambassador in Granada, King Pere explained that these *jenets*—representatives of a captain named "Çahim Abennaquem"—had agreed to enter the Crown's service.

Aragon	Castile	Naṣrids	Marīnids	Ḥafṣids	‘Abd al-Wādids
Jaume I (1213–76)	Ferdinand III (1217–52)	Muḥammad I (1232–73)		Abū Zakariyyā’ (1229–49)	Abū Yaḥyā, Yaghmurāsan (1236–8)
Pere II (1276–85)	Alfonso X (1252–84)	Muḥammad II (1273–1302)	Abū Yūsuf (1258–86)	al-Mustanṣir (1249–77) al-Wāthiq (1277–79) Abū Isḥāq (1279–83)	
Alfons II (1285–91) Jaume II (1291–1327)	Sancho IV (1284–95) Ferdinand IV (1295–1312)		Abū Ya‘qūb (1286–1307)	interregnum Abū Ḥafṣ (1284–95) Abū ‘Aṣīda (1295–1309)	Abū Sa‘īd, ‘Uthmān b. Yaghmurāsan (1283–1304)
		Muḥammad III (1302–9)	Abū Thābit (1307–8)		Abū Zayyān (1304–8)
		Naṣr (1309–14)	Abū’l-Rabī‘ (1308–10)	interregnum	Abū Ḥammū (1308–18)
	Alfonso XI (1312–50)	Ismā‘īl I (1314–25) Muḥammad IV (1325–33)	Abu Sa‘īd (1310–31)	Abū Yaḥyā al-Liḥyānī (1311–17)	Abū Tāshufīn (1318–3)
Alfons III (1327–36)		Yūsuf I (1333–54)	Abū al-Ḥasan (1331–48)		
Pere III (1336–87)	Pedro I (1350–69)	Muḥammad V (1354–59; 1362–91) interregnum Muḥammad V (1354–59; 1362–91)			

1. The Crown of Aragon (ca. 1300). Courtesy Dick Gilbreath, Gyula Pauer Center for Cartography and GIS, University of Kentucky.

It is the nature of archival research, however, that one can follow a narrative thread like this, stitched across several folios, and at the next turn of the page find it abruptly and agonizingly cut. From here, the registers reveal nothing more about the five *jenets* riding mules.

An Inner Solidarity

These were not the first or only *jenets*.

Over the course of the late thirteenth and fourteenth centuries—as they subdued, expelled, and enslaved Muslim populations—the Christian kings of the Crown of Aragon recruited thousands of foreign Muslim soldiers from al-Andalus (Muslim Iberia) and North Africa.[7] Across hundreds of Latin, Romance, and Arabic accounts, letters, court cases, spy reports, and diplomatic agreements, the *jenets* appear in far-flung battlefields across the Mediterranean as well as in the royal court, where they served as members of the king's entourage, his bodyguards, his diplomats, and even his entertainment. Put simply, this book seeks to explain how and why the Christian Aragonese kings and Muslim *jenets* came into an alliance with one another. It uses their relationship not only to offer a novel perspective on interactions between Muslims and Christians in the Middle Ages but also to rethink the study of religion more broadly.

The *jenets* immediately provoke the kinds of questions that have consumed scholarship on medieval Iberia since the nineteenth century: Was this a world of religious boundaries or democratic frontiers? When and how did religion shape or limit interaction? When did it lead to violence? These types of questions attempt to locate religion within complex interaction, to discover when and why it mattered. They have been and remain anxious questions because they were and are inextricable from contemporary concerns about the relationship of religion to politics and the sources of religious violence. This book argues that they are also the wrong kinds of questions because they already hold their own answers.

Despite an abundance of surviving records and the provocative questions that they elicit, the *jenets* have received surprisingly scant scholarly attention. They are absent from general histories of medieval Iberia.[8] And in the handful of previous studies of these soldiers, there has been no agreement about who they even were.[9] Why the *jenets* have been more or less ignored is inextricable from how historians have approached them—or indeed, parallel figures such as Christian soldiers in the service of medieval Muslim rulers.[10] Particular methodological and philosophical assumptions have contributed to the marginalization and misunderstanding of these men.

With respect to methodology, although these Muslim and Christian soldiers crossed political and linguistic boundaries, scholars have hesitated to do the same. Earlier studies of these soldiers have employed either Latin and Romance sources, focusing on Christian Iberia, or Arabic sources, focusing on al-Andalus and North Africa. The result is that significant connections and continuities have fallen into the divide. This scholarly dyspraxia, as if the right and left hands are ignorant of one another, has only reinforced the artificial divisions between the study of Christianity and that of Islam.[11] In this respect, recent efforts within Mediterranean studies to overcome such divisions are welcome. A new generation of scholars has profitably combined the study of Latin, Romance, Arabic, and Hebrew texts in order to reveal new histories and overturn old biases.

With respect to philosophy, over the past century, across deeply opposing methods, there has also been a surprising consensus about the motivations of these boundary-crossing soldiers. For Spanish liberals, writing in the early twentieth century, these Christian and Muslim soldiers were heroes who had cast off the chains of religious delusion. For their Catholic, conservative opponents, these soldiers were traitors who had undermined Spain's essential religious and national spirit. These opposing positions were part and parcel of the bitter "convivencia" debates.[12] Superficially, these were historical debates about the coexistence of Christians, Muslims, and Jews in medieval Iberia, but more fundamentally, they were moral disputes about the value of tolerance in modern Spain. More recent and far more temperate cultural historians have sought to distance themselves from and circumvent these earlier polemics. Instead, they have seen these soldiers as evidence for the essential malleability of religious identities. Nevertheless, these different paths have led all these scholars to much the same outlook. All have seen these soldiers as driven by secular rather than religious motivations, by rational self-interest rather than abstract belief—in short, by a rather mercenary logic.

This conclusion is not a coincidence. It has not persisted because it is empirically correct, but, rather, it points to an inner solidarity between these seemingly opposed approaches: a shared secular bias. By secularism, I mean not the liberal doctrine but more fundamentally the assumption that religion and politics are distinct, separate, and competing forces.[13] To put this differently, secularism is not an intellectual position but rather an intellectual background that underwrites certain self-satisfying accounts of history.[14] Through this bias, the cultural history of religious interaction remains unwittingly bound to the very polemics it hopes to overcome.[15] It remains bound to the value of tolerance. Across this book and particularly, in the epilogue, I discuss the nature and consequences of this implicit secularism, but for the moment, my point is simply this: Why could religious beliefs not have motivated the *jenets*? The preemptory exclusion of religion represents a significant analytical foreclosure.

If we can only imagine the *jenets* as motivated by politics as opposed to religion, then perhaps, our understanding of "politics" and "religion" needs some adjustment. In the late medieval Mediterranean, multiple

[margin: law + theology → divine + human authority]

conceptions of the relationship between divine and human authority, between theology and law, circulated within and across Christian and Islamic contexts. As the case of the *jenets* will demonstrate, these ideas overlapped to such a degree that to say Christians and Muslims met in the medieval Mediterranean begs the question. Christianity and Islam were already inextricably intertwined there. Abandoning stable conceptions of politics and religion does not mean casting one's hands up in surrender, collapsing into relativism or confusion. Instead, it enables and has enabled more capacious and faithful versions of analysis.[16] When we remove these tired lenses, the history of the *jenets* comes into focus.

[margin: Blurring Boundaries of politics + religion as stable/fixed]

Imperial Desire

[margin: Crown of A centralized confederation]

The dynastic union between the counts of Barcelona and the kings of Aragon in the twelfth century began the process of transforming a loose assemblage of archaic counties and administrative units into the centralized confederation that would eventually be called the Crown of Aragon and become a Mediterranean empire (map 2). The medieval kingdoms of Aragon and Catalonia occupied the diverse terrain of northeastern Iberia, extending from the high Pyrenees southward to fertile Ebro Valley in Aragon and the coast of Catalonia. From these shores, a thriving merchant class shipped wine, wood, wool, and other wares across the middle sea. Taking advantage of their economic and demographic strength, as well as the political disorder in al-Andalus, the first "count-kings" pushed their borders southward and aggressively settled new lands. Their efforts at unifying these disparate realms, however, were less than successful. In promulgating a new law code, the *Usatges of Barcelona*, Ramon Berenguer IV (r. 1131–1162) spoke of himself in Roman imperial terms, as "Prince (*princeps*)," and claimed for himself absolute jurisdiction. Such grandiose rhetoric provoked tensions both at home and abroad, tensions that foreshadowed the events of the following century. On the one hand, these kings faced resistance from powerful Aragonese and Catalan noblemen. As they would when later confronting the alliance of the Crown with the *jenets* in the thirteenth and fourteenth centuries, these noblemen blended complaints of overreaching royal authority with accusations of Islamophilia (and indeed, of Philo-Judaism).[17] On the other hand, this magniloquence heightened competition with the French and Castilian kings. In a subtle but telling indicator of an emerging anti-Frankish sentiment, after 1180, the Aragonese began to date their charters according to the

[margin: thriving merchant class]

[margin: political disorder in A]

[margin: unification unsuccessful]

[margin: count kings/ Roman Empire terms]

[margin: tensions]

[margin: resistance from Nobles]

[margin: complaints of Islamophobia]

[margin: Anti-Frankish Sentiment 1180]

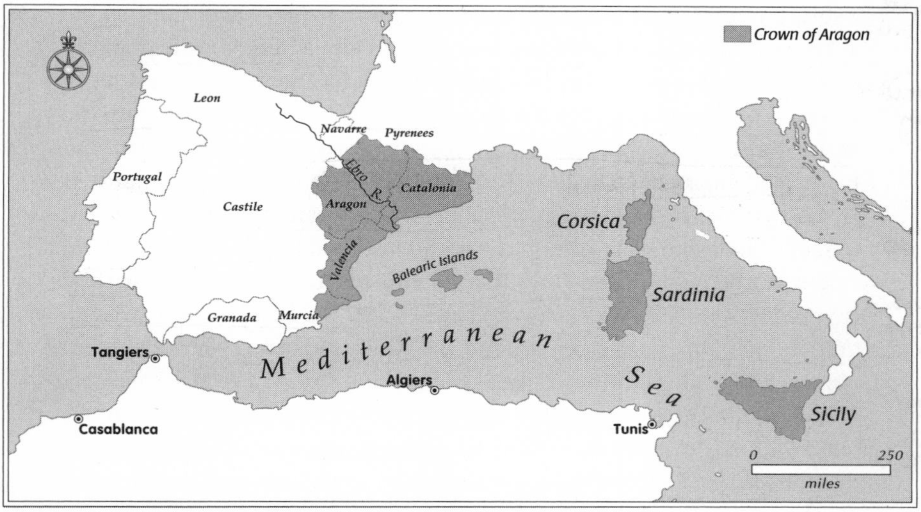

2. The Aragonese Empire (ca. 1300). Courtesy Dick Gilbreath, Gyula Pauer Center for Cartography and GIS, University of Kentucky. *Mediterranean Empire*

year of the incarnation rather than the regnal year of France. More than by ambition, however, the Aragonese kings survived this early period *personal loyalty* through bonds of personal loyalty.[18]

The vague imperial aspirations of the twelfth-century Aragonese kings *Imperial aspirations* found their concrete manifestation in the thirteenth century. The decisive turning point came with the reign of King Jaume I (r. 1213–1276). Over the course of four decades, Jaume managed to double the size of his king- *James I increased* doms, expanding further southward and into the sea. His conquests began *Empire → more* in the Balearic Islands, where he seized Mallorca and Ibiza in the 1230s, *Medit. Crown* thus bringing the Crown of Aragon further into the Mediterranean. In 1238, Jaume conquered Islamic Valencia, a fertile agriculture plain *1238 Valencia* shielded by mountains. This sudden expansion presented new challenges. For instance, it brought large Muslim and Arabic-speaking communities *Muslim comm* under the control of the Crown of Aragon. In Valencia, the subject Mus- *Crown of Aragon* lim population, the Mudéjares, far outnumbered Christians, a fact that *mudejars out number +* has made this kingdom the subject of intense interest for scholars of re- ligious interaction. Attempts to pacify these Muslim communities would *Political experimentatio* continue for centuries. But these new conquests also offered an opportu- nity for political experimentation, inspired not only by the earlier *Usatges* *revival of Romanist legal tradition* but also by the revival of Romanist legal traditions across Europe in this period. In parallel with French and Castilian kings, Jaume implemented

religious interaction

a series of legal, fiscal, and administrative reforms that imagined the king as the ultimate source of the law and granted him a decisionistic power.[19]

Although this process of bureaucratization has been seen as evidence of secularization—of the turning away from theological and charismatic and toward legal and rational justifications for power—for Jaume and his immediate successors, Pere II, Alfons II (r. 1285–1291), and Jaume II (r. 1291–1327), these reforms were understood differently.[20] They reflected a deeper and enduring effort to cast themselves as divinely authorized rulers, as the heirs of the Holy Roman emperors, above all Frederick II (r. 1220–1250). Frederick, in turn, had drawn influence from Christian and Islamic imperial courts around the Mediterranean. Thus, the Aragonese kings adopted the trappings and traditions of Frederick's court, including his employment of a Muslim royal guard. The *jenets*, in other words, were a central part of this imperial posture and performance of divinely inspired authority.

The Aragonese kings' ambition to style themselves as Holy Roman emperors also materialized in the decision to capture the island kingdom of Sicily in 1285, the seat of Frederick's court, thereby gaining control over much of the central and western Mediterranean. Over the following century, Sardinia and Corsica were also brought under their sway. The Crown of Aragon thus became a Mediterranean empire.

While the chronicler Ramon Muntaner (d. 1336) considered the Aragonese kings "sovereigns (*sobirans*) over all the kings of the world and princes, whether of Christians or Saracens," I employ the term "sovereignty" to describe their *aspirations* to supremacy, underscored because these aspirations were challenged on every side.[21] The claim to sovereignty and unimpeded authority not only obscured an irreducible context of competition but also the very practice of Aragonese royal power. For example, the Aragonese conquest of Sicily led to two centuries of furious struggle with the Angevins, what David Abulafia has felicitously called the "Two Hundred Years' War."[22] The authoritarian impulses of the Aragonese also drew the ire of the popes as well as of the French and Castilian kings, who considered themselves more worthy of the imperial title. These aspirations brought Pere II into open war with France and Castile, and, later, they would bring Pere III (r. 1336–1387) into a protracted and debilitating conflict with Castile, the so-called "War of the Two Peters" (1356–1375). As in the twelfth century, Aragonese and Catalan noblemen rose to challenge their kings in the thirteenth and fourteenth centuries. In 1283, 1286, 1301, and 1347 confederations of noblemen and municipalities, called *Unions*, revolted in order to assert their customary rights against the Aragonese kings' claims to supreme authority, forcing these kings repeatedly to capitulate, to surrender their sovereignty. These internal and external conflicts over the expansion of Aragonese royal power form the broader context for the alliance between the Crown of Aragon and the Muslim *jenets*. From the reign of Pere II to that of Pere III, across a century, every Aragonese ruler employed *jenets* in his courts and armies, in battles against external and internal enemies, against the French, the Castilians, and the *Unions*.

Who were these soldiers and where did they come from? The evidence for the *jenets* comes principally from the chancery registers in the Archive of the Crown of Aragon. These documents are summaries of royal correspondence and orders, a product of the administrative reforms begun by King Jaume I. The registers place two major obstacles before any study of the *jenets*. First, these mostly uncatalogued records constitute one of the largest medieval archives in the world. For the reign of King Alfons III (r. 1327–1336) alone, there are 1,240 registers, each holding thousands of documents. Second, beyond the overwhelming quantity of documentation, the nature of the evidence concerning the *jenets* is partial and fragmentary. Across hundreds of pay registers, dispatch and requisition orders, letters, reports, and court cases that refer to *jenets*, the royal officials of the Crown of Aragon say little to nothing about the origin or organization of these soldiers.

A full account of the Crown of Aragon's relationship with the *jenets* therefore demands a different approach, a view from the south. If imperial desires drew the Aragonese kings into the Mediterranean, then they also drew them into the affairs of North Africa. Thus, we need to tell the story again, beginning on the other side of the sea. In the same period that the Aragonese kings were consolidating their authority over the territories of northeastern Spain, North Africa and al-Andalus underwent radical transformation as a result of the collapse of the Almohad Caliphate (1121–1269) (map 3).

Sometime after 1120, the Berber religious scholar Ibn Tūmart (ca. 1080–1130) claimed for himself the title of al-Mahdī, the divinely guided one, and began preaching in the vernacular to the tribes of southern Morocco.[23] This was the beginning of the last of three successive revolutions that swept across North Africa, each led by a Muslim prophet appealing to the Berber population, each opposed to the one before. Blending Sunnī and Shīʿī theological and mystical traditions, Ibn Tūmart espoused a seemingly simple monotheism, one that emphasized the unity (*tawḥīd*) of divinity and criticized what he perceived to be the anthropomorphist or polytheist

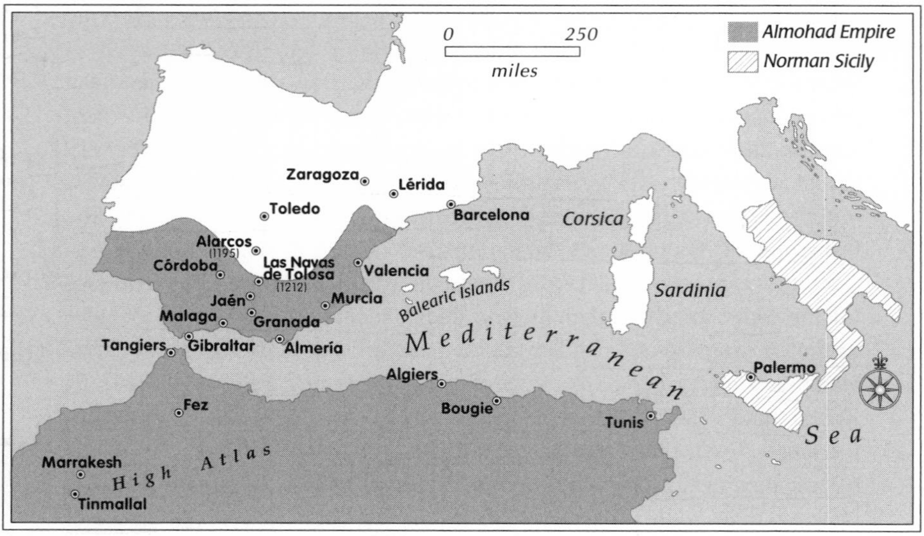

3. The Almohad Caliphate (1214). Courtesy Dick Gilbreath, Gyula Pauer Center for Cartography and GIS, University of Kentucky.

tendencies of the prevailing Muslim orthodoxies of North Africa. His followers took the name the Almohads (al-Muwaḥḥidūn), meaning the "Unitarians." Their revolution began in the High Atlas at Tinmallal (Tinmal), but it was only after Ibn Tūmart's death that the Almohad armies found success beyond these mountains. By 1159, the Almohads held the North African coast from Tripoli to the Atlantic, and by 1172, they held all of al-Andalus.

Within the historiography of medieval Iberia, the arrival of the Almohads has often been viewed as a step in the wrong direction, a moment at which a world of secular tolerance and cultural efflorescence gave way to blind religious intolerance and violent oppression. Amira K. Bennison and Maribel Fierro have recently challenged this view.[24] First, they have reevaluated the Almohads' restrictive policies toward Christians and Jews within Ibn Tūmart's efforts to reform Islam, his claim to have restored an authentic and universal monotheism for all believers. Second, they have emphasized the influence of the Almohad rationalist political theology upon European rulers from Frederick II to Alfonso X of Castile. The full understanding of the history of *jenets* both hinges upon and extends the significance of these insights.

The territorial and ideological strength of the Almohads, however, did not hold. At the Battle of Las Navas de Tolosa (1212), the typically fractious Christian kingdoms of the Iberian Peninsula united to deliver the Almohads a crushing defeat. The caliph narrowly avoided capture. The tapestry that covered his royal tent remains on display as a trophy at the Abbey of Las Huelgas, near Burgos. Although the enthusiasm for crusading quickly dissipated, the Almohad caliphs had already begun to lose authority throughout their empire. In the following decades, after a series of civil wars, the regions of al-Andalus threw off their allegiance. The Almohad ruler of Valencia, Abū Zayd, the last Andalusī governor loyal to the caliphs, turned to King Jaume I for assistance against rebels only to find himself and his lands subject to the Crown of Aragon. In North Africa, three successor states rose up: the Ḥafṣids at Tunis, who claimed to be the successors of the Almohads, the ʿAbd al-Wādids at Tlemcen, and the Marīnids at Fez, the last of whom dealt the final blow to the Almohads at Marrakesh in 1269 (map 4).

The Latin, Arabic, and Romance diplomatic correspondence in the Archive of the Crown of Aragon not only reveals extensive interactions

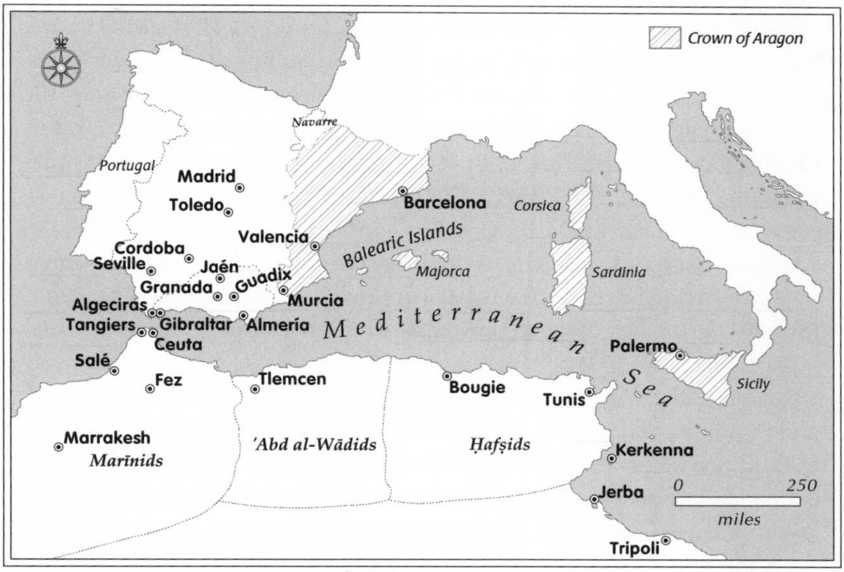

4. The western Mediterranean (ca. 1300). Courtesy Dick Gilbreath, Gyula Pauer Center for Cartography and GIS, University of Kentucky.

between the Aragonese kings and each of these successor states but also brings to light a critical, triangular tension. The Ḥafṣids, once tributaries of the Hohenstaufens, soon became the target of Aragonese predation. Kings Alfons II and Jaume II invoked the legacy of Frederick II to claim authority over Tunis. The Marīnids, by contrast, who carried forward a militant messianism, posed a threat to the Crown of Aragon. Like the Almohads before them, these Berber rulers crossed the Strait of Gibraltar for the sake of jihād in order to aid the Muslims of al-Andalus. In addition to several large-scale invasions, the Marīnids also permanently settled a contingent of holy warriors, known as al-Ghuzāh al-Mujāhidūn, composed of Arab and Berber troops from across North Africa and commanded by three Marīnid princes, on borders of the lands of the Crown of Aragon and Castile in 1262. From this moment until their dissolution at the end of the fourteenth century, the Ghuzāh remained a powerful and independent force on the Iberian Peninsula.

Through a Mediterranean approach, this book makes two central arguments about the history of the *jenets* that confound secular expectations for religious interaction. First, in recruiting and employing Muslim soldiers, the Aragonese kings not only expressed pragmatism in the face of political crisis but also drew upon an ancient and evolving Mediterranean tradition, far deeper than that of the court of Frederick II, one that bound legal and theological conceptions of imperial authority to the servitude of religious others. This tradition ties the history of the *jenets* not only to the longer history of Christian soldiers in Muslim armies but also to the history of military slavery in the Islamic world. Rather than ignoring religious difference, the Crown of Aragon's use of the *jenets* emphasized—often spectacularly so—their status as non-Christians. Put differently, the Crown of Aragon's claims to divinely sanctioned authority and absolute jurisdiction found their clearest and perhaps only expression over and through the bodies of non-Christians, whom they saw as their personal possessions, their slaves.

Second, in their written agreements and negotiations with the Aragonese kings, the *jenets* justified and expressed their service through a tradition of jihād. Indeed, rather than free-wheeling soldiers-for-hire, as earlier studies have presumed, the Marīnid Ghuzāh, holy warriors who had and would continue to threaten the lands of the Crown of Aragon, were the principal source of the Aragonese *jenets* and their leaders. Across the thirteenth and fourteenth centuries, the Crown of Aragon recruited *jenets* from Granada and North Africa and placed them under the command of the Ghuzāh leaders and soldiers in their lands. Moreover, the Aragonese kings agreed to and accepted limits on the use of these soldiers, limits by which, for example, Muslims could only fight Christians. Thus, far from marking the collapse of religious boundaries or the triumph of toleration, the relationship of the Aragonese kings to the *jenets* both depended upon and reproduced ideas of religious difference. This history forces us to reconsider the relationship between ideas of sovereignty, religion, and violence in the Middle Ages.

While these overlapping political and theological claims help to elucidate the logic that bound Christian kings and Muslim soldiers, they nevertheless also fall short, as David Nirenberg has recently argued, of a total explanation of the practice of royal power in the Middle Ages.[25] The Aragonese kings' claims to sovereignty masked a context of competing claims to jurisdiction and authority by the French, the Castilians, the Papacy, their own subjects, and most strikingly, by the *jenets* themselves. Indeed, far from slaves, as the kings imagined them, or practical rationalists, as historians have imagined them, the *jenets* continued to see themselves as members of the Ghuzāh, holy warriors who rejected the Aragonese kings' authority altogether. Significantly, however, none of these many challenges undermined the Crown of Aragon. The practice of Aragonese power differed from its lofty rhetoric and performances. Indeed, the Aragonese kings remained resilient in this period not through coercive violence or decision, which have been seen as constitutive features of political sovereignty, but rather through a politics of continual evasion and indecision.[26]

* * *

Across six chapters, *The Mercenary Mediterranean* approaches the history of the *jenets* at a variety of scales and from multiple points of view, gradually shifting its perspective from that of the Aragonese kings to that of the *jenets* themselves. Chapter 1, "Etymologies and Etiologies," begins where others have begun, in the Archive of the Crown of Aragon, in order to explain why a reliance on either Latin and Romance archival sources or Arabic chronicles can offer only a partial view of the *jenets*. Careful comparison of these seemingly incommensurate sources, however, unearths the unexpected source of these soldiers, members of a motley corps of North African cavalry, al-Ghuzāh al-Mujāhidūn, a band of holy warriors who entered the Iberian Peninsula for the purpose of defending Muslims. This fact raises the questions that frame the remainder of the book: How and why did the Aragonese kings rely on soldiers who had and would again threaten their lands to serve in their armies and, more stunningly, as their personal protectors? What was the logic that bound Christian kings and Muslim holy warriors?

Chapter 2, "A Sovereign Crisis," and chapter 3, "Sovereigns and Slaves," work together to reveal the context and motivations for the Crown of Aragon's decision to ally itself with its former enemies, the Marīnid Ghuzāh, and thus reconsider the narrative for the emergence of ideas of political sovereignty in the later Middle Ages. Following in the steps of two ambassadors on the first known mission to recruit *jenets*, chapter 2 argues that an emergency, prompted by the Aragonese conquest of Sicily, first led the Crown of Aragon to pursue a wider alliance with these soldiers. Chapter 3 traces earlier ways of accounting for the alliance between the *jenets* and the Aragonese kings: rational pragmatism and cultural accommodation, both of which suggest that something other than religious belief united these figures. In contrast to these views, it contends that the Aragonese kings' alliance with *jenets* can be fully understood only within their political and theological claims to be the heirs to the Holy Roman emperors. The employment of the *jenets* drew upon the spectacular tradition of cameral servitude at the court of Frederick II, in which both Jews and Muslims were simultaneously spoken of in exceptional terms, as privileged agents and slaves of the emperor. In this context, claims to political sovereignty emerged not against religious authority but rather through legal and theological concepts that bound emperors and religious others. Rather than seeing the emergence of sovereignty as a uniquely Christian and European narrative, this history places religious interaction at its heart.

Chapter 4, "A Mercenary Economy," extends this analysis into the wider scope of the medieval Mediterranean by examining the relationship of the Crown of Aragon to North Africa, regions that are too often studied apart. Through a study of Latin, Romance, and Arabic treaties as well as records of negotiation, this chapter connects the employment of the *jenets* to the more ancient service of Christian soldiers for the Muslim rulers of al-Andalus and North Africa. Together, Christian and Muslim rulers and soldiers developed norms and traditions for the use of foreign armies that respected religious and political boundaries. The intersection of these traditions also points to a deeper genealogy for the relationship of sovereign claims to "infidel" soldiers, namely the tradition of military slavery in the Islamic world. As such, the case of the *jenets* provides evidence for the transfer of certain imperial conceptions and practices from the Islamic to the Christian Mediterranean.

Chapter 5, "The Unpaid Debt," provides an account of the lives of the *jenets* beyond the royal court and beyond ideas of privileged servitude. How did the Aragonese kings use these soldiers in practice? How did Christians view Muslim soldiers in the service of their kings? And how did the *jenets*, in turn, make their way through these foreign lands? This chapter begins with the *jenets*' families, the women and children who accompanied them into the lands of the Crown of Aragon, and then examines the *jenets*' encounters with local Christian officials and villagers. It turns finally to the relationship between the *jenets*, as foreign Muslims, and the Mudéjares, the subject Muslim population of the Crown of Aragon. This evidence points to the numerous challenges and threats to the kings' and *jenets*' claims to power and privilege. It reveals an irreducible context of indeterminacy, one of competing claims to law and legitimacy. On a local level, the effect of the Crown's alliance with the *jenets* was to heighten tensions between Christians and Muslims. Far from being naïve or unaware of these challenges, the Aragonese kings turned this competition and disorder to their advantage.

Chapter 6, "The Worst Men in the World," turns to the point of view of the *jenets*. The career of one fourteenth-century *jenet* commander, al-'Abbās b. Raḥḥū, whose troops were called "the worst men in the world" by an Aragonese royal official, offers an opportunity to examine the motivations of these Muslim soldiers. Al-'Abbās and his *jenets* understood their service to the Aragonese king on limited terms. More precisely, they saw their service not as a transgression but rather as an extension of their commitment to the Marīnid Ghuzāh, with whom their loyalty ultimately lay. This not only forces us to reconsider the meaning and practice of jihād in medieval al-Andalus and North Africa but also underscores the thinness of the Aragonese kings' claim to sovereignty. The Aragonese kings depended upon soldiers who were not in fact their slaves or servants, empty ciphers for their will, but rather holy warriors, who denied their divinely sanctioned authority altogether.

In the light of these considerations of sovereignty, religion, and violence, the epilogue, "Medievalism and Secularism" returns to and explores more fully the origins and consequences of an implicit secular bias in the study of religious interaction in the Middle Ages and beyond.

CHAPTER ONE

Etymologies and Etiologies

The scholar reading through the chancery registers in the Archive of the Crown of Aragon, turning page after page of brittle paper, will find the Latin and Romance terms *jenetus* and *genet* (as well as a handful of other orthographic variants) scattered throughout the copious thirteenth- and fourteenth-century documentation, terms referring to certain but not all Muslim soldiers. By and large, historians have ignored these words in this context. In his handwritten, partial eighteenth-century catalog to the registers—the only such guide for contemporary researchers—the archivist Jeroni Alterachs y Avarilló mistakenly read *jenet* as a surname belonging to a Mudéjar, a subject Muslim.[1] And thus, these soldiers have remained mostly buried in these paper books. Only four scholars have seen something more.[2]

In these four earlier studies, however, the identity of the *jenets* has been a matter of confusion. For Andrés Giménez Soler, writing in 1905, their origin seemed obvious: they were Zanāta Berbers from North Africa. He saw the word *jenet* as a Romanization of the name of the tribe.[3] In 1927, when Faustino Gazulla wrote a second study of the *jenets*, he followed his predecessor on the matter of origin. A significant entanglement, however, arises from this etymological claim. To say that the *jenets* were Zanāta Berbers—a broad ethnic category—is only slightly more revealing than calling them North African. After all, from which Zanāta tribes did they come? And how, when, and why did they end up in the Iberian Peninsula?[4] The two more recent studies have challenged this North African origin. In 1978, Elena Lourie suggested that the *jenets* were in fact Iberian Muslim cavalry soldiers, members of the Banū Ashqilūla who had rebelled against the Naṣrid rulers of Muslim Granada and were therefore predisposed to trade allegiances.[5] And in 2003, Brian Catlos suggested that although the word *jenet* derived from the name of the Berber tribe, by the thirteenth century it "became a generic term for all foreign Muslim soldiers."[6] Each of these possibilities would lead to drastically different readings of this history. Therefore, it is worth asking the deceptively simple question: Who were the *jenets*?

Jennets for Germans

The confusion surrounding and scant scholarly attention upon the *jenets* stands in sharp contrast to the wide diffusion of the term and its linguistic descendants across the early modern and modern periods.[7] Tracing the word forward from the Middle Ages reveals a rapid dilation of its meaning and a web of significations. In thirteenth-century Iberian Latin and Romance sources, the first to use the term, *jenet* referred only to specific Muslim soldiers and their military accoutrements: *jenet* saddles, *jenet* stirrups, and *jenet* lances. However opaque to readers centuries later, the word had been specific in this context. By the early modern period, *jenet* had already expanded in meaning, referring to both Muslim and Christian cavalry, the so-called *jinetes*, who rode in the fashion of these earlier soldiers. According to Covarrubias in his 1611 dictionary, the *Tesoro*, it meant "a man on horseback, who fights with a spear and a leather shield, his feet gathered into short stirrups, which do not reach below the belly of the horse."[8] And by the time one reaches modern Castilian and Catalan, even this degree of specificity had dissolved. The linguistic descendants of *jenet*—the Castilian *jinete* and the Catalan *genet*—simply and generically mean "horseman," a fact that might explain why so many scholars have passed over the term in earlier sources: it seemed unremarkable and obvious. Precisely because of this linguistic genericide, a steady semantic slippage toward generality, I have chosen to use the term *jenet* (a truncated form of the Latin *jenetus*) in order to refer to this particular thirteenth- and early fourteenth-century Muslim cavalryman, to avoid confusion with these later variants.

Beyond the Iberian Peninsula, particularly in French and English, the term evolved differently, demonstrating again how "the words of things entangle and confuse."[9] From at least the early modern period, the term transferred its meaning from rider to mount: *jennet* refers to a diminutive and much prized horse or palfrey (*roncino*) of mixed Spanish and North African stock.[10] That detail makes sense of Iago's famous barb about Othello: "[Y]ou'll have/coursers for cousins and jennets for germans!"[11] The breeding of jennet horses made them a ready symbol of not only racial transgression but also sexual excess throughout early modern literature, propelling the semantic afterlife of the *jenets* forward in new ways: "A breeding jennet, lusty, young and proud," according to *Venus and Adonis*; "Glew'd like a neighing Gennet to her Stallion," for salacious Massinger in *Renegado*; or in Fletcher's *Thierry and Theodoret*, "power they may love, and like Spanish Jennetts Commit with such a gust."[12] It is worth mentioning that hippological metaphors for race were not an innovation of early modern literature. In late medieval Iberia, the Castilian word *raza*—from which the English "race" derives—referred first to the breeding of horses before it moved to men.[13] But jennet horses were not only "good to think" in the early modern and modern periods.[14] They also carried the Spanish conquistadors to the New World. Wealthy European gentlemen prized them for their speed and strength as well as their multitude of colors and patterns, their beauty, which made them a regular feature in eighteenth-century portraiture and literature. In *Ivanhoe*, for instance, one reads: "A lay brother, one of those who followed in the train, had, for his use upon other occasions, one of the most handsome Spanish jennets ever bred in Andalusia, which merchants used at that time to import, with great trouble and risk, for the use of persons of wealth and distinction."[15] And if only for the irrepressible pleasure of pulling a loose thread, even later in English, the word also attached itself to a mule, the modern *jenny*. Thus, from *jenets* riding mules, we come to *jenets* as mules.

The contorted afterlife of the word *jenet* is rather like the scattershot cosmic microwave background, the remnants of an explosion, in this case, one that leads back to the medieval Iberian Peninsula. At the beginning of the thirteenth century, Christian Iberian knights rode into battle in the manner of heavy cavalry. They sat low in their saddles, anchored with their legs outstretched—a style known as *a la brida*—in order to bear the weight of their armor and long lances.[16] And while these soldiers were expensive and slow, like high-maintenance armored vehicles, they could deliver granite blows to their enemies. Although the cause of this transformation is not well understood, by the late medieval or early modern period in Iberia and Europe more widely, this style had shifted.[17] The majority of Iberian Christian knights were now lightly armored. They rode smaller horses, bearing the so-called *jineta* saddle, with a low pommel and short stirrups, which allowed them to stand when in gallop. These saddles also

FIGURE 1. Granello-Tavaron-Castello y Cambiasso, *Battle of Higueruela* (1431). Skirmish of the Jinetes. Monasterio-Pintura, San Lorenzo de El Escorial, Madrid. Photograph: Album / Art Resource, New York.

gave cavalry soldiers the striking appearance of having their legs trussed beneath them, like chickens heading to the oven, making them readily identifiable and easily distinguishable from heavy cavalry in the famous sixteenth-century murals depicting the Battle of Higueruela (1431) in the *Sala de Batallas* of the monastery of San Lorenzo de El Escorial (fig. 1). This new Spanish knight carried a short throwing lance, called a *jineta*, as well as small leather shield, called an *adarga* (derived from the Arabic *daraqa*, meaning "shield").[18] His military advantage lay in the ability to attack and flee, a tactic known as *tornafuye*, which allowed him to harass and scatter heavy cavalry without engaging them directly.[19] As sixteenth- and seventeenth-century riding manuals like Tapia y Salcedo's *Exercicios de la gineta* demonstrate, the steady diffusion of this style—appropriately called *a la jineta*—led to the decline of heavy cavalry, which had dominated Iberia.[20] Indeed, so thorough and successful was this revolution that eventually in Spain *jinete* and *genet* simply came to mean horseman.[21]

As is well attested to in Arabic sources, this lightly armed style of riding as well as the tactic of attacking and fleeing (known as *al-karr wa'l-farr*) began among the Arabs and Berbers of North Africa, in particular members of the Zanāta tribes.[22] According to the eleventh-century historian

Ibn Ḥayyān (d. 1097), lightly armored Berber troops rode on saddles with low pommels, the so-called *sarj 'udwiyy* (racing saddle), that allowed them greater maneuverability on horseback.[23] While seeing this technique as strategically and morally inferior to closed formations, which had been the style employed by the early Islamic armies, Ibn Khaldūn (1332–1406) confirmed that light cavalry was the only style employed in the Maghrib in his time: "Fighting in closed formation (*zaḥf*) is steadier and fiercer than attacking and fleeing. . . . [But] the fighting of people of their country [i.e., North Africa] is all attacking and fleeing."[24]

This North African origin was not lost upon early modern Spaniards. In 1599, Juan de Mariana recommended the technique for training Christian princes while nevertheless admitting its "Moorish (Mauricae)" derivation.[25] A year later, Bernardo de Vargas Machuca bragged of this style's effectiveness in combatting the "barbarians" of the New World while also acknowledging—without a hint of irony—the fact that the Berbers, who were once Greece's quintessential "barbarians," had first innovated this technique: "Although it is true that Barbary (Berberia) first gave it to Spain, and Spain to the Indies, it has been perfected here more than elsewhere."[26] And Covarrubias recorded that some in his time ascribed the style specifically to "a certain nation or caste of Arabs called 'Cenetas' or 'Cenetes,' who lived in the mountains of Africa."[27] Despite the willingness of Spanish noblemen and princes to adapt and adopt this Moorish style, the popularity of riding *a la jineta* struck foreign travelers to Spain as something strange and exotic.[28] So, the thirteenth-century *jenets* stood at the heart of the transfer of this effective but culturally troubling cavalry style to the Iberian Peninsula, a significant military transformation in need of an explanation. And it thus might make sense to leap to the conclusion, as Giménez Soler did in 1905, that the *jenets* were Zanāta Berbers.

There are at least two problems with this leap. First, as noted earlier, to say that the *jenets* were Zanāta Berbers—a broad ethnic group—reveals little. Second, given the wide-ranging path of the term *jenet*, one must ask: by the time the word reached the Archive of the Crown of Aragon, had it already swung out of orbit, coming to signify the light style of riding over the ethnicity of the rider? For instance, writing in the thirteenth century, Ramon Lull (ca. 1232–1315), the Mallorcan mystic, described all Iberian Muslim cavalry—not just Berbers—as lightly armed: "They neither arm their bodies nor horses but rather ride into battle almost nude."[29] The same generalization, but with admiration, was made later by Don Juan Manuel (1282–1348) in his *Libro de los Estados*.[30] In other words, even if the Berber Zanāta inspired the term, it does not follow that the thirteenth-century *jenets* were Zanāta.

To press this point as far as it goes: the etymology upon which Giménez Soler relied in fact reflects this ambiguity precisely. Although philologists and historians have generally accepted that the words *jinete* and *genet* (as well as related terms) derive from *Zanāta*, the transformation of one word into the other—*Zanāta* into *jinete*—presents a difficulty for linguists.[31] In only one other case has an Arabic word with the letter zāy entered into Castilian with a *c* or Catalan with an *s*. Thus, for instance, the name of the Zanāta tribe was rendered in medieval Castilian as *Cenete*.[32] What the curious initial letter might suggest is that the path from the Arabic *Zanāta* to *jinete* and *genet* was indirect, passing through some intermediary language. Using contemporary evidence, Helmut Lüdtke has proposed that the word was brought to Spain in the mouths and on the tongues of Berber tribesmen, who pronounced the Arabic zāy in a fashion that more closely approximated the Castilian *j* (ž) or Catalan *g* (ẑ) in *jinete* and *genet*.[33] While this is a tempting and elegant explanation, the likeliest one, it also has to be admitted that other paths remain open. Indeed, in the one other case—the transformation of the Arabic *zarafa* (giraffe) into the Castilian *jirafa* and the Catalan *girafa*—the Italian *giraffa* served as an intermediary.[34] Thus, again, although the word *jenet* likely derived from the Berber *Zanāta*, there is no reason to conclude that Berbers directly introduced the term into Romance, or that the first *jenets* were themselves Zanāta. In brief, this etymology tells us more about the importance of the style of the *jenets*, their unacknowledged impact on military history, than about the identity of the thirteenth-century *jenets* themselves.

A Threshold of Indistinction

Although they have never been employed in etymological studies, the earliest references to the word *jenet* appear in the thirteenth-century Latin and Romance sources of the Archive of the Crown of Aragon.[35] Before examining this evidence, however, the words of Arlette Farge are worth remembering: "History is never the simple repetition of archival content, but a pulling away from it, in which we never stop asking how and why these words came to wash ashore on the manuscript page."[36]

The records of the Crown of Aragon are a miracle of sorts.[37] Unlike the French royal archives, they avoided destruction in the medieval and modern periods, providing us with a near continuous record of the Barcelonan counts and Aragonese kings' activities through the fifteenth century. The earliest documentation relates to the ninth-century counts of Barcelona, and the first explicit mention of an "archive," which is to say, of a conscious effort to maintain royal documents, dates to the reign of King Alfons I (r. 1164–1196). Across its history, the Crown's administrators held on to royal letters, account books, court records, and an often-overlooked but vital collection of Arabic charters, the so-called Cartas árabes, which hold correspondence with and from Muslim rulers. Nevertheless, the importance of the Archive of the Crown of Aragon rests principally upon the wealth of its paper registers, a wealth that borders on scribomania. After the conquest of Islamic Valencia (and its paper mills) in 1236, and in imitation of the Papacy and French kings, King Jaume I (r. 1213–1276) adopted this practice of maintaining registers. Jaume's registers, thirty-three in total, begin as brief but increasingly become more extensive summaries of the most important letters and orders sealed and dispatched by the royal chancery.[38] Jaume's successor and son, King Pere II (r. 1276–1285), later redacted these early records, raising the specter of manipulation, but he also recognized the value of these records and expanded the practice of keeping registers. At this stage, organizational habits remained inchoate. Rather than self-consciously burnishing the image of the king, the first eighty registers record unexpected details such as what the prince and princess ate and wore each day. This remained the practice until King Jaume II, whose reign (r. 1291–1327) corresponded with the greatest expansion of royal power and administrative prowess. He ordered all the existing registers as well as records from the royal treasurers, some of which remained in the private hands, be brought under one roof, an archive in the former chapel of Great Royal Palace.[39] Simultaneously, he ordered royal scribes to copy systematically and completely *all* correspondence, leading to the production of 342 registers. By the reign of Alfons III (r. 1327–1336), these paper registers would grow in size to 1,240, becoming impossible for a single scholar to survey, particularly in the absence of a catalog. This shifting terrain of paper is our principal source for the early history of the *jenets*, where we first find them riding. What do these Latin and Romance registers reveal about these Muslim soldiers?

Although Faustino Gazulla began his study of the *jenets* in the year 1284, a watershed moment after which the Crown's use of these soldiers dramatically increased, the *jenets*' Aragonese story does not in fact begin here but earlier, at the end of King Jaume I's reign and at the very beginning of King Pere II's.[40] These were precisely the unstable moments when these records were coming into existence, a fact that complicates a search for origins, an etiology.

The final years of Jaume's reign were troubled. Inspired by an invitation from the Mongol Khan and a desire to curry favor with Pope Clement IV (r. 1265–1268), Jaume planned and led a crusading expedition to the Holy Land in 1269.[41] It ended in failure when the king and the majority of his host prematurely disembarked at the marshy port of Aigues-Mortes in Southern France. Rumors spread that Jaume had landed because he wished to return to his mistress, adding insult to injury. Stung, Jaume tried to muster support for a new crusade at the Council of Lyon in 1274 but, once more, had little success. At home, he fared even worse, facing querulous barons: their criticisms of royal power had crystallized around Jaume's taxes to support Castile in its war against Muslim Granada. Tired, it seems, of the king's efforts to play the crusader at their expense, the barons revolted. Although Jaume's instinct was to show leniency and negotiate, his aggressive son Pere crushed the baronial rebellion in 1275, displaying a penchant for violent force that would carry into his kingship.[42] This fire was temporarily put out, but a worse one flared.

Although known as el Conqueridor, that is, "the Conqueror," for his capture of the former Almohad province of Valencia, Jaume's epithet-granting achievement became his undoing.[43] After decades of unrest, and following closely on the heels of a similar revolt in Castile-controlled Murcia (1264–1266), a Muslim uprising under the leadership of al-Azraq, "the Blue," erupted in 1275 and threatened to overturn Aragonese rule.[44] The aged king died on June 27, 1276, at Valencia, uncertain of the kingdom's future. The famous inscription on Jaume's tomb, "He always prevailed over the Saracens," was only added a century later.[45] The future king Pere left the battlefront briefly several months after Jaume's death to be crowned and then labored on, effectively having to conquer the kingdom for a second time. He extinguished the Mudéjar rebellions and reduced al-Azraq to a half-forgotten myth. Robert Ignatius Burns suggested that one still hears a hint of al-Azraq in the bogeyman of contemporary Valencian children's tales, el Drach. "¡Que vindra el Drach!" say admonishing mothers to their wayward children.[46]

With a single exception, to which I return later, the *jenets* first appear in the records of the Crown of Aragon during events surrounding these Muslim uprisings in Murcia and Valencia—not as soldiers of the Crown of Aragon but rather as invaders into its kingdoms. Speaking of the Murcian rebellion, which threatened Castile, King Jaume recorded in his autobiography, the *Llibre dels feyts*:

> And we had already heard that the king of Castile [Alfonso X (r. 1252–1284)] had fallen out with the king of Granada [Muḥammad I (r. 1232–1273) of the Naṣrids] and that the king of Granada had, for a long time, had recourse to the Moors on the other side of the sea; and that *jenets* had crossed to his land and could take all the king of Castile's land.[47]

Jaume specifies that these *jenet* soldiers were from "the other side of the sea (*d'allèn mar*)," a claim corroborated by the fourteenth-century Castilian *Crónica del Alfonso XI*, which adds, "they say these were the first *jenet* knights that crossed the sea."[48] In his *Llibre dels feyts*, Jaume also tells us something of their numbers and movements, which he observed with concern:

> While we were in Oriola, where we stayed well for eight days, one night two *almogàvers* [fighters who specialized in cross-border raids on Grenada] of Lorca came to us, and knocked on our door near midnight. They reported to us that eight hundred *jenets*, with two thousand loaded mules and two thousand men-at-arms guarding them, were entering supplies into Murcia.[49]

During the Muslim rebellion in the kingdom of Valencia a decade later, the *jenets* appeared again. In this case, King Pere moved to contain the threat. In a circular dated May 15, 1277, to the vicars and bailiffs of Gerona, Besalú, and other locations, Pere ordered export restrictions:

> Because in the kingdom of Valencia many of the *jenets* have risen up, and the *alcaydus* and Saracens of the castle of Montesa have broken the agreements that we had with them for the restitution of this castle; therefore, we are at war with them. We order you immediately to forbid the export from our land to any parts horses or large palfreys under the penalty of the loss of said horses and palfreys.[50]

And although such export restrictions were not usual, Pere does specify that these foreign cavalry soldiers were a central threat. Palfreys (*roncinos*) were preferred by the *jenets*. Nevertheless, like Jaume before him, Pere reveals little about the identity of these soldiers. They are distinguished from the "Saracens" of Valencia—which is to say, the Mudéjares. These subject Muslims are cited for having "broken agreements" and failing to deliver a castle to the king, complaints that have the tempered air of feudal disloyalty rather than religious contempt. In the same vein, King Jaume had referred to al-Azraq, the leader of the Mudéjar rebellion, as "our traitor (*proditor noster*)."[51] In other words, from the perspective of the Crown of Aragon, the Mudéjares were definitively insiders—disloyal and treacherous but feudal subjects nonetheless. Their treason was not only rebellion but also conspiracy with outsiders:

> The Saracens [of Valencia] rebelled with soldiers from castles and forts against the Lord King and his land, leading, moreover, Saracen spies from Granada and North Africa into Valencia at the greatest cost and dishonor to his land and all of Christendom.[52]

Only in speaking of the Mudéjares in this second sense—as conspirators—did King Pere's language take on the cast of eschatology, presenting them as enemies of Christendom.

The *jenets*, by contrast, are never spoken of as rebels. In fact, they are never spoken of as the king's subjects or, indeed, subjects of any one king or kingdom in these early documents. While some appear to be attached to specific castles within Valencia, others, one learns from war reports, have entered Valencia by land from Naṣrid Granada or by sea from North Africa during the rebellion.[53] A surrender treaty—negotiated directly with Mudéjar leaders—reveals, moreover, that the Crown was fully aware of the *jenets*' disaggregated organization.[54] At the end of August 1276, Pere signed an agreement with "shaykh Abrurdriz Hyale Abenayech, knight Abenzumayr Abenzaquimeran, and the *wazīr* Abulfaratx Asbat," who represented several castles in Valencia. The Muslim leaders would pay the Aragonese king an unspecified amount and vacate their strongholds within three months. And significantly, they agreed that none of their "*jenets* and other cavalry of Moors, in this land, in Granada, or any other place . . . would do harm to the kingdom of Valencia or any other part of the king's land."[55] In addition to confirming that the *jenets* were scattered "in this land," "in Granada," and indeed, "any other place," the surrender treaty appears to insist that the *jenets* were a particular and distinct form of cavalry—different from "other cavalry of Moors"—although in what sense remains unclear.

What might the term *Moor* tell us about the *jenets*? Although the origins of this word are unknown—perhaps Semitic (*mahourím*) or Greek (*Μαύροίςτιος*)—by the classical period, the Latin *Mauri* indicated the inhabitants of the Roman provinces of Mauretania.[56] And at least in a general sense, it referred to the Berber inhabitants of North Africa, which is promising. The word functions in this manner in the anonymous *Mozarabic Chronicle of 754*, an eighth-century text written by Christians living under Islamic rule in al-Andalus, which distinguishes consistently and accurately between "Arabs and Moors (Arabes et Mauri)," the Arabs and Berbers, among the Muslim invaders.[57] The *Miraculos romanzados*—which record miracles between 1232 and 1293 of Christians who escaped captivity among Muslims through the intercession of Saint Dominic of Silos—make mention of two "Moorish" captains of *jenets* who in 1283 terrorized the Murcian frontier: "Zahem and Zahet Azenet came with a thousand horsemen and killed two hundred Christians and took as many captive."[58] The name "Azenet" suggests that these men were Berber Zanāta tribesmen. Moors, in other words, consistently seem to be Berbers.

Does this mean that when Aragonese royal administrators wrote "*jenet*" in the thirteenth century, they understood that these soldiers were ethnically Berber? In fact, there is some indication that they were making such a distinction. For instance, in November 1290, the Crown's royal treasurer, Arnaldus de Bastida, was ordered to issue two sets of payments, one to a company of *jenets* and another to "certain Arab Saracens."[59] Similarly, on another occasion, in March 1291, King Jaume II dispatched a letter to an Arab soldier, "Mahomat, son of Abulgayri el Arabi," agreeing to his terms to bring "good Arab knights" into the Crown.[60] Nevertheless, among the hundreds of documents referring to Muslim cavalry in the service of the Crown, these are the only two occasions that refer specifically to Arab cavalry as opposed to *jenets*, which might weaken the conviction that something deeper was at play. Moreover, not unlike the term *jenet*, "Moor" shifted its meaning over the Middle Ages. In the twelfth-century *Crónica Najarense* or the thirteenth-century *Primera crónica general*, "Moors" were not simply Berbers but any and all Muslims living in the Iberian Peninsula.[61] Somewhere along the line, the matter-of-fact-sounding ethnic denominations of earlier texts had given way: "The Moors of the host wore silks and colourful cloths which they had taken as booty, their horses' reins were like fire, their faces were black as pitch, the handsomest among them was black as a cooking-pot."[62] All the same, even if one argued that archival documents were less susceptible to confusion than literature, "Moor" gives us only the impression that the *jenets* were Berbers, but not when and how they arrived or who they were.

Relying on the Latin and Romance sources, even unexplored sources, from the chancery registers, brings us only so far in our search of the origins of the *jenets*. For all the wealth of the Archive of the Crown of Aragon, it cannot be used unproblematically as a window onto the past. It inevitably reflected a certain perspective on the world, that of the royal court, and one that in this early period is partial or inchoate at best. We, the solitary readers, holding these remarkable papers some eight hundred years later, can only join the story in that epic fashion, in the middle of things.

A Curious Embrace

Arabic sources present new opportunities to break through this impasse and new challenges. Although we find a great deal written about the Berbers of North Africa, by and large our sources are chronicles rather than archives. These narratives served and responded to different pressures than the documents in the chancery registers and also cannot be used as a window onto the past. The earliest accounts of North Africa, for instance, were filled with embellishments and legends that coded political and ethnic tensions between Arabs and Berbers.[63] From the tenth century onward, however, written materials on the Berbers increased. And of these sources, the most thorough and complete, the *Kitāb al-ʿibar* (The Book of Lessons) of Ibn Khaldūn, a near contemporary of the *jenets*, devoted its longest section to a description of the Zanāta.[64] At different stages of his life, Ibn Khaldūn served in the major courts of North Africa and al-Andalus, giving him a unique but complicated vantage point.

A great deal has been written about Ibn Khaldūn, and it is worth reiterating some of those arguments.[65] Nineteenth-century European Arabists stressed Ibn Khaldūn's exceptional status and his rather unorthodox opinions. They cast him as a premodern materialist and as the father of secular social science.[66] Aziz al-Azmeh and others have strongly rejected these approaches. Although Ibn Khaldūn pursued a rational explanation of historical and religious development, his views were, in fact, traditional and unexceptional for his period, which is to say that they were fully compatible with a widely held understanding of divinity in medieval Islam and with his position as an Islamic jurist (*faqīh*).[67]

Nevertheless, his *Kitāb al-ʿibar* is somewhat unusual, and self-consciously so. What began as a conventional introduction to his theory of history developed into a universal history, a detailed elaboration of the cyclical nature of society, in which nomadic and tribal groups settle, lose their spirit of cohesion (*ʿaṣabiyya*), and are overtaken by hardier ones.[68] This dynamic not only shaped Ibn Khaldūn's exposition of history but also explains why he emphasized the centrality and vitality of nomadic warriors such as the Zanāta to the universal mission of Islam.[69] Thus below, wherever possible, I have attempted to balance Ibn Khaldūn's text with other sources.

In his time, Ibn Khaldūn described the Zanāta as an ethnic grouping comprising numerous tribes that dominated the central Maghrib (contemporary Morocco and Algeria), so numerous, in fact, that the entire region was colloquially known as the "land of the Zanāta (*waṭan al-zanāta*)."[70] He roughly divided the history of these tribes into two periods of ascendancy, key examples of his recurrent cycle: in the tenth century, under the Maghrāwa (specifically, the Banū Khazar and Banū Yifran), and again, in the thirteenth century, under the two great Berber dynasties, the Marīnids (Banū Marīn) and the 'Abd al-Wādids (also known as the Zayyānids).

In that first period, according to Ibn Khaldūn, although these tribes were composed of a variety of transhumant stockbreeders, cultivators, and city dwellers, the Zanāta had already developed a singular reputation for their formidable warriors, above all their cavalry (*fāris*, pl. *fursān*), who were lightly armed and specialized in raiding.[71] The Zanāta, in particular the Maghrāwa tribe, formed the backbone of the Andalusī Umayyad's resistance against the Fāṭimids, *shī'īs*, who—supported by the traditional rivals of the Zanāta, the Ṣanhāja—were making inroads into central North Africa.[72] And although the Zanāta eventually agreed to become clients of the Umayyad Caliphs, as Ibn Khaldūn described, this alliance involved a curious embrace of reciprocal manipulation.[73] Ruling from a distance, the Umayyads played the various Zanāta tribes off of one another, showering honors and titles on one chief in order to incite the jealousy of others.[74] Through this policy, engineered by the ambitious chamberlain (*ḥājib*) and later sultan, Ibn Abī 'Āmir al-Manṣūr (Almanzor in contemporary Spanish sources), the Umayyads pursued a short-lived but failed imperial project in North Africa.[75] For their part, the Zanāta chiefs, above all those of the Maghrāwa, turned this strategy to their own advantage by using the threat of rebellion to negotiate for land grants (*iqṭā'*), rights, and honors.[76]

Throughout this first period of ascendancy, the Umayyads recruited Zanāta and Ṣanhāja troops into al-Andalus, that is, into the Iberian Peninsula.[77] They referred to these new troops generically as the Tangerines (Ṭanjiyyūn) because they arrived from the port of Tangiers. And in the period of the Caliph al-Ḥakam II al-Mustanṣir (r. 961–976), these paid troops entirely displaced Arab Syrian armies, becoming the dominant force on the Muslim-Christian frontier. Simultaneously, the Berber tribes also became a powerful political force in al-Andalus. Their involvement in the succession crisis following the death of al-Ḥakam II led to a civil war (*fitna*), the bloody sack of Cordoba—which had actively resisted the Berber candidate—in 1013, and ultimately, the downfall of the Umayyad Caliphate in al-Andalus.

It is worth underscoring, again, that Ibn Khaldūn's version of these events is refracted through the prism of the politics of fourteenth-century North Africa, a period and region with a strong identification with the Berber past. And in this sense, as M'hammad Benaboud and Ahmad Tahiri have warned, his clear distinctions between Andalusīs and Berbers as well as the seeming solidity of tribes should be approached with caution.[78] All the same, two broad conclusions can be drawn from this material. First, a large and influential contingent of Zanāta soldiers settled permanently on the Christian-Islamic frontier in Iberia in the tenth century, more than two centuries before the chancery registers of the Crown of Aragon began. Second, the Umayyad-Zanāta history also reveals a mutually coercive dynamic—between royal court and warrior—that would echo throughout the history of the *jenets* in Islamic and Christian lands.

Zanāta Kingdoms

Ibn Khaldūn's first period of Zanāta ascendency ended with the rise of the Almoravids (al-Murābiṭūn) in the eleventh century, backed by Ṣanhāja Berbers, and subsequently the Almohads in the twelfth century, supported by Maṣmūda Berbers.[79] During the periods of Almoravid and Almohad rule in North Africa and al-Andalus, the Zanāta tribes found themselves widely dispersed: some, like the Maghrāwa, who had dominated the first period, were entirely destroyed; others submitted to the new powers; and yet others declared short-lived independence on the frontiers.[80] According to Ibn Khaldūn, the old Zanāta tribes showed little desire or ability to rise above this condition: "They are, up to this day, a people taxed and besieged by states."[81] Only with the collapse of the Almohad power, Ibn Khaldūn explains, did a new set of Zanāta tribes—the Marīnids and 'Abd al-Wādids—a "second wave (*al-ṭabaqa al-thāniyya*)," untouched by luxury, seize the opportunity to build new states:

> [The Zanāta] remained in that land [the desert], wrapped in clothes of pride (*mushtamilīn lubūs al-'izz*) and ceaseless disdain (*mustamirrīn li'l-anafa* [sic]) for others. The majority of their earnings were from livestock (*an'ām wa'l-māshiya*),

and they satisfied their desires for wealth by pillaging travelers (*ibtighā'ahum al-rizq min taḥayyuf al-sābila*) and by the ends of the spears (*fī ẓill al-rimāḥ al-mushra'a*). They made war with other tribes, fought against other nations and states, and had victorious battles over kings, of which little is known. . . . During these ancient periods (*al-aḥqāb al-qadīm*), no king of this generation of Zanāta encouraged men of letters (*ahl al-kitāb*) to record events or write history (*taqyīd ayyāmihim wa-tadwīn akhbārihim*).[82]

While this stylized description emphasizes the military prowess of these new tribes, reflecting his basic typology, Ibn Khaldūn's image of the Berbers as marauding nomads, innocent of civilization (what he calls *'umrān ḥaḍārī*) in fact fits poorly with the story he tells.[83] In the period before the Almohad collapse, the 'Abd al-Wādids had already established an alliance with the Almohad Caliphs; their foundation of a kingdom at Tlemcen (Tilimsān) reflected only one of many ways their rule developed out of Almoravid and Almohad models.[84] For their part, the Marīnids, based in Fez (Fās), employed religious ideals to their advantage by establishing alliances with religious leaders in urban centers, building *madrasas*, and establishing a messianic mission through jihād.[85] In other words, these redoubtable Zanāta tribes of the "second wave" were canny and well suited to take advantage of the religious and political situation of the Maghrib and the Iberian Peninsula at the end of the thirteenth century.

The appearance of these new Zanāta kingdoms reminds us that in the decades preceding 1284—the year when the *jenets* begin to appear in the records of the Crown of Aragon in large numbers—the political order of North Africa shifted dramatically (map 4). From the wreck of the Almohad Empire, three new successors—the Ḥafṣids (an offshoot of the Almohads) at Tunis, the 'Abd al-Wādids at Tlemcen, and Marīnids at Fez—emerged, effecting a profound shift in the political and commercial landscape of the western Mediterranean. The Ḥafṣids declared themselves independent in 1229, and the 'Abd al-Wādids in 1239. The Marīnids dealt the final blows, conquering Marrakesh (Marrākush) in 1269 and Tinmallal, the sacred center of the Almohads in the Atlas Mountains, seven years later. While only the latter two were Zanāta, all three employed Zanāta cavalrymen, which is to say, all or any of the three could have been the source of the Muslim soldiers called *jenets*.[86]

The rivalry between these three states produced a complex array of diplomatic arrangements with Christian Iberian kings. For instance, despite their initial hostility during the Aragonese conquests of the Balearics (1229) and Valencia (1238), the Ḥafṣids eventually developed a consistent and pacific relationship with the Crown of Aragon, continuing up to 1282.[87] This relationship developed out of and depended upon the influence already established by Christian adventurers—merchants, missionaries, renegades, and soldiers—who lived at or attended the Ḥafṣid court.[88] Aragonese soldiers, in particular, helped to defend Tunis from its predatory neighbors, both Christian and Muslim. In 1285, at Coll de Panissars, where the five *jenets* riding mules were headed, King Pere agreed to a monumental fifteen-year peace with Tunis, temporarily defusing the emerging tension between them.[89]

Like the Ḥafṣids, the ʿAbd al-Wādids sought alliances across the Mediterranean to defend themselves against their ambitious neighbor, the Marīnid sultan.[90] A powerful contingent of Christian soldiers, including the captain "Bīrnabas," served valiantly in the struggle against the Marīnids and facilitated connections between the ʿAbd al-Wādids and the Christian Iberian kingdoms.[91] The tripartite alliance between the ʿAbd al-Wādids, Castilians, and Naṣrids against the Marīnids ended abruptly with the death of the founder of the ʿAbd al-Wādid dynasty, Abū Yaḥyā Yaghmurāsan, in 1283. At the advice of his ailing father, Abū Saʿīd ʿUthmān b. Yaghmurāsan (r. 1283–1304) decided to sue for peace with the Marīnids.[92] Thus, by 1285, the ʿAbd al-Wādids had taken an introverted posture, hoping that the sultan of Fez would focus his attention elsewhere.

The Marīnids followed a different path from the Ḥafṣids or ʿAbd al-Wādids. With the exception of the year 1274—when they struck a brief alliance with the Aragonese king—the Marīnids were openly hostile toward both the Crown of Aragon and Castile.[93] The sultan Abū Yūsuf (r. 1258–1286) displayed a particular passion for jihād and conducted four expeditions for the purpose of aiding the Mudéjares in 1275, 1276, 1283, and 1284: "From the beginning, the commander of the Muslims, Abū Yūsuf, was disposed to perform jihād (*kāna . . . mu'thiran ʿamal al-jihād*), addicted to it (*kalifan bi-hi*), and opting for it (*mukhtāran lahu*) to such a degree that it became the greatest of his hopes."[94] The anonymous *al-Dhakhīra al-saniyya* described in vivid terms the appearance of the first Marīnid army as it departed for Spain:

> In the year 674 (1275 CE) on the first day of Muḥarram, the commander of the Muslims Abū Yūsuf arrived at the Fortress of the Crossing (*qaṣr al-majāz*) and settled there. He undertook transporting the holy warriors to al-Andalus with

swift horses (*bi'l-khayl al-'itāq*), equipment (*al-'udda*), and weapons. It was a mercy of God that every day crossed a tribe of the Banū Marīn and groups of volunteers (*muṭṭawwi'ūn*) as well as tribes of Arabs. . . . [T]hey crossed, company after company (*fawjan ba'da fawj*), tribe after tribe, group after group. The boats and ships journeyed morning and evening from the break of day to night (*kānat al-marākib wa'l-sufun ghādiyāt wa-rā'iḥāt ānā' al-layl wa-aṭrāf al-nahār*) from the crossing to Tarifa (Ṭarīf), and they crowded the passage (*ma'bar*): "They crossed morning and evening to assault the foe /As if the ocean were a pavement for their steeds, / With the seaweed bearing the chargers up/As if the two shores were joined together,/And all had become a single causeway to tread." And when all had crossed and had settled (*istaqarrū*) in al-Andalus, the Muslim armies spread from the city of Tarifa to Algeciras, then Abū Yūsuf crossed last with his noblemen, ministers, officials of state, along with a group of holy men (*ṣulaḥā'*) of the Maghrib.[95]

Thus, in the period of the Muslim uprisings in Murcia and Valencia—which is to say, when *jenets* first begin to appear in the records of the Crown of Aragon—Abū Yūsuf had transferred a large body of volunteer and salaried Zanāta and Arab troops onto the Iberian Peninsula. He had established a beachhead at Algeciras, where he constructed the fortress, al-Binya ("the Edifice") not only to house these soldiers but also to isolate them and thus protect the local populations from their depredations.[96]

According to Ibn Khaldūn, the Marīnid attack began with a vanguard of five thousand cavalry soldiers, whom he simply calls "the Zanāta," under the command of Abū Ya'qūb, the sultan's son. The expedition ravaged the frontier, and in these raids, Ibn Khaldūn adds, the Zanāta knights distinguished themselves: "The Zanāta once more showed their clear-sightedness and determination; their zeal was roused. They proved their loyalty to their lord (*ablat fī ṭā'a rabbihim*) and were restless in the cause of their religion."[97] Were these Marīnid soldiers the *jenets* first mentioned in the chancery registers as invaders? During Abū Yūsuf's third incursion in April 1284, King Pere sent the following letter to the Master of the Templars and various castellans:

We know for certain that *jenets* and armies of the King of Morocco [i.e., Abū Yūsuf] and many others are coming shortly to inflict harm to the kingdom of Valencia. Therefore, we tell, urge, demand, and counsel you to prepare yourselves and your soldiers, weapons, foodstuffs, and other equipment for the defense of the aforementioned kingdom.[98]

Pere's warning explicitly connects the *jenets* to Abū Yūsuf's jihād. This connection not only provides an explanation for the *jenets*' appearance during the Valencian uprising but also suggests that the term *jenet* or Zanāta, as Ibn Khaldūn used it, functioned in a broad rather than ethnic or tribal sense, as a synecdoche for the Marīnid cavalry, composed, as the *Dhakhīra* noted, of both Berber and Arab soldiers from the Maghrib. Thus, we can identify some of the hostile *jenets* in the Iberian Peninsula as members of the Marīnid cavalry.

When Abū Yūsuf departed the Maghrib for his fourth jihād in August 1284, however, Marīnid ambition in al-Andalus was already waning. After the death of King Alfonso X in April 1284, the Castilians petitioned for and eventually signed a peace with Fez. This treaty removed levies on the merchandise of Muslim traders, forbade Christians from meddling in the affairs of Muslims (*tark al-taḍrīb bayn mulūk al-muslimīn wa'l-dukhūl baynahum fī fitna*), and perhaps reflecting an awareness of new translation and missionizing efforts by the Dominicans, requested that all Arabic science books (*kutūb al-'ilm*) that had fallen into Christian hands be returned to Morocco.[99] Foreseeing the departure of the Marīnids, the rulers of Granada agreed to cobble together alliances with both Castile and the Crown of Aragon. Abū Yūsuf died a year later, and his son and successor, Abū Ya'qūb (r. 1286–1307), decided to abandon the Marīnid's foothold in al-Andalus, renouncing all but a handful of his fortresses, and return his armies to North Africa, where he became embroiled in a struggle to secure his own authority.[100] In a few short years, the political scene of the Iberian Peninsula had been radically transformed. The only remaining warfront lay between the Crown of Aragon and Castile, two Christian kingdoms, a hostility that would continue for twenty years. Put most succinctly, 1284 saw the beginning of a dramatic demobilization of the Marīnid cavalry along the Christian-Islamic frontier, a seeming end to their decades-long jihād.

Holy Warriors

The soldiers who accompanied Abū Yūsuf across the straits joined a second and separate branch of Marīnid cavalry, known as al-Ghuzāh al-Mujāhidūn, the Holy Warriors, who had settled permanently in Granada decades earlier and remained the most enduring and influential cavalry on the Iberian Peninsula.[101] Ibn Khaldūn devoted the final part of his *Kitāb al-ʿibar* to the history of these soldiers from 1262 until the arrest of their last leader in 1369.[102] He traced the origin of this corps to the revolt around the year 1260 at Salé (Salā) by a grandson of the founder of the Marīnid dynasty against the sultan Abū Yūsuf.[103] The rebellion was supported by Christian merchants living in the port city as well as three nephews of the sultan, whose names are mentioned here because they are critical to the history of the Aragonese *jenets*: Muḥammad b. Idrīs, ʿĀmir b. Idrīs, and Raḥḥū b. ʿAbd Allāh.[104] Nevertheless, this putsch failed. Abū Yūsuf massacred the Christian community at Salé and then marched against the three princes and their followers, who had retreated to their tribal homeland in the Rīf Mountains, in the western Maghrib, beyond Marīnid control.[105] Anticipating their own defeat, the young rebels repudiated their rebellion and negotiated terms. Crucially, rather than killing these princes, the sultan strong-armed them into accepting his terms.[106] According to Ibn Khaldūn, "He forced (*intadaba*) them to perform jihād (*ghazw*) and to cross the sea because of the cries of the Muslims of al-Andalus."[107] In short, they were exiled, banned from the kingdom. In this sense, Abū Yūsuf kept these quarrelsome competitors at a distance, while nevertheless using them to support his overarching efforts to aid the Muslims of al-Andalus. In 1262, therefore, the cousins, now bandits, crossed into the Iberian Peninsula at the head of three thousand cavalry soldiers.[108]

The Naṣrid ruler in Granada greeted these exiles with honors, as new allies against the encroaching Christian kingdoms to the north, and named them the first leaders of the Ghuzāh:

> They pressed the *amīr* of al-Andalus to give them the leadership [of the Ghuzāh] on the coast. So he ceded to them (*tajāfā lahum*) the battlefront, command of the Ghuzāh living on the shore (*ahl al-ʿudwa*) as well as the other tribes and factions of Berbers. They passed [command] to one another and shared the tax revenues (*jibāya*) with him [the *amīr*]. He also generously paid the salary of their soldiers (*bi-farḍ al-ʿaṭāʾ waʾl-dīwān fa-badhalahu lahum*). They continue in this manner until today. Their impact on [al-Andalus] was great, as we will note in the history that follows.[109]

By uniting various Berber tribes on the frontier of al-Andalus, these men wielded enough force to demand a portion of the Naṣrid tax revenue, military supplies, including a regular supply of horses, and control of any lands they conquered.[110] Although the commander of the Ghuzāh took his title from the Naṣrid sultan, Granada's authority over these soldiers appears to have been no more than nominal.[111] Until the Ghuzāh's dissolution, their leaders were almost exclusively elected from among a handful of the descendants of the three Marīnid princes.[112] The two neighborhoods in Granada in which contingents of these troops were settled were known as and continue to be known as "Cenete" and "Gomerez"; the latter alludes to the Ghumāra, the Zanāta tribe of these three exiled princes.[113]

These princes' promotion of jihād lent them a fame and authority beyond the scope of al-Andalus.[114] Ibn Khaldūn captured the messianic fervor that surrounded these troops:

> The Banū Idrīs and 'Abd Allāh . . . arrived in al-Andalus at a time when it lacked protection (*aqfara min al-ḥāmiya jawwuhā*). The enemy (*al-'aduww*) seized its frontier (*ista'sada*); their mouths drooled (*taḥallabat*) with anticipation of the pleasure [of seizing it]. But they [the Ghuzāh] took hold of it like vicious lions with sharpened swords, accustomed to encountering champions and striking them down with one deadly blow (*mu'awwadīn liqā' al-abṭāl wa-qirā' al-ḥutūf wa'l-nizāl*). Toughened by life in the desert (*mustaghliẓīn bi-khushūna al-badāwa*), the rigor of holy war (*ṣarāmat al-ghazw*), and intrepid barbarity (*basālat al-tawaḥḥush*), they inflicted great harm to their enemy. . . . They inspired zeal in the weakened Muslims behind the sea (*warā'a al-baḥr*) [i.e., in al-Andalus] and gave them hope of overcoming their oppressor.[115]

The successes of the Ghuzāh inspired other Zanāta princes, Marīnid and 'Abd al-Wādid, to imitation and their own crossing into al-Andalus.[116] Most but not all were Berbers: Mūsā b. 'Alī, a Kurd who had served as chamberlain to the 'Abd al-Wādids, joined the Ghuzāh after a fall from grace.[117] Eventually, the Ghuzāh incorporated a miscellany of mainly Zanāta tribesmen—some salaried, others volunteers, from across the kingdoms of North Africa—all devoted to the defense of the frontier. From here, they regularly invaded Aragonese and Castilian lands.

Lisān al-Dīn Ibn al-Khaṭīb (1313–75), the fourteenth-century polymath and rival of Ibn Khaldūn, surveyed the status of Granada's military and provides a more precise picture of the Ghuzāh, distinguishing them from the other Muslim cavalry of al-Andalus. In his time, Ibn al-Khaṭīb explained, the Naṣrid military was divided into two distinct armies, one Berber and the other Andalusī, by which he meant one comprising the North African soldiers and the other the Iberian Muslims.[118] Confirming what Ibn Khaldūn had told us, Ibn al-Khaṭīb explained that the "Berber" army was in fact made up of a variety of Zanāta and Arab tribes from

[margin note: Who N Africans answer to]

[margin note: Berber troops did not dress Andalusi leads or id]

the Maghrib: "As for the Berber, who come from the Marīnid, Zayyānid, Tijānī, 'Ajīsa, and North African Arab tribes, they fall under the jurisdiction of their own captains and leaders who, in turn, answer to the leader of them all, who is drawn from the eldest of the Marīnid tribe."[119] These Marīnid leaders, he continued, dressed like their Andalusī counterparts, but the majority of the "Berber" troops did not.[120] Nevertheless, Ibn al-Khaṭīb was frustratingly terse in describing how the majority did dress, saying only that these "Berber" soldiers used a throwing weapon called a *madas* (pl. *amdās*), a two-headed lance made of two sticks joined by a grip in the middle, which is likely the precursor of the *jineta* lance used by early modern Spanish *jinetes*.[121] By the fourteenth century, he added, these soldiers had also mastered the use of the Frankish arblete or crossbow (*qusiyy al-firanja*) to complement the throwing lance.[122]

When describing the Andalusī troops, however, Ibn al-Khaṭīb was clearer. They were commanded by relatives of or men close to the Naṣrid sultan. In the past, he continued, these Andalusī soldiers were outfitted in the same manner as their Christian counterparts.[123] They wore long coats of mail, carried heavy shields and long lances, and traveled with a squire, which is to say that they rode in the fashion of other European heavy cavalry. By his time—that is, the late fourteenth century—however, this style had changed. The cavalry now wore shorter coats and gilded helmets; they used "Arab saddles," North African leather shields, and light lances.[124] Importantly, therefore, Ibn al-Khaṭīb's description reveals that Iberian Muslim cavalry underwent a military transformation parallel to that of their Christian counterparts, but well before them. In other words, Muslim cavalry in al-Andalus had not always been light cavalry. At some point before 1363 (when the *Lamḥa* was completed), they adopted and adapted the Zanāta style; they started to ride in *a la jineta*. The illuminations from the late thirteenth-century *Cantigas de Santa Maria* by Alfonso X of Castile indicate the coexistence of both styles of dressing—with and without armor—and riding—*a la brida* and *a la jineta*—in the Granadan army, suggesting that the transformation was not complete at this moment (fig. 2).[125] And thus, the question is: were these light soldiers depicted in the *Cantigas* Iberian or North African troops? A description by the historian Ibn Saʿīd al-Andalusī (d. 1286) strongly suggests the latter. In his time, he explains, the Andalusī cavalry was still comprised singularly of heavily armed knights.[126] If one accepts Ibn Saʿīd's portrait, then the only light cavalry in the Iberian Peninsula in 1284 were the North African arrivistes—mainly but not exclusively Zanāta Berbers—under the command of the

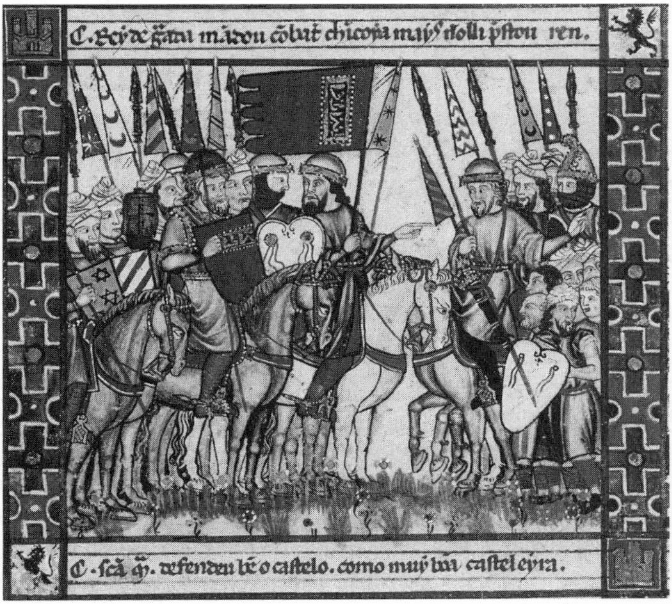

FIGURE 2. Alfonso X, *Cantigas de Santa Maria* (no. 187) (ca. 1284) (detail, middle-left panel). Heavy and light cavalry in the Granadan army. Monasterio-Biblioteca-Colección, San Lorenzo de El Escorial, Madrid. Photograph: Album / Art Resource, New York.

Marīnid sultan or the Marīnid princes who led the Ghuzāh. These North African soldiers who had come to the Iberian Peninsula for the sake of jihād must have become the Aragonese *jenets*.

Is there definitive proof of this transformation? Ibn Khaldūn did tell us that a handful of the commanders of the Ghuzāh sought refuge in Christian courts across the thirteenth and fourteenth centuries.[127] But he never says that the Ghuzāh sold their services to the Aragonese kings in large numbers at that time. Indeed, from his perspective, the Ghuzāh were admirable defenders of Islam, true holy warriors. This is the limitation of the *Kitāb al-ibar*, which strongly identified with these Berber warriors and saw them as the vital spirit of renewal.

Latin and Romance archival records, on the one hand, and Arabic chronicles, on the other, thus appear incommensurable. Each set of sources presents us with a partial view. Each possesses its own concealments and biases. While Latin and Romance sources speak of *jenets*, they tell us little to nothing about the origin of these troops. In fact, the success of these soldiers or, more precisely, the style of riding associated with them has only further obscured their history and allowed them to hide in plain sight. In these paper records, the word *jenet* has become unremarkable, trivia for hippologists. Arabic sources speak of the Ghuzāh, one of many waves of holy warriors, Islamic heroes who crashed upon the shores of al-Andalus. But the Aragonese *jenets* and the Marīnid Ghuzāh never clearly meet.

A careful comparison of all these sources does reveal that they, the *jenets* and the Ghuzāh, were one and the same soldiers. As Arabic names enter into Romance sources, they are often mangled and misshapen beyond recognition. Letters are transposed, dropped, or changed as a scribe strains to make sense of what he has heard. But occasionally and particularly in the case of prominent figures, their names can be reconstructed. Across the thirteenth and fourteenth centuries, in missions to recruit *jenets*, contracts for service, and records of employment, some familiar-sounding names appear in the Crown's archive. For instance, one reads: Iça Abenadriz, Muça Abenrohh, Alabes Abarraho, Iyca Abenrraho, Baratdin Abarraho, Greneladim Abarraho, and Hali Ebemuca Abenrraho among others.[128] In Arabic sources, one finds: 'Isā b. Idrīs, Mūsa b. Raḥḥū, al-'Abbās b. Raḥḥū, 'Īsā b. Raḥḥū, Badr al-Dīn [b. Mūsā.] b. Raḥḥū, Jamāl al-Dīn [b. Mūsā] b. Raḥḥū, and 'Alī b. Mūsā b. Raḥḥū, among others. These men were members of the Marīnid royal family, relatives and descendants of the three Marīnid princes, exiled to al-Andalus, who were the founders of al-Ghuzāh al-Mujāhidūn.[129] Some of these men would command the Ghuzāh, and some would also command the Aragonese *jenets*. These names tell us without a doubt that the Ghuzāh were also members of the *jenets*.

This realization presents a new challenge. How and why did the Aragonese kings turn to the Ghuzāh, men who as late as 1284 were invading its lands and would continue to invade it, to serve in their armies and more strikingly, as their personal protectors? Why would the Ghuzāh seemingly abandon their cause? What bound these Christian kings to Muslim holy warriors over the period of a century?

CHAPTER TWO

A Sovereign Crisis

Six months before the arrival of the five horsemen riding mules, in October 1284, King Pere II ordered Conrad Lancia, his master of accounts (*maestre racional*), as well as a Jew named Samuel Abenmenassé, a physician and translator, to prepare for a journey to Granada.[1] The Crown had recently concluded a truce with the Muslim kingdom, and this mission seemed routine.[2] Before their departure, Pere had ordered the release of all Granadan captives in his territories. He had instructed a royal official to give each prisoner a tunic and sufficient money to "return to their king."[3] In return, Pere asked his ambassadors, Conrad and Samuel, to confirm the release of two Valencian captains and their crews held in Granada.[4] Curiously, Pere also asked a local Muslim leader (*alaminus*, from Ar. *al-amīn*), Abrahim Abençumada, to cover the cost of Conrad's mission to Granada.[5] Why were the Crown's Mudéjares being asked to finance what seemed like a diplomatic effort? The king described the mission's intent in a letter of introduction:

> Know all that we, Don Pedro, by the grace of God, king of Aragon and Sicily, order you, our special procurator, noble and beloved, Conrad Lancia, chamberlain of our house, and master of accounts, to speak with the captains of the *jenets* and with others regarding the date of their arrival and stay with us in our service. And regarding what we must give them [i.e., salary], we hold firmly to whatever will be said and done or promised by the said Conrad in this [negotiation], and this we will observe. And that this charter should be firm and no doubt enter, we order it sealed.[6]

Conrad and Samuel had been ordered to recruit Muslim soldiers from Granada. They were about to depart on the first known mission to recruit *jenets* for the Crown of Aragon.[7]

To pursue the question of how and why the Aragonese kings turned to their former enemies, the Marīnid Ghuzāh, it serves us to follow these two ambassadors as they made their way into the kingdom of Granada in 1284. This was a watershed moment, after which the Crown's use of these soldiers increased dramatically. An overlooked list of names and locations, scribbled alongside the letter of introduction above, enables us not only to recreate these ambassadors' itinerary and to confirm the identity of the soldiers that they hoped to recruit but also to place this mission in a broader social, political, and intellectual context. This story spans the Mediterranean—from Spain to Sicily and North Africa—and draws upon Latin, Romance, and Arabic sources in order to demonstrate that this alliance not only responded to immediate circumstance—to extreme crisis—but was also a piece of political theater. It grew out of a much longer and deeper history of Aragonese aspiration.

A Rupture?

Claiming that there is no evidence of their use prior to 1284, Faustino Gazulla began his history of *jenets* with the date of this mission to recruit these soldiers.[8] Indeed, from the perspective of the chancery registers, the year 1284 seems to be a levee-breaking moment, after which *jenets* flood these pages. Is this the beginning of our story, the start of something new? To call something a first is no minor or middling matter: it imposes a certain interpretation on all the documents that follow. In this case, to begin in 1284 implies a rupture: one moment the Muslim *jenets* were raiding Valencia; the next, they were trotting in as soldiers-for-hire with letters of invitation from the Aragonese king. Accepting this narrative raises a challenge—which Gazulla, perhaps wisely, sidestepped—the challenge of accounting for sudden change.

Aside from a general suspicion of ruptures, two significant factors impede writing a study of the origins of the Aragonese *jenets*. First, in this period, the chancery registers remained nascent; they were kept irregularly, unsystematically, or simply not at all.[9] Thus, any starting point may be nothing more than a fiction of the documents themselves, a mirage of paper and ink. Second, and more significantly, evidence from the earliest registers hints at a longer and more convoluted history of interaction between the Aragonese kings and *jenet* soldiers before this mission.

An overlooked fragment from the archives—the earliest surviving reference to the *jenets*—demonstrates the problem. Dated October 13, 1265, during the reign of King Jaume I, twenty years before the mission of Conrad Lancia and Samuel Abenmenassé, this document is brief—a list of expenses, copied into the registers:

> Also, for the expenses of the *jenets*, 6 *denarii*. . . .
> Also, for the clothes of [i.e., given to] the *jenets*—903 *solidi*
> Also, for the clothes of the representatives of the *jenets*—86 *solidi*
> Also, for the cloth (*pannus*) of the *jenets*—35 *solidi*
> Also, 140 *solidi*, 6 *denarii* for cloth, tunics (*aflabays*), and thread
> Also, for the shoes of the *jenets*—15 *solidi*
> Also, for the shirts (*camisis*) of the *jenets*—35 *solidi*
> Also, for thread—8 *solidi*, 8 *denarii*
> Also, for the shirts of the representatives of the *jenets*—5 *solidi*, 8 *denarii*
> Also, for tunics and thread—9 *solidi*, 8 *denarii*.[10]

While desultory, this list of accounts, recorded three years after the establishment of the Ghuzāh in al-Andalus and well before the first Marīnid incursion into the Iberian Peninsula, is the earliest proof of an encounter between the Muslim *jenets* and the Crown of Aragon. What was happening here? A payment was made for expenses to *jenets*. Cloth and clothes were distributed to the representatives (*nuncii*) of the *jenets* as well as the *jenets* themselves. As we shall see, payments for travel expenses and gifts were typical of later negotiations for recruitment. The presence of an Arabic translator at this encounter also suggests that these are the traces of a negotiation.[11] Clothing was generally given to soldiers who had agreed to enter the service of the Crown, and thus one might contend that this was also a successful recruitment effort. The terse language—the fact that the scribe did not explain who or what the *jenets* were—may also imply that this was also not the Crown's first encounter with these soldiers. One can push further. These expenses appear in the account books of Prince Pere. In fact, there is no evidence that King Jaume ever employed *jenets*, suggesting that Pere may have been the first to show an interest in these soldiers, a claim that is borne out by the story told below. Additionally, these records appear tucked among the expenses of the prince's household—his personal expenses—including, for instance, 11 *solidi*, 7 *denarii* to buy a tunic for "a Saracen of the Lord Prince," perhaps, a domestic slave.[12] Pere as well as later Aragonese and Castilian kings did employ Muslim soldiers in their households—as members of their entourage and as their personal protectors.[13] And although these shreds of evidence cannot give confidence to the assertion, perhaps the prince was already using these soldiers in this intimate capacity.

For the two decades after this brief notice, during the period of the massive Mudéjar rebellions that shook Valencia, there is no indication of *jenets* in the Crown's employ, only as enemies of it. But in the months just before Conrad and Samuel's departure, hints of *jenets* in the service of the Crown begin to appear again. For instance, the chancery registers record that in August 1284, a *jenet* named Muçe (Mūsā) received "53 *solidi* and 4 *denarii* that remained of his salary."[14] And in the same month, Pere ordered an official to give traveling expenses to Aixe ('Ā'isha), the wife of a *jen*[illegible]ervice, such that she could move to Valencia.[15] In N[illegible] bailiff of Valencia was asked to pay three *jenets* who had already agreed to enter the king's service.[16] All of these documents suggest the continued use of *jenets* between 1265 and 1284. In the first case, Muçe received the remainder of his salary, which is to say that he had been paid before and had completed some service without leaving any imprint upon the documentation. Even if these early registers limit our ability to know the extent of the use of *jenets* before 1284, they confirm that King Pere had successfully recruited and employed these soldiers before the mission of Conrad and Samuel.

It is also worth adding that the *jenets* were not the first or only Muslim soldiers in the employ of the Aragonese kings. Although early studies of the Mudéjares rejected the fact, both Burns and Boswell have shown that the Crown of Aragon did in fact use subject Muslims in its armies.[17] In part, the evidence of their service is negative. Surrender agreements, such as those at Tudela (1115) or Chivert (1234), agreed to limit the service owed by Mudéjares to local or municipal defense.[18] Similarly, the chancery registers preserve certain exemptions from military service (*exercitus*) given to prominent or skilled Muslims.[19] For instance, in 1259, two brothers, Mahomet and Abdela, were granted freedom from military service because of "certain work" they provided the king.[20] Of course, the implication of such documents is that the Crown expected the rest of the Mudéjares to provide military service.[21] But one also finds more explicit evidence, such as assurances from the king to Mudéjar soldiers that their goods would be protected in their absence during war or that they would be exempted from any extraordinary taxes related to war.[22] In 1285, for example, Pere asked the Mudéjares of Valencia to deliver over four thousand *solidi* "in one bag" to pay the salaries and expenses of the Muslim soldiers that they had already sent to the king.[23] What is more, the Aragonese kings

[margin note: prized archers]

openly prized and praised their Muslim archers—who specialized in using the heavy "two-foot crossbow," so called not because of its length but because archers used both feet to tense it.[24] Christian Aragonese soldiers, by contrast, only employed a light crossbow. Relatedly, the Crown employed Mudéjares for the purpose of weapon making. In 1280, an engineer (*faber*) named Mahomet (Muḥammad) arrived at the court and so impressed the king with his metalwork, in particular crossbow bolts (*cairells*), that the king placed him in his private employ.[25] And in 1295, the king called upon the Mudéjares of Daroca and Calatayud to make weapons for his armies.[26] There is, however, no evidence of Mudéjar cavalry, a fact that may provide an explanation for the need to recruit North African soldiers for this role.

Significantly, the Crown's experience with Mudéjar soldiers was not without problems. During al-Azraq's second uprising, when the *jenets* were attacking the lands of the Crown, King Jaume expressed anger and surprise at the refusal of certain Mudéjares to come to his aid:

> While we were in Valencia, the leader (*alcait* from Ar. *al-qā'id*) of Játiva came to us with a large group of Saracens and about ten elders from the village. He entered very happily and kissed my hand and asked how we were. And we said, "Well by the grace of God, but that we are very distressed by the wrongs al-Azraq has committed in [taking] our castles and marvel at your allowing it." [And he said:] "Lord, if it distresses you, know that it distresses us and causes grief." But they seemed happier and more content than we had ever seen them. We thought that they would be distressed by the wrong al-Azraq had done us and offer help, but none of them offered it.[27]

[margin note: mudejars unwilling to fight muslims]

Thus, while the Crown was willing to use its Mudéjar soldiers against other Muslims, at least on this occasion, it found the Mudéjares unwilling to serve. Eventually, both Jaume and his successor Pere agreed to commute military service into a payment for several Mudéjar communities.[28] In 1277, for instance, numerous Mudéjar villages in Aragon were given the choice of serving in the army or paying to support the army.[29] Nevertheless, despite questions of their loyalty, with regard to the military, the Aragonese kings ultimately treated their Mudéjar subjects just as they did their Christian ones: they expected service in men or in kind, which is to say that the Mudéjares were regarded as members of the Crown's feudal army.

Three important facts thus emerge from these crucial fragments belonging to the earliest registers. First, not all *jenets* were hostile to the

Crown. Before the mission of 1284, some *jenets* were already willing to enter into its service. The relationship of the *jenets* and the Crown of Aragon may have been as old as the Ghuzāh. In other words, the cluster of documents highlighted in the previous chapter, in which the *jenets* appear attacking the lands of the Crown of Aragon during the Mudéjar uprising in Valencia, represents only part of the picture and masks a deeper continuity. Second, the evidence for these early dealings point exclusively to the future King Pere. During his lieutenancy, Pere may have employed the *jenets* in his personal entourage, as members of his household. Third and finally, the Crown had not only used Muslim soldiers in its armies but also experienced challenges in dealing with them, a fact that would shape its history with the *jenets*. The first known recruitment of the *jenets* therefore did not represent a clean rupture from this past.

The Sicilian and the Jew

In and of itself, Pere's choice of leaders for the mission to Granada to recruit *jenets* was telling. One of Pere's closest confidants, his childhood companion, and relative of his wife, Conrad Lancia was not an Aragonese nobleman but rather a Sicilian one. More precisely, he was the illegitimate grandson of the Holy Roman emperor Frederick II (1194–1250).[30] With Pere's ascent to the throne, Conrad rose to fortune as well, becoming commander of the Aragonese navy in 1278.[31] A year later, in that capacity, Conrad boldly invaded the North African port of Ceuta (Sabta), from which the Marīnid sultan had been providing support for al-Azraq's rebellion in Valencia.[32] In the same year, Conrad participated in the dramatic coup that placed Abū Isḥāq (r. 1279–1283) on the Ḥafṣid throne at Tunis.[33] According to the chronicler Muntaner, Conrad had the Aragonese flag raised above Tunis' citadel.[34] For such service, Pere rewarded him with a castle and lands and made him governor of the Mudéjar-dominated kingdom of Valencia in 1280.[35] By 1284, Conrad was also the head of the king's household as well as his master of accounts.[36]

Although his name does not appear in the letter of introduction above, the prominent figure Samuel Abenmenassé accompanied Conrad.[37] A member of the royal household (*de domo regis*), Samuel served as the king's physician (*alfaquimus et fisicus*) as well as his Arabic secretary (*scriptor de arabico*), a dual role that was not uncommon for Jews at the court.[38] Like Conrad, Samuel was a confidant and intimate of Pere. The king, for instance, entrusted his doctor to carry special messages to the queen and prince, and the letters between these men evince an unusual familiarity in both tone and content.[39] But Samuel's superior knowledge of Arabic also made him indispensable to the Crown.[40] For instance, in 1280, when negotiating with the Mudéjares of Játiva, King Pere signed a "certain Arabic letter," trusting only in Samuel's translation.[41] Samuel wrote and delivered the peace treaty with Granada in 1282 that paved the way for this mission.[42] He traveled on secret missions to Tunis.[43] On the domestic front, he managed the sale of captives from Valencia's Mudéjar rebellion.[44] And most significantly, Samuel had already acted as a recruiter among Muslims. Three months prior to the mission to Granada, he visited the Mudéjar communities of Aragon and Valencia, seeking "well-appointed crossbowmen and lancers" in return for a "good salary," suggesting that these Muslim soldiers were needed for extraordinary service.[45] As a reward, Pere similarly granted Samuel privileges as well as lands in Valencia.[46]

Thus, as leaders for this mission, Pere chose two trusted representatives with ties to local Muslims as well as sultans. One might be tempted to argue that this mission both reflected and leveraged the cosmopolitan character of the Aragonese court, and that it demonstrated the manner in which religious and political boundaries were easily pierced or ignored in this world. The deeper implication of this presumed cosmopolitanism is that religious and political identities were shibboleths that could be shrugged off by men of a certain perspective and status like old clothes. But such logic, however much it satisfies a democratic and inclusive vision of the world, did not drive Pere's choice. Indeed, the fact that Pere relied heavily upon a foreigner and a Jew brings to the surface a rather different motivation for his recruitment of the *jenets*.

The Sicilian Vespers

What follows is a story that revolves around Sicily, a history of repetitions: the first time as tragedy, the second as farce.[47] It begins twenty years earlier, in 1262, around the same time the Ghuzāh first arrived in the Iberian Peninsula, when Pere's father, King Jaume I, arranged the marriage of the young Prince Pere to fourteen-year-old Constanza (1249–1302), the granddaughter of the Emperor Frederick II and daughter of Manfred of Sicily as well as half-cousin to Conrad Lancia.[48] Constanza arrived at the Aragonese court with her royal household, including a school-aged

Conrad, our main protagonist, as well as Roger de Lauria, the future admiral of fame.[49] This marriage alliance, which drew together the Aragonese and Hohenstaufen dynasties, immediately met objections from many, including King Louis IX of France (r. 1226–1270). Both Jaume and Louis desired control of the central Mediterranean and through it, right to the title of Holy Roman emperor.[50] And the tension between them only mounted when four years later, in 1266 at Benevento, Louis' brother, Charles of Anjou, killed Constanza's father and then seized the island kingdom. These maneuvers marked the beginning of a protracted and violent struggle between the Angevins and the Aragonese.

Initially, Hohenstaufen loyalists and rebels, championing a young nephew of Manfred, sought refuge with Sicily's longtime tributary, the Ḥafṣid sultan of Tunis.[51] Among those who traveled to North Africa was Federico Lancia, Conrad's father, who subsequently entered the service of the sultan as a member of his Christian guard, a phenomenon that ran parallel to and intersected with that of the *jenets*.[52] Federico and other exiles defended the city from Louis' crusaders in 1270, extending the Hohenstaufen and Angevin war into North Africa.[53] In fact, Conrad's support of a coup in Tunis less than ten years later should be seen as a continuation of this same struggle, the effort to restore Hohenstaufen rule to Sicily.[54] Nevertheless, when the efforts of these rebels in Tunis were foiled in 1268, King Jaume pushed Constanza, his daughter-in-law, to proclaim herself the rightful heir to the Hohenstaufen throne. And thus, in the years that followed, a variety of Sicilian exiles—noblemen, jurists, officers, and administrators—arrived in the lands of the Crown of Aragon, where they would gain extraordinary sway over Prince Pere.[55]

In the decades after this marriage, the Aragonese court also took on the appearance of Frederick's. For instance, under Constanza's influence, Pere issued a set of sweeping palatine ordinances that implemented sophisticated innovations from Sicily related to dress, diet, and diversion.[56] Like Frederick, Pere now maintained Arabic secretaries—including Samuel Abenmenassé—for translating "Saracen books."[57] Institutionally, Pere borrowed whole cloth the idea of an independent royal treasury as it existed in Sicily and tellingly made Conrad Lancia its first *maestre racional,* master of accounts.[58] He established the royal pantheon at Santes Creus on the model of the Sicilian one at Palermo.[59] Most significantly, it is also at Frederick's court that one finds a precedent for the *jenets*. Both Frederick II and Manfred had recruited Muslim soldiers from the colony of Lucera in Apulia to serve in their armies as well as their courts as bodyguards, a fact that drew more than passing notice from visitors.[60] That Pere also called upon Conrad Lancia, the grandson of Frederick, to recruit his own Muslim guard reveals the clear path of influence from Sicily to Aragon. Collectively, these courtly and administrative reforms aimed at imagining, performing, and ultimately realizing a vision of imperial authority modeled upon the Hohenstaufens' lofty conception of empire.

Given all these Sicilian echoes, it is not surprising that from 1279, if not earlier, Pere directed his foreign policy toward the goal of retaking that kingdom from the Angevins.[61] An aggressive maritime strategy along the North African littoral was part and parcel of a desire to control the central Mediterranean, an effort to envelope the island of Sicily. In 1282, while the Aragonese navy—captained by the Hohenstaufen exiles, Roger de Lauria and Conrad Lancia—was fumbling a putsch to impose a puppet ruler on the throne of Tunis, a rebellion erupted in Angevin Sicily, perhaps kindled by Aragonese agents.[62] Samuel Abenmenassé was one of many Aragonese representatives to travel to Sicily just before the uprising. Upon receiving news of the rebellion, the ships of Roger de Lauria temporarily abandoned the North African coast and succeeded in capturing the island kingdom from Charles of Anjou, returning Sicily to the heirs of the Hohenstaufens.

Having accomplished his singular ambition, however, Pere ironically unleashed the greatest threat to his sovereignty, a French invasion and one of the worst wars suffered by the lands of the Crown of Aragon.[63] Enraged by the conquest of Sicily, the French pope, Martin IV, excommunicated King Pere, undercutting the Crown's claim to divinely sanctioned authority. Martin offered the Crown of Aragon to the Capetians. When the French ruler accepted in 1284, a crusade against Pere was launched. Meanwhile, the situation within the Crown of Aragon deteriorated dramatically. Pere's uncle, Jaume of Mallorca, threw his lot in with the Papacy. The powerful nobleman Juan Nuñez de Lara declared Albarracín, a region in Aragon, an independent lordship in support of the French. Half of Pere's other vassals declared themselves unwilling to defend him, rising up in rebellion. In their first forays across the Pyrenees, the French committed horrible excesses, killing men, women, children, and nuns. Panicked villagers fled the lands north of Barcelona. Whole cities were abandoned.

Pere thus faced a major crisis in 1284. With his navy in Sicily and Calabria, many of the Aragonese and Catalan noblemen in open revolt, and the threat of a massive French invasion gaining support from his own men, King Pere could only muster a scant force—thirty-eight knights and seventy foot soldiers—at Coll de Panissars to prepare for war.[64] He was capable of little more than hurling invectives through his court jongleur at the French.[65] And it is precisely at this point that he ordered Conrad and Samuel to depart for Granada to seek new allies. In responding to this crisis, Pere's decision to reach out to the *jenets*, his former enemies, reflected desperate necessity, but he also traveled upon well-worn tracks, following a model of authority that led back to the Holy Roman emperors.

All the Names

From this point, we would be lost if it were not for a list of names recorded alongside Lancia's letter of introduction, a list that recorded with whom he was to meet:[66]

> Also, we made for him [Conrad Lancia] a letter of introduction to the below named:
>
> > Abzultan Hademi, the chief minister (*alguazir*, from Ar. *wazīr*) of the king of Granada,
> > Muça Abenrohh,
> > Guillelmus Nehot, consul of Almería,
> > Raiz Abuabdille Abenhudeyr, the lord of Crevillente,
> > to Iça Abenadriz, captive of the king,
> > Raimundus de Santo Literio,
> > Petrus Morelle, that he should transfer to Raimundus de Santo Literio custody of the aforementioned Iça,
>
> Also, we gave Conrad a letter of passage, addressed to Castilian officials. Later, we gave him letters of introduction and also procurement regarding the *jenets* named below:
>
> > Çahit Azanach,
> > Çahim Abebaguen,
> > Tunart.

These names allow us to track Conrad's progress toward Granada and confirm the source of the soldiers he aimed to recruit (maps 1 and 3). Conrad first sought a meeting with "Iça Abenadriz" through his custodians. Abenadriz was a captive of the Crown of Aragon, a prisoner held in the

Castle of Empostà (Amposta), south of Teruel in Catalonia, by the Hospitaller Knights. Both Kings Pere II and Alfons II treated Abenadriz and his wife with some deference.[67] Three years later, the Marīnid sultan, after extended negotiations, would secure Abenadriz's release for an astonishing 3,600 gold dinars.[68] Abenadriz would also return freely to the Crown of Aragon in 1291 as an ambassador from the Marīnid court.[69] All this suggests that he was a man of some importance, and indeed, he is easily identified in Arabic sources. He was 'Īsā b. Idrīs, a nephew of Abū Yūsuf, the Marīnid sultan. The significance of Conrad's visit with this prince becomes clearer in the light of his whole itinerary.

Conrad then carried on to Crevillente (Qirbilyān), where he held a letter of introduction to the Muslim ruler (*Raiz* from Ar. *al-ra'īs*), Abuabdille Abenhudeyr (Abū 'Abdallah b. Hudhayr).[70] Crevillente was a curiosity, a neutral "village-state" near Murcia that nominally paid homage to the Castilians in this period but would eventually come under the protection of the Aragonese kings.[71] Its leaders, the Banū Hudhayr, maintained their independence until 1318 by serving as intermediaries between the Crown of Aragon and Granada.[72] In later periods, part of their service to the Crown of Aragon included acting as recruiting agents for *jenets*. As early as 1286, one finds evidence of *jenets* entering and departing the realms of the Crown of Aragon through Crevillente.[73] Later, in 1303, King Jaume II would write to the Muslim ruler of Crevillente to inform him that he had hired forty *jenets* and was returning the remaining forty, whom he did not require, suggesting that Ibn Hudhayr facilitated their recruitment.[74] And on at least two occasions, moreover, the Muslim ruler would write to Jaume II reporting on the activities of the *jenets* in Valencia and Ghuzāh across the border in Granada.[75] In short, Conrad's arrival in Crevillente may have marked the beginning of their long-standing intermediary role with the *jenets*.

Conrad continued south in order to meet the consul of Almería (al-Mariyya), a strategic port city in southeastern Spain, where almost all Mediterranean powers had interests and representatives. Although it was momentarily under Christian rule, Almería was a contested zone that changed hands regularly.[76] Its desirability derived from the fact that it served as the major commercial artery between Valencia and Granada.[77] And as a hub of legal and illegal trade, Almería represented a quintessential zone of overlapping jurisdictions.[78] Significantly, it was also famous for its *ribāṭs*, military-religious fortresses for those devoted to jihād, which had been and would be used by Ghuzāh soldiers for raids into Christian Spain.[79]

Finally, Conrad arrived in Granada, where he met the chief minister of the Naṣrid sultan as well as man named Muça Abenrrohh, who was the well-known figure, Mūsā b. Raḥḥū. The fact that Conrad met both ʿĪsā b. Idrīs and Mūsā b. Raḥḥū is extremely revealing. These men were the sons and nephews of the three Marīnid princes—Muḥammad b. Idrīs, ʿĀmir b. Idrīs, and Raḥḥū b. ʿAbd Allāh—who had crossed into Spain in 1262 at the head of three-thousand Marīnid cavalry to become the first commanders of al-Ghuzāh al-Mujāhidūn, the Holy Warriors. According to Ibn Khaldūn, Mūsā b. Raḥḥū was commander of these soldiers (*shaykh al-ghuzāh*) on three occasions.[80] His brother al-ʿAbbās b. Raḥḥū would later serve the Aragonese kings as commanders of their *jenets*.[81] In other words, from the outset, Conrad and Samuel aimed to recruit the Marīnid Ghuzāh, a band of holy warriors who only a few months earlier had served alongside the armies of Abū Yūsuf's fourth and final jihād against Castile and the Crown of Aragon.

band of holy warriors

The Arrivals

Conrad received his final letters of introduction to three *jenet* corporals (*cabos*) named "Çahit Azanach, Çahim Abebaguen, and Tunart." While of lower rank than Mūsā b. Raḥḥū, they nevertheless found themselves in the company of rather prominent men. Their names appear on a short list of dignitaries whom Conrad and Samuel met, including two Marīnid princes and the chief minister (*wazīr*) of Granada. None of these three names—muddled in transliteration to Romance—are identifiable in Arabic sources. By chance, however, these soldiers left an imprint elsewhere, confirming once again the source of the soldiers whom Pere had chosen to recruit.

Not in arabic sources—elsewhere

Sometime after the arrival of the Ghuzāh in 1262, a monk named Pero Marín at the monastery of St. Dominic of Silos near Burgos began to record the testimonies of Christian villagers, who claimed to have escaped from the hands of these North African raiders.[82] His *Miraculos romanzados* provides important evidence about captivity and slave markets, as well as the effects of Ghuzāh raids on the Murcian frontier. The economy and demography of regions like Lorca, for example, would not recover for more than a century.[83] But miraculously for the historian, across several of these accounts, we hear of two captains, named "Zahem and Zahet Azenet," who in 1283 raided the Murcian frontier with 1,000 *jenet* soldiers, killing 200 men and taking many captives.[84] If these were the same men as

from monastic testimony

slave market

jenet raiders

Çahim and Çahit, then within a year, the Crown was aiming to recruit these notorious Ghuzāh leaders.

The name Çahim Abebaguen also provides us with proof that Conrad and Samuel's recruitment effort ended in success. The five horsemen, with whom this book began, riding mules borrowed from a Jew in Granada, were in fact the representatives of "Çahim Abennaquem." Several months after meeting Conrad Lancia and Samuel Abenmenassé in Granada, these horsemen, among the first to respond to the call, crossed into the lands of the Crown of Aragon. At the border of Valencia, after examining their letters of introduction, royal officials impounded the *jenets'* swords, indicating a well-earned distrust of these raiders.[85] The soldiers next appeared in the city of Valencia, where they met with the local Muslim leader, Abrahim Abençumada, who had helped to finance Conrad's mission, suggesting that the Mudéjares, who once sought aid from these soldiers against the Crown, were now supporting their recruitment for the Crown.[86] Some days later, the *jenets* stayed in the Christian town of Vilafranca, some one hundred miles north of Valencia, after which a royal official wrote a letter to the king, complaining that these Muslim travelers had borrowed fifteen *solidi* from him and failed to repay him.[87] These soldiers then passed into and through the kingdom of Catalonia, but we learn nothing more of their journey through this predominantly Christian kingdom. Finally, having crossed the length of the realms of the Crown of Aragon, they arrived at the base of the Pyrenees, at Coll de Panissars, where they received an audience with King Pere, who was preparing for battle against the French crusaders.

Some months later, King Pere would write a letter to Samuel, who had apparently remained in Muslim Granada, to announce the success of his negotiations at Coll de Panissars.[88] He ordered that Abrahim Abençumada should cease interfering "because we [the king] got along well with them [the *jenets*]," confirming the Mudéjar governor's role in the recruitment.[89] But Pere's insistence on dealing directly with the *jenets* hints at a certain wariness of interactions between the Mudéjares and the *jenets* that is borne out by later history.[90] This letter also solves a more mundane mystery when Pere explains that he has decided to give these soldiers Samuel's mules, items of great value, as a gift.[91] The royal physician, in other words, was the Jew who lent the *jenets* the mules that they rode the long distance from Granada.

Having successfully completed the negotiations, Pere paid for the expenses of the five *jenets* in traveling to the Crown and returned their swords.[92] He further issued an expense account (*expensarium*) to cover the costs of Çahim and the rest of his troops in coming to Coll de Panissars.[93] As he would on later occasions with other soldiers, he showered the *jenets* with gifts. All five received "Saracen" tunics and stirrups, but he singled out three.[94] Alaçen, "Saracen soldier and representative to Çahim, son of Abennaquem," was given a tunic (*aliuba*) of multicolored cloth and red Parisian silk shoes; Hamet Abenobrut received a tunic from the city of Jalón and shoes of colored cloth; and Mahomet de Villena accepted clothes of plain cloth and shoes from Narbonne.[95] Alaçen and Hamet also received saddles and horse bridles. Alaçen was given a "good bridle," whereas Hamet was given "one of lesser price," a distinction that indicates that Alaçen was the mission's leader.[96] And while it appears that Çahim's company of *jenets* agreed to enter into the service of the king, after this moment, definitive evidence of these five soldiers disappears from the royal records.

All the same, Pere's decision to recruit Muslim soldiers to aid in the defense against a French invasion led to a successful outcome. During the siege of Gerona, the chronicler Bernat Desclot recorded that over six hundred Mudéjar crossbowmen valiantly defended the city alongside Count Ramon Folch.[97] The city would eventually fall, but in the meantime, Roger de Lauria's fleet returned from Sicily. Lauria destroyed Philip III's ships in the Bay of Roses in September 1285, cutting off the French forward position in Gerona and sending their armies into retreat. The arrival of ten thousand *jenets* (*deu milia Serrayns ginets*), according to Desclot, pushed the French back toward Perpignan, where King Philip died at the beginning of October.[98] While the number of *jenets* is suspect, it nonetheless suggests that Desclot considered Muslim support essential to this victory. The papal legate, who had preached the French crusade against the Crown of Aragon, agreed that the Crown's reliance upon Muslim soldiers was not only decisive but also, for that very reason, damning: "He [King Pere] has joined with himself Saracens to destroy the Christian faith, and with their aid he strives to withstand us, for by his own strength, which is naught, he could not stand alone."[99] Although Pere hoped to press on from this victory and punish his uncle, Jaume of Mallorca, for insubordination, the king died a month later on November 11, 1285. The success of the *jenets*, however, would fix their place in the lands of the Crown of Aragon for decades to come.

payment

crucial to success

CHAPTER THREE

Sovereigns and Slaves

The Crown of Aragon's decision to recruit large numbers of Muslim *jenets* initially emerged out of extreme circumstances—an existential threat. In 1284, facing a French invasion and the rebellion of his own noblemen, King Pere II could only muster a handful of men to his defense. Thus, at some level, his alliance with his former enemies, the Marīnid Ghuzāh, reflected practical necessity—the desire for professional soldiers, at any cost, who would answer his commands. Nevertheless, for decades to come, until the dissolution of the Ghuzāh at the end of the fourteenth century, Aragonese kings continued to recruit and employ *jenets* across their far-flung empire, in their armies and courts, against their enemies and their own rebellious subjects. What began as an emergency measure, in other words, became a permanent one, a fixed feature of royal power. Why did these rulers continue to rely on their former enemies? Did anything more than practical necessity bind these Christian kings to these Muslim soldiers? And what does this alliance reveal about the nature of Aragonese kingship?

Salary

The *jenets* were mercenaries. They were soldiers-for-hire, men who received payments from the Crown of Aragon for the services that they offered. Indeed, the vast majority of the records in the Archive of the Crown of Aragon concerning the *jenets* deal with the disbursement of salaries. Seen from the perspective of these receipts, piles of medieval pay stubs, the Aragonese kings' relationship with these soldiers seems decidedly professional and uncomplicated. This was a clean and clear financial transaction: the kings paid, and these soldiers fought their wars.

It was pecuniary nature of the professional or contractual bond, however, that led Machiavelli to warn rulers against relying upon mercenaries. Nothing binds the soldier-for-hire, he said, nothing, that is, but greed.[1] Mercenaries are faithless (*infedeli*). In the case of the *jenets*, they were rather literally infidels. So why did the Aragonese kings then put their faith in the hands of non-Christians?

The arrival of the *jenets* in the armies of the Crown of Aragon coincided with and accelerated the decline of the feudal army. In principle, the Aragonese king could expect all his subjects to contribute to the defense of his kingdoms without remuneration.[2] This obligation had been enshrined, for instance, in the article "Princeps namque" of the twelfth-century *Usatges de Barcelona*, the basic customs of Catalonia.[3] In this law code, war was a matter of custom—grounded in rituals, in which vassals kneeled and kissed, exchanged sweet words and signs, and swore allegiance to their lords—not business. Over the course of the late thirteenth century, however, as the Aragonese kings embarked on a new path of sovereign self-fashioning, bureaucratic centralization, and aggressive expansion, this feudal system came under stress. Cash-starved kings replaced feudal duties with war taxes and increasingly relied on salaried soldiers, whom they could manage directly, resulting in a move toward smaller armies and new military strategies.[4] Alongside and in parallel with the royal administration, the military was professionalized in the service of an emerging ideal of authority. Under these pressures, by the end of the thirteenth century, the demise of the feudal army seemed all but inevitable. Joseph Strayer understood the emergence of professionals and bureaucrats as part of the broader "laicization" of Europe, that is, the transfer of power from the hands of religious clerics to educated laymen.[5]

These laicizing trends were evident in the fact that upon arriving for service in the lands of the Crown of Aragon, the *jenets* first met with royal bureaucrats. Generally, they encountered the royal treasurer or in later periods, the king's master of accounts (*maestre racional*) from whom they gathered a series of official documents—expenses, requisitions, promissory notes, and marching orders—that may have been issued in both Latin and Arabic.[6] At first irregularly but later more systematically, these slips were then copied into the chancery registers or account books, where the historian can now find them. What one discovers is that King Pere's treasurer, Arnaldus de Bastida, interacted almost exclusively with the *jenets* through 1294.[7] After this period, Guillelmus Dufort, who was master of accounts after Conrad Lancia, played this central role for a while.[8] Only a handful of other men, also royal administrators, dealt with the *jenets*. The Crown's grip on these soldiers, in other words, was relatively direct and tight.

Despite obvious differences in language, the encounter with elite Aragonese bureaucrats may have been familiar to the *jenets*. As a centralized system for dealing with royal correspondence, land tenure, taxation, and the military, the Crown's nascent chancery mirrored the Marīnid *dīwān al-inshā'*, with which the *jenets* would have been familiar.[9] The Crown's key legal instrument, the *albaranum*—a promissory note used to pay *jenets*—derived its name and function from the Arabic *al-barā'a*, meaning the same.[10] The *jenets* may have also seen something familiar and not strange in the Crown's reliance upon Jewish bureaucrats. Jewish administrators served at both the Marīnid and Naṣrid courts.[11] What is more, Jews like Samuel Abenmenassé, who spoke Arabic fluently, likely served under the Almohads before serving the Aragonese, making them perfect interlocutors and intermediaries. Finally, it should be added that even Christian bureaucrats like Pere's treasurer Arnaldus de Bastida would have been very familiar with Muslim foreigners. Arnaldus dealt regularly not only with the *jenets* but also with Muslim diplomats, captives, and slaves across his career.[12] In short, the arrival of the *jenets* may have been a matter of business as usual.

As members of a professional army, all *jenets* received a salary that was managed centrally, as it would have been in the Marīnid *dīwān*. During the late thirteenth century, Arnaldus de Bastida personally handled the vast majority of disbursements, paying the soldiers directly or, occasionally, authorizing local officials to do so if time was limited.[13] Soldiers or their companies were paid upon receipt of a promissory note (*albaranum*). Determining the average monthly salary of a *jenet* based upon these documents, however, poses several problems.[14] Not all promissory notes given to *jenets* specify the number of months' service or the number of soldiers being compensated, and as the case of one *jenet* named Muçe demonstrates, payments were occasionally made in installments.[15] To add further confusion to the matter, the Crown of Aragon relied upon several standards of currency.[16] In general, coinage followed the Carolingian system: *librae*, *solidi*, and *denarii*.[17] However, each kingdom employed a different standard: that of Jaca, Barcelona, or Valencia.[18] In addition, gold coins, the Castilian *dobla* and Islamic *dīnār*, circulated and were used to pay *jenets* on occasion.[19] Setting aside equivocal data, however, the handful of remaining documents indicates that a *jenet* earned approximately four *solidi* per diem.[20] The Crown paid the same to Christian light cavalry during the conquest of Sardinia, suggesting that the Aragonese kings valued their *jenets* no more or less than their Christian counterparts.[21] In addition, Christian militias operating in Muslim lands during King Alfons II's reign received roughly the same compensation, three to six *solidi*.[22] In assigning these wages, the Crown of Aragon may have been adhering to the unspoken professional standards of a broader mercenary economy. All this is to say that the Aragonese kings did see it necessary to offer the *jenets*, their former enemies, exceptional remuneration in order to ensure their loyalty. They seemed to compensate them just like other soldiers.

Profession

From the perspective of the Crown of Aragon, the *jenets* were not simply bodies to add to its armies, cannon fodder: these horsemen also brought with them a military innovation. Despite being less well armed, or precisely because they were, the *jenets* had an advantage over the traditional heavy cavalry that dominated Muslim and Christian Iberia. These light cavalry soldiers specialized in small, rapid, and organized incursions that the Crown's records refer to as "*jenet* raids."[23] They employed a tactic of attacking and fleeing, which allowed them to harass heavy cavalry, with the aim of drawing them away from the protection of archers and infantry.[24] With a mixture of horror and admiration, Don Juan Manuel (1282–1348), the prolific writer and nephew of the Castilian king Alfonso X, said, "The war of the Moors is not like that of the Christians. . . . In every way, it is very different."[25] If hyperbolic, the Castilian prince was correct in this respect: the military advantage offered by the *jenets* and sought by the Christian kings was not their strength but rather their difference from other types of soldiers. The same desire for strategic difference, Ibn Khaldūn noted, inspired Muslim rulers to recruit Christian heavy cavalry (fig. 3).[26]

While the *jenets* differed from other soldiers in the Aragonese armies in terms of language, religion, and style, they were not isolated from them. During the many wars against France and Castile, these horsemen found themselves fighting shoulder to shoulder with a variety of Christian troops, both professional and feudal.[27] Indeed, the extent of this collaboration is occasionally surprising. In 1289, for example, King Alfons issued the following order protecting a company of *jenets* and their Christian associates, departing for raiding activities together:

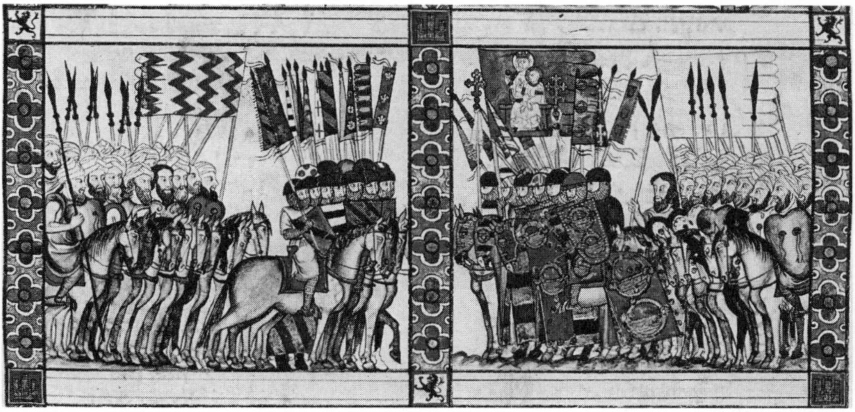

FIGURE 3. Alfonso X, *Cantigas de Santa Maria* (no. 181) (ca. 1284) (detail, middle-left and -right panels). Christian militias, Marrakesh, North Africa. Monasterio-Biblioteca-Colección, San Lorenzo de El Escorial, Madrid. Photograph: Album / Art Resource, New York.

> To all men of whatever frontier location of our land: Because Mahomet el Viello, our *jenet*, and others, both Christian and Saracen associates of the aforementioned Mahomet, have gone to conduct *jenet* raids (*vadunt ad jenetiam*) by our mandate, they must travel to frontier regions in order to defend our land and also inflict damage on our enemies.[28]

Mahomet el Viello was not unique in this regard. For their part, the *jenet* commanders Mahomet Abenadalil and al-ʿAbbās b. Raḥḥū both either led or fought alongside Christian soldiers, including, in the latter case, heavily armed Templar knights: men who, like the Ghuzāh, were devoted to holy war.[29] Another captain, Moxarref Abenhalbet, who came from Castile, brought Christian troops with him, suggesting not only that the *jenets* collaborated with Christian soldiers of their own accord but also that these interreligious mercenary associations existed independently of the Christian and Muslim rulers of the Iberian Peninsula.[30] We also know that two *jenets*, who operated alongside Christian soldiers in the Aragonese navy, named Machamet Almenochoxi and Athame Benbrahi, also went by the names George (Georgius) and Peter (Petrus).[31] Nothing indicates that George and Peter were converts. Thus, perhaps, these names give us a glimpse at the sorts of accommodations, camaraderie, or even good humor that resided among these companies as they fought side by side.

Finally, one also finds the *jenets* fighting alongside almogàvers and *adalids*, lightly armored Catalan and Aragonese foot soldiers who specialized in cross-border raids against Muslim Granada, soldiers who were in some sense a mirror image of the Ghuzāh.[32] Desclot described these soldiers vividly:

> These men, called almogàvers, live only by their weapons. They do not live in villages or cities but rather in the mountains and forests. They fight every day with the Saracens, entering into their lands for a day or two, raiding and seizing many people and goods, and that is how they live. They endure many terrible things that other men cannot: they go many days without eating, and survive on grass at no harm to themselves. The *adalids* who guide them know the lands and the paths. They wear no more than a tunic (*gonella*) and a shirt in summer or winter. On their legs, they wear leather pants; and on their feet, leather sandals. They carry a good knife and scabbard, strapped to their belts. Each one has a javelin, two arrows, and a leather purse to carry food. They are very strong and very fast to flee and chase.[33]

Despite being raiders against Muslims but as the Arabic origin of their names hints—*mughāwir* (raider) and *dalīl* (guide)—these soldiers likely had their genesis in the Islamic armies that swept through Iberia centuries earlier.[34] All the same, like the *jenets*, these raiders of obscure origin and composition increasingly moved from the political and social margins into the bureaucratic control of the Crown in the thirteenth century.

The extent of these collaborations raises a critical question: Did an emerging military profession override religious profession in medieval Iberia? If one takes into account the long-standing use of Christian soldiers by Muslim rulers, then it would seem that men on both sides of the Mediterranean seemed to value good soldiers and good salaries above religion. Did these fighters cast aside their beliefs for money? Did they rise above their differences?

These were precisely the questions that most concerned the first studies of these soldiers. For Giménez Soler, the first to write about the *jenets*, this history evinced a wider spirit of tolerance.[35] In this context, tolerance did not signify religious openness but rather, in the vein of classical liberalism, signaled a criticism of religion itself. At the turn of the twentieth century, Spanish liberals like Giménez Soler saw religion as a primitive form of politics, as a cunning ideology used to manipulate credulous masses.[36] They saw religious beliefs as delusions that stifled free and rational thought and, as such, promoted violence. In short, they dismissed belief as blind adherence. Thus, in the alliance of the Crown of Aragon with the Muslim *jenets*, Giménez Soler saw a welcome turn toward political secularization, away from superstition and toward self-interest, away from medieval ways of thinking and toward modern ones.[37] Not surprisingly, Spanish Catholics vigorously objected to these interpretations. They saw these kings and soldiers as traitors and transgressors, as men whose greed had undermined the authentic religious and national spirit of the Spanish people.[38] They saw religion as an absolute and necessary commitment without which community could not survive. These competing interpretations of mercenaries were part of the bitter and deadlocked twentieth-century *convivencia* debates, debates between Spanish liberals and conservative Catholics about the nature of religious coexistence in Spain's medieval past and the value of secular tolerance for the present.

Medievalists now view these disputes as a scholarly embarrassment.[39] They have criticized both the liberals and the conservatives for distorting the past in the service of the political extremes that provoked the bloody Spanish Civil War. They have challenged the empirical value of tolerance for understanding religious interaction.[40] And most assuredly, they have rejected the essential contention, shared by both liberals and conservatives, that religious beliefs were inflexible commitments which impeded and opposed peaceful interaction. But how have they made sense of figures like the *jenets*?

Privilege

The relationship of the Crown to the *jenets* was not limited to a financial transaction. In addition to regular salaries, the Crown also conferred upon the *jenets* numerous gifts and privileges—small and large—that, in fact, distinguished them from other soldiers on the battlefield and thus offer a different perspective on how the Aragonese kings might have viewed these foreign Muslim soldiers.

To begin with the smallest and least significant of such privileges, all *jenets* regularly received basic clothes (*vestes*) and cloth (*pannus*) for making clothes.[41] In 1290, for example, King Alfons II reminded his tax collectors not to assess a port duty (*lezda*) on cloth destined for his army of *jenets* in Valencia precisely because it was a privilege and not a sale.[42] Nothing indicates that the *jenets* wore or were made to wear uniforms or distinguishing marks like the Christian soldiers of North Africa.[43] For instance, Alfons offered to provide the troops of the captain Mohamet Abenadalil with either clothing or money to buy their own clothing, suggesting it did not matter much to him how they dressed.[44] In addition to basic clothing, *jenets* also received compensation for all travel related to their duties, both within and beyond the king's territories, a privilege not granted to feudal troops.[45] Moreover, unlike Aragonese feudatories—but like the Marīnid Ghuzāh—*jenets* received horses and military equipment.[46] In some cases, money was disbursed for a *jenet* to purchase these items;[47] in other cases, horses, mules, or equipment were distributed directly by royal officials;[48] and in yet other cases, *jenets* commandeered horses, whose owners were later reimbursed.[49] It should be added that the Crown also insured these animals and goods against loss or harm.[50] In one of many such instances, in July 1289, Arnaldus de Bastida compensated Hahen Abenhali 500 *solidi* for "a certain horse of his that he lost in our service."[51] This privilege was broadly and generously applied: for example, Arnaldus de Bastida paid a *jenet* named Maymon 400 *solidi* to recover a horse that he had pawned in Valencia to cover a debt.[52] Similarly, in 1310, King Jaume II paid a Christian nobleman 180 *solidi* in compensation for a mule taken by a *jenet* when he departed the lands of the Crown of Aragon.[53] The Crown also extended these indemnities to the bodies of the *jenets* themselves. The captain, Abduluahet ('Abd al-Wāḥid), who served at Albarracín, received compensation rather matter-of-factly for "two animals and two soldiers" that he lost in battle.[54] Similarly, the Crown intervened to redeem *jenets* from captivity. In 1290, for example, King Jaume II demanded the release of *jenets* held prisoner by his own subjects.[55] And in 1292, Jaume also reimbursed Paschasius Dominici for paying the ransom for several *jenets* held captive in Castile.[56] In short, the Crown provided for these soldiers in all aspects of their service, from stipends to sustenance, whatever they might need while in its lands. The fact that other soldiers in battle did not receive these same privileges suggests that the king valued his Muslim *jenets* differently and, perhaps, more than the rest.

The Aragonese kings heaped even more privilege, honor, and one might say, affection upon *jenet* captains and commanders.[57] For instance, in February 1290, King Alfons issued three letters, each to a captain of *jenets* residing in the kingdom of Granada, inviting them to enter his service:

> Don Alfons, by the grace of God, king of Aragon, Mallorca, Valencia, and Count of Barcelona, to you, Don Iuceff Abenzubayba, greeting and good will. We have understood from Adabub Adalil that you with a company of *jenets*

wish to enter into our service, which pleases us greatly. And we hope that after seeing this letter, you will come to Valencia, where we have ordered our faithful scribe, Raimund Escorne, to collect from us your salary (*quitacio*) and whatever you require. And we promise you that when we have won with the aid of God a settlement to the war, if you have not returned to the land of the King of Granada, that as long as you wish to stay in our land you will lack nothing (*no vos faleçremos de lo que ayades menester*) until you win the love of the king of Granada, because we know that every man who serves us, serves the king of Granada (*tot homne qui a nos sierva, sierve al Rey de Granada*). Dated Zaragoza, 24 February.

Likewise to Don Mahomet al Granadaxi.

Likewise to Don Mahomet Abenadalil.[58]

In this invitation, Alfons not only expressed great pleasure at the possibility of the service of these three new captains of *jenets* but also revealed the context for their arrival, namely, that they have had a falling out with the sultan of Granada, Muḥammad II (r. 1273–1302). One can only speculate about the cause of this rift, but what is significant to note is the nature of Alfons' entreaty. In a rather ecumenical tone, Alfons appealed to these exiles by invoking both the divine ("with the aid of God") and political justness ("every man who serves us, serves the king of Granada") of his impending war, which to say that although these soldiers were seeking refuge, he nevertheless hoped to dissuade them from seeing their crossing as a transgression.

Some *jenet* leaders received elevated positions at the Aragonese royal court. Mahomet Abenadalil, from the letter above, and al-'Abbās b. Raḥḥū, whom King Jaume II referred to as "beloved (*amado*)," became vassals of the Crown.[59] Both of these men as well as several other *jenets* were also members of the king's household (*de domo regis*), where they joined his entourage and served as his guardsmen.[60] It is worth adding that they would not have been the only Muslims in court: the Crown's chief veterinarian and horse smith, known as the *menescallus*, was typically a Mudéjar.[61] Given the presence of *jenets* in the royal entourage, perhaps, it is also no coincidence that the modern Castilian *jinetear*, another relative of the word *jenet*, signifies to ride in a public procession, a meaning suggestive of the kind of public and performative role that the *jenets* might have once played.

Several of the *jenets* in the king's entourage also served as ambassadors to and from Muslim courts. Both Mahomet Abenadalil and al-'Abbās b. Raḥḥū visited the Aragonese court from Granada and Fez, respectively, after their tenures of service had ended.[62] In 1290, when King Alfons II was facing a combined French and Castilian threat, three *jenets* of his household traveled to Granada "at the king's wish."[63] And in 1295, during another crisis over Sicily and an impending war between Morocco and Castile, Jaume II dispatched the *jenet* Muça Almentauri, perhaps the longest standing member of this royal guard, to Sicily and Ḥafṣid Tunis for negotiations.[64] The Aragonese kings thus not only trusted the *jenets* in this intimate context but also saw value in the fact that the *jenets* could serve as intermediaries with Islamic courts.

It is also as a member of the king's household that one finds the sole instance of a Jewish *jenet*, Abrahim el Jenet.[65] Elena Lourie, who first mentioned Abrahim, unearthed much of the evidence related to him in the chancery registers. She suggested that Abrahim might have come from either Granada or North Africa alongside the Muslim *jenets*.[66] She concluded that he reflected the essentially pluralist character of the *jenet* military bands.[67] It may go too far to call Abrahim a soldier. Although we see Abrahim with the *jenets* at court, receiving privileges and salaries parallel to those of other *jenets* of the king's household, we have no evidence that he fought alongside them.[68] Thus, it was more likely that Abrahim was a *jenet* in name only, someone who held an honorary association with these soldiers. But even an honorary association speaks to a surprising pluralism.

In addition to welcoming the leaders of the *jenets* into their entourage, the Aragonese kings also presented lavish gifts to them. Some of what the kings gave could be considered martial frippery. For instance, in 1291, King Alfons II honored Abutçeyt Asseyt with a beige horse, three silver bridles, three pairs of *jenet* spurs, and a saddle embossed with lions that was in the possession of a Mudéjar.[69] It should be added that specialized *jenet* horses, *jenet* saddles, *jenet* bridles, and *jenet* weapons are mentioned throughout these archival records as gifts given to both Muslim and non-Muslim elites, indicating not only an admiration for but also a steady diffusion of the style of riding *a la jineta*.[70] For example, the Jewish physician, Samuel Abenmenassé, who served in King Pere II's mission to recruit *jenets* from Granada, had in his possession a *jenet* saddle, *jenet* sword, and *jenet* shield.[71]

The circulation of these gifts among Aragonese elites suggests that the *jenets* were not only an object of military but also aesthetic fascination. Some of this fascination is reflected in the fact that the *jenets* became a form of courtly entertainment. On two occasions, the registers make mention of *jenets* participating in games or tournaments (*ludere ad jenetiam*), perhaps precursors to the early modern *juego de cañas*, an equestrian game

FIGURE 4. *Juego de Cañas* in Valladolid (1506). Bibliothèque Royale Albert I, Brussels. Photograph: Album / Art Resource, New York.

in which participants dressed as "Moors," or the *moros y cristianos* festivals, mock battles between light cavalry, dressed as Muslims and Christians (fig. 4).[72] A *jenet* named Gaylen, for example, was compensated the remarkable sum of 500 *solidi* for wounds that he sustained during one such event at the pleasure of the king.[73] In other words, well before early modern Spanish noblemen and princes rode *a la jineta* as a matter of taste and social distinction, thirteenth- and fourteenth-century Aragonese elites—both Christian and Jewish—already considered this style worthy of admiration and imitation. This fascination may have also spread further afield. In 1356, King Pere III (r. 1336–1387) arranged to have a small contingent of Muslim knights sent to the French court.[74] This ability to translate from one context to another is what Georg Simmel had in mind when he said that "style is always something general."[75]

Prominent *jenets* also received other valuable gifts. The Crown presented a handful of *jenets* with falcons.[76] Over the course of his career, for instance, the *jenet* captain Mahomet Abendalil received five falcons, including a goshawk (*austurcus*), which was a rarity in North Africa.[77] The most common gift given to these soldiers, however, was sumptuous cloth. At first blush, these rich cloths seem fancy but rather utilitarian: capes, shoes, bolts of cloth, and tunics. Among numerous other examples, two *jenets*, Muçe and Çahit, received leather-lined capes made with Parisian chiffon as well as tunics and boots made from colored cloth.[78] The representatives of Çahim Abennaquem received colored tunics and shoes made with silks imported from France and the Levant.[79] Other sumptuous cloths mentioned include vermillion *presset* and colored chiffon from Saint Denis, the cult center of the Capetian kings.[80] These cloths may have been used to make tunics or tie turbans.

What do all these lavish gifts tell us about the Aragonese kings' understanding of the *jenets*? Far from an empty ritual, gift giving holds deep social significance.[81] Gifts materialize bonds and obligations between men, and thus they might also help to reveal an unspoken but shared symbolic vocabulary between the Aragonese kings and their Muslim soldiers. The falcons they gave, for instance, were admired throughout Spain and North Africa.[82] Red cloth was favored by both Aragonese and Naṣrid knights.[83] What is more, honorific gifts (*tashrīfāt*), including robes (*khila'*), featured regularly in ceremonies (*marāsim*) at Islamic courts.[84] Strong parallels between Christian ideas of chivalry and the Islamic concept of *murū'a* may have further strengthened these connections. For both parties, the significance of these martial and vestiary trifles was familiar. These gifts formed part of a common cultural ground and a shared script. More precisely, they were elements of both Christian and Islamic courtly rituals, rituals that bound kings and elite soldiers. In other words, not only salaries but also gifts tied kings to these elite soldiers. Thus, these gift-giving rituals offer us another way to understand the authority of the Aragonese kings. As opposed to purely bureaucratic rationalism, these gifts point to the continuing charismatic power of Aragonese kingship in this period.[85]

This shared sense of style and mutual esteem speaks to a bond between Christian, Muslim, and Jewish elites that transcended religious difference. It suggests, as Robert Ignatius Burns and others have argued, the existence of a common "military-aristocratic" culture, a set of values—above all, wealth and honor—that bridged elite men.[86] This shared culture allowed them to see each other as equals, as members of the same community. And it suggests despite the claims of earlier liberals and conservatives, that religion was ultimately no impediment, that the Aragonese kings and Muslim *jenets* were capable of seeing themselves and each other as something more than merely Christians and Muslims.

Exception

While this cultural reading is satisfying, there are other ways to make sense of these privileges and gifts. If the privileges that the Aragonese kings conferred upon the *jenets* could be read as evidence of honor and esteem, then they might also be read as evidence of caution and unease. As in the case of *jenets* captured by Aragonese villagers in 1290, mentioned above, the Crown was fully aware of the threats and challenges that these soldiers faced when traveling around Christian territory.[87] Christian villagers regularly barred these soldiers from entering towns and violently attacked them, sometimes raiding their camps in the middle of the night.[88] Thus, perhaps in granting these soldiers basic military and nonmilitary necessities, the Aragonese kings may have hoped to minimize encounters between its Christian subjects and the *jenets*.[89] From this perspective, such privileges served to isolate these soldiers and made them dependent on royal administrators.[90] In short, they did not mark the *jenets* as favorites but rather exceptions.

This sense that the *jenets* were exceptional is further underscored by the fact that the Crown also granted them the privilege of keeping the king's customary fifth or *quinta* of all war spoils.[91] Whereas other soldiers were required to share their spoils with the king, the *jenets* were not. What is more, Christians who raided alongside the *jenets* were required to give a fifth of their spoils to the *jenets*, a fact that occasionally led to violent confrontation within mixed companies, complicating any claim that these were easy collaborations.[92] It is worth adding that this privilege was not an Aragonese innovation but rather the customary right of the Marīnid Ghuzāh. The Naṣrid rulers had always granted these soldiers their fifth (*khums*) of all war spoils (*ghanīma*).[93] Thus, whereas salaries and other privileges kept the *jenets* tightly bound to royal administrators, the fifth share marked the *jenets*' independence from them. By surrendering its fifth of spoils, the Crown permitted the *jenets* to operate outside of its purview and more problematically for the historian, outside of the view of the chancery registers. Moreover, since these spoils may have outweighed salaries, it could be argued that raiding rather than salaried service was the principal motivation for *jenets* in entering the lands of the Crown of Aragon. In other words, rather than as professional soldiers, who traded their roles in the Granadan army for ones in the Aragonese army, *jenets* might be seen as raiders and bandits, who belonged to neither kingdom. Despite their crossing into the lands of the Crown of Aragon, they essentially remained Ghuzāh.

Can one say, at least, that the *jenets* found some common ground at the Aragonese court among elites of similar tastes and values? To see the gifts of cloth that the *jenets* received as style as opposed to substance, as objects that could freely move from Christian to Muslim bodies, overlooks the fact that clothing was freighted with spiritual and moral danger in the medieval Crown of Aragon. Indeed, clothing was deeply bound up in social and religious identity throughout medieval and early modern Europe.[94] Clothes *were* a matter of religious concern.[95] In other words, these gifts demand not a sociological explanation but rather a soteriological one.[96] For instance, Christian legislation specified how non-Christians should dress, comport themselves, and wear their hair. The *Customs of Tortosa* stated: "Saracens must wear their hair cut round and wear long beards, unlike the Christians, and their outer garment must be the *aljuba* or *almexia*."[97] The *aljuba* and *almexia*—from the Arabic *al-jubba* and *al-maḥshiya*—were long tunics worn over clothing, to mark the Mudéjar population as distinct and to prevent miscegenation.[98] Subject Muslims were required to make these tunics from plain cloth, underscoring their abject and inferior status.[99] Christians, in turn, were forbidden from wearing the *aljuba* or *almexia* at all.[100] One might protest that such sumptuary laws were more honored in the breach than in the observance: evidence of punishments is rare, and the punishments, when they exist, varied widely from fines to enslavement.[101] Nevertheless, Muslims and Jews regularly sought and received privileged exceptions from these restrictions, indicating that even the arbitrary application of these laws remained a threat.[102] In 1290, for example, the king wrote to his justices in Valencia to remind them that although the Jews of Barcelona and Valencia were required to wear capes, two Jews of the royal household, Abrahim Abennamies and Abrahim el Jenet, should not be compelled to wear them.[103]

From the perspective of these sumptuary laws, the fact that the Aragonese kings presented elite *jenets* with not simply tunics but also rich and colorful *aljubas* or what they sometimes called "Saracen" tunics is ambiguous at best. If, on the one hand, the sumptuous cloth implied the *jenets*' freedom from the discriminatory laws that threatened non-Christian subjects, on the other, the *aljuba* itself continued to mark them as Muslims. In other words, one cannot say that these gifts were properly gestures of inclusion or exclusion. Instead, they underscored the *jenets*' exceptional status within in the lands of the Crown of Aragon. The cultural account of the relationship between the Aragonese kings and *jenets*, which emphasized their shared sense of community, conceals this meaning. It leaves "a bit of undigested theology" in the throat.[104]

The trouble with these tunics is placed in even sharper contrast by examining a later echo of the *jenets*, the Moorish Guard (*guardia morisca*) of the fifteenth-century Castilian kings. In a period of even deeper hostility towards Muslims and Jews, the Trastámara kings also maintained a corps of Moorish knights as their personal guard, who appeared in parades alongside them, physically marking out the space of the sovereign. And as Ana Echevarría has shown, despite the fact that many of these soldiers had converted to Christianity, the Castilian kings continued to dress them lavishly as "Moors"—adorned in turquoise tunics, sheepskin garments, doublets, and laced boots. To put this clearly, the Castilian kings continued to dress their soldiers as Muslims even after they had become Christians. And although the practice of recruiting and hiring Muslim soldiers had disappeared in this period, the spectacle and indeed, more precisely, the display of Muslim soldiers continued to have importance to Christian kings.[105] What was the relationship of these kings to these ersatz *jenets*? What notion of authority was being performed in these processions?

The challenge of reading these tunics reveals the limit of recent approaches to religious interaction in medieval Iberia. In step with the wider historical discipline, many medievalists have come to see religion as an aspect of culture, which is to say that they see religion as part of a broader set of norms and rules that clothe individuals in identity and dress their choices in a deep sense of pragmatism, purpose, and order.[106] They see religion as a lived, pragmatic, and flexible system that responds to the needs of individuals in community.[107] Thus, rather than stifling agency, religion can express agency. Rather than inevitably leading to collision or transgression, religious interaction becomes a process of encounter and acculturation.[108]

Although I am not alone in making this critique but precisely because this cultural approach continues to hold power among scholars of medieval Iberia, I want to suggest that the time has come to shift the furniture piled up in the lumber room once again.[109] As Steven Justice has recently argued, in a quest to provide rational and coherent explanations *for* religious belief, the cultural account of religion has provided a familiar understanding *of* religious belief.[110] If one contends that believers were aware of the underlying reasons for their beliefs, then they also held a curious detachment from them. If one contends they were unaware of those reasons, then they appear to be in bondage to their beliefs. In other words, one must either see believers as cunning manipulators, who secretly disbelieved, or delusional fools, who believed unblinkingly.[111] Sincere belief remains, as it had for Spanish liberals and conservatives, a form of blind adherence and constraint. As such, the cultural theory of religious identity can not provide a genuine alternative to views it seeks to overcome.[112] If one begins with the understanding that religious belief is a form of community, then religious interaction can only be read as transgression.

Indeed, recent accounts of Muslim and Christian mercenaries in the medieval Mediterranean have come to the same understanding of them as their liberal and conservative predecessors. If for an earlier generation, these soldiers crossed lines in spite of religion, in either heroic or treasonous transgression of it, then for contemporary scholars, they crossed regardless of their religious beliefs. In spite of religion or regardless of it, the conclusion is the same: this religious encounter curiously has nothing to do with religion. In the century of scholarship on Christian and Muslim mercenaries, every historian has concluded that social and economic interests, secular and pragmatic motivations, drove these kings and soldiers.[113]

My argument is not that this reading of the *jenets* is wrong but rather that it underdescribes their relationship to the Crown of Aragon. To imagine the Aragonese kings' employment of the *jenets* solely as a matter of rational pragmatism or cultural accommodation not only excludes the question of religion from the outset but also, as a result of that exclusion, reproduces an enduring historiographical bias that sees the Middle Ages as a period of incomplete secularism, a way station on the road to a disenchanted modernity. What then would it mean to write the history of the Crown of Aragon's reliance upon the *jenets* beyond secular terms that oppose political and religious impulses?

Law and Theology

Given the sustained efforts of the Aragonese kings to style themselves the heirs of Frederick II, which is to say, as the heirs to the most successful thirteenth-century Holy Roman emperor, it is necessary to consider the model of authority that Frederick himself embodied.[114] Armed with his own professional bureaucrats and lawyers, Frederick II had transformed his court at Sicily into a miracle of fiscality and centralized authority. This change bore the influence of two overlapping traditions. First, from North Africa, the rationalist political philosophy of the Almohads entered Sicily through translations of the works of Ibn Tūmart and Ibn Rushd, known more famously as Averroes, the Arabic commentator on Aristotle. The Almohads had imagined their ruler, the caliph, as a supreme lawmaker, a "lamp of reason," and an earthly reflection of the divine sovereign, who they understood as radically distant and utterly inscrutable, unique and transcendent.[115] Second, Frederick's court was a center for the revival of Roman law. In this regard, beginning with the argument that "every king is an emperor in his own domain (*rex est imperator in regno suo*)," jurists

[handwritten margin notes: "wrong to see as incomplete secularism (middle age)"; "central auth (Sicily)"; "earthly reflection of divine sovereign"; "Roman law revival"]

sought to ground royal authority and legitimacy upon the Roman idea of royal law (*lex regia*), which is to say upon the exclusive power of the emperor to make law—upon his sovereignty, his absolute jurisdiction (*merum imperium*).[116] For scholars like Joseph Strayer and Ernst Kantorowicz, the intellectual work of these jurists marked a turning away from theological towards legal, rational, and secular justifications for political authority across thirteenth-century Europe.[117]

From the perspective of medieval jurists, the glossators who read and commented on Roman law, however, the line between law and theology was not so clean and clear. For instance, in reading the *Digest*, the sixth-century law code of the Emperor Justinian I (r. 527–565), these glossators recognized something exceptional in the twin adages, "whatever pleases the Prince has the force of law (*quod principi placuit legis habet vigorem*)" and "the Prince is free from the laws (*princeps legibus solutus est*)."[118] If the sovereign was the source of law, then it followed that his authority could never fully be contained within or restrained by law.[119] Conservative and liberal historians, political philosophers, and legal theorists from Carl Schmitt to Giorgio Agamben, John Austin to Hans Kelsen, have recognized an absolutist streak in these ideas—an arbitrary and violent potential in the notion of the sovereign exception that posits an absent foundation of the law.[120] Nevertheless, as Brian Tierney has argued, for influential medieval glossators such as Accursius (ca. 1182–1263), sovereignty was not ungrounded or unbound.[121] Although the king could not be forced to obey the law, Accursius nevertheless expected him to respect it voluntarily because law was a gift from God.[122] That is, if the king stood above human or positive law, then he also lay beneath and subject to divine or natural law.[123] In other words, political ideas were inextricable from theological ones precisely because earthly order mirrored divine order. The Accursian gloss of *legibus solutus est* depended upon a particular theology and understanding of nature. Following but also responding to Schmitt, Kantorowicz borrowed the mixed expression "political theology" to describe this medieval juridical discourse. Although Kantorowicz saw the connection between theological and legal concepts as purely formal, a matter of borrowing, I employ the expression here to emphasize the continual and dynamic exchange between legal and theological ideas.[124]

If one accepts that law and theology were interrelated in this period, then it also follows that ideas about political sovereignty both shaped and were shaped by ongoing debates about God's sovereignty, about the nature of divinity and its relationship to man. It mattered deeply, for instance, whether God's will was bound (*potestas ordinata*) or unbound (*potestas absoluta*) by reason and good.[125] If bound, then it seemed, as Accursius argued, that the king's, too, must be restrained. But it is significant that over the course of the later Middle Ages, the balance of opinion on such matters tipped. As the early medieval realism that characterized Accursius' solution increasingly gave way to late medieval nominalism and Averroism—which is to say, as a God approachable through and limited by reason (*logos*) became a distant and inscrutable will (*voluntas*), as Aquinas turned into Ockham—so the meaning of earthly sovereignty shifted towards a greater emphasis on absolute and unpredictable will; towards a more extreme sense of exception, free from *any* impediment.[126] It is in this evolving theological context that one should understand Frederick II's claim that he was the *lex animata*, the living law, and his dramatic self-coronation in Jerusalem in 1229.[127] Thus, rather than ushering in secularism, as Kantorowicz argued, the language of law—jurisdiction—was infused with theological assumptions that allowed medieval kings and royal jurists to make arguments about political sovereignty that ranged from minimalist and restrained to radical and unbound.[128] The potential for both was embedded in the late medieval theological tradition. To put this differently, political sovereignty is not the secularization of theology but rather an extension of it.[129]

Before the arrival of the Hohenstaufen exiles at Pere's court, Romanist legal traditions had already taken root in the lands of the Crown of Aragon.[130] In part because of proximity, in part because of a powerful and aspiring merchant class, significant numbers of Catalan students attended the schools of Roman law at Bologna and Montpellier.[131] Among those educated at Bologna, for instance, were the jurists and royal advisors Ramon de Penyafort, Vidal de Canyelles, Pere Albert, and Guillem Çassala. By the thirteenth century, Romanist legal concepts had penetrated both local custom and new legislation.[132] Well before its official approbation in the sixteenth century, Roman law had in practice steadily replaced customary law as the common law (*ius commune*) of the kingdoms of the Crown of Aragon.[133]

For their part, the Aragonese kings clearly understood that they could employ novel ideas of royal jurisdiction to extend their authority.[134] King Jaume I, for instance, invoked *merum imperium* in his newly conquered kingdom of Valencia.[135] But when he made the same claim in the Aragonese heartland, he faced challenges. The well-established nobility, some of whom commanded more wealth and arms than the king himself, balked. They complained of "innovations," of the intrusion of foreign law.[136] They blamed the preponderance of "legists" and "decretalists," by which they meant men trained in Roman law, at the king's court.[137] These pretensions to absolute sovereignty and royal jurisdiction as well as conflicts with the nobility peaked again during the time of King Pere II. Both Sicily and North Africa became zones in which the king hoped to free himself from the grip of his noblemen and express a new independence, a full sovereignty. Indeed, there may be some truth to the Franciscan writer Francesc Eiximenis' (d. 1409) record of Pere's fondness for the radical and voluntaristic expression "the law goes wherever the king wills (*lla va la llei on vol lo rei*)."[138] These pretensions to imperial authority were challenged not only at home but also abroad. The French and Castilian kings competed to cast themselves as the heirs of the Holy Roman emperor, as universal sovereigns.[139]

In addition to sharing its extreme political theology, the Aragonese court took on the appearance of Frederick's, adapting its institutions, habits, and rituals in order to elevate the image of the king. Among these, as I have argued, was the tradition of maintaining Muslim guardsmen. Beginning with the reign of Alfons III, it should be added, the fourteenth-century Aragonese kings also adopted the tradition of self-coronation, mirroring the brashness of Frederick's own act at Jerusalem in 1229.[140]

What, however, did these performances and ideologies of omnipotence have to do with the employment of Muslim soldiers? Importantly, just as enthusiastic new readings of Roman law elevated the king to near divine status, they had profound but opposite implications for non-Christians, stripping them of all rights. And precisely for this reason, like the Sicilians before them, the Aragonese kings found in religious others not only skilled agents but also symbolic expressions of their own power.

As John Boswell has explained, from the twelfth century, religious minorities—Muslims and Jews—enjoyed a consistent if ambiguous legal status in the kingdoms of the Crown of Aragon. The Aragonese kings first referred to Jews and, later, Muslims as well as "their property" or "servants of the royal chamber (*servi camerae regis*)."[141] These ideas placed Jews and Muslims at the whim of kings.[142] Nevertheless, despite this rhetoric, and as has been noted before, in the early years of the reign of King Pere II the political status of Jews in particular appeared to improve dramatically. Several highly educated and influential Jewish families—including that of Samuel Abenmenassé—came to hold elite positions in the royal administration.[143] Against a backdrop of new efforts to convert, expel, and demonize Jews throughout thirteenth-century Europe, the rise of these Jewish royal administrators has led some historians to speak of a "Golden Age of Aragonese Jewry"—a period of toleration and intellectual creativity that belied the language of servitude.[144]

Rather than measuring religious interaction in terms of tolerance and intolerance—which is to say, in modern liberal terms—it might be better to ask what, if anything, drew together slavery and privilege in this period. For instance, while speaking of his Muslim soldiers as *servi camerae regis*, Frederick granted them exceptional privileges such as knighthoods.[145] David Abulafia has suggested that this notion of Jewish and Muslim servitude in fact reflected the conflation of two traditions: first, a more ancient Augustinian tradition that emphasized the debased status of Jews on account of their rejection and murder of Christ; and second, a German and Sicilian tradition of privileged Jewish and Muslim cameral servitude, regularized by Frederick II. Frederick's use of the ambiguous term *servus*, Abulafia has further contended, also reflected a shift away from a sense of the word as "servant" and toward "slave" or "possessed," as it had signified in Roman law.[146] As a whole, the expression *servi camerae regis* marked Frederick's attempt to assert exclusive jurisdiction over non-Christians, a pointed challenge to the counterclaims of the Church and the nobility. By this logic, these soldiers' increased privilege derived from rather than stood in opposition to their enslavement by the king.

In precisely the same fashion as Frederick II, the Aragonese kings used non-Christians to challenge the authority of the Church and nobility as well as assert their exclusive and exceptional right of jurisdiction.[147] Pere relied upon Jewish administrators to lessen his dependence on the nobility, to create a body of bureaucrats who were personally dependent upon him.[148] Similarly, he turned to the Muslim *jenets* to serve as his personal protectors and fill his armies. In brief, he used Jews and Muslims not only to defend but also to articulate his claims to absolute authority.

While this relationship may seem counterintuitive to modern sensibilities, in the wake of his conquest of Sicily in 1282, Pere's own noblemen recognized this pattern and connection. Rising up in rebellion, a large coalition of Aragonese noblemen, calling themselves the *Unions,* explicitly challenged the king's claim to sovereignty (*merum imperium*).[149] They called for a reduction of royal jurisdiction and a return to respect for customary law, rejecting "the *imperium* . . . which was never known in the kingdom . . . and other new things without following the custom."[150] More significantly, they demanded that Pere dismiss "the Jews and foreigners" in his administration, indicating their awareness of the relationship between non-Christians, Sicilian exiles, and the new imperial pretension. Under threat on all sides, Pere was forced to compromise. On October 3, 1283, he approved the Privilegio General in Aragon, agreeing to dismiss all his Jewish bailiffs.[151] The same concession was granted to the kingdoms of Valencia and Catalonia a few months later.[152]

The rebellions, however, continued, and Pere and his successors continued to maintain the practice of relying on privileged non-Christians.[153] Local Jewish bailiffs indeed disappeared, but the Crown's use of Jews as privileged agents of the royal court continued unabated. The recruitment of the *jenets* was an expansion of this system. And significantly, in this context, rather than referring to his Jewish and Muslim agents as *servi*, as he had in the past, Pere now prevaricated, speaking of them obliquely and innocuously as "our faithful (*fidelis noster*)" and "of our household (*de domo nostra*)."[154] Abrahim el Jenet, for instance, was simply "our Jew."[155] In other words, these expressions and others like them did not suggest equality, community, or even affection—an ability to see these men as something other or more than Muslims and Jews—but rather were an ambage that masked ideas of possession and ownership.

In all but name, the Aragonese practice of using Jewish and Muslim *servi* remained the same. King Alfons II used the *jenets* to attack the *Unions*. From 1285 to 1287, the *jenets* were operating not only in foreign theaters but also in the Aragonese towns of Cutanda, Alfamén, and Calatayud, centers of rebellion.[156] The Crown's dependence on these soldiers is perhaps best illustrated by the fact that they actively prevented others from recruiting them. In 1293, Artal de Alagón, one of the leaders of the *Unions*, sent representatives to Granada—including a *jenet* already in his service—to request the support of the Ghuzāh for his rebellion against King Jaume II. Learning of this mission, Jaume moved immediately to block the alliance:

> We have learned for certain that some Aragonese noblemen have recently sent representatives to the king of Granada, asking for and seeking assistance from him. . . . We have also learned that the nobleman Artal de Alagón sent his majordomo to said king as well as a certain Saracen *jenet* to request an army of *jenets* to do us harm, and we plan to resist these efforts so that no one can inflict harm or injury on our land and people.[157]

If the *jenets* were an extension of the royal body, an expression of its power, then they could only belong to the king.

Thus, in employing the Muslim *jenets*, King Pere and his successors were not merely acquiring skilled soldiers but also satisfying a certain vision of imperial power, an extreme political theology. They were not recruiting men that they saw as equals or boon companions but rather men that they saw as wholly dependent upon them—as their slaves. The privileges that they heaped upon these warriors, in other words, also symbolized their perfect submission. "Beware of all enterprises that require new clothes," Thoreau wrote.[158] Indeed, the sumptuous clothes granted to the *jenets* were freighted with danger. These new clothes indexed the king's claim to transcendence, his desire to stand apart from and above the law, to be sovereign. By putting on these rich silks, the *jenets* risked becoming embodiments of the king's assertions of exceptional authority and extensions of the king's body. To state this more provocatively, rather than religious indifference or cultural accommodation, the Crown's relationship with the Muslim *jenets* both depended upon and reinscribed the fact that these men were non-Christians.

CHAPTER FOUR

A Mercenary Economy

Tracing the Crown of Aragon's efforts to recruit *jenets* across the later thirteenth and fourteenth centuries reveals not only the broader scope of their ambitions but also the deeper history of their imperial ideals.[1] As evidenced by Latin, Romance, and Arabic treaties in the Archive of the Crown of Aragon—which include the Cartas árabes, one of the most important and underexamined collections of medieval Arabic chancery material in the world—King Pere II and his successors recruited *jenets* not only from Granada but also from the rulers of North Africa. These new soldiers joined the ranks of the Marīnid Ghuzāh already in the service of the Aragonese kings. Beyond bringing more soldiers into the lands of the Crown of Aragon, however, these recruitment efforts demonstrate two significant facts. First, they show that the Aragonese kings' efforts to rule Sicily were inextricable from their desire also to rule Tunis. While these kings claimed the legacy of the Holy Roman emperors to justify their conquest of Sicily, they invoked the memory of the Almohad caliphs to justify their authority in North Africa. In other words, they cast themselves as the heirs of not only the Hohenstaufens but also the Almohads. Second, these records show the recruitment of Muslim soldiers was not merely a curious parallel to but also developed out of the well-known and longer-standing use of Christian soldiers by Muslim rulers. In this period, Christian and Muslim troops were exchanged for one another through agreements by which Aragonese and North African rulers accepted limits upon the use of foreign soldiers that respected political and religious boundaries. As such, Christian militias in North Africa provide another important precedence for the *jenets*. These connections to the history of North Africa point to a deeper genealogy for the ideas that linked emperors to privileged servants, one that led beyond Sicily and into the ancient Mediterranean. These same ideas would also rattle forward into the modern world.

The Tunisian Matins

The wars between the Aragonese and Angevins over claim to the title of Holy Roman emperor—which framed the first part of this book—were also fought in North Africa. After the Angevin seizure of Sicily in 1266, Hohenstaufen loyalists, men like Federico Lancia, who was Conrad Lancia's father, took refuge in Tunis.[2] The Ḥafṣid sultan, al-Mustanṣir (r. 1249–1277), had been a tributary of Frederick II and refused to recognize the authority of the Angevins. It was in this context that King Louis IX decided to launch a crusade against Tunis in 1270. Louis, who supported the Angevin claim to Sicily, aimed to destroy the remaining Hohenstaufens.

As these events unfolded, King Jaume I watched cautiously from the margins. He tacitly offered support to the Hohenstaufen loyalists in Tunis by permitting Aragonese subjects abroad to participate in defense of the city. Pleading before the pope, Jaume even gained approval for the Christian militias in the service of the Ḥafṣids.[3] To put this plainly, both French crusaders and Aragonese defenders of Tunis had papal permission for their opposing actions. In the end, however, the destructive effect of the French crusade convinced Tunis to pay both allegiance and annual tribute to the Angevins at Sicily. Many of the surviving Hohenstaufen loyalists thus fled to the Aragonese court, to the protection of Constanza, the wife of the future King Pere II.

Given Pere's pretension to style himself the rightful heir to Frederick II, it is not surprising that he was more aggressive than his father on the matter of Tunis. A new sultan, al-Wāthiq (r. 1277–1279), was patently hostile to the Aragonese.[4] Thus, in an effort to find a more pliable and predisposed ruler, Pere entered into an alliance with a Ḥafṣid prince named Abū Isḥāq, who was living in exile in Muslim Granada. Ten Aragonese galleys, under the command of Conrad Lancia, supported the coup that placed Abū Isḥāq (r. 1279–1283) on the Ḥafṣid throne.[5] This sultan, however, was less of a puppet than Pere had hoped. In response, the king briefly contemplated imposing "Peter of Tunis," a son of Abū Isḥāq who had converted to Christianity, on the Ḥafṣid throne but abandoned this prospect.[6]

The aggression against Tunis continued. In 1282, an Aragonese fleet landed at Collo (al-Qull) to support a rebellion against Abū Isḥāq.[7] Although the rebellion failed, the Aragonese navy was perfectly placed to take advantage of a sudden uprising against Angevin rule in Sicily, the episode known as the Sicilian Vespers. Nevertheless, what is striking is that despite the fact that the conquest of Sicily had been the Crown of Aragon's highest ambition for over a decade, the Aragonese navy immediately turned around, as if before the matins, and attacked North Africa once again. Tunis remained central to the Crown of Aragon's unfolding ambitions in the Mediterranean.

When the French crusade against the Crown of Aragon was announced, however, Pere halted these raids along the Tunisian coast.[8] In 1285, at Coll de Panissars, where he was preparing his scant armies to face a massive French invasion and where he was awaiting the arrival of the five *jenets*, riding mules borrowed from a Jew in Granada, Pere also met ambassadors from Tunis. These ambassadors agreed to peace and agreed to pay an annual tribute to the Crown of Aragon.[9]

Before his death a few months later, Pere stipulated the division of the lands of the Crown between his sons, Alfons and Jaume. Jaume, who would later become King Jaume II (r. 1291–1327), inherited the island of Sicily, while Alfons II (r. 1285–1291), his elder son, inherited the remaining kingdoms and the crown itself. The purpose of this division was to free Sicily from the prying hands of Catalan and Aragonese noblemen, who had threatened Pere's authority with rebellion. But this division had little effect on the dangers that Alfons and later Jaume would face. The Crown of Aragon remained under threat from the *Unions* within and the Papacy, the French, and the Castilians without. Thus, for his part, King Alfons responded to these threats just as his father had. He turned to the *jenets*. And as three interlocking missions to recruit these soldiers from North Africa in 1286 reveal, in the midst of crisis, he also held on to his father's ambition of mastering North Africa. Pere's early attempts at asserting his authority over Tunis foreshadowed Alfons' own.

Three Missions

In December 1286, two ambassadors, Pere de Deo and Abrahim Abengalel, a Jew, were issued instructions for a mission to the court of the Marīnid sultan Abū Ya'qūb.[10] The first half of their negotiations was intended to deal with the recruitment of *jenets*. Alfons instructed his ambassadors to convey two sentiments to Abū Ya'qūb: first, that "from Pere, his father, and Jaume, his grandfather, he has learned of the good will of the sultan," and second, that "from his father, Pere, he also has learned of the aid (*valença*) of his [the sultan's] knights (*companya sua de cavalers*) that profited the king in his war against the French." Significantly, this document reveals that the Marīnids had acknowledged if not authorized the participation of their cavalry in the defense of the Crown of Aragon against the French crusade in 1285. Alfons further instructed his ambassadors to tell Abū Ya'qūb that "he [Alfons] has learned that the sultan can offer him 2,000 *jenets* for his mission (*II mile janets ab sa messio*)." He therefore authorized Pere and Abrahim to conclude a peace treaty with the Marīnids. According to its terms, Abū Ya'qūb would initially provide Alfons with 500 *jenets*, and Alfons, in turn, would provide the sultan with five galleys or more if required.[11] The rulers also agreed to place restrictions on the use of these troops and navies: Alfons promised only to assist the sultan against Muslims, and the sultan would only aid Alfons against Christians.[12]

The deeper purpose of this exchange of troops was revealed by the remaining instructions, namely a proposed joint invasion of Tunis. First, Alfons promised to release into Marīnid custody a captive referred to only as "Margam" in this document as well as others in the registers of the Archive of the Crown of Aragon. "Margam" was undoubtedly Murghim b. Ṣābir, whose captivity in Barcelona was noted by Ibn Khaldūn.[13] Murghim was also a chief of the Banū Dabbāb, an Arab tribe, and more importantly, a prominent enemy of the Ḥafṣids. Second, Alfons instructed his ambassadors to tell Abū Ya'qūb that any ships supplied by the Crown of Aragon must immediately be employed against Tunis. Third and last, in the event the Marīnids captured Tunis, the annual tributes and other rights (*els los tributz els altres dretz*) of the Aragonese kings would be maintained.[14] The importance of these negotiations to understanding the Aragonese king's goals is not mitigated by the fact that a signed agreement with the Marīnids never followed.[15]

At the same time that Pere and Abrahim traveled to Fez, an Aragonese ambassador named Pedro Garcia succeeded in signing a treaty with the 'Abd al-Wādid ruler, Abū Sa'īd 'Uthmān b. Yaghmurāsan (r. 1283–1304), for the exchange of troops.[16] In this case, however, the Christian soldiers in question were already in the service of Abū Sa'īd. They were members of a militia under the command of Jaume Pere, an illegitimate son of King Pere II.[17] Alfons' instructions to Pedro Garcia began by asking the ambassador to "express his desire to be friends with him [the sultan] just as his father, King Pere, and grandfather, Jaume, were."[18] The focus of these negotiations, however, was the treatment of Christian soldiers in Tlemcen. Alfons requested that all these Christian troops, regardless of origin, be placed under Aragonese law (*fuero d'Aragon*) and under the command of an *alcaidus* or *alcayt*, nominated by the Aragonese king. (The Arabic *al-qā'id* comes into Latin as *alcaidus* or *alcaldus* and into Romance as *alcayt* or other similar variants. Although the Arabic simply means leader, in the context of Christian militias these terms specifically meant captain.)[19] Alfons also stipulated the amount of these soldiers' salaries, the manner in which they would be housed, that they should be properly provisioned with horses, camels, and mules, and finally, that they should have a priest accompanying them.[20] In short, Alfons was aiming to gain control over all aspects of the soldiers' physical, legal, and liturgical lives. He sought to mark these soldiers out not only as Aragonese subjects in North Africa but also as Christians.[21] In return for the service of these Christian mercenaries, Alfons requested that Abū Sa'īd supply the Crown with Muslim troops whenever their help was required (*cada que mester oviere su aiuda*).[22] Thus, again, the *jenets* were linked to soldiers of the other faith, moving in the other direction.

At the same time as the embassies to Fez and Tlemcen, Alfons order another mission under the leadership of Conrad Lancia to travel to the Ḥafṣid court.[23] Lancia's instructions were short and his purpose narrow. He was meant to renew and enlarge the parts of the treaty signed by King Pere at Coll de Panissars, particularly those parts related to the treatment of Christian soldiers in the service of the sultan. As with Garcia's mission to Tlemcen, Alfons requested that all Christian soldiers, regardless of origin, should be placed under the jurisdiction of an Aragonese *alcayt*.[24] Provisions were also made for salaries and housing.[25] But Lancia's instructions make no mention of recruiting *jenets*. These final negotiations merely aimed at maintaining the status quo, and the fact that no treaty followed them meant little to the Aragonese king. Lancia's mission to Tunis masked the most fascinating part of Alfons' Mediterranean strategy.

The Last Almohad

In order to understand what followed, what grander plan lay behind these three missions, one must step back fifteen years to the collapse of the

Almohad Empire. On August 31, 1269, as the Marīnid cavalry approached the rose walls of Marrakesh, the last Almohad caliph, Abū Dabbūs (r. 1266–1269), rode into battle, fell from his charger, and was killed.[26] His family fled high into the Atlas Mountains, the sacred center of the Almohads, where their mission began, and hid until Marīnid troops finally captured them in 1276, putting an end to their rule in North Africa.[27] In his account of the empire's fall, the historian Ibn Khaldūn added the following detail:

> [Abū Dabbūs'] sons scattered and were overthrown in the land. One of them, 'Uthmān, fled to eastern al-Andalus and settled with the tyrant of Barcelona (*ṭāghiyat Barshilūna*) and was treated well. There, he found the sons of his uncle (*a'qāb 'ammihi*), the Almohad lord (*al-sayyid*) Abū Zayd, the false convert (*al-mutanaṣṣir*; this may be translated as "convert" or "impostor"), brother of Abū Dabbūs, living in the lands of the enemy. They [the sons] held an esteemed position (*makān wajāh*) on account of the flight (*nuzū'*) of their father from his religion [Islam] (*dīnihi*) to theirs [Christianity].[28]

Abū Dabbūs' son, 'Uthmān, had chosen exile in Iberia, where he sought the protection of his cousins. These were the sons of the Almohad governor of Valencia, Abū Zayd, who had converted to Christianity after the kingdom's conquest by the Crown of Aragon.[29] But from this moment, Ibn Khaldūn said nothing more about 'Uthmān until his sudden reappearance in North Africa in 1289. What became of this Almohad prince during the twenty years when he disappeared from the Arabic record? Although Elena Lourie noted the presence of not one but several "Almohad princes" living in Valencia in 1285, she dropped the matter, unaware of the larger context.[30]

Between 1262 and 1285, there is also no evidence of 'Uthman in the records of the Archive of the Crown of Aragon. We cannot confirm whether he did indeed seek refuge with the sons of Abū Zayd, but the history of Abū Zayd himself provides an important precedent for Alfons' later dealing with 'Uthmān.

Decades earlier, in 1225, facing rebellions against Almohad rule in al-Andalus, Abū Zayd fled to the court of King Jaume I. In exile and with the hope of regaining Valencia, he signed a series of agreements with the Crown of Aragon, each one progressively eroding his authority.[31] On the eve of Jaume's conquest of Valencia in 1238, Abū Zayd became a vassal of the king, and as a single charter of donation to the Bishop of Segorbe betrays, Abū Zayd also converted to Christianity. What is striking, however, is that he would keep this conversion a secret for another twenty-eight years.[32]

In his relationship with Abū Zayd, the secret convert, Jaume established a pattern that later Aragonese kings would follow, one in which they would assert their authority over Muslims through the legacy of the Almohads rather than against it. After his conquest of Valencia, Jaume faced both challenges and opportunities. On the one hand, he now ruled over a majority-Muslim population, one that would remain restive for decades to come. One the other hand, the conquest of Valencia allowed Jaume and his advisors to experiment with new ideas of royal authority.[33] In Valencia, Jaume invoked the Roman principle of absolute jurisdiction (*merum imperium*) and established the first fully Romanized law code in Europe. These traditions marked a profound shift in Christian political theology, which is to say, ideas and claims about the relationship of divine to earthly authority. Enthusiastic legists tried to recast the Aragonese king as a divinely inspired lawmaker and judge over all his subjects, Christian, Jewish, and Muslim.

Recently and provocatively, Maribel Fierro has also argued that these ideas bear more than a passing resemblance to Almohad concepts of universal sovereignty.[34] The revolutionary ambitions of the Almohads had been grounded in the theological doctrine of *tawḥīd*, radical monotheism or unitarianism. And although earlier historiography saw this fervent belief as a source of intolerance, Fierro has argued that Almohad policies toward Jews and Christians aspired less toward their conversion than the reversion of all believers, above all Muslims, to an uncorrupted monotheism.[35] Ibn Tūmart, the founder of the Almohads, had developed a messianic and universalist political theology that aimed at the integration of all Muslims, Christians, and Jews into one community under the leadership of the caliph.[36] Far from blind adherence to dogma, the Almohads argued for the supremacy of knowledge and reason as an instrument for this social, moral, and political transformation.[37] They developed high degrees of legal and administrative centralization.[38] And most famously, they patronized the rationalist political philosophy of Ibn Rushd (Averroes), whose works would have a profound impact on Europe.[39] Within all these ideas, the Almohads saw the caliph as a divinely inspired and sovereign lawmaker. Although North Africa and al-Andalus eventually rejected the Almohads, their ideas arrived in Latin Christendom through the translation of key texts.[40] In the figure of Abū Zayd, a Muslim before Muslims and a Christian before Christians, these overlapping and competing political theological traditions, Aragonese and Almohad, intersected.

When ʻUthmān finally appears in the chancery registers in 1285, we find him living in the kingdom of Valencia. In addition to ʻUthman, who is called "Açmon," we find his brothers, ʻAbd al-Raḥmān (Abderamen), Muḥammad (Mahomet), and ʻAbd al-Wāḥid (Abdeluaheyt). The presence of ʻAbd al-Wāḥid is significant. The eldest of Abū Dabbūs' sons, he was technically the last Almohad caliph because he held the title for five days after his father's death.[41] As these records show, the Aragonese kings had been providing houses and living expenses for these men and their families, in essence treating them as dependents and dignitaries.[42] What is more, from 1285 to 1288, during the period that Pere II and Alfons II were facing a French crusade and the *Unions*, these four brothers also served as leaders of *jenet* companies, which is to say, they served as leaders of the very same Marīnid cavalry that had overrun the Almohads a generation earlier.[43] For this service, the Almohad princes were paid twice what the average *jenet* received. The Aragonese kings, however, had a different purpose in mind for these men.

On July 29, 1287, in the city of Jaca, near the border with France, ʻAbd al-Wāḥid, the eldest of the Almohad princes, signed a treaty, written in Latin and Arabic (*bi'l-ʻajamī wa'l-ʻarabī*), agreeing to a lifelong alliance with the Crown of Aragon in return for financial and military support for the conquest of Ḥafṣid Tunis and the restoration of the Almohad Caliphate in North Africa.[44]

The treaty was wide-ranging. ʻAbd al-Wāḥid promised to welcome and protect Aragonese merchants as long as they respected the rights and customs of Tunis.[45] He agreed to pay annual tributes to King Alfons and his brother King Jaume of Sicily of 33,333 ⅓ silver (*fiḍḍa/argenti*) dīnārs and 16,000 silver dīnārs respectively, the former the traditional tribute paid by the Ḥafṣids to the Holy Roman emperor. The remainder of the treaty concentrated on matters related to Christian soldiers serving in Tunis. The Almohad prince agreed to transfer all of these Christian soldiers, regardless of their origin, to the jurisdiction (*ṭāʻa wa-ḥukm/jurisdiccione et dominacioni*) of the Crown of Aragon and its royal captain (*al-qā'id/alcaldus*), who alone would adjudicate all civil and criminal law cases.[46] ʻAbd al-Wāḥid agreed to maintain the customs established "during the time of Guillem de Moncada," a captain appointed by Alfons' grandfather, King Jaume I.[47] He also agreed to provide these soldiers with regular salaries, armed horses, mules, and other necessary provisions, mirroring the treatment of *jenets* by the Crown of Aragon.[48] Differently than for the *jenets*, he promised to make alcohol available, one wine barrel (*barīl* [sic] *al-sharāb/barrile vini*) every five days for a knight and every seven days for a squire.[49] In addition to matters of jurisdiction, pastoral concerns were also addressed. ʿAbd al-Wāḥid authorized the Aragonese soldiers to establish a merchant hostel (*funduq/alfundicum*) with the customary right to possess a church, celebrate rituals such as "[raising] the body of Jesus Christ (*jāshū qarīsit/Iehsu Cristi*) while ringing bells," receive communion, and use a censer (*mibkhara/turibula*) for burial services.[50] Finally, the prince promised to aid the Aragonese against all their enemies, whether Christian or Muslim:

> Moreover, we promise you upon our word (*ʿalā ʿahdinā/bona fide*) that whenever you call upon us (*nuṭlabu ʿankum/a vobis fuerimus requisiti*) by letter or messenger, we will help you with all our might to oppose anyone, whether Christian, Muslim, or otherwise, of whatever community (*umma/condicionis legis*), religion or creed (*dīn aw iʿtiqād/fidei*), and we will do this without deceptions, malice, or treachery (*khuduʿ wa-khubth wa-ghadr/dolo, malo, et fraude*).

The imbalance between the parties of this contract is underscored by the fact that Alfons, in turn, only promised to offer ʿAbd al-Wāḥid support against his Muslim enemies.[51] Finally but rather typically for such interreligious agreements, the Almohad prince and Aragonese king swore on the Qur'ān and Bible respectively.[52]

In this treaty, Alfons asserted his dominion not only over Tunis but also over the Christian troops living there, who served in the armies and courts of the Ḥafṣids. Like his predecessors, Alfons was attempting to place a puppet on the throne at Tunis. This desire to ventriloquize, to speak through Almohad authority, is most obvious in the fact that the Arabic of this charter is a slavish copy of the Latin. The script is Maghribī but written unsteadily and riddled with errors, unusual word choices, and curious vocalization marks. All the witnesses to the charter are, moreover, Christians. In other words, this treaty was most likely the product of the Aragonese chancery, an agreement thrust upon ʿAbd al-Wāḥid. One might even be tempted to conclude that the whole document was a forgery if not for the events that followed.

After signing this agreement, it took some time for ʿAbd al-Wāḥid to depart for North Africa. In October 1287, Alfons transferred 2,000 *solidi* to ʿAbd al-Wāḥid for his journey.[53] But as late as April 1288, the Almohad princes were still in Valencia, attempting to settle the debts owed to them for their service as *jenets*. In the meantime, in 1287, an Aragonese fleet, under the command of Roger de Lauria, had captured the Kerkenna (Qarqana) islands, an archipelago off the coast of Tunis, from which they terrorized the North African coast, carrying off Muslim captives, whose last traces can be found in the receipts of slave markets in Italy.[54]

From this point, Ibn Khaldūn picked up the narrative thread again, offering more detail than can be found in the chancery registers. Speaking not of 'Abd al-Wāḥid but rather his younger brother, 'Uthmān, Ibn Khaldūn explained that this Almohad prince had long maintained the hope of restoring the caliphate. And in an Aragonese captive by the name of Murghim b. Ṣābir, whom Ibn Khaldūn called the chief of the Dabbāb tribe in Tripoli, 'Uthmān saw his opportunity to secure a foothold in North Africa.[55] Using his influence at the Aragonese court, 'Uthmān secured the release of Murghim and arranged to hire ships and soldiers with the promise to reimburse the Crown. The two conspirators, 'Uthmān and Murghim, made landfall in 1289 in North Africa where, with the aid of Murghim's tribe and the Aragonese fleet, they undertook the siege of Tripoli, just beyond the grasp of the Ḥafṣid sultan. According to Ibn Khaldūn, the siege lasted only three days before the coalition began to unravel. The historian al-Nuwayrī (d. 1333) clarified, moreover, that 'Abd al-Wāḥid died in these early battles, leaving 'Uthmān in command, a fact that may explain 'Abd al-Wāḥid's total elision from Ibn Khaldūn's later account.[56]

Perhaps seeing the mission as failed, the Aragonese chose to leave the fight. Alfons was facing an emerging Castilian alliance with the French and decided reluctantly to reestablish diplomatic ties with the Ḥafṣid sultan. In December 1290, an Aragonese ambassador was dispatched to Tunis to renew the terms of Pere's treaty at Panissars.[57] Abandoned by the Aragonese, 'Uthmān decided to take refuge with the Dabbāb tribe.[58] But at some point, the Almohad prince must have fallen out with his Arab allies as well. According to Ibn Khaldūn, 'Uthmān died on the Aragonese-controlled island of Jerba (Jarba).[59] His last gasp in exile was also that of the Almohad Caliphate.

Das ist der doux commerce![60]

Mapping Alfons' effort to recruit *jenets* reveals a broad network of Christian-Islamic interaction, of which Conrad Lancia and Samuel Abenmenassé's mission to Granada in 1285 was only a part. The Crown of Aragon regularly sent ambassadors to each of the major kingdoms of North Africa in order to recruit *jenets* for decades to come.[61] The three interlocking missions above also formed part of an ambition to control Tunis, the last representative of Almohad authority in North Africa and the great rival of the Marīnids. The *jenets* were not disconnected from this ambition. As the accounts of Roger de Lauria held in the Cathedral of Valencia reveal, several *jenet* companies served aboard Aragonese ships, alongside both Mudéjar oarsmen and Christian knights from Rhodes and Lucera, as they raided the Tunisian coast.[62] The strategy of the Aragonese kings in Tunis, however, was never to rule directly but rather over and through representatives of Almohad authority. Indeed, this policy continued well after the death of 'Uthmān b. Abī Dabbūs, the last Almohad. Following repeated attacks by Roger de Lauria's fleet along the Tunisian coast in 1313, Jaume II reprised this strategy with the sultan Abū Yaḥyā al-Liḥyānī (r. 1311–1317), a latter day Abū Zayd, who may have also been convinced to convert to Christianity.[63] This was not mere politics. Just as the Aragonese kings cast themselves as heirs to the universal claims of the Holy Roman emperors before their Christian subjects, they also borrowed and adapted the universal claims of the Almohad caliphs before Muslims.

These missions also reveal a fact that has otherwise gone unnoticed. Over the late thirteenth and early fourteenth centuries, the Aragonese kings and North African sultans exchanged soldiers, Muslim *jenets* for Christian militias. As these treaties make clear, these rulers were not indifferent to belief. They neither employed religion as mere ideology nor were blindly obedient to it. Instead, in these treaties one finds creative attempts to navigate and negotiate emerging spiritual and pastoral concerns. Indeed, these concerns were a central aspect of the instructions issued to Aragonese ambassadors. But perhaps more strikingly, a regular feature of these exchanges was the mutual agreement on limitations for the use of these soldiers. Sultans regularly agreed to use their Christian militias only against their Muslim enemies, and the Aragonese kings agreed to use their *jenets* only against their Christian enemies.[64] On some occasions, the limits followed political lines, as in the willingness of the Marīnids to let the Aragonese use *jenets* against the Ḥafṣids. Among these many treaties, 'Abd al-Wāḥid's agreement in 1287 to aid the Aragonese against *all* their enemies, whether Christian or Muslim, was unusual. To give one salient example of the degree of the respect for these limits: in 1323, the Marīnid sultan refused to return Christian troops in his service to support Jaume II's conquest of Sardinia, which is to say, he refused to let these troops fight against other Christians, saying this would break with custom, but offered Muslim soldiers in their stead.[65] Far from belying religious boundaries, these agreements for the exchange of soldiers proved to be a surprising confirmation of those boundaries. Religious commitments did not impede these exchanges but rather channeled them through certain types of interaction. To be certain, all interaction, all trade across the Mediterranean, was not bound and determined by belief or religious law, but the perduring assumption that interaction occurred despite or regardless of religion, that all commerce was what Montesquieu called "sweet commerce," risks running so far in the opposite extreme only to achieve the same reductive end.

Christian Militias

The connection of the *jenets* to the longer-standing service of Christian soldiers to Muslim rulers exposes another narrative thread. It suggests a more profound ancestry for the *jenets* than that of the Hohenstaufen court. Indeed, by the late thirteenth century, when the Crown of Aragon moved to bring them under its jurisdiction, Christian militias had been well entrenched for centuries. What kind of precedent for the *jenets* did these militias offer?

Although the earliest evidence is sparse, within the Iberian Peninsula the use of foreign Christian soldiers by Muslim rulers can be traced at least as far back as the Umayyads (711–1031).[66] As part of a wider military reform, the *amīr* al-Ḥakam I (r. 796–822) established an army of foreign, salaried troops, known as the *ḥasham*, composed of both Europeans and Berbers.[67] Simultaneously, he also organized a palatine guard (*dā'ira*), a bodyguard, composed of Galician (Eastern European) and Frankish slaves or former slaves (*'abīd* or *mamālīk*).[68] Called "the Mute" (*al-khurs*) in chronicles—perhaps because they could not speak Arabic—these guardsmen were led by a Mozarab (*must'arab* or *must'arib*), that is, an Arabic-speaking Christian, captain (*qā'id*), named Rabī' b. Teodulfo.[69] Al-Ḥakam's son, 'Abd al-Raḥmān II (r. 822–852) continued this tradition, employing foreign soldiers in both his armies and his personal guard.[70] The palatine guard of slave soldiers is attested to again during the reign of 'Abd Allāh (r. 888–912).[71] The first Umayyad in al-Andalus to proclaim himself caliph, 'Abd al-Raḥmān III (r. 912–961), also employed foreign soldiers in his armies and entourage.[72] Finally, the historian al-Maqqarī described Christian soldiers, dressed in parade uniforms, paying obeisance to the caliph al-Ḥakam II (r. 961–976).[73] However scattered and fleeting this evidence from the Umayyad period may be, key elements of the later tradition were already in place.

The decline and splintering of Umayyad authority in Iberia that followed, known as the Ṭā'ifa period, increased the opportunities for military alliances between Muslims and Christians.[74] In this climate, various rulers competed to cast themselves as the legitimate successors to the Umayyads. For instance, in imitation of the caliphs, the ruler of Valencia, Ibn Jaḥḥāf, was said to parade with an army of Christian military slaves (*'abīd*) before him.[75] The fragmentation of political authority also precipitated the movement of free Christian political exiles into Islamic courts.[76] For one example among many, one need only mention the nobleman, Rodrigo Díaz de Vivar, also known as El Cid, who served the Muslim ruler of Zaragoza in the eleventh century before establishing his own principality.[77]

Superficially, the events of the eleventh and twelfth centuries appeared to be less propitious to such border-crossing activity on the peninsula. Two Berber dynasties, the Almoravids and Almohads, successively united al-Andalus under a single authority and appeared hostile to religious interaction. Simultaneously, from north of the Pyrenees, crusade ideology entered into the Iberian Peninsula from as early as the reign of Pope Alexander II (r. 1061–1073). All this did little, however, to impede the movement of men and arms into armies of the other faith. The enthusiasm for crusading quickly dissolved.[78] And individuals like Fernando Rodríguez de Castro (1125–1185), a Castilian nobleman, enrolled in the armies of the Almohads seemingly without compunction. His son, Pedro Fernández, fought with the Almohads at the battle of Alarcos in 1194 against Alfonso VIII of Castile.[79]

Although the Christian realms of Iberia united briefly to deal a devastating blow to the Almohads at the Battle of Las Navas de Tolosa in 1212, the fragmentation of political authority that followed—a second Ṭā'ifa period—encouraged political exiles and warlords to cross into Islamic kingdoms once again. Despite papal censure, noblemen from Navarre, Castile, and Aragon regularly took up residence in Muslim territory.[80] For instance, during the reign of King Jaume I, several rebellious Aragonese knights took refuge in Islamic Valencia, perhaps the most famous of these being Blasco de Alagón, who defected during Aragon's crusade against

Valencia to the court of Abū Zayd. According to Jaume's autobiography, Blasco's brother Giles converted to Islam, taking the name Muḥammad.[81] It is worth repeating in this context that Blasco's son, Artal, had *jenets* in his employ, underscoring that the family resemblance between these Christian and Islamic military traditions was more than coincidence.[82] All the same, during this second Ṭā'ifa period, the flow of soldiers was sufficient such that Ibn Hūd, a rebel against Almohad rule, could maintain a guard of two hundred Christian soldiers in his service.[83] This trading of allegiances continued well into the rule of the last Islamic principality on the Iberian Peninsula, the Naṣrids (1232–1492), who relied heavily upon foreign soldiers, both Berber and European, to serve in their armies and courts.[84]

The use of Iberian Christian soldiers in Islamic armies was not limited to the peninsula. The Almoravid ruler 'Alī b. Yūsuf b. Tāshfīn (r. 1061–1106) was said to have first introduced the practice to North Africa.[85] According the *Chronica Adefonsi Imperatoris*, the chronicle of the reign of Alfonso VII of Léon (r. 1126–1157), these soldiers had been captives of war, who eventually rose to a privileged position:

> At that time, God granted His grace to the prisoners who were in the royal court of their lord, King 'Alī, and moved His heart toward them in order to favor the Christians. 'Alī regarded them above all of the men of his own eastern people, for he made some of them chamberlains of his private apartments, and others captains of one thousand soldiers, five hundred soldiers, and one hundred soldiers, who stood at the forefront of the army of his kingdom. He furnished them with gold and silver, cities and strongly fortified castles, with which they could have reinforcement in order to make war on the Muzmutos [Almohads] and the king of the Assyrians, called Abdelnomen ['Abd al-Mu'min], who attacked his territories without interruption.[86]

Precisely where these Iberian Christians came from remains unclear. They may have been among the Mozarabs deported by the Almoravids following a rebellion in 1125.[87] The status and history of the leader of these troops between 1135 and 1137, Berenguer Reverter, the viscount of Barcelona and lord of La Guardia de Montserrat, is similarly obscure. Reverter likely came to North Africa of his own volition.[88] Several letters held at the Archive of the Crown of Aragon suggest that this was the case.[89] Moreover, Reverter served the Almoravids loyally, dying in battle against the Almohads.[90] The careers of Reverter's sons, however, underscore the complexity of parsing these soldiers' motivations. One, known as Abū'l-Ḥasan 'Alī b. Ruburtayr, converted to Islam and served the Almohads.[91] The other, also Berenguer Reverter, moved between North Africa and Barcelona, signed his letters in Arabic and Latin, and eventually joined the Knights Templar, a crusading order.[92]

Although the same *Chronica Adelfonsi Imperatoris* reported that many Christian soldiers fled from Islamic lands to Toledo after the siege of Marrakesh in 1147 by the Almohads, within a year, the Almohads, too, began to employ Christians in their armies in North Africa.[93] In fact, the rise of the Almohad Empire marked an important step toward the institutionalization of Christian militias. Like their predecessors and contemporaries, the Almohads maintained a palatine guard of Christian slaves or former slaves, whom they referred to as "Ifarkhān" or "Banū Farkhān," an enigmatic term whose meaning is contested.[94] Yet the Almohads also recruited large numbers of apparently free Christian soldiers from the Iberian Peninsula.[95] The well-known Portuguese warlord Geraldo Sempavor (the "Fearless") and the Castilian prince Don Enrique are worth mentioning in this context.[96] For his part, Geraldo Sempavor pledged loyalty to the Almohad caliph Abū Ya'qūb (r. 1163–1184) and was rewarded with lands in the western Atlas.[97] According to Ibn Khaldūn, the caliph al-Ma'mūn (r. 1227–1232) reportedly recruited some 12,000 Christian soldiers through an agreement with Fernando III of Castile.[98] Significantly, these soldiers were allowed to build a church at Marrakech.[99]

After the rise of the Almohads, the influence of these soldiers in royal courts appeared to increase. Once in the corridors of power, Christian militias and their captains became embroiled in intrigues and palace coups.[100] Nevertheless, as Ibn Khaldūn explained, they held a reputation for fierce loyalty and were prized as heavy cavalry, which was unknown in North Africa (fig. 4):

> We have mentioned the strength that a line formation [of heavy cavalry] behind the army gives to fighters who use the technique of attacking and fleeing (*al-karr wa'l-farr*). Therefore the North African rulers have come to employ groups of Franks (*ṭā'ifa min al-Ifranj*) in their army, and they are the only ones to have done that, because their countrymen only know how to attack and flee.[101]

These knights collected taxes for the caliphs, suppressed rebellions, and participated in demonstrations of force (*maḥalla*) among the nomadic tribes at the empire's fringes.[102] The Almohads only seemed to have hesitated to use these soldiers against other Christians.[103] In practice, this trust was well placed. Christian militias played a prominent role in the defense of the Almohads against the advancing Marīnid armies.[104] In one striking example of loyalty, after the conquest of Fez in 1248, two Christian captains, who were called Zunnār and Shadīd, conspired with the inhabitants of Fez to expel the Marīnids.[105]

Despite the fact that the Almohads had depended upon Christian soldiers in their wars against them, the new North African kingdoms—the Ḥafṣids at Tunis, the ʻAbd al-Wādids at Tlemcen, and the Marīnids at Fez—systematically recruited these very same men to serve in their armies and in their courts.[106] In a telling instance, after their victory over the Almohads, the ʻAbd al-Wādids incorporated their rival's Christian guard, mainly men of Castilian origin, into their armies and royal entourage:

> After the death of al-Saʻīd [Abū'l-Ḥasan ʻAlī al-Saʻīd (r. 1242–48)] and the defeat of the Almohad army, Yaghmurāsan employed some of the corps of Christian troops that were in al-Saʻīd's army (*qad istakhdama ṭā'ifa min jund al-naṣārā alladhīna fī jumlatihi*), grateful to add to their number to his army and as well as display them in his military processions (*al-mawāqif wa'l-mashāhid*).[107]

But these troops remained loyal to the Almohads and eventually rebelled, leading the ʻAbd al-Wādids to expel them. In the wake of this rebellion, however, rather than ending the practice of using foreign militias, the sultan in Tlemcen simply sought replacements from the lands of the Crown of Aragon.[108] The value of these Christian soldiers thus outweighed the threat of subversion.

In general, the use of Christian soldiers by these three kingdoms followed the pattern established in earlier periods. Independent warlords and political exiles—for example, the sons of the Castilian king Ferdinand III (r. 1217–1252) and the nobleman Alonso Perez de Guzmán (1256–1309), also known as Guzmán el Bueno—traveled to North Africa.[109] Like their predecessors, these kingdoms also recruited soldiers directly from the kings of the Crown of Aragon and Castile. Moreover, these sultans continued to employ royal guards, composed of slaves or former slaves.[110] And most significantly, they never employed Christian militias against Christians on the Iberian Peninsula. As Ibn Khaldūn underscored in his discussion of these militias in the fourteenth century, "The rulers in the Maghrib do this [use Christians] only in wars against Arab and Berber nations, in order to force them into submission. They do not use them for holy war, because they are afraid that they might take sides against the Muslims. Such is the situation at this time."[111] Despite such constraints, the use of Christian was widespread.

By the time one reaches the thirteenth and fourteenth centuries, the period best illuminated by the chancery registers of the Archive of the Crown of Aragon, the employment of soldiers was not only thoroughly entrenched but had also become an "affair of state," a fact that brought these armies greater legitimacy, authority, and influence in North Africa and the Iberian Peninsula.[112]

As seen in the case of Alfons' three missions above, the Aragonese kings were concerned principally with asserting their jurisdiction over Christian soldiers in North Africa.[113] In this regard, they were most successful in Tunis and Tlemcen. By contrast, in Fez, their influence was split: Aragonese and Castilian troops competed with each other for control, backing different factions at court, leading to decades of intrigue.[114] Nevertheless, control over the traffic in Christian soldiers to all three North African kingdoms was an Aragonese diplomatic priority in the thirteenth century.[115]

The earliest Aragonese intervention into the lives of Christian militias in North Africa can be roughly dated to the 1250s. In that period, the captain William de Moncada approached the Aragonese king to help settle a salary dispute with the Ḥafṣid sultan in Tunis.[116] The resulting agreement with the sultan would become the standard invoked during later negotiations, as it was, for instance, in the treaty of ʿAbd al-Wāḥid, the Almohad prince.[117] In accepting the service of Christian knights, Muslim rulers had to confirm what they recognized as customary privileges related to pay and religion.[118] They agreed to salaries for different ranks of soldiers from squire to knight. They recognized pastoral concerns and made assurances that these soldiers would be free to perform religious services.[119] The Aragonese kings assigned Christian militias uniforms and banners, bearing the colors of the Crown of Aragon, a white cross on a colored background, an image that reportedly drew complaints from some Muslims in North Africa.[120] But perhaps most significantly, the Aragonese king gained the right to name a captain (Lat. *alcaidus* or Rom. *alcayt*) over these soldiers, who would administer justice on the king's behalf.[121]

In an effort to appeal to the powerful captains of these Christian militias, the Aragonese kings extended them honors and privileges. These captains were called upon to serve as ambassadors and translators, as representative of the Crown of Aragon in North Africa.[122] The first

Aragonese captain named at Tlemcen, William Gauceran, was forgiven his participation in rebellion against the king.[123] Kings also granted these soldiers immunity from any religious crimes that they might incur or had incurred while aiding non-Christians.[124] This privilege could also be granted to an entire family line in perpetuity.[125] Honors and privileges such as these were expressions of the new jurisdictional prerogatives of the Aragonese kings and mirrored their treatment of *jenet* elites.

Earlier studies of Christian militias in North Africa have concluded that these soldiers were consciously transgressing or ignoring religious boundaries.[126] These negotiations and privileges from the thirteenth century suggest, in contrast, that religious or, more precisely, pastoral concerns were of central importance to the soldiers. North African caliphs and sultans permitted Christian militias to build and maintain churches and to celebrate public rituals. Soldiers sought absolutions from the Aragonese kings for their sins in serving Muslim rulers.

What is more, popes and religious lawyers were both more permissive of and involved in these activities than one might imagine. It is true that in 1214, after the Battle of Las Navas de Tolosa, Innocent III (r. 1198–1216) excommunicated all Christians who offered military aid to Muslims.[127] Within the peninsula, the archbishop of Toledo similarly condemned the mercenaries in North Africa in 1222 or 1223.[128] Nevertheless, as Simon Barton and Michael Lower have shown, these rigid attitudes masked flexibility.[129] Over the thirteenth century, the papacy eased or added subtlety to its stance toward Christian militias in North Africa. Fearing that they would alienate Christians living abroad, some popes began to recognize the spiritual needs of Christian mercenaries. Honorius III (r. 1216–1227) absolved these soldiers of their sins and urged the Almohad Caliph to allow them to practice Christianity freely.[130] For his part, Innocent IV (r. 1243–1254) saw the Muslim sultans' dependence upon these troops as an asset and used the threat of withdrawing his approval of their residence in North Africa for diplomatic leverage. By the time of Nicholas IV (r. 1288–1292), the pope claimed that the presence of Christian soldiers might have a positive effect on the conversion of the Muslims.[131] Ramón de Penyafort (d. 1275), the master-general of the Dominican Order and advisor to Jaume I, clarified that only soldiers who had the king's permission to serve in North Africa should be considered licit.[132] For his part, the bishop of North Africa openly acknowledged the leadership of Bernat Segui in Morocco.[133] Were these venal gestures or attempts to justify political ends? Just like the Aragonese kings, the Papacy and religious authorities moved belatedly to legitimize the enduring presence of Christian soldiers in Muslim kingdoms, but they also bent to meet the desires of these soldiers for spiritual recognition. These thirteenth-century popes were not indifferent to the beliefs and practices of Christian soldiers in North Africa.

The Aragonese control over Christian militias in North Africa peaked during the thirteenth and the early fourteenth centuries. By the middle of the fourteenth century, both Aragonese and Castilian influence appeared to have waned.[134] In Tunis, where the Aragonese had been strongest, one finds a Genoese captain in 1358.[135] The movement of fifty thoroughly assimilated families of Christian soldiers, known as the *farfanes*, from Fez to Castile at the end of the fourteenth century may have indicated that the political climate in Morocco had shifted away from reliance on non-Muslim troops.[136] Nevertheless, these militias continued to exist elsewhere in North Africa. Roser Salicrú has found permissions for individual Castilian soldiers to depart for North Africa as late as the fifteenth century.[137] When the friar Juan Gallicant arrived in Tunis in 1446 to negotiate the release of captives, he sought the assistance of the captain of the Christian militia, Mossen Guerau de Queralt.[138] The pilgrim Anselm Adorno found a thriving and well-assimilated Christian community at Tunis a few decades later.[139] Almost at the end of Ḥafṣid rule, Leo Africanus (d. 1552) attested to the continued existence of a Christian "secret guard" in Tunis.[140] In other words, while official exchanges of soldiers had vanished, Christian royal guardsmen, at the very least, continued to serve in North African courts.

The use of Christian Iberian soldiers by the Muslim rulers of al-Andalus and North Africa provides an important precedent for the *jenets*. From at least the eighth century, Christian soldiers were present in Islamic armies and courts. In the twelfth and early thirteenth centuries, the Almohads institutionalized the use of these soldiers. Their agreements with Christian kings regularized customs and practices concerning pay, limitations on use, and spiritual and liturgical practices. When the Aragonese kings ultimately sought to recruit *jenets* from North Africa in the late thirteenth and early fourteenth centuries, these customs were either implied or explicitly invoked. The employment of Muslim *jenets* grew out of and into an already established tradition. The Mediterranean trade in "infidel" soldiers also declined in tandem. In parallel with the case of the *guardia morisca* of the Castilian kings, after Christian soldiers disappeared from the Islamic armies of North Africa, they remained a regular feature of North African courts. In other words, in both regions, the performative and ornamental function of these soldiers also outlasted the military and practical one.

There is, however, one important distinction between these intertwined histories. Unlike the *jenets*, a large number of Christian troops in North Africa were, in fact, slaves or converts of slave origin. Although earlier studies have tended to emphasize the presence of mercenaries and warlords, men who were attracted by the prospect of making their fortunes or seeking political refuge, these free men were also employed alongside slave soldiers.[141] Indeed, there were large Christian slave populations in North Africa serving in a variety of roles. Eva Lapiedra has argued that Arabic texts were intentionally ambiguous in distinguishing between free and slave soldiers. Chronicles refer to Christian militias sometimes specifically as slaves (*'abīd* or *mamālīk*) and other times more generically as barbarians (*'ulūj*) or simply Christians (*rūm* or *naṣārā*).[142] If one wanted to generalize, then the term "slave" does appear more frequently to describe members of the royal entourage (*biṭāna*, *dā'ira*, *ḥāshiya*, *khāṣṣa*, *'abīd al-dār*, or *sanī'a*).[143] But for Lapiedra, this ambiguity reflected the fact that these distinctions in status were essentially irrelevant to Islamic rulers.[144] From the perspective of the royal court, all foreign Christian soldiers, whether they were free or not, were still thought of as slaves, as royal possessions.[145] This perspective not only resonates strongly with the Sicilian and Aragonese tradition of the *servi camerae regis* but also points us toward an even earlier precedent for the employment of "infidel" soldiers in western Mediterranean courts.

Military Slaves

Although armed slaves can be found in numerous contexts from ancient Greece and Rome to Revolutionary America, the scope and significance of military slavery in the Islamic world is unparalleled.[146] Beginning at least with al-Mahdī (r. 775–785) and more fully under al-Mu'taṣim (r. 833–842), the 'Abbāsid caliphs imported Turkic slaves to serve in their armies, transforming the nature of Islamic military forces for centuries to come.[147] As young boys, these soldiers were trained in both martial and courtly arts. Although they continued to be called slaves (*'abīd*, *ghilmān*, or *mamālīk*), they were usually at least nominally converted to Islam and manumitted.[148] Occasionally, these soldiers became part of the ruling elite, enjoying extraordinary wealth and power. This military servitude, in other words, was different from the "social death" associated with Atlantic slavery, different from domestic slavery or slavery in the service of great state enterprises.[149] Strangers to the Islamic heartlands and cut off from their lineages, these men nevertheless celebrated their servile status as a sign of privilege in the 'Abbāsid context. Their servitude was understood as a form of clientage (*walā'*), of obedience and loyalty to the 'Abbāsid caliphs, whom they protected against internal and external threats.[150] Indeed, these slave soldiers depended upon and reflected the power of the 'Abbāsid caliphs. They were a simultaneously powerful and vulnerable figure.

Although the origins and nature of Islamic military slavery remain under dispute, the strongest influences for this idea of servitude appear to have been the pre-Islamic Turkic and Iranian royal guards.[151] For example, the imperial guardsmen of the Sāsānid shahs were known as the *bandagān*, meaning "bondsmen" or "slaves."[152] The *bandagān* wore a distinctive dress—earrings or belts that symbolized servitude. They received certificates of manumission (*āzād nāma*) as a reward for extraordinary service. But critically, they were not slaves. Instead, as Peter Golden has argued, in this case an ideal of "political dependence was expressed in the vocabulary of slavery."[153] This background to the Islamic tradition of military slavery, in which slavery was symbol more than reality, underscores again the fact that the performative value of military slaves to imperial authority was as central as if not more so than their military function.[154]

The 'Abbāsids not only adapted this tradition of military service but also expanded it dramatically, making it a central feature of Islamic rulership until the nineteenth century. For instance, in Khurasān, a region that now covers eastern Iran as well as parts of Central Asia and Afghanistan, the Samānids (819–999) and their successors, the Ghaznawids (977–1186) and Seljuqs (1037–1194), each employed Turkic military slaves. The Ayyūbids (1171–1250) also relied upon military slaves, who eventually established their own political authority in the form of the Mamlūk Sultanate in Egypt (1250–1517).[155] Finally, the Ottomans maintained this practice into the modern period. As Yaacov Lev has recently contended, scholars have insufficiently examined the use of military slaves in North Africa as an extension of this phenomenon.[156] North African rulers did not rely upon Turkic slaves, who lay at a distance, but rather European and black slaves (*saqāliba* and *'abīd*), who lay closer at hand.[157] The Aghlabids (800–909), Ṭūlūnids (868–905), Ikhshīdids (935–969), and Fāṭimids (909–1171) all employed black African slaves.[158] The Ibāḍī imām Aflaḥ b. 'Abd al-Wahhāb (r. 832–872) had a royal guard composed of Christians.[159]

Thus, when the Umayyads and later the Almoravids and Almohads first employed Frankish and Galician military slaves—whom they also called *'abīd* or *mamālīk*—they were intentionally invoking and drawing comparison with the practices of their contemporaries and rivals to the east. Although it has not been, the history of Christian mercenary soldiers in North Africa in the thirteenth and fourteenth centuries should be also understood as an important extension of this tradition of military slavery.

The 'Abbāsids may have also influenced other emperors around the Mediterranean. For instance, in the ninth century, the Byzantine emperor established the Hetaireia (ἑταιρεία), an imperial bodyguard composed of mainly of Turkic Khazars, which is to say, the very same soldiers who were used in caliphal military retinues.[160] Indeed, contemporary observers saw the 'Abbāsid and Byzantine practices as indistinct.[161] And as discussed above, the Holy Roman emperor Frederick II also maintained a palatine guard of Muslim slave soldiers.

From here, one need only travel a short distance to close the circuit of ideas. The thirteenth-century Aragonese kings not only styled themselves the heirs to the universal claims of the Holy Roman emperors before Christians but also invoked the supreme authority of the Almohad caliphs in North Africa before Muslims. Like each of these emperors and caliphs, they employed foreign soldiers, whom they treated as legal slaves, in their armies and in their courts as their personal protectors. The fact that the *jenets* were not actually slaves or of slave origin mattered little to the Aragonese kings just as it mattered little to Islamic rulers. The Aragonese tradition was not an aberration from the tradition of military slavery but a reflection of its deepest logic. In addition to adding military might, these soldiers brought imperial prestige to rulers. By treating these soldiers as slaves, as their possessions, the Aragonese kings articulated their claims to absolute authority and universal jurisdiction. The *jenets* were just another in a line of military slaves belonging to Mediterranean emperors.

This tradition, which intimately bound emperors and religious others across the Mediterranean, outlasted the Middle Ages. It was not simply a premodern mode of governance. In the nineteenth century, for example, rulers from the Ottoman governor of Baghdad to Napoleon Bonaparte employed mamlūks as elite guardsmen.[162] But the most fascinating and relevant modern case comes from twentieth-century Spain. In addition to casting himself as the new El Cid, a preserver of Spanish Catholicism, General Francisco Franco (1892–1975) also established a Moorish Guard (Guarda Mora) of some 80,000 troops brought from Morocco, who served in his armies and as his personal protectors.[163] These troops fiercely attacked Republican sympathizers, suppressed rebellions, and appeared in parades alongside Franco, riding white horses, dressed in scarlet tunics with white capes, bearing turbans, and carrying lances. From a distance, Franco's employment of these Muslim soldiers was seen as a failure of his Spanishness, his descent into "Moslem fatalism."[164] The service of these soldiers was seen as expression of their "semi-oriental loyalty," of their slavish obedience.[165] Seen from the history of the *jenets*, however, there was nothing surprising about any of this, or about the fact that when he was forced to disband the Moorish Guard, Franco dressed his new Spanish Christian protectors in the same red and white clothes, which is to say that he continued to dress them as Muslims. The fiction of sovereignty persisted.

religious others as protectors

CHAPTER FIVE

The Unpaid Debt

In the summer of 1292, several men arrived at the houses of Muça Almentauri and Maymon Avenborayç, *jenets* in the service of the Crown of Aragon.[1] They had come to settle a stunning debt of 900 *solidi*, money that their wives had borrowed with usurious interest, and an amount that each man might expect to earn as salary in half a year.[2] The angry creditors threatened to seize what they could. A royal document listed some examples in passing: household utensils, wine jugs, oxen, horses, tack, weapons, and plows. The *jenets* were members of the king's household, a fact that helps to account for the appearance of this incident in the chancery registers. But the list—household utensils, wine jugs, oxen, horses, tack, weapons, and plows—also paves another path of inquiry. It suggests a different story from that of privilege and exception, which was the perspective of power. While perhaps only a moment of scribal emphasis, this list of mundane items spiders outward to the mess of living: eating, drinking, and laboring. And the questions multiply: From whom did these Muslims buy wine? Indeed, did Muslims drink wine?[3] Who tilled their fields? Who lent their wives money at exorbitant interest? And so on.

These small but significant questions highlight the limits not only of archival documents but also of an approach that overemphasizes sovereignty and therefore risks confusing a formal description of power with its performance and effects. The lives of the *jenets* were not neatly confined to the purview of the chancery registers or to their relationship with the Crown. So what were the experiences of the *jenets* in the lands of the Crown of Aragon beyond the royal court? How did these experiences shape the lives of the *jenets* in ways the Aragonese kings did not intend? Did these soldiers find a place, a sense of belonging on their own? What challenges did they face? If the gift helped to reveal the sovereign ambitions of the Aragonese kings, then the unpaid debt, the other half of the transaction, opens a door to the lives of the *jenets* in the kingdoms of the Crown of Aragon and the quotidian practices of royal power.

Life Is Elsewhere

The case of Muça Almentauri and Maymon Avenborayç reveals something simple but easily overlooked: the *jenets* did not come into the kingdoms of the Crown of Aragon alone. Indeed, the Crown issued a safe-conduct in 1290 to three *jenets*, Muça Abenbeyet, Açe Parrello, and Yoniç, permitting them to enter Valencia with their "wives and families."[4] At the opposite end of their service, in 1286, five other *jenets* received permission to return home with their wives and children:

> Because Giber, Jahia, Jucef, Hiahiaten, and Dapher, *jenets*, brothers, served us, therefore they may return [home] with their families, wives, and sons, in all forty-seven people. We order you [all officials], immediately, to put no impediment or obstacle in [the way of their] return but rather you should provide them safe passage.[5]

These *jenets*, five brothers, had lived in and departed these Christian lands with forty-seven members of their family. Between their arrival and departure, what did their families do? How did they survive in the kingdoms of the Crown of Aragon while these men served the king?

The Crown did, in fact, extend some of the same privileges and protections that *jenets* received to their wives.[6] Luxurious gifts were rare. Exceptionally, for instance, the wife (referred to simply as "his wife") of Çeyt Abdela received a gift of colored cloth "for clothing" alongside her husband.[7] But by and large, soldiers' families received basic provisions: plain cloth, clothes, and food.[8] Some families were also provided with houses. Muça Hivanface and his wife, Axone, were given several houses in the *morería*, the Muslim quarter, of Valencia, a rather grand gesture but nevertheless one that parallels the equivocality of the *aljuba*, which is to say, if on the one hand, this gift signified privilege, the location of these houses nevertheless marked this *jenet* and his wife as non-Christians.[9] The wives of the Almohad princes, perhaps less generously, received one "suitable" house also in Valencia.[10] Other women appear to have traveled alongside their husbands, who received additional compensation for their expenses.

Mahomet Abolxahe was granted 15 *duplas* to cover the cost of bringing his wife, Horo, and family to him.[11] Although no evidence indicates such a thing, it is not unreasonable to imagine that some women accompanied their husbands to the battlefront.[12] Ibn Khaldūn recorded the presence on the battlefield in North Africa of Berber women, who lifted their veils "to incite the men."[13] Regardless of whether they settled or followed their husbands, the wives of *jenets* received some financial support from the Crown.[14]

To conclude from these privileges and protections, however, that the lives of these women were privileged and protected—that they shared in their husbands' exceptional status—would be to leave the curtain half drawn. The fact that the wives of Muça Almentauri and Maymon Avenboraуç accrued significant debts may indicate that their stipends, of which little detail exists, were minimal.[15] The challenge of making ends meet may have been compounded or perhaps caused by the difficulties some women encountered in obtaining disbursements from royal officials.[16] In the case of Muça and Maymon, their wives sought help by turning to moneylenders, who lent them cash at precipitous interest.[17] Their decision to take usurious loans underscores not only the depth of their crisis but also these women's lack of real social protection.

What became of the wives of Muça and Maymon? Two documents, separated by over five hundred folios in the chancery registers, reveal that Muça and Maymon used their influence with the Crown to defer this debt and deter these creditors.[18] On July 23, the *jenets* managed to appeal directly to King Jaume II in Barcelona. They arranged to have their salaries, two hundred *solidi* each, paid directly to their wives in Valencia.[19] Just over a week later, on August 3, King Jaume wrote to the local justice to offer the *jenets*' wives protection, arrange a six-month extension on the loan, and adjust its interest to a "more appropriate" amount, four *denarii* per *libra*.[20] While these *jenets* of the royal household used their influence with the Aragonese king to solve this problem, it cannot be said that the problem was truly solved for their wives, who lived far from the court. Despite the king's intervention, the unnamed wives of Muça and Maymon still had to face their creditors and the unpaid debt.

The Bestial Floor

Family, however, was not just a matter of what one might call private life for the *jenets* but rather overlapped with the history of their professional service. As in the documents above, passing remarks suggest that these mercenary companies were agnatic groups, extended families.[21] Sons served alongside their fathers, and brothers appeared together to collect their salaries. They were *familia* in all senses of the Latin: army, servants, and family. All this, however, seemed to be of little concern to the Crown's bureaucrats, who preserved almost no detail about the organization or composition of *jenet* companies. Should it have mattered? The *jenets* served, and the Crown paid them all the same.

At least on one occasion, the king's failure to understand the structure of the companies under his command led to tense negotiations for service. To the scholar's benefit, exasperated messengers had to shuttle back and forth between the king and the *jenets*, leaving a paper trail that offers a unique insight. In January 1304, Pere de Montagut, procurator of Murcia, and Ferrer des Cortey, bailiff of Murcia, wrote to Jaume II to acknowledge that they had received two letters of instruction with regards to incorporating the troops of al-ʿAbbās b. Raḥḥū, a prominent Marīnid prince and member of the Ghuzāh.[22] Before enlisting al-ʿAbbās' *jenets*, these two royal officials were meant to take hostages (*rahenes*) from among these soldiers.[23] By taking hostages, Jaume intended to insure against the *jenets*' disloyalty, but from the surviving documentation in the archives, it is unclear whether this was a customary practice with all the *jenets*, as it had been in Mudéjar surrender agreements decades earlier, or a special arrangement.[24] In this case, Jaume had sent these two administrators a list of men to be taken, the sons of four leaders: Alabes Abarraho (al-ʿAbbās b. Raḥḥū), Baratdin Abarraho (Badr al-Dīn b. Mūsā b. Raḥḥū), Greneladim Abarraho (Jamāl al-Dīn b. Mūsā b. Raḥḥū), and Jahia Abenmudahar. It is worth highlighting again that the first three names corresponded to leaders of the Ghuzāh.[25] But the two administrators now responded to Jaume that al-ʿAbbās refused to turn over the four men, his son and the sons of these three other men. Al-ʿAbbās explained that these hostages represented only two of the four family lineages in his company of soldiers, and thus "it would be much more effective if each [family] provides its own hostage, because if he provided them all, the others would be free to leave whenever they want (*valia molt mes que cascun linatge donas lo seu per ço con si ell ab son linatge donas tots les dites rahenes los altres tota ora ques vulgessen sen hieren*)." Thus, the royal officials laid out the lineages of each family for the king, mentioning the tribes to which they belonged, adding, "Believe, my lord, that from what he says, al-ʿAbbās and the others want to serve us and in this [respect], they are worth more than all other armed knights, and know, my lord, that throughout the frontier, your enemies tremble and have great fear of them." Finally, the officials pleaded with the king for a quick response, explaining, "as you already know they make many excuses," hinting at a tense relationship, which will be described in detail in the following chapter. A letter held in the Archive of the Crown of Aragon, written in Arabic some six months later, likely by al-ʿAbbās himself, confirms that these adjustments were ultimately made and the four hostages were handed over.[26]

Montagut and Ferrer's letter to Jaume casts light on not only the process by which the *jenets* were integrated into the Crown's service but also the dynamics of these companies themselves. Although the distant view of the chancery registers makes it rather easy to forget, the *jenets* were not homogeneous units but rather alliances of members of various tribes, a fact that opens up the possibility of competing loyalties within and between companies.[27] However obvious this point seems, it only further underscores the significance of the king's failure to recognize it. Put simply, in this case, Jaume presumed that authority resided solely in the figure of the captain, al-ʿAbbās b. Raḥḥū, who in turn had the absolute fidelity of his troops. By contrast, Montagut and Ferrer's negotiations reveal that the structure of these companies served to distribute authority and responsibility horizontally across the group. This misunderstanding highlights again that the convergence of the *jenets* and the Aragonese kings was not a seamless union, a moment of immediate and mutual recognition but rather one of competing, overlapping, and often incommensurate claims, values, and jurisdictions.

The Aragonese kings' decision to recruit *jenets* grew out of a Mediterranean tradition that saw ethnic and religious others as slaves of emperors. But does this mean that the real lives of the *jenets* were of no concern to the Aragonese kings? This bleak vision of Aragonese sovereignty does not reflect the reality of the kings' treatment the *jenets*. After all, the Aragonese kings listened and responded to the demands of the *jenets*. What is more, several particular incidents evidenced by the chancery registers suggest a deeper bond. For example, when several *jenets* along with their wives and children were captured by Castile in 1292, the Crown moved to secure the return of all of them rather than just the soldiers.[28] In another instance, when two *jenets* retired, which is to say, when their martial utility came to an end, the Crown continued to extend their privileges.[29] A *jenet* named Daut was given sufficient funds to live out his life in Valencia.[30] And at the end of his career and "because of his many acts of service (*propter plurima servicia*)," Muça Almentauri received lands in Murcia, which, intriguingly, had been confiscated by the Crown from someone else.[31] Were these selfless acts on the part of the Aragonese kings? Or were they merely efforts to play the part of the good employer, to ensure the *jenets*' loyalty? To put the matter in different terms, did the king care for his *jenets*? Can one detect an intimacy between the Christian kings and their Muslim soldiers based on a shared sense of humanity?

Perhaps a final example will suffice to lay bare the problem of appealing to an essential and universal humanity as the basis for understanding the relationship between the Crown and its Muslim mercenaries. In 1289, King Alfons II intervened on behalf of the wife of Abdalla Abençiça, a *jenet* in his service. Alfons explained his actions in a promissory note directed to Arnaldus de Bastida, his royal treasurer:

> Since Ali Amari bought at our command in Jaca the horse of Abdalla Abençiça, a certain *jenet* of ours, who died in Jaca, for the price of 55 *duplas* that we ordered him to give, we order you, immediately, to pay Ali [back] for the said *duplas*, which he gave to the wife of Abdalla.[32]

While still on the field of battle at Jaca, King Alfons had ordered a Muslim named Ali Amari to pay a fixed price for the horse of a *jenet*, Abdalla Abençiça, who had just died in battle, and give that money immediately to Abdalla's widow. Was this command an act of compassion? Perhaps, in this moment, one can glimpse a connection between the Christian kings and their Muslim soldiers beyond religion or politics. If not grounded in a shared military ethos or even a shared understanding of family, then perhaps one can speak here of a genuine sense of human community grounded on a small outcrop of suffering. Then again, perhaps, it was nothing of the sort, merely an order to get on with the battle and put the horse back to use. For the historian holding this faded and age-worn document, it can only remain an open question.[33]

Lawless

The *jenets* were principally raiders and bandits both before and after they entered the service of the Crown. The Aragonese kings let these soldiers loose along the frontiers of their lands and turned them against their Christian enemies: the French, the Navarrese, the Castilians, and even their own rebellious noblemen. Raiding, occasionally alongside Christian soldiers,

FIGURE 5. Alfonso X, *Cantigas de Santa Maria* (no. 165) (ca. 1284) (detail, top-left panel). Muslim raiders with Christian captives, Syria. Monasterio-Biblioteca-Colección, San Lorenzo de El Escorial, Madrid. Photograph: Album / Art Resource, New York.

the *jenets* terrorized local populations, laying waste to their villages, and ransacking houses for everything of worth: goods, weapons, animals, and captives (fig. 5). But unlike Christian soldiers, many, if not all, *jenets* had the privilege of retaining their spoils without paying a customary fifth (*quinta*) to the Aragonese kings, a fact that highlighted the unique relationship between the Aragonese kings and the *jenets*.[34] Paradoxically, the law permitted the *jenets* to remain lawless, to remain bandits. But just like the unpaid debt with which this chapter began, these spoils—household goods, weapons, animals, and captives—point to the material limits of this privilege of exception. Selling these goods meant finding markets and depending upon local Christians and royal officials. How did these kinds of men react to the arrival of the uniquely privileged *jenets*? And how did the *jenets*, in turn, deal with them?

An episode from the career of Mahomet Abenadalil provides a dramatic example of what the privilege of raiding meant in practice. Abenadalil, the subject of a detailed study by Brian Catlos, entered the service of King Alfons II in February 1290, following the mission of the Jewish ambassador Abrahim Abennamies to Granada. The Crown awarded Abenadalil the highest honors and privileges. On August 10, 1290, Alfons made the *jenet* his vassal and commander of all *jenets* in his service. In addition, Abenadalil received a salary of almost twenty-four *solidi* per diem (six times the rate of other *jenets*) as well as the right to the king's fifth share of spoils from raids.[35] And in turn, the Aragonese king put his vassal to work. Alfons first sent Abenadalil and his troops to the French and Navarrese borders.[36] Abenadalil spent the following months fighting along the Castilian border in various locations.[37] Finally, in December 1290, after only ten months in the Aragonese king's service, and back in the good graces of the Naṣrid sultan, Abenadalil and his troops returned home to Granada.[38]

In Abenadalil's surprisingly brief career, the events that took place in villages in the region of Calatayud, along the Castilian border, demand deeper investigation (map 1). Although Abenadalil and his *jenets* held the right to maintain the king's fifth of spoils, their desire to convert any spoils into profits presented them with significant challenges. In November 1290, King Alfons wrote to Petrus Sancii, the justice of Calatayud. He explained that after a raid into Soria, just across the Castilian border, Abenadalil and his soldiers had brought back certain goods (*prede*), worth 2,200 *solidi*, that the Christian inhabitants of Calatayud accepted and agreed to pay for on an appointed day.[39] Apparently, as later correspondence revealed, these "goods" also included Castilian captives, for whom the locals had acted as guarantors.[40] In any event, despite their initial promise, the villagers now refused to pay the *jenets*. King Alfons therefore ordered Petrus either to compel the villagers to pay the *jenets* or to confiscate their property and levy a fine of 2,200 *solidi*. A month later, however, the matter had grown worse. Several men from nearby Calatayud attacked Abenadalil's *jenets*, making off with "horses, shields, and other things (*roncincos, adargas, et alias res*)."[41] On December 13, frustrated with Petrus' lack of response, Alfons addressed a letter to Calatayud's council, indicating that none of the money or the fine against the villagers had been paid and asking them to determine whether the local justice, Petrus, was acting "maliciously (*maliciose*)."[42] The king simultaneously wrote to the justice of Aragon, Petrus' superior, and the justice of Valencia, asking them to take an interest in the matter.[43] Finally, in the archival equivalent of raising his voice, the king also issued a circular to *all* royal officials in the kingdom of Aragon, reiterating the right of the *jenets* to raid from his lands and sell any captives or goods that they brought back from enemy territory, suggesting that he thought that the attacks were related to this privilege.[44] Although nothing is known of what ultimately came of the captives, goods, or debt, the tension between the king, royal administrators, *jenets*, and the villagers of Calatayud is what concerns us.

What motivated the villagers' attack on the *jenets*? Canon law, which is to say, the law of the Catholic Church, banned Muslims from buying or selling Christian captives. Thus, one could argue that in trying to sell their goods to villagers, the *jenets* were crossing a well-established legal boundary.[45] This transgression, moreover, may have been felt less abstractly and more viscerally by Christian frontiersmen, who were themselves regularly victims—in person and property—of Ghuzāh raids from Granada. In addition, Soria was a short distance from Calatayud, meaning robbers and captives may have known one another and may have felt some sense of community on account of their shared suffering at the hands of the Muslim Ghuzāh. Should one say, then, that this transgression of religious law motivated these assaults? In his reading of the Calatayud episode, Catlos suggested that this motivation is "a convenient rationalization."[46] After all, Christian soldiers from Castile also raided these regions, taking their own captives and ransacking homes. What is more, Christian soldiers ran into similar problems in selling goods from raids. At the same time that Abenadalil complained of trouble, a Christian almogàver, Vincent de Sayona, informed the Crown that a villager from Calatayud, Johannes Petri, still owed him 50 *solidi* for a captive.[47]

For his part, Catlos attributed the attack on Abenadalil's troops not to the privilege of raiding, as King Alfons had, or to religion but to the *jenets*' own vulnerability as foreigners. In 1286, for instance, the king ordered Muçe de Portella, the Jewish bailiff of Aragon, to compensate a *jenet* named Abduahet for goods that were stolen from him by a Christian.[48] Similarly, in 1290, the king ordered the arrest of Mosse Maymono, a Jew from Valencia, who had stolen (*surripuit*) promissory notes from some *jenets*.[49] Catlos saw these incidents as evidence that the *jenets* were easy prey for petty criminals. Thus, the events at Calatayud, like frontier war in general, better reflected greed rather than grievance. They were the actions of men accustomed to "the misery and opportunity" of the frontier, something like what Hobbes saw as "the war of all against all."[50] And while the villagers' decision to free the Castilian captives displayed a "spirit of confessional cohesion," Catlos suggested that this, too, should ultimately be accounted for by self-interest rather than religious belief.[51]

If these Christian villagers, rescuers and captives, were on opposite sides of a political border, freeing each other's captives of war served their local and financial interests in the long run.

Catlos' reading of this episode offers an opportunity to consider his broader attempt to rethink the dynamics of religious interaction in medieval Iberia.[52] Rather than a monolithic clash between religions, as historians of an earlier generation imagined, or a subtler process of acculturization, as more recent scholarship has envisioned, Catlos has contended that interaction between Christians, Jews, and Muslims followed a different logic. To his mind, religious abstractions like crusade and jihād were not determinants but rather later justifications for and explanations of events.[53] Similarly, "confessional," "sectarian," or "ethno-religious identities" did not determine but were rather the consequences of interaction.[54] In other words, religion, whether understood as ideology or identity, was an afterthought to practices on the ground. Catlos has suggested instead that interactions between Muslims, Jews, and Christians followed a social calculus, an equation of competing individual and communal interests. In a witty play on and criticism of *convivencia*, religious tolerance, Catlos calls this the principle of *conveniencia*, convenience.

Catlos is certainly right that an overemphasis on religion or identity risks dissolving agency and contingency, but he risks running too far in the opposite direction, sacrificing agency and contingency to another all-consuming principle: convenience. Again, my point is not to say that self-interest played no role in such interaction but to ask why this kind of reading presumes that religion is divorced from rational thoughts and practical motivations, to ask why religion can only be a dependent variable.[55] Ultimately, the principle of convenience dismisses religion on precisely the same terms as liberal positivists and cultural theorists. It casts religion as either ideology or identity, as either political manipulation or reflexive adherence to community. If one starts with these familiar explanations of religion, then beliefs can never play a role in explaining events like those at Calatayud.

What is more, in the case of Abenadalil, convenience and rational self-interest fall short of fully explaining the villagers' actions. While, as foreigners, the *jenets* may have appeared to be easy marks for rogues and grifters, the Calatayud villagers took enormous risks in attacking them. The *jenets* were not only well armed but also protected by the Crown. And, by targeting the *jenets*, these Calatayud villagers immediately incurred the wrath of the Aragonese king. Initially, they faced extraordinary fines, 2,200 *solidi*. Eventually, King Alfons ordered both the villagers' arrest and the seizure of their property throughout *all* the kingdoms of the Crown of Aragon.[56] One can safely say then that the frontiersmen were not acting in their own best interest. So why would they take such individual risks and openly challenge the king?

The Calatayud villagers' actions are better approached from the history of their previous encounters with these soldiers. Significantly, the earliest recorded appearance of Muslim *jenets* in the region dates to 1287, during the rebellion of the Aragonese *Unions* against the Crown. King Alfons employed the *jenets* to pacify the kingdom; thus, the residents of Calatayud would have known the *jenets* not only as foreign raiders but also as agents of royal repression.[57] This ironic disjunction can only have resulted in confusion and tension. On October 14, 1287, for example, the justice of Calatayud—perhaps the same Petrus Sancii above—was reprimanded for seizing and ordered to return several Christian captives that *jenets* had brought back from a raid on the Aragonese village of Cutanda, near Teruel.[58] Royal administrators, in other words, and not simply villagers found themselves in conflict with the *jenets*. Significantly, these officials' caution and suspicion was not unjustified. Just over a week later, *jenets* operating from the villages of Alfamén and Almonacid were accused of raiding a Christian village, Aguaro, which was under the protection of the Crown of Aragon.[59] In this case, the Crown ordered the *jenets* to return any goods or captives that they had seized, but otherwise, the soldiers went unpunished. Whether resulting from the complex and ambiguous political situation or the *jenets*' obvious impunity, a climate of accusation and recrimination had reigned on the Aragonese frontier. Tensions remained high after the rebellion of the *Unions*. In October 1289, several villagers from Alfamén—the same village that hosted the Muslim raiders above—decided to take some *jenets* captive, marking a new boldness and daring in these villagers' dealings with royal agents. King Alfons ordered the justice of Calatayud—in all likelihood, now Petrus Sancii—to free the *jenets* and to safeguard their journey out of the region.[60] The fact that Alfons withdrew his *jenets* and insisted on their protection suggests that the Crown not only saw the villagers as dangerous and unpredictable but also the entire situation as untenable.

This pattern of conflict across various locations reveals two critical things about the encounter between Abenadalil's *jenets* and the Calatayud villagers in 1290. First, these frontiersmen had challenged and attacked the *jenets* before and had been rebuked by the king, suggesting that they cannot have been innocent of the consequences of their assaults. These were not spontaneous acts of greed. Second, the justice of Calatayud was deeply involved in this resistance. He did not simply represent royal authority. He not only treated the *jenets* with some suspicion but also, given the raids on Aguaro, had good reason to do so. In this light, the fact that Petrus Sancii dragged his feet in implementing the Crown's justice for Abenadalil in 1290 looks less like bureaucratic inefficiency and more like defiance of royal authority, a vestige of the anger that drove the *Unions*.[61] One could therefore argue that the villagers who attacked Abenadalil's *jenets* were not acting selfishly or blindly but rather with the knowledge that royal officials—if only tacitly—would support their actions.[62] This kind of local and strategic solidarity in Calatayud suggests a more complex approach to the question of motive than self-interest. While these attacks appeared illegal in the eyes of the king, there is no reason to assume that the people of Calatayud saw them the same way. The tensions at Calatayud reflected competing ideas of law and legitimacy. Such competition rendered visible the obvious limits of the Crown of Aragon's claim to absolute jurisdiction and sovereignty. More to the point, it undermined the value of the exceptional privilege of the *jenets*.

Although tensions in Calatayud appeared to be particularly high because they were particularly well recorded, it is worth mentioning that this was not the only region where the presence of *jenets* led to tension and conflict. In March 1290, for instance, royal officials from Játiva took captive several *jenets* serving in Villena, near Alicante. The king "angrily (*irato*)" rebuked them, his words indicating that he saw their actions as malicious and defiant.[63] In November 1290, immediately before they arrived in Calatayud, Abenadalil's also troops ran into problems on the Navarrese front. The troops of the Aragonese nobleman Lope Ferrench de Luna, who participated with the *jenets* in raids, despoiled Abenadalil's soldiers after they returned from battle.[64] The attack reveals that military cooperation between the *jenets* and Christian soldiers did not necessarily imply acceptance or equivalence. In brief, these conflicts demonstrate that Christian villagers, local administrators, and soldiers, all took issue with the *jenets* and their privilege. The incidents in Calatayud in 1290 were neither isolated nor passing.

In this context, one can ask again, why were the *jenets* attacked? To ask whether these attacks were religiously or politically motivated only begs the question. Religion was neither a thin mask for selfish desires, an ideology, nor a reflexive sense of communal belonging or identity. Rather than suggesting that the villagers were cold and calculating manipulators or blind to the reasons for their actions, the foregoing documents reveal many overlapping motivations: opportunism, revenge, criticism of royal power, and religious animus. The nature of these conflicts could have been simultaneously private, local, and public to varying degrees. One has no reason or means to discount any of these readings. Religion is not separable from other processes or from material circumstances. While complex matters resist systematization, the violence was also not arbitrary or chaotic. Just as King Alfons made clear in his circular to all royal official in Aragon, the *jenets'* raiding—or more particularly, their taking and ransoming Christian captives—was the occasion and catalyst for the pattern of events above.[65] In other words, it was the blatant transgression of a legal boundary—understood rationally and felt viscerally—that shaped and channeled the multiple motivations of the attackers, made them take excessive and bold risks, giving them a sense of legitimacy. By extension, moreover, beliefs and practices gained greater meaning and power through these local acts, through their iteration. A moment of boundary crossing became a moment of boundary making. For the case at hand, this understanding allows us to speak of the complex motivations for violence without reducing actors to ciphers and history to a painted backdrop.

Killed but Not Murdered

The vulnerability of the *jenets* derived not from their physical weakness but rather from the weakness of their claim to privileged exception. These attacks on the *jenets* also highlighted the impotence of the Aragonese kings, their inability to either enforce or realize their claims to absolute jurisdiction and sovereign authority. The story of Abenadalil and his troops in Calatayud holds a final chapter that suggests that the Aragonese kings both were well aware of these challenges to their authority and navigated them with canny ability. The practice of royal power differed sharply from its towering rhetoric.

This story begins with a murder. A month after the controversial raids into Soria and during the furious exchange of letters between King Alfons II and the various justices of Aragon, two curious attacks were recorded in the chancery registers. First, a group of Christian almogàvers—Paschasius Valentini, Matheus de Galera, Juanyes Bono, Raimundus Petri, Galmus Petri, and others—attacked and killed a man named Puçola, the "Big Flea," who had raided alongside Abenadalil's troops into Navarre.[66] The local justice—Petrus Sancii—convicted Puçola's murderers and seized their property.[67] In the second attack, just a few days later, the same almogàvers turned their sights on three of Abenadalil's *jenets*—Masset, Assager, and Alabes—attacking them and making off with their horses.[68] Did anything link these two moments of violence?

If not for a letter, another complaint from King Alfons to Petrus Sancii, the fact that the same men perpetrated these attacks would only be a coincidence. Alfons explained that at the time of his death, Puçola owed a debt to Abenadalil. Puçola and his troops had agreed to pay Abenadalil in return for the privilege of raiding alongside his *jenets*. On the eve of the second attack on the *jenets*, Alfons had ordered Petrus Sancii to use Puçola's goods to pay that debt "so that [Abenadalil] should not have to complain of defective justice."[69] In other words, the goods seized by Petrus Sancii from the almogàvers had made their way into the possession of Abenadalil's *jenets*, providing a material link between the two episodes.

The Crown's response to this outburst of violence is telling. While it appears that King Alfons supported the *jenets*, his privileged agents, against the almogàvers, he, in fact, played both sides. Indeed, after the initial attack on Puçola, Alfons wrote to the Petrus Sancii, insisting that the Christian almogàvers—however guilty—should have their goods returned and moreover, be sent back into service in Valencia, which is to say, to fight the Marīnid Ghuzāh, their traditional Muslim enemies, who were actively raiding the frontier at this moment.[70] One could argue that Alfons' decision to exculpate the almogàvers precipitated the second act, not only in giving them a sense of immunity but also legitimacy in attacking the *jenets*. Demonstrating that his response was not unique, Alfons responded to the second attack even more equivocally than the first. Caught between his *jenets* and almogàvers, he ordered Petrus Sancii to return the *jenets*' horses but not to arrest the almogàvers.[71]

Perhaps then to call Puçola's death a murder obscures more than it reveals. The Aragonese king let his almogàvers attack Abenadalil's associate with impunity, which, to put it differently, is to say that Puçola was killed but not exactly murdered. The king, who embodied the law, was indifferent to the matter. Similarly, these Christian raiders received a slap on the wrist for attacking the *jenets*, making Alfons' complaint against Petrus Sancii for "defective justice" appear absurd. Did Alfons, one must then ask, similarly abandon justice in the case of the Calatayud villagers once Abenadalil's troops had moved on? Better yet, did these frontiersmen know that the king's threats were only that, rhetoric and nothing more?

To say then that the *jenets* were above the law, exceptions to the law, means little in practice to the unfolding of the events above. Circumstance and practice brought the *jenets* into contact with royal officials, Christian soldiers, and Christian villagers, each of whom understood law and legitimacy in their own terms. In other words, this contested territory was a zone of overlapping and competing jurisdictions. But as the case above demonstrates, the Aragonese kings were able to turn these complications to their advantage. If, in the abstract, sovereignty is defined by coercion and decision, then in practice, Aragonese royal power succeeded through deflection and indecision. If the Crown permitted the Muslim *jenets* to stand outside the law, to be lawless, then it only partially enforced that privilege. It tacitly legitimated violent attacks against its disposable agents, the *jenets*. The overall effect of privileged exception and royal indecision were the same: the Aragonese kings profited from the violence of these soldiers while simultaneously disavowing them, marking them as outsiders and non-Christians.

Blood and Belonging

In November 1290, in the midst of Abenadalil's struggles in Calatayud, King Alfons wrote the following letter to the Mudéjar *çalmedine* (*ṣāḥib al-madīna*), a community leader, of nearby Zaragoza:

> We know that a certain Saracen named Mahumet Sugeray, a soldier of our esteemed nobleman, Abenadalil, captain of the *jenets*, very much loves (*diligit multum*) a certain Saracen woman of Zaragoza, named Fatima, daughter of Abdullasis, whom he wants to lead into marriage. Therefore, we tell and order you immediately to arrange that this Saracen man should have that Saracen woman in marriage.[72]

Set against the violent and exclusionary acts above, this document offers a way to imagine how and why the *jenets* remained and lived in the kingdoms of the Crown of Aragon. If marriage suggests affiliation, then perhaps one can argue that interactions between the Crown of Aragon's Mudéjares and the *jenets* fostered a sense of brotherhood and community. What was the nature of this community? Was religion a sufficient condition for inclusion? How did the unique relationship that each of these groups had with the Crown shape and affect their bond? And finally, how did the Crown react to their association?

On closer inspection, this document—recording the marriage of a *jenet* to a Mudéjar woman—opens itself to many possible readings. One could read it as congratulatory, as a pure formality, which would suggest that the king was merely adding honor to the occasion. Thus, one could argue that the letter speaks of the Crown's approval of interaction between the *jenets* and the Mudéjares. Sensitive to the dialogic quality of texts, one could read this document as a response. Did the Mudéjar *çalmedine*, who was technically in the king's employ, first seek approval for the marriage, knowing that the king took a keen interest in the affairs of his Muslim subjects, his possessions, with these foreigners, who were servants and agents of his authority? In this scenario, the Mudéjares might have been taking tentative steps in their relationship with the *jenets*. Perhaps again, one could take a less subtle view of the king and see this document as a monologue, as the "order (*mandatum*)" that it claims to be and nothing more. This perspective might suggest that the king, an aspiring sovereign, was pressing his will on the Mudéjares, staving off any stated or potential objections to the marriage. Did Abdullasis or the local Muslim leader disapprove? This is all to say, given the fact of the relationship of the *jenets* to the Mudéjares, one must still ask whether theirs was a happy or unhappy marriage.

Arriving by land or sea, *jenets* entering the service of the Crown of Aragon found a world simultaneously familiar and strange. Like the five *jenets* with whom this book began, most entered through the kingdom of Valencia. Crossing over the rough and arid hills that surrounded this territory, they would have caught sight of an expansive green plain, covered with an arterial network of canals, all framed by the blue Mediterranean. Pope Gregory IX (d. 1241) once remarked upon this land's wealth and beauty.[73] But one might say that it was Valencia's delicate nature, environmental and political, that lent its inhabitants an unusual mixture of ironic detachment and nostalgia. The Muslim poet Ibn Ḥarīq, Gregory's contemporary, composed these lines on the eve of the kingdom's fall to the Aragonese:

> "Valencia is the dwelling of all beauty."
> This they say both in the East and the West.
> If someone protests that prices there are high
> And that the rain of battle falls upon it
> Say: "It is a paradise surrounded by
> Two misfortunes: famine and war!"[74]

After the conquest of Valencia, the remaining Muslims, now Mudéjares, maintained considerable military strength—castles and soldiers—that they alternately employed against and in aid of the Crown of Aragon.[75] These Mudéjar strongholds also received support from the North African arrivistes and holy warriors, the Ghuzāh, whom the Aragonese called *jenets*. Nevertheless, the overall tendency in Valencia was toward disunion. Muslim resistance to the Aragonese peaked during the second revolt of al-Azraq, from 1275 to 1277, when Pere finally wrested control of the last independent Muslim castles and pushed the *jenets* from his territory.

This brief recapitulation of Islamic Valencia's history was meant to say two prefatory things about the relationship of the *jenets* to the Mudéjares. First, these soldiers had surrendered Valencia less than a decade before Pere's efforts to recruit them in 1285.[76] Their arrival, in other words, was more properly a return. Second, at the time the *jenets* abandoned Valencia, they were still newcomers. Thus, while they were not outsiders, they were also not insiders—not interchangeable with the Mudéjares. Their return was not a homecoming, and their journey cannot be considered simply in terms of an encounter between Islam and Christianity.

Despite the loss of Muslim control, the Valencia to which the *jenets* returned would have appeared mostly unchanged. Muslims still dominated the landscape, above all, the agrarian landscape, and possessed a degree of autonomy.[77] Indeed, throughout the lands of the Crown of Aragon, the Mudéjares maintained their own mosques,[78] merchant hostels,[79] community leaders,[80] law,[81] and language.[82] The *adhān*, the call to prayer, could still be heard, marking not only a familiar time but also space.[83] In these respects, as Burns has argued, the Mudéjares represented a "species of state within a state."[84] Muslim life was enfolded within a Christian kingdom—simultaneously included and excluded.

Earlier, it was demonstrated that the Mudéjares played a role in recruiting the *jenets*. They not only participated in negotiations but also helped to pay for the *jenets* who served in the defense of Valencia.[85] But these groups were not simply connected through the questions of military service. Some *jenets* sought to live alongside the Mudéjares. For example, although operating in the Christian-dominated kingdom of Aragon, the *jenets* raiding from Alfamén and Almonacid in 1287 were in fact residing with local Mudéjares, not Christians.[86] In addition to their taking up temporary residence, there is also evidence that *jenets* and their families settled permanently among Mudéjar communities. Muçe Hivanface, a *jenet*, and his wife Axone owned several houses in the *morería* of Valencia.[87] When he retired from the king's service, a *jenet* named Daut settled in the city of Valencia.[88] And after more than a decade of service, Muça Almentauri, the indebted *jenet* with whom this chapter began, settled in Murcia.[89] A great deal recommended these places. Among the Mudéjares, the *jenets* would have found speakers of Arabic, Islamic institutions, and people who adhered to the same or familiar customs, rituals, and practices. One might imagine that all this promoted a sense of belonging for the *jenets* and the potential for the uncomplicated marriage of these communities.

Islamic belief and practice, however, were not uniform. Indeed, it is worth recalling that the opinions of jurists varied widely on the status and requirements of Muslims living in non-Muslim territories. Mālikī jurists, jurists from the school of law that dominated Spain and North Africa, however, took a relatively consistent position on the matter.[90] Most considered emigration (*hijra*) from conquered territories obligatory (*farīḍa*) upon all Muslims who were physically and economically capable. In failing to do so, Mudéjares had also failed in their religious duties.

Is it possible that the *jenets*, relative newcomers from North Africa, shared the Mālikī's contempt for the Mudéjares and their leaders? From this perspective, one might read as significant the fact that the *jenet* Daut, who retired to Valencia, chose to reside in the city—that is, the Christian city—rather than in the nearby *morería*. Although the *morería* was by no means a ghetto—which is to say that there was no rigid line between dwellings of Muslims and those of Christians—the privilege of living within the city walls of Valencia specifically was unusual for a Muslim, shared only by the occasional visiting Muslim dignitary.[91] By living near but nevertheless apart from the Mudéjares, was Daut asserting his superiority? In a similar vein, in December 1286, Çehit, a *jenet*—perhaps the same notorious Ghuzāh captain of the *Miraculos romanzados* (there called "Çahit")—was accused of attacking a Mudéjar judicial official (*alaminus*) and his son.[92] Although the cause of the conflict is unknown, the incident required the intervention of a royal bailiff, who stepped in to free the *jenet* and absolve him of any charges, circumventing Mudéjar leaders and perforating the illusion of communal autonomy. This kind of privilege was not occasional but rather continual and manifest: the *jenets* were exempted from the sumptuary laws that bound all but a few of the most privileged Mudéjares; they could ride horses and wear rich and colorful garments without fear of the law.[93] The Crown, in other words, was an unavoidable presence in the relationship of the Mudéjares and the *jenets*, a third party to their marriage. And these privileges could only have driven a wedge between these Muslims.

Two seemingly contradictory examples from the Crown's chancery registers will suffice to lay bare the problem of defining this community.

Despite Jaume's conquest of Mallorca in 1229, the smaller (as the name indicates) neighboring island of Minorca remained under Muslim control until 1287.[94] After its conquest in that year by King Alfons II, those Muslims who could not buy their freedom made their way into the slave markets of Barcelona and Mallorca. And it is precisely in this unexpected and uninviting context—at the Muslim slave market—that several *jenets* appear, performing the rather curious act of buying slaves.[95] Were they freeing their coreligionists? The fact that these soldiers exclusively chose "black Saracens" from among the captives from Mallorca troubles this suggestion, opening up the possibility that religious affiliation mattered less than other prejudices, needs, or calculations.[96]

Nevertheless, a poorly preserved chancery document at the mangled edge of a folio presents a different view of the *jenets*' relationship with Muslim captives of war. In 1285, six Muslim prisoners—five men and a woman—fled from their Christian owners in Barcelona. Local officials were immediately informed of the escape but also warned, "Take sufficient care of Albohaya, Cassim, and Sahat, *jenets*, who by action or insinuation are said to have caused said Saracens to have fled."[97] These may once again have been the notorious *jenets* from the *Miraculos romanzados*. Nevertheless, the document paints a striking portrait, the image of *jenets* encountering and conspiring with Muslim captives in the city of Barcelona. Whereas before, the *jenets* seemed to be profiting from the capture of Minorca without care for religious affiliation, here they seem to have taken a personal risk—by deed or word—to help these six Muslim captives. Or was this the insinuation of the king's royal administrator alone? The opposing events make only one thing clear: while shared beliefs and practices may have connected the *jenets* to the Mudéjares, they did not determine their relationship alone. Religion cannot be understood simply as community.

Conspiracy

In the prison break above, one also detects a whisper of fear in the king's letter. Regardless of the *jenets*' involvement, the king saw sufficient reason to suspect them: in what might be coincidence, he chose instead to see conspiracy. This attitude was not isolated. The Crown of Aragon saw all the Muslims living in its kingdoms as potential insurgents or worse, a fifth column for an invasion from Granada, a lesson it learned from the revolt of al-Azraq. All the same, throughout the period of sovereign crisis, the Aragonese kings continued to recruit *jenets* and allow their interaction with the Mudéjares. Why did the Mudéjares and the *jenets*, who had surrendered Valencia to the Crown in recent memory, not unite to seize the kingdom back? Why did a new al-Azraq not present himself in these moments? And why were the Aragonese kings so confident in their use of these foreign Muslim soldiers?

At the end of 1286, while his *jenets* were dispatched to Aragon to fight the *Unions*, King Alfons began to mobilize a mass of forces to send to the Valencian frontier. Among others, he called upon Templars, Hospitallers, the Knights of Calatrava, and almogàvers in order to prepare for a rumored attack of "*jenets* from Granada," which is to say, of Ghuzāh.[98] By the following April, the calls became more urgent as Granadan attacks began, threatening to overrun Valencia.[99] Bishoprics were called upon to lend horses, and royal revenue from the kingdom was redirected to pay the salaries of troops on the frontier.[100] The battle, which the Crown came to call the Guerra Jenetorum, the War of the *Jenets*, lasted only a few months.[101]

Given the fact that two decades earlier the *jenets* had been so integral to al-Azraq's uprising against the Crown of Aragon, one might have expected the Valencian Mudéjares to embrace the Guerra Jenetorum as a new opportunity for rebellion.[102] In this case, however, the threat seemed more contained, and the Mudéjar response, muted and uncertain. In April 1287, for example, the Mudéjares of Alhavir received permission to withdraw from service in the king's army, citing their fear of both "the Moors entering Valencia" and the almogàvers.[103] On the one hand, the Crown may have thought better of testing the Mudéjares' allegiance. On the other hand, caught between warring armies, the Mudéjares may have recognized that they were in a vulnerable position and earnestly sought to stay out of the battle. Indeed, even the rumor of a *jenet* attack was fuel enough for local Christians, some "young men," to attack the Valencian Muslim communities.[104] In other words, the constant threat of *jenet* raids from Granada may have ironically promoted Mudéjar quietism and passivity. Some Muslims, to be sure, did choose to throw in their lot with the *jenets*, and in the wake of the war's failure, they retreated into Granada alongside these soldiers. Despite this treason, the Crown of Aragon welcomed some of them back after the war's cessation.[105] Others chose to remain loyal to the Crown throughout: in his accounts for the war, for example, King Alfons recorded a payment to a "Saracen spy."[106] Thus, during the last two decades of the thirteenth century, the threat of another Mudéjar rebellion with the support of *jenets* remained no more than a rumor. In November 1294, for instance, several Granadan *jenets* were arrested carrying letters from the Naṣrid ruler urging the Mudéjares to revolt.[107] Nothing, however, came of the proposal; Granada soon entered into another alliance with the Crown.[108] Thus, a combination of canny royal policy, political circumstance, and conservative local dynamics stood in the way of uniting the *jenets* and Mudéjares and forged another surprising sort of exclusion.

Conclusion

The Aragonese kings alone did not define the *jenets*. If they granted these soldiers a privileged exception from the laws that bound the citizens and subjects of their kingdoms, then they could never in practice command those citizens and subjects to accept that privilege. The lives of the *jenets* in the lands of the Crown of Aragon were replete with challenges and opportunities beyond royal control. Nevertheless, the kings of the Crown of Aragon relied upon these soldiers with confidence to defend their authority against their external and internal enemies. This is nowhere clearer than in the fact that the Crown of Aragon maintained a defensive front against the Marīnid Ghuzāh during the Guerra Jenetorum while simultaneously employing *jenets* to suppress a rebellion of its own subjects. This confidence reflected a royal flexibility in practice, an ability to play and placate all sides at once. But if these kings used the *jenets* without hesitation, then it is also true that they did not test these soldiers' loyalty. By keeping the *jenets* on the Castilian and French fronts or by deploying them in battles against their own Christian subjects, during the rebellion of the *Unions*, the Aragonese kings were not only defending their claims to sovereign authority but also respecting the terms of treaties that brought these soldiers into the lands of the Crown of Aragon. Precisely because and as long as France and Castile continued to threaten the Crown of Aragon, this circumscribed use of the *jenets* suited the Aragonese kings, and they felt no need to complicate it. What would happen if this balance shifted?

CHAPTER SIX

The Worst Men in the World

For a period of seven months, from December 1303 to July 1304, the Marīnid prince and Ghuzāh leader al-'Abbās b. Raḥḥū served as commander of the Aragonese *jenets*, leaving in his wake a lengthy trail of Latin, Romance, and Arabic evidence in both archives and chronicles. Not only the paper chase that he initiated but also the moment that he chose to cross make al-'Abbās the ideal case for understanding the motivations of the Aragonese *jenets* and their relationship to the Marīnid Ghuzāh. In March 1304, just after al-'Abbās' entry into its service, the Crown of Aragon entered into negotiations with Castile that would lead to the signing of the Treaty of Agreda. For the first time in two decades, since the emergency that first led King Pere II to recruit *jenets* in 1285, the Crown of Aragon and Castile entered into an alliance and called for a crusade against Muslim Granada.[1] Although in earlier periods, as during the War of the *Jenets* (Guerra Jenetorum), *jenets* served the Aragonese kings while Ghuzāh raided Aragonese lands, where would the loyalties of the *jenets* fall in this moment?[2]

Born in Rebellion

In the century of collaboration between the kings of the Crown of Aragon and the Muslim *jenets*, it is the fact that these soldiers were recruited from and commanded by members of the Marīnid al-Ghuzah al-Mujāhidūn—holy warriors who had come to the Iberian Peninsula to defend Muslims and raiders who terrorized Christian villagers and incited Mudéjares to revolt—that is the hardest of swallow. Al-'Abbās b. Raḥḥū was not a marginal figure among the Ghuzāh. In fact, he was a son of one of the three exiled Marīnid princes who founded this corps, and across the late thirteenth and fourteenth centuries, numerous members of his family, the Banū Raḥḥū, would serve both as leaders of the Marīnid Ghuzāh and as Aragonese *jenets*. What then was the relationship of the Ghuzāh to the *jenets*? In order to answer this question, it is worth standing back to consider the history of these holy warriors.

While Aragonese archival sources tell us little about the origin and nature of the Ghuzāh, the situation in Arabic chronicles is better but still problematic. Only two historians spoke of these Marīnid soldiers in any detail. The Andalusī polymath and politician Ibn al-Khaṭīb, who dealt directly with the leaders of the Ghuzāh at the Naṣrid court, left brief descriptions and biographies of them in his works. More substantially, Ibn Khaldūn devoted the final part of his *Kitāb al-ʿibar* to an account of the leaders of the Ghuzāh, whom he called "the princes (*qarāba al-murashshaḥīn*) of the family of ʿAbd al-Ḥaqq [the founder of the Marīnid dynasty] among the holy warriors (al-Ghuzāh al-Mujāhidūn) in al-Andalus who shared power with the Naṣrid ruler and distinguished themselves in the leadership of jihād."[3] Ibn Khaldūn's history of the Ghuzāh is the only systematic record of them from their rise in 1262 to the imprisonment of their last leader in 1369.[4] Thus, the limitations of Ibn Khaldūn's history are also, to a great extent, the limitations for understanding the Ghuzāh.

The Ghuzāh were born out of rebellion in North Africa. Their first leaders, members of the Banū Idrīs and Banū Raḥḥū, two closely related branches of the Marīnid royal family, arrived as men banished from their homeland following an uprising against the Marīnid sultan Abū Yūsuf in 1262.[5] This was not their first or last rebellion in North Africa. Nine years later, in 1271, a second uprising pushed more members of these princely families into al-Andalus. This second wave included Mūsā b. Raḥḥū, the first to receive the title of commander (*shaykh al-ghuzāh*) from the Naṣrid sultans and the man to whom Conrad Lancia and Samuel Abenmenassé held letters of introduction.[6] In 1286, a third princely branch, the Banū Abī al-ʿUlā, known as the Fijos de Ozmín in Castilian chronicles, joined the Ghuzāh in exile.[7]

The Naṣrid rulers of Granada greeted these North African exiles with extensive privileges and placed them in command of the various soldiers along their frontiers with the Crown of Aragon and Castile. Ibn Khaldūn did question the motivations of the first Marīnid princes to arrive in the Iberian Peninsula: "They entered al-Andalus under the pretense of performing jihād (*tawriyatan bi'l-jihād*) but they were only seeking refuge, fleeing from his [the Marīnid sultan's] authority (*maḥallihi*)."[8] Nevertheless, military successes rapidly brought them tremendous authority and enthusiastic acolytes.[9] Princes and soldiers from the kingdoms of North Africa crossed the sea to join the Ghuzāh, replenishing their ranks continually. Ultimately, these Marīnid princes commanded a motley crew of Zanāta and Arab soldiers as well as a mixture of salaried soldiers and ascetic warriors. These ascetic warriors were men who had devoted themselves voluntarily to holy war. The Ghuzāh resided both at the city of Granada, where they protected the Naṣrid sultans, and in frontier fortresses, which were simultaneously military and religious institutions from which they conducted raids into Christian territory.[10] As Romance and Arabic sources confirm, the Ghuzāh played a decisive role the battles of Moclín (1280), Alicún (1316), de la Vega (1319), and Teba (1331), triumphs that resonated across the peninsula and the Mediterranean.

The extensive success of the Ghuzāh for a period of a century reflected not only their military strength but also the delicate balance of power in the western Mediterranean after the collapse of the Almohad Caliphate. For the Marīnid sultans in North Africa, the existence of the Ghuzāh served two purposes. First, this institution offered a tidy solution to the problem of royal succession at Fez. By banishing competitors, sending them across the sea, the Marīnid rulers aimed to free themselves from internal threats while nevertheless keeping these pretenders within reach. For instance, when the Marīnid sultan sent the powerful prince ʿAbd al-Ḥaqq b. ʿUthmān to Iberia to join the Ghuzāh, he asked that the Naṣrids imprison ʿAbd al-Ḥaqq upon his arrival in Granada.[11] This caution was wise: the prince escaped from prison; fled to "Christian territory (*dār al-ḥarb*)"; and ultimately returned to North Africa, where he continued to conspire against the Marīnids.[12] Second, the Marīnid sultans' creation of and support for the Ghuzāh demonstrated their commitment to jihād.[13] From the Aghlabids to the Almohads, Islamic rulers in the North Africa and al-Andalus had employed holy war against not only Christians but also other Muslims to establish their temporal and spiritual authority, to gain approval from jurists and warriors.[14] By choosing to call these troops "al-Ghuzāh," these sultans may have also intended to draw a comparison between themselves and the Almohads, who maintained a homologous military division. In other words, in the eyes of the Marīnid sultans, the Ghuzāh were an important symbol of their claim to be the rightful heirs of these caliphs.[15]

For the exiled Marīnid princes, al-Andalus offered not only refuge but also opportunity. Their participation and success in jihād lent these princes an authority that came to rival that of the Marīnid sultan. For instance, with renewed prestige, Mūsā b. Raḥḥū was able to reconcile with the powers in Fez. He arranged for the marriage of his daughter to the Marīnid sultan Abū Ya'qūb.[16] Rather differently, 'Uthmān b. Abī al-'Ulā, who first commanded the Ghuzāh at Málaga in 1302, took advantage of a dispute between the Naṣrids and Marīnids over the port of Ceuta to declare his candidacy for the Marīnid throne. With Naṣrid support, he returned to North Africa, gathered a large following among his tribesmen, and besieged the Marīnids.[17] Significantly, after his defeat in 1308, 'Uthmān was welcomed back to Granada, where he would eventually become the most famous commander of the Ghuzāh, conducting some 732 raids into Christian territory.[18]

As the cases of 'Abd al-Ḥaqq and 'Uthmān demonstrate, from the perspective of the Naṣrids, the Ghuzāh provided a useful counterweight to the Marīnids, who were the most powerful Islamic force in the western Mediterranean. Although they had withdrawn many of their own forces after 1285, the Marīnids maintained a handful of fortresses on the Iberian Peninsula, the most prominent of which was the fortress at Algeciras, al-Binya, which served as a beachhead for troops arriving from their lands.[19] Thus, while the Naṣrids relied upon Marīnid military assistance, they also worried that these North Africa sultans secretly planned to overrun them. In this sense, the Ghuzāh were ideal. They not only protected the Naṣrids but also chastened the Marīnids. Indeed, 'Abd al-Ḥaqq and 'Uthmān were not the only princes whom the Naṣrids supported in rebellion against the Marīnids. Fifty years later, 'Uthmān's son, Idrīs b. 'Uthmān Abī al-'Ulā also attempted and failed to seize the Marīnid throne. Idrīs sought refuge in Barcelona for a period of two years and then was recalled to Granada, where he took command of the Ghuzāh from 1359 to 1362.[20]

These Marīnid scions also proved beneficial to the Naṣrids in other, familiar ways. They served in the Naṣrid court as members of the sultan's entourage, as his protectors, advisors, and ambassadors.[21] By taking command of the salaried troops and volunteer warriors from North Africa along the weakened frontiers with the Crown of Aragon and Castile, they helped to secure the fragile kingdom of Granada. In addition to combatting external threats, the Ghuzāh also suppressed internal rebellions, a fact that occasionally drove a wedge between local Muslims and these North African arrivistes.[22] In return, the Naṣrids compensated the leaders of the Ghuzāh handsomely, granting them a share of tax revenues and permitting them to retain all spoils and lands that they seized in battle.[23] In short, the Naṣrids employed and compensated the Ghuzāh in almost precisely the same fashion as Crown of Aragon did its *jenets*.

Rivalries among the leaders of the Ghuzāh also emerged as a defining feature of their history, one that ultimately led their downfall. Across a hundred years, command of the Ghuzāh fell almost exclusively into the hands of one of two families, the Banū Raḥḥū and the Banū Abī al-'Ulā.[24] With one significant interruption, discussed below, the Banū Raḥḥū dominated this post until 1314. Mūsā b. Raḥḥū was succeeded by his brother, 'Abd al-Ḥaqq, who was then succeeded by his son, Ḥammū.[25] In 1314, however, a rebellion backed by 'Uthmān b. Abī al-'Ulā forced the Naṣrid sultan Naṣr (r. 1309–1314) to flee Granada with his protectors, the Banū Raḥḥū, and ultimately abdicate the throne in favor of Ismā'īl I (r. 1314–1325).[26] Once in command of the Ghuzāh, 'Uthmān greatly expanded the authority of the post, provoking the jealously and anger of the Marīnid sultan.[27] He had his Berber competitors, the members of the Banū Raḥḥū, deported to North Africa.[28] According to Ibn Khaldūn, he also arranged to have Ismā'īl assassinated and replaced by a minor, Muḥammad IV (r. 1325–1333), effectively seizing direct control of the Naṣrid state.[29] Although 'Uthmān's rivals at court managed to recall the Banū Raḥḥū from North Africa to challenge his position, 'Uthmān clung to power and managed to pass command of the Ghuzāh to his son in 1330.[30]

The fortunes of the Banū Abī al-'Ulā and Banū Raḥḥū reversed after the involvement of the Ghuzāh in the assassination of Muḥammad IV. Fearful of their growing power, the new Naṣrid sultan, Yūsuf I (r. 1333–1354), had the Banū Abī al-'Ulā deported to Tunis and placed a member of the Banū Raḥḥū, Yaḥyā b. 'Umar b. Raḥḥū, in command of the Ghuzāh in 1337.[31] With the exception of a brief interruption in the reign of Muḥammad V from 1359 to 1362, when Idrīs b. 'Uthmān b. Abī al-'Ulā arrived from Barcelona to take command of the Ghuzāh, a member of the Banū Raḥḥū held this position from 1337 to 1367.[32] The last commander of the Ghuzāh, who held the post until 1369, was from neither the Banū Raḥḥū nor the Banū Abī al-'Ulā.[33]

For some time before 1369, however, the Naṣrids had grown tired of the machinations of the Marīnid princes. Ibn al-Khaṭīb, the chief minister (*wazīr*) at the Naṣrid court of Muḥammad V, resented the strong influence of these Berber princes.[34] Taking advantage of the weakness of the Marīnids as well as the Christian Iberian kingdoms in 1363, he convinced Muḥammad to imprison Yaḥyā b. 'Umar b. Raḥḥū and place a Naṣrid prince in command of the Ghuzāh.[35] This initial attempt to suppress the Marīnid leaders of the Ghuzāh was rejected by their soldiers, and the Banū Raḥḥū clung to power. In 1369, Ibn al-Khaṭīb conspired again. This time, he forged letters implicating the Ghuzāh in a coup plot, which convinced the sultan to arrest the last known commander of the Ghuzāh and take direct control of these soldiers himself. With this act, the Ghuzāh ceased to be an independent institution. According to Ibn Khaldūn, the remaining Marīnid princes in Granada held only an honorific role at court.[36] And in that same year, underscoring his shift away from dependence on North African military support, Muḥammad captured the fortress at Algeciras and dismantled its massive fortifications, an enduring symbol of Marīnid influence in Granada.[37] The suppression of the Ghuzāh, however, did not end the trade in soldiers. In 1377, Muḥammad and King Pere III signed a bilingual truce, in which Granada promised to continue to supply the Crown of Aragon with soldiers, referred to simply as "knights" (*fursān*/*caballeros*) rather than *jenets*, so long as they were only used against mutual enemies.[38]

As a whole and across their history, the Ghuzāh were riven by tensions. They were caught between the motivations of the Marīnids and the Naṣrids, motivations that occasionally aligned and occasionally ran contrary to one another. They were also divided by the ambitions of their leaders, the members of the Banū Raḥḥū and the Banū Abī al-ʿUlā, who not only struggled among themselves for position at the Naṣrid court in Granada but also harbored desires to return to power at the Marīnid court in North Africa. Although Ibn Khaldūn made no mention of the fact that the Ghuzāh sold their services to the Crown of Aragon, he did tell us that these kinds of intra-Muslim tensions occasionally compelled leaders of the Ghuzāh, like Idrīs b. ʿUthmān b. Abī al-ʿUlā, to seek refuge at the Aragonese court.[39] Thus, he offered us one explanation and justification for the presence of Ghuzāh elites in the lands of the Crown of Aragon. These Marīnid princes were rebels (*muradā'*) against what they saw as the unjust authority of the Marīnids or Naṣrids.[40] They understood their service for the Aragonese king as a temporary measure as they struggled to return to power. While a spirit of rebellion explains some cases, it does not explain them all. The Crown of Aragon also recruited its *jenets* in high-level and sweeping agreements with Granada and all of the kingdoms of North Africa.[41] From the beginning, these rulers permitted their soldiers to fight for and live in a Christian kingdom. In other words, the Marīnid Ghuzāh and the Aragonese *jenets* were sometimes an inversion and at others an extension of one another. Given their ready willingness not only to fight other Muslims but also to fight for Christians, in what sense were the Ghuzāh really holy warriors, *mujāhidūn*? What did their commitment to jihād mean?

The Skeletonization of Fact

From the beginning of Islamic history, the meaning of jihād has been *contested* [handwritten margin note: *contested*]
contested.[42] Political leaders, jurists, and soldiers drew upon a variety
sources—the Qur'ān, the Ḥadīth (the sayings of Muḥammad), and historical narratives of the early Islamic conquests—and developed competing
and contradictory understandings of the term, which ranged from seeing
jihād as an inward spiritual struggle to a code of conduct in war. The question of who defined jihād was as fraught as the question of against whom
could jihād be directed. Did frontier warriors, jurists, or rulers lead these
wars? Was jihād an individual or a collective responsibility? Could Muslims also be legitimate targets of jihād? Such questions highlight the fact
that jihād was not a rigid and abstract ideology but rather a terrain of
shifting ideals and practices. It cut to the very heart of struggles *within* in
the Islamic world to define the relationship of divine to human authority.
More particularly, in the context of thirteenth-century North Africa and
al-Andalus, as Abigail Krasner Balbale has argued, jihād was central to
the struggle to define and claim authority after the collapse of the Almohad Caliphate.[43] Indeed, both the Naṣrids and Marīnids employed the
Ghuzāh to assert their power over their Muslim and Christian rivals.

If the Ghuzāh were therefore a normative expression of jihād in this
period, then can one say the same of the *jenets*? Surveying the opinions
of Mālikī jurists—that is, jurists from the school of Islamic law that domi- [handwritten margin note: *beyond boundary of jihad?*]
nated Spain and North Africa in this period—one might quickly conclude
that these soldiers' actions were beyond the boundary. According to the
Tunisian jurist Saḥnūn (d. 854), Mālik (d. 796), who founded this school of
law, disapproved of Muslims even traveling to non-Muslim territory (*dār
al-ḥarb*).[44] Thus, it is not surprising that after the twelfth century, when
greater numbers of Muslims found themselves under Christian rule in the
Iberian Peninsula, a general consensus emerged among Mālikī scholars [handwritten margin note: *emigration later*]
that emigration (*hijra*) was obligatory for all able-bodied Muslims in con-
quered territory. This was the legal opinion (*fatwā*) of the highly influential chief *muftī* (one who is authorized to issue legal opinions) of Fez,
Aḥmad b. Yaḥyā al-Wansharīsī (d. 1508).[45] Al-Wansharīsī's *al-Mi'yār al-
mu'rib wa'l-jāmi' al-mughrib 'an fatāwā 'ulamā' ahl Ifrīqiya wa'l-Andalus
wa'l-Maghrib* (The Clear Standard and Extraordinary Collection of the
Legal Opinions of the Scholars of North Africa and al-Andalus) was a vast
compilation of legal opinions from the year 1000 to around 1491. It was a

standard reference work for Mālikī jurists. In this collection, al-Wansharīsi considered it impossible for Mudéjares, subject Muslims, to fulfill the basic requirements of Islam—prayer, alms, fasting, pilgrimage, and jihād—under Christian rule.[46] In making this claim, he drew upon the precedents of the Andalusī jurists Ibn Rushd al-Jadd (d. 1126) and Ibn Rabī‘ (d. 1319), which is to say that his position was neither unique nor extreme, as has been occasionally argued.[47]

Most relevantly, all three of these jurists also spoke with some disdain of Muslim soldiers who served in Christian armies. For instance, in a section entitled, "Refusal of Jihād (*Tamannu‘ al-Jihād*)," Ibn Rabī‘ explained, "They [Muslim soldiers in Christian armies] boldly embark on the very opposite of it [jihād] (*naqīdahu*), by supporting their allies (*awlīyā'ihum*) against the Muslims, either physically or financially (*immā bi-l-nufūs immā bi-l-amwāl*), and thus, they become at that point hostile combatants (*ḥarbiyīn*) with the polytheists."[48] In explaining their views on the matter, both al-Wansharīsī and Ibn Rushd al-Jadd cited a legal discussion recorded by the Andalusī jurist al-‘Utbī (d. 869) regarding Muslims who remained in Barcelona after its conquest in 801:

> I [Yaḥyā b. Yaḥyā] asked him [Ibn al-Qāsim] about [the case of] a Muslim from Barcelona who failed to move away from them [the Christian conquerors] after the year which had been set [by the Christians as the grace period] for their departure on the day it [the city] was conquered, and then attacked Muslims (*aghāra ‘alā al-muslimīn*), seeking to protect himself, because he feared being killed if he was defeated [by Muslims retaking the city]. He [Ibn al-Qāsim] said: I do not see his status as any different from that of the criminal or illegitimate rebel (*al-muḥārib*) who steals from Muslims in Islamic territory (*dār al-Islām*); this is because he remains within the religion of Islam.[49]

To these jurists, not only should no Muslim remain in conquered territory, but also those who did and allied themselves with Christians against Muslims had become enemies (*ḥarbiyūn*) or at best criminal and illegitimate rebels (*muḥāribūn*), whose lives and property could be legitimately seized.[50] Given the circumstances that led some Ghuzāh to move to Christian courts, it should be underscored that al-Wansharīsī considered any rebellion that sought the aid of non-Muslims as illicit.[51] In other words, the *jenets* seemed to have little room to stand on with respect to Islamic law.

Nevertheless, as others have amply demonstrated, these opinions were not fully representative of the Mālikī tradition in particular or Islamic law in general.[52] As opposed to legal theory (*uṣūl al-fiqh*), these opinions were born out of practice and reflected specific social and historical circumstances.[53] Rather than blindly enforcing tradition, jurists sought to reconcile precedents with the exigencies of the present.[54] In the cases above—of Ibn Rushd al-Jadd, Ibn Rabīʻ, and al-Wansharīsī—each scholar wrote in and responded to a particular moment of crisis and territorial contraction: the fall of Toledo, the fall of Murcia, and the Portuguese occupation of North Africa respectively.

Although al-Wansharīsī drew on earlier opinions, he in fact selectively cited and rearranged these arguments to suit his purposes and audience. For instance, he trimmed the words of al-ʻUtbī, who qualified his view of Muslim soldiers in Christian armies, by adding: "If he [a Muslim soldier] was forced and commanded to do what he did (*yukrih alayhi wa-yūmar bi-hi*), and was unable to disobey his commander out of fear for his life, then I do not see that he is an enemy (*ḥāriban*), or that he should be killed if captured; nor is he punished, if it is clear that he was commanded to do this and feared for his life."[55] Leaders and not regular soldiers, in other words, bore the moral burden. Elsewhere, al-ʻUtbī also considered the presence of Christian soldiers in Islamic armies licit under certain circumstances.[56] He established rules, for instance, on how to share spoils of war with Christian soldiers.[57] If he could permit this relationship within constraints, then could he have permitted the opposite—Muslim soldiers in Christian armies—in another context? Facing a Portuguese occupation, al-Wansharīsī was not interested in making such qualifications or even considering such possibilities.

It should be added, however, that although he appears rather categorical on the matter of Muslims living with Christians and serving in their armies, al-Wansharīsī did nevertheless make room for competing opinions elsewhere. For instance, he cited the opinion of the Mālikī jurist al-Māzarī (d. 1141), who considered it licit for Muslims to enter non-Muslim territory in hopes of guiding (*li-rajā' hidāya*) those there or turning them away from error (*naqlihim ʻan ḍalāla*).[58] In short, within the Mālikī school, there was room for debate and discussion. This was not a closed tradition.

Examining views beyond those of the Mālikīs reveals an even wider divergence on the questions of residence in Christian territories and jihād. Facing circumstances similar to the Mālikīs—the expansion of non-Muslims into Muslim territory—Shāfiʻī and Ḥanafī scholars, which is to say, scholars from two of the other four orthodox schools of Islamic law, responded very differently.[59] They held that any territory in which Islamic jurists continued to practice should be considered part of Islamic territory (*dār al-Islām*).[60] And to cite one example relevant to this discussion, the Shāfiʿī jurist Ibn Ḥajar al-Haytamī (d. 1566) urged Muslims to offer military support to any territory that allowed Islam to be performed fully and openly.[61] In other words, he argued that one might correctly fulfill the obligation of jihād by defending a Christian territory. Could such distant opinions have influenced Muslims living in the Iberian Peninsula? As van Koningsveld and Wiegers have shown, Mudéjares did not limit themselves to the advice of Mālikī jurists.[62] Some Iberian Muslims traveled as far as Egypt to seek legal opinions, which is to say that in practice, not only jurists but also individuals pursued interpretations of the law to suit their purposes.

In order to make moral determinations, Clifford Geertz argued, the law inevitably leads to "the skeletonization of fact."[63] Jurists must reduce the complexities of the veridical to the clarity of the instrumental.[64] Nevertheless, the tension between legal theory and legal practice helps to reveal how contested questions of legitimacy were. When examining the Islamic legal traditions concerned with residence in Christian territories or the performance of jihād, one cannot speak simply and clearly of licit and illicit actions but rather competing norms and sensibilities. Thus, the case of the *jenets* cannot be summarily dismissed from court. There may be some room for them to stand on.

The treaties between Christian and Islamic rulers, which arranged for the exchange of Christian and Muslim soldiers, are exceptionally relevant in this regard.[65] Precisely because these agreements received the approval of Islamic jurists who were trained the Mālikī tradition, they offer yet another perspective on legal practice.[66] By regularly insisting that Muslim soldiers could be used only against Christians, these treaties suggest that jurists both responded and offered a creative solution to the repeated prohibition of Muslim soldiers voluntarily serving in Christian armies *against* other Muslims. These rulers and jurists attempted to accommodate the exchange of soldiers to existing norms and rules. Given these limits upon use, there is no reason to conclude that the *jenets*' actions were illegitimate or, so to speak, beyond belief.

Rebels

The case of al-ʿAbbās b. Raḥḥū offers us a closer look at the lives of the *jenets* in the lands of the Crown of Aragon and demonstrates that not only jurists but also soldiers struggled to reconcile their service for a Christian king with their beliefs and with their status as members of al-Ghuzāh al-Mujāhidūn. This final story weaves between Latin, Romance, and Arabic sources in archives and chronicles to reconstruct the history of a powerful Marīnid prince and the soldiers under his command.

A political tumult first swept al-ʿAbbās into the lands of the Crown of Aragon. In April 1302, the Naṣrid sultan of Granada, Muḥammad II (r. 1273–1302), died suddenly and left the throne to his son, Muḥammad III (r. 1302–1309)—known to posterity as the Deposed (*al-Makhlūʿ*). Despite a longstanding alliance with the Crown of Aragon, Muḥammad III decided upon his ascension to enter into negotiations with King Fernando IV of Castile (r. 1295–1312) and drifted away from King Jaume II. Fearful of this alliance, Jaume sent an ambassador to the Marīnid sultan Abū Yaʿqūb, promising Aragonese knights and ships for the sultan's war against the ʿAbd al-Wādids but hoping, through this gesture, to repair their lapsed relationship.[67] This series of events produced bafflement among their contemporaries just as it has among modern historians.[68]

Why did the Naṣrid sultan trade allegiances from the Crown of Aragon to Castile? Upon his ascension to the throne, Muḥammad III, in fact, faced an uprising by the commander of the Ghuzāh. In 1302, Ḥammū b. ʿAbd al-Ḥaqq b. Raḥḥū and other members of the Banū Raḥḥū revolted. They seized the fortress of Bedmar near Jaén and declared themselves independent of the new sultan. When Fernando's ambassadors arrived at Muḥammad's court in 1303, they offered to aid in the conquest of Bedmar; in other words, to protect Muḥammad from the rebellious Ghuzāh.[69] Muḥammad's decision to accept Castilian rather than Aragonese assistance at this moment only makes sense in light of the overlooked connection between the Marīnid Ghuzāh and the Aragonese *jenets*. Of course, neither the Aragonese, for whom this alliance threatened control of the Mediterranean straits, nor the members of the Banū Raḥḥū welcomed the alliance between Castile and Granada.

Events began to converge towards a new confrontation, a new crisis. As early as September 1303, Muḥammad complained to Jaume that Aragonese *jenets* were raiding Granadan and Castilian territory.[70] In the same month, Jaume's ambassador departed once again for the Marīnid court, from which he requested and eventually secured the transfer of another one to two thousand *jenets* specifically for use against Castile.[71] Perhaps most tellingly, Bernat Sarria, an Aragonese ambassador, reported through a Muslim agent in Granada that some noblemen and knights (*alguns rics homens e cavalers*) were so displeased with Muḥammad's recent alliance that they were willing to join the Crown against Castile.[72] In other words, the Crown of Aragon had become a refuge for Muslim soldiers, not (or not merely) seeking profit but rather hoping to continue to fight against the sultan of Granada and the king of Castile. It was this climate of rebellion that motivated al-ʿAbbās b. Raḥḥū—who was an uncle of Ḥammū and had also been held prisoner in Almería for his attempts to thwart a Granadan alliance with Castile—along with a handful of other prominent members of the Banū Raḥḥū to cross into the service of the Crown of Aragon.[73] An Aragonese royal official reported to King Jaume: "Believe, my lord, that from what he says, al-ʿAbbās and the others want to serve us and in this they are worth more than all other armed knights (*quens hic valen mes que no farien atretans cavayls armats*), and know, my lord, that throughout the frontier, your enemies tremble and have great fear of them."[74]

Mutual Exception

On December 22, 1303, al-ʿAbbās signed a contract for service and presented it to King Jaume II.[75] He swore allegiance to the king on behalf not only of the other members of the Banū Raḥḥū in his entourage but also of all the *jenets* and corporals (*cabos*) of the *jenets* in Valencia and Murcia, suggesting that al-ʿAbbās was now commander of these Muslim troops in the lands of the Crown of Aragon. Al-ʿAbbās agreed to place hostages (*rahenes*) in the king's charge in return for three Murcian castles—Negra, Lorquí, and Ceutí—which he would hold as a vassal of the king and from which he would collect income (map 5).[76] Al-ʿAbbās also agreed to seek permission from the king or his royal procurator before leaving the Crown's service. Finally and most significantly, he promised to support the Aragonese king against all his enemies whether Christian or Muslim (*si quiere Christianos si quiere Moros*) and more particularly, against the kings of Granada and Castile, with whom the Banū Raḥḥū were in dispute. But in this final regard—his willingness to attack other Muslims—al-ʿAbbās' terms of service were all but unique.[77] Al-ʿAbbās appeared to place no limits on his service. He, the other members of the Banū Raḥḥū, and a handful of other Ghuzāh leaders in their company sealed this commitment by swearing on the Qur'ān: "And we swear in the presence of you, Lord King, by the Qur'ān that everything above will be held and completed by us in good faith and without trickery."[78]

5. The Aragonese-Granadan frontier (1304). Courtesy Dick Gilbreath, Gyula Pauer Center for Cartography and GIS, University of Kentucky.

At the same moment al-'Abbās presented Jaume with this agreement, the Aragonese king signed and returned his own, which offers an opportunity to see this alliance from the other perspective.[79] Jaume promised to inform all his officials of al-'Abbās' new service as well as to establish the *jenet* as his vassal in the aforementioned castles. He promised al-'Abbās and his troops ample food supplies.[80] The *jenets* were guaranteed freedom of movement, except travel into enemy territory. They were allowed to keep the king's *quinta* from all spoils as well as what was owed to the Crown by any Christian soldiers who raided in their company.[81] The king also promised them the freedom to leave his service whenever they wished, an understanding slightly inconsistent with al-'Abbās'. Nevertheless, to this point, Jaume's terms seemed to be the same that he had offered other *jenets*.

Three final stipulations, however, throw their relationship into sharper relief. Rather than a moment of good faith and agreement, these terms expose a deep-seated mistrust at the heart of this contract. First, Jaume insisted that al-ʿAbbās neither allow other *jenets* to enter his kingdoms nor hire new soldiers without the consent of the Crown. In short, he charged these *jenets* with policing the frontier and preventing raids from Granada.[82] However paradoxical it may seem, Jaume's use of these soldiers as border guards perfectly expresses their intertwined history: the service of the *jenets* for the Crown of Aragon only confirmed and achieved their exclusion from its communities. These boundary-crossers were also boundary-makers.

Second, Jaume consented that the *jenets* could retain any land or castles that they seized from the king of Granada, a fact that casts a different light on al-ʿAbbās' motivations and his willingness to attack Granada. Any raids into Muslim territory would ultimately benefit the Ghuzāh under the command of the Banū Raḥḥū and not the Crown. Thus, the strategic alliance against Granada did have its qualifications. Al-ʿAbbās was not a servant of the king but rather served his own interests and those of the Ghuzāh who were loyal to the Banū Raḥḥū.

Finally and most curiously, the Crown requested that on raids against Christians, the *jenets* neither capture nor kill women because "it is not our custom (*no es costumpne nuestra*)."[83] The specter of *jenets'* taking Christians captive—more particularly, Christian women—one that was raised over and over in the circulating *Miraculos romanzados* of Pero Marín, brought to the surface an acute need for boundaries—even for the Aragonese king. In Jaume's language, the *jenets* possessed a dangerous alterity. Thus, far from inviting community and shared interest, this alliance seemed deeply concerned with inscribing difference. These negotiations underscore the very complexity and instability of the bond that tied the *jenets* to the Crown of Aragon. The alliance between the Crown of Aragon and the *jenets* was fragile and grounded in a sense of mutual exception.

Conspirators

Although in theory the strategic aims of al-ʿAbbās' *jenets* and the Crown coincided well, in practice problems quickly mounted. While Jaume still hoped to avoid or delay an open confrontation with Granada, to maintain a semblance of peace, al-ʿAbbās and his troops were less restrained. In

January 1304, Jaume received a complaint from Muḥammad III that al-'Abbās and his troops had attacked a Granadan ambassador near Guadix.[84] A month later, Jaume wrote to al-'Abbās to deal with yet another complaint.[85] While praising the *jenet* for his service, Jaume explained that on a recent raid into the region of Cuenca, in Castile, al-'Abbās' soldiers had seized goods and captives from villages under the protection of Don Juan Manuel, who was, in fact, an ally of the Crown.[86] Given that alliance, the king ordered al-'Abbās to return the goods and captives. Jaume also informed the *jenet* captain that the Crown had signed a temporary truce with Castile, a truce that would ultimately lead to the Treaty of Agreda.[87] For his part, al-'Abbās wrote back not only to contest the charges against him but also to complain of mistreatment.[88] He claimed that as his *jenets* returned from Castile, the local governor of Jarafuel (in Valencia) sent robbers in the middle of the night, who made off with their sheep and cows. At Játiva, where the *jenets* hoped to sell their remaining spoils, the residents sealed the town gates and armed themselves against the Muslim soldiers. The food supplies that were promised to al-'Abbās and his soldiers by the Crown, moreover, were also never delivered.[89] Separately, al-'Abbās would also write to the king to complain that villagers on the lands that he held as a vassal refused to pay their rents.[90] Thus, as in the case of Mahomet Abenadalil, Christian administrators and villagers continued to treat the *jenets* as enemies and outsiders. Despite these setbacks, the agreement between the king and the *jenet* commander remained intact. Jaume issued new orders to have supplies delivered to al-'Abbās and his troops. They were ultimately delivered in April.[91] Foreseeing war with Granada, Jaume also sent an ambassador along with a messenger from al-'Abbās to Fez to seek approval for the *jenets*' continued service.[92] Abū Ya'qūb responded with appreciation for the good treatment his soldiers had received from the Aragonese king.[93] And al-'Abbās consequently wrote to Jaume, agreeing to cease attacks against Castile and "obey [the king's] command in all matters."[94]

Private dispatches among the royal letters, however, reveal that the seeming good will between these parties masked a great deal. Bertran de Canelles, the procurator of Valencia, wrote to inform the bailiff of Valencia and the king that despite making several requests, he had failed to convince al-'Abbās to return the goods belonging to Don Juan Manuel.[95] To Canelles, however, the *jenet* commander's refusal did not reflect greed but rather defiance of the king. Al-'Abbās had not sold these goods and seemed to have no intention to do so. Moreover, Bertran reported that al-'Abbās' attitude had grown increasingly bad, particularly after receiving news of the king's truce (*la carta dels Seynor Rey de la treva*) with Castile.[96] And even more startlingly, Bertran reported that three *jenets*, bearing letters from the king of Granada, had visited with al-'Abbās, which was a cause for great celebration (*fort alegrats*) among his soldiers. Thus, Bertran requested that Templar knights be sent to the kingdom for its protection. Seeing the *jenets*' lack of loyalty to the Crown, Bertran warned the king that al-'Abbās and his men were "the worst and the most evil men in the world (*la pigor gent e la pus avol del mon*)."

In a separate letter to the king, Bernat de Libia, the bailiff of Valencia, also reported that the situation in the kingdom had grown worse and potentially dire.[97] Every day, he wrote, al-'Abbās met with Valencian Mudéjares, who were pleased to see him. He had also heard rumors that after meeting the *jenet* commander, some of these subject Muslims sold their possessions and made preparations to leave the kingdom. Had the *jenets* convinced the Mudéjares that it was their duty to emigrate? Bernat also warned that since al-'Abbās' arrival, Muslim preachers (*moradins*) in Valencia had become more outspoken. "For certain," he added, "to my understanding and that of others who know the Moors, they would not behave like this unless they were going to rise up like the other time [i.e., the revolt of al-Azraq]."[98] This notice suggests coordination or collaboration rather than tension between the *jenets* and Mudéjar preachers. It gives a glimpse of the support that local religious leaders had for the *jenets*, something that legal sources from North Africa masked. In other words, in this case, the Mudéjares saw the *jenets* not as agents of the Crown or traitors but rather as their protectors. Bernat explained finally that he had spoken with al-'Abbās extensively and that the *jenet* captain swore that he remained loyal to the Crown of Aragon but that many of his soldiers said that "they would do no harm to the king of Granada (*que ells no farien mal al Rey de Granada*)."

Thus, not only had the changing political climate affected al-'Abbās and his troops but also the presence of the *jenets* had had a profound influence on the Mudéjar population. Nevertheless, Jaume's response to the claims that the *jenets* were a threat was as equivocal as that of his predecessors. On the one hand, he ordered the arrest of a Muslim preacher by the name of Alhaig (al-Ḥājj), "the pilgrim," for incitement.[99] He also commanded the Templars to enter Játiva for its protection.[100] On the other hand, he ignored al-'Abbās' conspiratorial behavior and passed over complaints that the *jenets* would not support the Crown against Granada in the coming war.

The Limit of Loyalty

The situation, however, could not hold. After several raids from Muslim Granada and pressure from the Templars, Jaume was forced to authorize reprisals, new attacks against Granada.[101] It was in this context that in May 1304, the Templar knight Berenguer de Cardona issued a report on a five-day raiding mission that the Christian Templars conducted alongside the Muslim *jenets* into the Granadan marchland. Berenguer's account, which is preserved among the king's letters in the Archive of the Crown of Aragon, not only offers a detailed look into raiding but also self-consciously addresses the issue of the *jenets'* loyalty to the Aragonese king.[102] Would the *jenets* still fight against Granada?

On Thursday, May 15, the knights left Lorca, on the Granadan border of the kingdom of Murcia, in the company of al-'Abbās as well as his cavalry, totaling in all 1,500 foot soldiers and 300 horsemen. They traveled night and day until they arrived at Zurgena (Sugena), near Almería, along the Almanzora River (map 5). Here, they "pillaged all the fields and did great damage (*e aqui talam tota lorta e fem hi gran dan*)." After Zurgena, the army turned towards Vera, along the coast of Almería. Near the hill of Nabez they were met by a messenger, who informed them that 350 horsemen from the cavalry of Vera were approaching. Al-'Abbās' *jenets* charged (*algareyan*) these troops, engaging them close to Vera, killing 13 horsemen and 30 foot soldiers and sending the rest into retreat within the city walls. The Templars and *jenets* consequently laid waste to the surrounding area, seizing all horses and burning the harvested wheat (*cremam tot lo blat que havien cullit*), and finally forced their way through the city gates of Vera. They turned next to Cuevas de Almanzora (Les Coves), where again they laid waste to its fields and spent the night. On the following day, Sunday, they moved on to Purchena (Porxena), burning mills and fields again. Their raid, however, took a turn for the worse as the soldiers laid siege to the castle of Huercal. Having surrounded the castle and set fire beneath its gates such that the men of Huercal could do nothing to defend themselves save throw stones (*haviem mes foch a les portes del Castell e aportatz los homens del Castell a aço [que] no podien als fer sino que gitaven pedres orbes*), the soldiers received a notice that the cavalry of the "King of Granada" was approaching. Deciding to abandon their siege, they gathered their horsemen, pack mules, and soldiers and turned to face the Granadan *jenets* (*los genetz*). Two hundred of al-'Abbās' men immediately charged (*algareyan*) and exchanged heavy blows with the

Granadan cavalry (*e aqui donaren se los uns abs los altres de grans colps*). For their part, the Templars dispatched several armed horsemen and ordered their crossbowmen to discharge a volley of bolts. "Through the mercy of Our Lord," Berenguer added, the Templars and *jenets* killed a hundred of the Granadan soldiers and pressed the rest into retreat within the castle of Huercal. The Templars suffered the loss of one foot soldier, and al-'Abbās, of four to six men. All the soldiers returned to Lorca the following day. Two days later, on account of the honor and profit gained by the Temple through this mission (*e los profit e la honor del Temple per aquesta raho vos scrivim aquestes novelles*), Berenguer de Cardona addressed this report to Bertran de Canelles, the very same man who had called al-'Abbās and his *jenets* the worst men in the world.

Berenguer's report is striking not only for its substance but also for its import. In the former respect, it provides unparalleled detail. Here, one witnesses the quintessential border raid, the primary aim of which was to plunder and create chaos rather than conquer: the soldiers ransacked and burned mills, fields, and towns; they operated in a small, light company with several scouts but nevertheless engaged in the siege of a castle. The military skill of the *jenets*, moreover, was manifest. Al-'Abbās' cavalry served as a frontline, and consequently suffered the only significant losses. By contrast, the heavily armed Knights of the Temple lagged behind with only a few horsemen capable of keeping pace with the *jenets*. Perhaps more striking than this wealth of detail is the document's import. First, the Templars, whom one readily associates with crusading, were riding alongside Muslim soldiers into Muslim territory, a fact that deepens the extent of Christian-Muslim military collaboration in this period.[103] Second, among the hundreds of documents involving *jenets*, this is the only surviving record of Aragonese *jenets* fighting Ghuzāh soldiers from Granada.[104] Despite the fact that al-'Abbās' *jenets* had refused to attack Granada when speaking with Bernat de Libia, it now appears that they underwent some change of heart.

In sharp contrast to the royal administrators, Berenguer de Cardona, who penned this report, appeared confident of al-'Abbās' loyalty to the Crown: "My Lord [Jaume II], know that al-'Abbās acted well and faithfully in this raid, and we saw and know that he desires to serve loyally. . . . It should be certain to you, Lord, that he is essential to you in this kingdom [Murcia]."[105] The Templars, it should be added, had strongly advocated a full invasion of Granada.[106] And to the degree that al-'Abbās' presence furthered that end, in Berenguer's eyes, this collaboration between

Templars and *jenets* could convey "profit and honor." While perhaps only rhetorical in intent, Berenguer unflinchingly invoked "the mercy of Our Lord" in the victory over the Granadan cavalry.

In an equally enthusiastic tone, Jaume wrote letters to congratulate both Berenguer and al-'Abbās on their victory "by the grace and mercy of God" and to praise them for their service and fidelity.[107] He urged them both to continue to defend his territory against its enemies. The king also acknowledged the losses that al-'Abbās suffered during these battles and promised that further supplies would be sent to the *jenets*.

Did al-'Abbās and his troops share the attitude that the raid was a matter of shared profit and honor? Did they see their actions as a legitimate? The consequences of the May raid must have troubled the *jenets*. Almost immediately, Granada launched a devastating sea attack on Valencia, causing panic throughout the kingdom.[108] As before, the threat of a Muslim invasion had a direct and negative effect on the Mudéjar population. In June, Jaume wrote to Bernat de Libia, the royal bailiff of Valencia—who earlier had feared a Mudéjar uprising. On this occasion, the king ordered his bailiff to protect the Muslim population from local attacks and to reassure the Mudéjares that they would not be punished for any conspiracies (*per raho daquels parlamens que avien hauts*) that they had with al-'Abbās. In offering this forgiveness, Jaume was hoping to divide the Mudéjares and the *jenets* and to defuse the potential for rebellion.[109] In order to further appease the Mudéjares, Jaume ordered the release of Alhaig, the preacher he had earlier imprisoned for incitement.[110] For his part, al-'Abbās also worked to relieve the tension. He offered to free a Muslim captive that he had taken from Granada, presumably a valuable one, in exchange for 220 or more Christians recently seized by the Granadan army.[111] Peace with Granada, however, could not be restored.[112] Aragonese reinforcements arrived at the Valencian frontier in preparation to meet another massive Granadan assault. Al-'Abbās' raid alongside the Templars, in other words, became an excuse for violence between Muslims and Christians on every level. Collaboration produced divisive results.

With open war on the horizon, Jaume's alliance with al-'Abbās collapsed. In July, the procurator of Murcia, Pere de Montegut, who gathered al-'Abbās' hostages earlier, wrote to Jaume II.[113] He informed the king that the Marīnid ruler, Abū Ya'qūb, had sent messengers to al-'Abbās, ordering him and his soldiers to return to Fez immediately.[114] In spite of their strident independence, the Ghuzāh remained under the authority of the Marīnid ruler. The Marīnid sultan asked Montegut to retake possession of al-'Abbās' castles in Murcia and return his hostages, while al-'Abbās would take his soldiers to Algeciras, where ships would be waiting. Upon receiving these instructions, al-'Abbās immediately came with his troops "en semble" to seek Montegut's advice. Montegut counseled the soldiers to go to the Aragonese king before taking a decision, advice consistent with the *jenets*' contract. Al-'Abbās replied that "he [al-'Abbās] knew what was in his heart (*ell se lo avia a coraçon*)." Montegut continued, "The next day he [al-'Abbās] returned and said . . . that nothing would make him go to you [King Jaume II], that his nephews and sons and other soldiers wanted to leave and nothing in the world would make them wait (*Otro dia torno a nos, et dixo nos que ell por ren del mundo no poria ir a vos, que los sobrinos et sus fijos et la otra cavalleria se le querian hir se carrera et que por ren del mundo no lo atendrian*)." With these lines, one finally strikes bedrock. Al-'Abbās' *jenets* rejected the possibility of continuing their service to the Crown of Aragon. In these circumstances, no stipend or salary could justify their remaining in Jaume's employ. Although these soldiers were in open rebellion against Granada and had come into the lands of the Crown of Aragon of their own accord, they now invoked the same boundaries found in the sweeping treaties approved by Islamic jurists. They would not support a Christian king who threatened Granada. Their loyalty had its limits. Thus, Montegut consented to discharge al-'Abbās on the king's behalf, take possession of his lands, and return his hostages. Just seven months after entering the king's service, al-'Abbās and the other members of the Banū Raḥḥū departed for North Africa.

A month later, the Crown of Aragon and Castile signed the Treaty of Agreda, by which they agreed to divide Murcia between them and prepare a joint crusade against Almería. And what followed leaves little doubt as to the motivation behind the *jenets*' sudden departure. In September 1304, Ghuzāh cavalry under the command of none other than al-'Abbās b. Raḥḥū attacked Murcia and Valencia.[115] Berenguer de Cardona and his Templar Knights were called to defend the kingdom from their former comrades.[116] The invasion of the Ghuzāh had precisely the result that Bernat de Libia, the bailiff of Valencia, had feared the most: the Mudéjares rose up in large numbers to join the Ghuzāh.[117] But the uprising failed.[118] In some regions, entire Mudéjar villages were forced to retreat alongside these cavalrymen, abandoning their possessions.[119] Other Mudéjares, including the young and the old, were imprisoned for their treasonous collaboration.[120] Nevertheless, al-ʿAbbās remained a staunch enemy of the Crown of Aragon and the subject of anxious royal correspondence for years to come.[121] In 1309, during the crusade against Almería, the Marīnid prince and his soldiers fought valiantly and repelled the Aragonese and Castilian armies from Granadan lands.[122] One of the worst men in the world, a seemingly faithless mercenary, had become a new al-Azraq and a champion of Islam.

Coda

Al-ʿAbbās' story did not end there. The fortunes of the Banū Raḥḥū in Granada were about to change. When in 1314 Ismāʿīl I seized the Naṣrid throne with support of the Banū Abī al-ʿUlā, the deposed sultan, Naṣr, fled to Guadix in the company of his protector, the Ghuzāh commander Ḥammū b. ʿAbd al-Ḥaqq b. Raḥḥū.[123] During battles in which Ghuzāh soldiers loyal to Ismāʿīl fought Ghuzāh soldiers loyal to Naṣr, Ḥammū was captured and brought to Granada as a prisoner. At the Granadan court, Ibn Khaldūn reported, Ḥammū's uncle, none other than al-ʿAbbās b. Raḥḥū, pleaded for clemency for his nephew.[124] Ismāʿīl begrudgingly agreed, and Ḥammū immediately fled to the safety of Christian territory.[125] For his part, Ibn Khaldūn said nothing more about al-ʿAbbās. Our villain or hero, depending on your perspective, disappeared from the Arabic record. But Romance letters lying in the Archive of the Crown of Aragon reveal that his history held one more chapter. In March 1317, Naṣr wrote the procurator of Valencia, indicating his willingness to send troops to support Jaume's war against Ismāʿīl.[126] And indeed, a month later, despite having invaded the lands of the Aragonese king a few years earlier, despite the deep mistrust they had for each other, al-ʿAbbās sent a messenger with a letter to King Jaume II offering his service once again. "Beloved al-ʿAbbās," Jaume responded, "we are ready and willing to have you in our service and prepared to offer you every honor that you deserve."[127] The curious collaboration of the Aragonese kings with the Muslim *jenets* continued.

EPILOGUE

Medievalism and Secularism

I set out to write a different book.

Long before I stumbled across the *jenets*, I knew the kind of story I wanted to tell. In the light of events that seemed to defy human reason, the distant past provided a way to make sense of the present. The ragged history of religious coexistence in medieval Iberia lay somewhere between a clash of civilizations and a world of interfaith harmony, between the poles of blind intolerance and benign tolerance. The steady movement of men and women across boundaries demonstrated that religious beliefs were not fate, that religious identities were flexible, negotiable, and permeable—subject to circumstance and human agency. In short, I postulated that these interactions demonstrated that religion was as poor an explanation of events—both violent and peaceful—then as now.

That was not the book that I wrote.

At every turn, the history of the *jenets* said something else. Religion reasserted itself in unexpected ways and ran out of its bounds. The alliance of the Muslim *jenets* with the Christian Aragonese kings both depended upon and reproduced ideas of religious difference. Although the Aragonese kings first recruited the *jenets*, a motley band of holy warriors, out of practical necessity to fill the lines of its armies, mere pragmatism failed to explain the significance of their enduring alliance. While marking the *jenets* as Muslims and outsiders to the Crown's laws and communities, the Aragonese kings nevertheless treated these soldiers as privileged agents, bringing them into their courts as members of their entourage, and parading with them as their personal protectors. Across this period and around the Mediterranean, the Muslim *jenets* fought in battles against the Crown's Christian enemies. These soldiers were conspicuous symbols and expressions of royal authority. And at every level from the court to the village, this strange alliance had a powerful and polarizing social impact. The presence of these Muslim soldiers did not inspire interreligious harmony or lift the veil from people's eyes but rather provoked deeper divisions and tensions between Christians and Muslims, a state of disorder that the Aragonese kings turned to their advantage, further entrenching their power.

What then was the logic that brought these Christian kings and Muslim holy warriors into an alliance? Neither high-minded tolerance nor simple indifference paved this path. The Aragonese kings' decision to recruit the *jenets* emerged from their inextricably entwined ideas of religious and political authority. Drawing upon novel and casuistic readings of Roman law, as well as precedents by Christian and Islamic rulers, the Crown of Aragon enacted its claims to sovereignty through and upon the bodies of privileged ethnic and religious others whom they also considered their possessions and slaves. To put this differently, these aspirations were not only partly influenced by Islamic models—the tradition of military slavery—but also partly enacted through Muslim agents. Nevertheless, these claims to transcendent authority were just that: claims. They were met with resistance from every corner, including from the *jenets* themselves. Indeed, the *jenets* understood their service in terms that denied the king's assertions of transcendent authority altogether and pursued their own agendas. For the *jenets*, service to the Aragonese kings was not a contradiction but rather a continuation of their role as al-Ghuzāh al-Mujāhidūn, the Holy Warriors.

What explains the disjunction between the book that I planned to write and the one that I eventually did? When religion was my central subject, why had I been inclined to minimize its effects, to see it as a minor variable?[1] What invisible hands nudged me toward certain paths rather than others? I was not alone in this regard. Across deeply opposing methodological, political, and philosophical positions, every scholar who has studied the *jenets* or their Christian counterparts has come to the same conclusion about these figures. All have seen these soldiers as transgressors, as men driven by secular rather than religious motivations. All have seen this alliance as a product of rational and pragmatic needs. If this book aimed to demonstrate how this kind of reading concealed more than it revealed, then here I want to explore more fully the origins and consequences of this secular bias. What explains this broad agreement? Why has it endured? Why should it trouble us? These concerns are not confined to the study of medieval Iberia. They sit stubbornly at the center of ongoing debates about religion and politics. And although they remain too often on the margins, medievalists still have the most to gain from and contribute to these urgent and unresolved discussions.[2]

Beyond *Convivencia*

No scholar of religious interaction in medieval Iberia can avoid the legacy of the bitter *convivencia* debates, debates over the nature and significance of the coexistence of Christians, Muslims, and Jews.[3] Across the twentieth century, these disputes pitted Spanish liberals against conservatives, each proposing a different understanding of the past and its consequences for the present. These debates about religion were constitutive of Iberian medievalism, and despite efforts to overcome them, they continue to set the terms in which religious interaction is studied.

Writing in 1905, Andrés Giménez Soler saw the *jenets* as evidence of the wider spirit of tolerance in medieval Iberia.[4] Giménez Soler admired these mercenaries' ability to place self-interest before religious commitment. This attitude, he argued, was exemplary of Muslims in general, who, since the earliest invasions, had been driven by material gain and martial glory rather than by eschatological fervor.[5] As such, Islamic warfare and commerce had a "civilizing" effect on the western Mediterranean, encouraging diplomatic and economic exchange with Christian kingdoms.[6] This admirable period of toleration, he concluded, lasted until the age of expulsions, the Inquisition, and the arrival of the Ottomans in North Africa.

Giménez Soler belonged to a wave of late nineteenth-century Spanish Arabists committed to the twinned ideals of positivism and liberalism.[7] Rejecting the romantic embellishments of earlier historians and under the influence of neo-Kantian thought, these scholars sought to write history with scientific rigor—"as it really was."[8] Nevertheless, as John Tolan has put it, their confidence betrayed a "blend of melancholy and nostalgia."[9] Witnessing the decline of Spain's imperial fortunes, its descent into religious and political extremes, liberals sought to revalorize and reorient modern Spain by casting medieval Iberia as the birthplace of the European Enlightenment. The invocation of tolerance was not an anodyne call for religious pluralism, as it is often meant today, but rather a rationalist critique of religion itself. Liberal Arabists dismissed religion as mere ideology, a thin veil for politics, and an archaic mode of thinking. To their minds, religion was a set of empty delusions employed by elites to manipulate credulous masses. In medieval mercenaries, Arabists like Giménez Soler saw men ahead of their times, secular and practical rationalists, individuals struggling to break free from religious bondage.

Catholics and conservatives met this skepticism of religion with strong resistance.[10] In his *La España del Cid* (1929), Ramón Menéndez Pidal, a Romance philologist, presented a very different image of the quintessential medieval soldier-for-hire, Rodrigo Díaz de Vivar, more widely known as El Cid, who spent part of his career in the service of the Muslim ruler of Valencia.[11] Challenging earlier studies that had portrayed El Cid as a faithless brigand, Menéndez Pidal recast him as a national and religious hero, as a champion of what he saw as an epic struggle between Christendom and Islam.[12] Menéndez Pidal did not deny the existence of pacific interactions between Muslims and Christians. Indeed, he first coined the term *convivencia*, by which he meant an unqualified "living together," to describe El Cid's temporary service for the Muslim ruler. In this history, El Cid emerged as a loyal, noble, and democratic figure, not a religious fanatic. But for Menéndez Pidal, Islamic Spain's tolerance of Christians, so admired by liberals, was also a sign of its fundamental weakness, of its dilution by rationalism.[13] Thus, despite his alliance with Muslims, Menéndez Pidal's El Cid remained a true believer who eventually rejected *convivencia* in order to become a passionate defender of the Castilian nation.

In his approach to this history, Menéndez Pidal mirrored other Romantic conservatives, who rejected what they saw as the shallow, cold, and foreign ideas of Spanish liberals.[14] In the midst of crisis, conservatives called for the revival of Spain's unique religious and national spirit. Adapting emerging theories of race, biology, and psychology, these traditionalists argued that religion was necessary for the health and function of society. These arguments shared the nostalgia that characterized postidealistic social thought from Herder's national soul, Fourier's theory of passionate attraction, Smith's invisible hand, and Freud's sublimation to Weber's concept of disenchantment.[15] Religious passions served as a salve for a modern sense of anomie.[16] In medieval mercenaries, these conservatives saw traitors to the faith.

This academic sparring was not insular and otiose but rather represented the political fault lines of early twentieth-century Spain. Willingly or unwillingly, both liberal and conservative scholars found themselves pulled into the ideological positions of the Spanish Civil War. Indeed, General Francisco Franco's regime enthusiastically drew upon Menéndez Pidal's own work to cast its leader as a new El Cid, a new Catholic hero.[17]

And in precisely the same fashion as medieval Aragonese and Castilian kings, Franco employed an elite guard of Moroccan soldiers, reviving the curious tradition that this book has sought to unravel.[18]

The tension between liberal and conservative Spaniards continued well into the twentieth century, as epitomized by the prolonged polemic between two scholars living in exile from Franco's Spain, Américo Castro and Claudio Sánchez Albornoz.[19] These men reversed the methodological poles of the debate. Castro, a romance philologist and student of Menéndez Pidal, transformed the notion of *convivencia* into a liberal value—the positive association that has since prevailed. He argued that the history of interactions between Christians, Jews, and Muslims had produced Spain's unique character, one that was grounded in pluralism and resistant to religious intolerance or what he called the "totalitarianism . . . of their belief."[20] Castro was challenged by the historian and positivist Sánchez Albornoz, who maintained the traditionalist argument. Sánchez Albornoz recapitulated the original, limited view of *convivencia*, seeing tolerance as a negative value, as a strategic and venal gesture by elites toward religious minorities. Like Menéndez Pidal before him, Sánchez Albornoz contended that medieval toleration had undermined "the vital passion" of Spanish Catholicism.[21]

These bitter and deadlocked debates continue to trouble the study of medieval Iberia. In the copious literature on *convivencia*, most contemporary scholars dismiss these positions as politically motivated distortions of the past.[22] They argue that the extremes of tolerance and intolerance fail by empirical standards and that these perspectives paper over the interplay and interdependence of the peaceful and violent interactions that comprised everyday coexistence. Some scholars have called for a return to strict empiricism; others, particularly in the American academy, have sought refuge in the seemingly neutral terms of cultural theory.[23] Neither response has managed to dislodge these debates or the question of religious tolerance from the center of public or scholarly discussion.[24] If the polemical tone of the *convivencia* debates has diminished, its essential dichotomies continue to motivate and pattern scholarship.

Cultural approaches have failed to overcome the polemics between liberals and conservatives because these twentieth-century debates were never methodological in nature but rather moral. The *convivencia* debates truly belonged to the fin-de-siècle derangements and the "crisis of culture" that gripped Europe in the years before and after World War I, an event that shook liberal confidence to its core.[25] To see the peninsular debates as part of wider disputes about the liberal values—above all, toleration—helps to bring the challenge of resolving them into full view.

Political Theology

The enemy of liberalism had another name: political theology. Although it has a longer history, this expression is now associated with Carl Schmitt's slim and gnomic text, *Politische Theologie*, which claimed, "All significant concepts of the modern theory of the state are secularized theological concepts."[26] In short, all politics derives from religion. A Catholic conservative and Nazi jurist, Schmitt believed that a liberal faith in secularism was flawed. Politics, he contended, can never divorce itself from religion, by which he meant its nonrational and transcendental foundation. Invoking the very same medieval legal traditions discussed in the chapters above, Schmitt argued that an authority that creates and sustains the law can never be fully included within the law; it logically stands prior to and outside of it. Political sovereignty, like divine sovereignty, he wrote, is fundamentally an exception to the order it creates. Thus, Schmitt saw the liberal ideal of separating religion from politics as impossible and naïve. Reviving the work of nineteenth-century Catholic counterrevolutionaries like Bonald and Maistre, he called for a redivinization of politics, a restoration of its religious and moral basis, and a return to an idealized synthesis of politics and theology, which he identified with the Catholic Middle Ages.[27] It is significant to underscore that this definition of sovereignty depended upon a certain periodization, a claim about what came before "the modern."

Schmitt's secular and liberal opponents defended the "legitimacy of the modern age" against what they saw as the rising threat of political religion.[28] Among them, it is worth highlighting the medievalist Ernst Kantorowicz, whose *King's Two Bodies* leaves a heavy impression on the pages above. Written after Kantorowicz's emigration to the United States in 1957, this book should be read as an apology for his first, an eccentric biography of the Hohenstaufen emperor Frederick II.[29] In that earlier work, Kantorowicz emphasized the near messianic quality of the German ruler, who, like the myth of the Last World Emperor, had united political and spiritual authority in one figure. Göring, Goebbels, and Hitler lauded the work as a celebration of the German national spirit, prompting some to call the biography a "fascist classic."[30] In *The King's Two Bodies*, however, Kantorowicz sought to place Frederick—or more precisely, the exceptional or dual nature of medieval kingship—within a longer narrative of the relationship between politics and religion:

> Taken all by itself, this transference of definitions from one sphere to another, from theology to law, is anything but surprising or even remarkable. The *quid pro quo* method—the taking over of theological notions for defining the state—had been going on for many centuries, just as, vice versa, in the early centuries of the Christian era the imperial political terminology and the imperial ceremonial had been adapted to the needs of the Church.[31]

As Roman imperial metaphors informed early Christological debates—the problem of Christ's humanity and divinity—so religious metaphors were in turn later adapted to answer political questions—the problem of the body politic. For Kantorowicz, this formal borrowing, a quid pro quo, did not reveal the religious origin of politics but rather the essential and necessary fiction at the heart of all politics.[32] Politics and religion simply met in the Middle Ages, like two cars weaving at an interchange, sharing a path briefly before diverging again. The convergence, however, was serendipitous: the language used to solve the riddle of Christ's two natures was also employed to justify representation, constitutionalism, and humanism. In this narration, secular liberalism proceeded from rather than against religion, as a fragile but admirable art of politics. *The King's Two Bodies* was a defense of secular modernity against the Middle Ages.

Although Schmitt and Kantorowicz represent only two of the variety of positions taken during the political-theological debates by Protestant, Jewish, and Islamic thinkers, they demonstrate that the polemics over *convivencia* between Catholic conservatives and secular liberals in Spain were part of a larger contemporary discussion about the relationship of politics and religion that was mediated through the medieval past.[33] Across Europe, liberals hoped to cure modernity of the ills of religion, and conservatives hoped to cure religion of the ills of modernity, understood as cold and excessive rationalism, a falling away from an idealized medieval past. These two essential positions were hopelessly locked.

Recently, Peter Eli Gordon has suggested that rather than seeing these debates as allegories of war and crisis, the political-theological debates should be seen as fundamentally philosophical disputes.[34] For Gordon, these debates were reprisals of the deeper tension between Enlightenment and Counter-Enlightenment, which is to say, the tension between rationalism and irrationalism, universalism and relativism, transcendentalism and hermeneutics. These remain the essential debates of modern philosophy and to recognize them as such means also to recognize that they were and are insoluble. As Gordon has explained, relativism amounts to a universal and transcendental claim: if historians claim that all meaning derives from context, then they also generalize that claim across all contexts, as something universally true.[35] This, in short, is the problem of self-defeating relativism. For Gordon, this insolubility, this nagging problem of transcendence, is an essential and inescapable feature of the post-Kantian intellectual tradition. From this perspective, the intellectual problem of sovereignty—what Schmitt identified as the exception and Kantorowicz as "the king's two bodies"—can never be resolved. One cannot ultimately choose between religion and politics or, as Leo Strauss put it, between Jerusalem and Athens.[36]

I would, however, like to push Gordon's insight further and contend that this insolubility—this haunting idea of transcendence—derives from a more fundamental agreement between the poles of these debates that is deeper than Kant. If liberals saw religious belief as an irrational and unnecessary delusion that impedes freedom, and conservatives saw it as a passionate and necessary force that binds community, then what is striking—but little mentioned—is that they both seem to be in agreement about the nature of religion and its relationship to politics.[37] Both see religion as a set of nonrational and premodern beliefs that served to create social cohesion.[38] Both find the meaning of religion in its extravert effects—in its worldly function.[39] And both see religion as essentially incompatible with modernity. In other words, they share an essentially secular understanding of religion, one that sees it as a category of abstract beliefs and transcendent claims distinct from and opposed to rational thought. Where they differ is simply upon its value: one sees religion as an impediment and the other as a fundament without which politics cannot function. More than opposing empirical, methodological, or even philosophical positions, therefore, they are better understood as competing moral narratives of modernity.[40]

This shared secular horizon accounts for both the ferocity of the political-theological debates and the manner in which these debates continue to ramify and reverse.[41] It explains how Giorgio Agamben has resuscitated Carl Schmitt or how Charles Taylor has revived Hans Blumenberg in order to act as a witness for the opposition.[42] One extreme readily collapses into another because they share the same beating heart. Indeed, this internal agreement casts a dark shadow over the recent recrudescence the political-theological debates.

The contemporary cultural approach to religion, epitomized by the work of Clifford Geertz, rejects this reductive view.[43] Geertz saw religion as an aspect of culture, as part of the webs of significance, the wider set of rules and norms that dynamically reflect and respond to the needs of individuals in a community. Balancing an appreciation of discourse and agency, he sought to find the reasons in and for religion. This pragmatic and culturally embedded understanding of religion promises to speak of belief as something other than blindness, as an expression of agency. To give one concrete example: to make sense of why medieval Christians attacked Jews, a cultural historian might argue that these Christians were expressing a criticism of royal power and fiscal policy. If this kind of reading offers a smart, satisfying, and coherent explanation *for* belief, then, as Steven Justice has recently argued, when taken as a full and systematic account, it offers a familiar picture *of* belief.[44] By reducing religion to the play of interests, to its societal value, this approach can only understand belief as a propositional matter. If one says that believers were aware of these reasons, then they appear as people who never really believed at all. If, on the other hand, one argues that they really *did* believe, then they appear as people who were unaware of the reasons for their beliefs. In other words, the cultural account of religion views belief as either an ideological mask or communal delusion.[45] Sincere belief, by extension, can only be a form of blind adherence, an irrational commitment. This coded but persistent attitude to belief helps to explain why cultural histories of religious interaction have done little to staunch the flow of liberal and conservative polemics. It explains why they continue to view religion with the same anticipatory nostalgia. Cultural history cannot overcome these polemics because it stands upon the same horizon.

The consequences of this agreement are acutely apparent in studies of religious interaction. Again, for the liberal neo-Kantian epigones, interaction provided evidence of man's ability to cast off the chains of religious delusion, to act freely and independently; for Catholic conservatives, interaction occurred at the expense of religion, at the expense of community; and for contemporary cultural pragmatists, it demonstrated that religious boundaries were permeable and flexible. At the risk of putting this too simply, these points of view respectively conclude that interaction occurs in resistance to, in spite of, or regardless of religion. All of these paths arrive at the same curious conclusion: religious interaction has nothing to do with religion. Indeed, in the century of scholarship on Muslim and Christian mercenaries, every historian has argued that these soldiers were driven by politics rather than religion. Why? Because if one begins with the implicit understanding that religion amounts to blind adherence to community, then interaction can only provide evidence of transgression and resistance.[46]

To be clear, my argument is *not* that this reading of religious interaction is wrong. Rather, cultural theory underdescribes the possibilities of encounter because it is essentially a moral tale.[47] However well-intending, the scholar who says that when Muslims and Christians interact they demonstrate an ability to act freely and rationally, comes dangerously close to the polemicist, who asserts that religion inhibits freedom and reason, that religion is inherently violent and intolerant.[48] But why couldn't religious beliefs have motivated pacific interactions? To ignore this possibility not only paints belief in a dull grisaille, in shades of black and white; it also reduces history to the terms and trajectory of a moral narrative of modernity that can only see the Middle Ages as a period of either serene faith or frustrated secularism.[49]

History from Theology

If this secular bias threatens to narrow the possibilities of medievalism, then medievalists have also been and remain best placed to challenge it. Sitting in the audience at the debate between Heidegger and Cassirer in Davos—the quintessential moment of the "crisis of culture"—Hans Blumenberg wrote perhaps facetiously that this was a reprisal of the debate at Marburg 400 years earlier between Martin Luther and Ulrich Zwingli over the nature of the Eucharist.[50] The connection is more than fanciful. Rather than a parochial discourse, theology was and remains an important source of philosophical and political commentary.[51] To see these debates as a continuation of theological ones helps to give us a grasp of the secular distinction between religion and politics that underwrites these competing perspectives on interaction.[52]

As Philippe Buc has argued, both liberal and conservative accounts of religion were heirs of the theological tradition.[53] Both perspectives developed as responses to the nineteenth-century Protestant-liberal synthesis—an attempt to reconcile religious belief with the liberal Enlightenment. For Friedrich Schleiermacher (d. 1834), religion and politics, belief and reason, were fully compatible because they were also radically different.[54] While belief was grounded in man's subjective, emotional, and nonrational experience of a transcendent divinity, politics was the public and rational unfolding of God's worldly plan. To save religion, Schleiermacher privatized and encastellated belief, removing it from the play of temporal concerns and concealing it from what Geertz called "the bitch-goddess seductions of secular life."[55] But the Protestant-liberal synthesis did not hold. Secular liberals drew upon Schleiermacher's basic distinction between religion and politics to dismiss religion as pure unreason.[56] Catholic conservatives like Bonald and Maistre rejected the Protestant solution and called for a reintegration of religion with politics, a return to what they imagined was the medieval Catholic synthesis, political theology.[57] Significantly, these conservative arguments for the necessity of religion to politics profoundly influenced the secular sociological tradition.[58] Catholic antimodernism and modern philosophy similarly went hand in hand. As Robert Nisbet demonstrated decades ago, while exchanging an emphasis on veracity for function, Durkheim's theory of the sacred, Weber's charisma, and Simmel's piety openly drew upon conservative theology.[59] In order to explain belief's social effect, its ability to create community, these ideas also openly accepted that belief was something fundamentally spontaneous and irrational. From here, it is a short step to the cultural theory of Geertz.

Schleiermacher's distinction between religion and politics does lead back to Protestant debates of the sort Blumenberg imagined. In their assaults upon Catholics as well as Jews, Muslims, and other non-Christians, Protestant theologians drew sharp distinctions between true belief and mindless ritual, between spirit and flesh, between ancient and modern religion.[60] True religion oriented men consciously toward inward belief, while false religions were merely political (*politia*), forms of primitive idolatry. To be sure, this distinction between religion and politics does not begin with or belong only to Protestantism. Medieval Catholics made it when they looked on China and the Islamic world with simultaneous admiration, for their political skill, and horror, for their false beliefs.[61] It can be found in medieval Islamic and Jewish theology, some of the very same ideas that shaped Mediterranean notions of imperial authority.[62] It can also be found in the writings of Augustine, the Gnostics, Paul, and even the Stoics. If anything, what distinguishes Protestant polemics from earlier ones is the fact that they circulated globally through modern imperialism.[63] But my central point is this: the rigid distinction between religion and politics, from which the secular critique of religion proceeds, is a polemical one. The radical purification of belief from practice, of being from substance, of unreason from reason, and of God from man was and remains disciplinary and hortatory.[64] It belongs to the language of disputation, not description. Yet this polemical ideal has enshrined itself at the core of the social sciences as the category of religion.[65]

When I first set out to write this book, I was also following the well-worn tracks of a long and unresolved intellectual tradition. Far from finding the past, I was seeking a version of it that satisfied a certain moral understanding of the present. My intention here is neither to mount a criticism or a defense of secularism as an ideal, nor is it to enter into the ongoing debates across the spectrum about the relationship of religion to politics. Instead, my intention is to question the value of these terms for scholars of religious interaction and scholars of religion more widely.[66] If a secular understanding of religion and politics depends upon a certain view of the medieval past, then medieval history also holds the key to shifting that understanding and reorienting these tired debates. Those medievalists that have questioned the seemingly natural distinction between religion and politics, body and spirit, matter and meaning have not impoverished the study of the past but enabled richer versions of it.[67] In the same fashion, abandoning these strict distinctions has brought and will bring new perspectives to urgent contemporary debates. Rather than seeking a transcendent definition, new scholarship must embrace religion as what Bruno Latour has called a "specific order of difficulty." [68]

To ask if the Aragonese kings and the *jenets* were motivated by religion or politics only beggars the past. It measures history according to its progress away from or toward a secular ideal. The sovereign ambitions of the Aragonese kings were grounded in tightly imbricated and impartible ideas of law and theology. The strategic choices of the *jenets* were also not beyond belief. For both, collaboration was neither opposed to something called religion nor reducible to it. Their alliance emerged within a context of evolving, competing, and overlapping claims to imperial authority across the medieval Mediterranean. It was grounded in mutual distrust and exception rather than agreement. While this kind of history cannot fully satisfy the needs of the present, it can help to direct it toward new futures.

Abbreviations

ACA	Arxiu de la Corona d'Aragó
ACB	Arxiu de la Catedral de Barcelona
ACV	Arxiu Capitular de la Catedral de València
AHM	Arxiu Històric de Mallorca
AHN	Archivo Histórico Nacional, Madrid
Ar.	Arabic
ARV	Arxiu del Regne de València
AS	Archivo de Segorbe
BNM	Biblioteca Nacional de España, Madrid
BNP	Bibliothèque nationale de France, Paris
Cast.	Castilian
Cat.	Catalan
CR	Cartes Reials
CYADC	*Constitutions y altres drets de Catalunya*
EI^2	*Encyclopedia of Islam*, ed. P. J. Bearman, C. E. Bosworth, E. van Donzel, and W. P. Heinrichs
fol.	folio
HEM	Évariste Levi-Provençal, *Histoire de l'Espagne musulmane*
Lat.	Latin
MR	Maestre Racional
Perg.	Pergamíns
r	recto
R.	Registre

Rom.	Romance
RP	Reial Patrimoni
v	verso

Notes

Introduction

1. See, for instance, ACA, CR, Jaume II, caixa 137, Templarios, no. 101. Cf. the description of the Marīnid prince Abū Ya'qūb's raid across the Spanish frontier in 1275: Ibn Khaldūn, *Kitāb al-'ibar wa-dīwān al-mubtada' wa'l-khabar fī ayyām al-'arab wa'l-'ajam wa'l-barbar wa-man 'āṣarahum min dhawī al-sultān al-akbar*, ed. 'Ādil b. Sa'd, VII: 200. For more on frontier warfare, see Rachel Arié, *L'Espagne Musulmane au temps des Nasrides (1232–1492)*; María Teresa Ferrer i Mallol, "La organización militar en Cataluña en la Edad Media," *Revista de historia militar* Extra 1 (2001): 119–222; Francisco García Fitz, *Castilla y León frente al Islam: estrategias de expansión y tácticas militares (siglos XI–XIII)*; and Josep Torró Abad, *El naixement d'una colònia: dominació i resistència a la frontera Valenciana, 1238–1276*.

2. On these revolts in Valencia, see Robert Ignatius Burns, *Islam under the Crusaders: Colonial Survival in the Thirteenth-Century Kingdom of Valencia*, 323–32; and idem, "The Crusade against Al-Azraq: A Thirteenth-Century Mudejar Revolt in International Perspective," *American Historical Review* 93 (1988): 80–106. The Castilian word *Mudéjar* (Cat. *Mudèixar*) comes from the Arabic *mudajjan*, literally "those who remain or lag behind." It should be noted, however, that the term rarely appears in Catalan or Castilian texts before the fifteenth century. More commonly, one sees "sarraceni," "moros," or "sarraï." See *EI*², s.v. "mudéjar," for more detail.

3. For translated documents, see ACA, R. 52, fol. 68v (4 Nov. 1284): ". . . sarraceni janeti [qui] in nostro servicio venerant sibi debebant cum duobus publicis instrumentis quorum unum est moriscum et aliud christianite scriptum. . . ." On impounding swords, see ACA, R. 58, fol. 22v (3 May 1285): "Baiulo Exatium quod donet Alaçeno militi Sarraceno nuncio Cahim filio Jahie Abennaquem quinquaginta solidos \regalium/ pro redimendis et quitandis ensibus quos idem Alaçenus et alii qui cum eo venerunt pignori obligaverunt in Exatium." By contrast,

Mudéjars from Almonezir, travelling to serve in the king's army, were protected from seizures. See ACA, R. 62, fol. 81v (7 Sep. 1284): ". . . Unde cum dicti Sarraceni sint in servicio domini Regis et nostro in hunc exercitum quem dominus Rex proponit facere contra regnum Navarre, mandamus vobis ex parte domini Regis et nostra quatenus dictos Sarracenos non pignoretis dum fuerint in dicto servicio. Immo restituatis eisdem [. . .]qua pignora eis fecistis." Muslim merchants from Granada and Jewish merchants from Castile were also protected from such seizures. See ARV, Justicia de Valencia, 1, fol. 10 (1279) and ARV, Justicia de Valencia, 1, fol. 10v (11 Mar. 1279).

4. For the requirement for foreigners to travel on public roads, see ACA, R. 48, fol. 135r (1280) and ACA, R. 66, fol. 152v (27 July 1286).

5. ACA, R. 56, fol. 93v (3 May 1285).

6. ACA, R. 58, fol. 22v (3 May 1285): "Bernardo Martini, baiulo Ville Franche, quod non exigat a nunciis Sarracenis de Cahim, filio Jahie Abebbaquem, illos quindecim solidos quos eisdem accomodavit. Immo si aliquos fideiussores ab eis recepit absolvat, cum dominus Rex mandet per presentes [dict]os quindecim solidi recipi in compotum per Guillelmum de Rocha a dicto Bernardo [Mar]tini."

7. I use North Africa as a synonym of what is called the "Maghrib" in Arabic sources, meaning northwest Africa, west of Egypt.

8. While general histories do not mention these soldiers, more specialized accounts of the Crown of Aragon do but rarely and without specificity. Among those that do see, Àngels Masià i de Ros, *La Corona de Aragón y los estados del Norte de África: política de Jaime II y Alfonso IV en Egipto, Ifriquía y Tremecén*; idem, *Jaume II: Aragó, Granada, i Marroc: apportació documental*; John Boswell, *The Royal Treasure: Muslim Communities under the Crown of Aragon in the Fourteenth Century*, esp. 186–87; María Teresa Ferrer i Mallol, *La frontera amb l'Islam en el segle XIV: christians i sarraïns al país Valencià*; and Elena Lourie, "Anatomy of Ambivalence: Muslims under the Crown of Aragon in the Late Thirteenth Century," in *Crusade and Colonisation: Muslims, Christians and Jews in Medieval Aragon*, 1–77.

9. There have been four articles or book chapters on the *jenets*: Brian Catlos, "'Mahomet Abenadalill': A Muslim Mercenary in the Service of the Kings of Aragon, 1290–1291," in *Jews, Muslims and Christians in and Around the Medieval Crown of Aragon: Studies in Honour of Prof. Elena Lourie*, ed. Harvey J. Hames, 257–302; Elena Lourie, "A Jewish Mercenary in the Service of the King of Aragon," *Revue des études juives* 137 (1978): 367–73; Faustino D. Gazulla, "Las compañías de Zenetes en el reino de Aragón," *Boletín de la Real Academia de la Historia* 90 (1927): 174–96; and Andrés Giménez Soler, "Caballeros españoles en Africa y africanos en España," *Revue Hispanique* 12, 16 (1905): 299–372. See also Ferrer i Mallol, "La organización militar," 186: "Por el momento, el cuerpo de la 'geneta' no está estudiado, aunque hay documentación para hacerlo." There is also a handful of studies of Muslim soldiers, who were not *jenets*, in the service

of Aragonese and Castilian kings in later periods. See Ana Echevarría Arsuaga, *Caballeros en la frontera: la guardia morisca de los reyes de Castilla, 1410–1467* [translated as *Knights on the Frontier: The Moorish Guard of the Kings of Castile (1410–1467)*, trans. Martin Beagles]; Roser Salicrú i Lluch, "Caballeros granadinos emigrantes y fugitivos en la Corona de Aragón durante el reinado de Alfonso el Magnánimo," in *II Estudios de la frontera: actividad y vida en la frontera*, ed. Francisco Toro Ceballos and José Rodríguez Molina, 727–48; and José E. López de Coca y Castañer, "Caballeros moriscos al servicio de Juan II y Enrique IV, reyes de Castilla," *Meridies: revista de historia medieval* 3 (1996): 119–36.

10. There are numerous studies of Christian soldiers in the service of the sultans of North Africa. Most significantly, see Eva Lapiedra Gutiérrez, "Christian Participation in Almohad Armies and Personal Guards," *Journal of Medieval Iberian Studies* 2, no. 2 (2010): 235–50; Alejandro García Sanjuán, "Mercenarios cristianos al servicio de los musulmanes en el Norte de África durante el siglo XIII," in *La Península Ibérica entre el Mediterráneo y el Atlántico. Siglos XIII-XV. Cádiz, 1–4 de Abril de 2003*, ed. Manuel González Jiménez and Isabel Montes Romero-Camacho, 435–47; Roser Salicrú i Lluch, "Mercenaires castillans au Maroc au début du XVe siècle," in *Migrations et diasporas Méditerranéennes (Xe–XVIe siècles)*, ed. Michel Balard and Alain Ducellier, 417–34; Simon Barton, "Traitors to the Faith? Christian Mercenaries in Al-Andalus and the Maghreb, C.1100–1300," in *Medieval Spain: Culture, Conflict, and Coexistence: Studies in Honour of Angus MacKay*, ed. Roger Collins and Anthony Goodman, 23–45; Carme Batlle i Gallart, "Noticias sobre la milicia cristiana en el Norte de África en la segunda mitad del siglo XIII," in *Homenaje al Profesor Juan Torres Fontes*, 127–37; and José Alemany, "Milicias cristianas al servicio de los sultanes musulmanes del Almagreb," in *Homenaje á D. Francisco Codera en su jubilación del profesorado*, ed. Eduardo Saavedra, 133–69.

11. For a recent assessment of the study of Spain and North Africa, see Andrew Devereux, Yuen-Gen Liang, Camilo Gómez-Rivas, and Abigail Krasner Balbale, "Unity and Disunity across the Strait of Gibraltar," *Medieval Encounters* 19, nos. 1–2 (2013): 1–40. There are important exceptions to this division. See, for instance, Olivia Remie Constable, *Trade and Traders in Muslim Spain: The Commercial Realignment of the Iberian Peninsula, 900–1500*; idem, *Housing the Stranger in the Mediterranean World*; Thomas E. Burman, *Reading the Qur'ān in Latin Christendom, 1140–1560*; and Kathryn A. Miller, *Guardians of Islam: Religious Authority and Muslim Communities of Late Medieval Spain*.

12. For an overview of the "convivencia" debates, see Maya Soifer, "Beyond Convivencia: Critical Reflections on the Historiography of Interfaith Relations in Christian Spain," *Journal of Medieval Iberian Studies* 1, no. 1 (2009): 19–35; Alex Novikoff, "Between Tolerance and Intolerance in Medieval Spain: An Historiographic Enigma," *Medieval Encounters* 1, no. 2 (2005): 7–36; and John Victor Tolan, "Using the Middle Ages to Construct Spanish Identity: 19th and 20th Century

Spanish Historiography of Reconquest," in *Historiographical Approaches to Medieval Colonization of East Central Europe*, ed. Jan Piskorski, 329–47.

13. Talal Asad, *Genealogies of Religion: Discipline and Reasons of Power in Christianity and Islam*, 27: "For these twentieth-century anthropologists, religion is not an archaic mode of scientific thinking, nor of any other secular endeavor we value today; it is, on the contrary, a distinctive space of human practice and belief which cannot be reduced to any other. From this it seems to follow that the essence of religion is not to be confused with, say, the essence of politics, although in many societies the two may overlap and be intertwined." See also idem, *Formations of the Secular: Christianity, Islam, and Modernity*; Hussein Ali Agrama, *Questioning Secularism: Islam, Sovereignty, and the Rule of Law in Modern Egypt*; Michael Warner, Jonathan VanAntwerpen, and Craig J. Calhoun, *Varieties of Secularism in a Secular Age*; and Elizabeth Shakman Hurd, *The Politics of Secularism in International Relations*. Cf. Brad Gregory, "The Other Confessional History: On Secular Bias in the Study of Religion," *History and Theory* 45, no. 4 (2006): esp. 136–37.

14. Hurd, *The Politics of Secularism*, 30; Bruno Latour, *We Have Never Been Modern*, 9–10.

15. Philippe Buc, *The Dangers of Ritual: Between Early Medieval Texts and Social Scientific Theory*, 94; and Steven Justice, "Did the Middle Ages Believe in Their Miracles?" *Representations* 103 (2008): 1–29. See also John Milbank, *Theology and Social Theory: Beyond Secular Reason*, 52–61; Robert A. Nisbet, *The Sociological Tradition*, 221–63; and Talal Asad, "Responses," in *Powers of the Secular Modern: Talal Asad and His Interlocutors*, ed. David Scott and Charles Hirschkind, 212.

16. Jonathan Sheehan, "Sacred and Profane: Idolatry, Antiquarianism and the Polemics of Distinction in the Seventeenth Century," *Past & Present* 192, no. 1 (2006): 35–66, esp. 65; and Elizabeth Shakman Hurd, "The Specific Order of Difficulty of Religion," 30 May 2014, *The Immanent Frame*, accessed 30 May 2014, http://blogs.ssrc.org/tif/2014/05/30/the-specific-order-of-difficulty-of-religion: "The approach proposed here resists adoption of any singular, stable conception of religion, and instead acknowledges the vast and shifting array of practices and histories that fall under the heading of religion as used today."

17. Thomas N. Bisson, *The Medieval Crown of Aragon: A Short History*, 52.

18. Bisson, *The Medieval Crown of Aragon*, 51; and Adam J. Kosto, *Making Agreements in Medieval Catalonia: Power, Order, and the Written Word, 1000–1200*, esp. chap. 3.

19. Kenneth Pennington, *The Prince and the Law, 1200–1600: Sovereignty and Rights in the Western Legal Tradition*; Walter Ullmann, "The Development of the Medieval Idea of Sovereignty," *English Historical Review* 64, no. 250 (1949): 1–33; Gaines Post, "Roman Law and Early Representation in Spain and Italy, 1150–1250," *Speculum* 18, no. 2 (1943): 211–32; Alfonso Otero Varela, "Sobre la 'plenitud o potestatis' y los reinos hispánicos," *Anuario de historia del derecho español*

34 (1964): 141–62; and Antonio Pérez Martín, "La institución real en el 'ius commune' y en las *Partidas*," *Cahiers de linguistique hispanique médiévale* 23, no. 1 (2000): esp. 313–17.

20. Joseph R. Strayer, "The Laicization of French and English Society in the Thirteenth Century," *Speculum* 15, no. 1 (1940): 76–86; idem, *On the Medieval Origins of the Modern State*; and Ernst H. Kantorowicz, *The King's Two Bodies: A Study in Mediaeval Political Theology*.

21. Ramon Muntaner, *Crònica* in *Les quatre gran cròniques*, ed. Ferran Soldevila, chap. 292: "[P]oden fer compte que seran sobirans a tots los reis del món e prínceps, així de crestians con de sarraïns." The French kings also spoke of themselves as "sovereigns" in this period. See Philippe de Beaumanoir (d. 1296), *Coutumes de Beauvaisis*, XXXIV, 1043 [my emphasis]: "Voirs est que li rois est *souverains par dessus tous*, et a de son droit la general garde de tout son roiaume."

22. David Abulafia, *The Western Mediterranean Kingdoms*, xvi.

23. Allen J. Fromherz, *The Almohads: The Rise of an Islamic Empire*, provides a useful and readable introduction to the dynasty.

24. Maribel Fierro, *The Almohad Revolution: Politics and Religion in the Islamic West during the Twelfth–Thirteenth Centuries*; Maribel Fierro, "Alfonso X 'The Wise': The Last Almohad Caliph?" *Medieval Encounters* 15, no. 2 (2009): 175–98, esp. 175; and Amira K. Bennison and Maria Ángeles Gallego, "Religious Minorities under the Almohads: An Introduction," *Journal of Medieval Iberian Studies* 2, no. 2 (2010): 143–54, esp. 143. For the broader religious context, see Mercedes García-Arenal, *Messianism and Puritanical Reform: Mahdīs of the Muslim West*.

25. David Nirenberg, *Neighboring Faiths: Christianity, Judaism, and Islam in the Middle Ages and Today*, 88.

26. A criticism also made by Ernesto Laclau, "Bare Life or Social Indeterminacy?" in *Giorgio Agamben: Sovereignty and Life*, ed. Matthew Calarco and Steven DeCaroli; and Agrama, *Questioning Secularism*, 27. On coercive violence, see Charles Tilly, *Coercion, Capital, and European States: AD 900–1990*; and Brian Downing, *The Military Revolution and Political Change: The Origins of Democracy and Autocracy in Early Modern Europe*. On the decision, see Carl Schmitt, *Political Theology: Four Chapters on the Concept of Sovereignty*, trans. George Schwab; and Giorgio Agamben, *Homo Sacer: Sovereign Power and Bare Life*, trans. Daniel Heller-Roazen.

Chapter One

1. The handwritten "Catálogo de los documentos de los registros," begun by Alterachs in the eighteenth century, is a partial catalog to the thirteenth-century documentation and resides on the shelves at the Archive of the Crown of Aragon.

2. Giménez Soler, "Caballeros"; Gazulla, "Zenetes"; Lourie, "A Jewish Mercenary"; and Catlos, "Mahomet Abenadalill."

3. Giménez Soler, "Caballeros," 348–49.

4. This confusion is paralleled in etymological studies. While Joan Coromines and J. A. Pascual, *Diccionario crítico etimológico castellano e hispánico*, 516–18, claims that "jinete" derives from the Berber tribe, the Zanāta, it also claims that "jineta" derives from the Arabic *gharnāṭa,* the city of Granada.

5. Lourie, "A Jewish Mercenary," 367–73; and idem, "Anatomy of Ambivalence," 8.

6. Catlos, "Mahomet Abenadalill," 259n6, citing Antoni María Alcover i Sureda and Francesch de Borja Molls y Casanovas, *Diccionari català-valencià-balear*, s.v. "genet." Boswell conflates Mudéjar and *jenet* soldiers, taking the term *jenet* to signify any light cavalry soldier, Mudéjar or foreign. See, for instance, Boswell, *Royal Treasure*, 186.

7. For the passage of other Arabic words into Romance and Latin, see Eva Lapiedra Gutiérrez, *Cómo los musulmanes llamaban a los cristianos hispánicos*; and Ana Echevarría Arsuaga, "La conversion des chevaliers musulmans dans la Castille du xve siècle," in *Conversions islamiques: Identités religieuses en Islam méditerranéen*, ed. Mercedes García-Arenal, 119–138.

8. Sebastián de Covarrubias, *Tesoro de la lengua castellana o española*, ed. Martín de Riquer, 640: "Hombre de cavallo, que pelea con lança y adarga, recogidos los pies con estirbos cortos, que no baxan de la barriga del cavallo," as cited with translation in Barbara Fuchs, *Exotic Nation: Maurophilia and the Construction of Early Modern Spain*, 92.

9. Wallace Stevens, "The Comedian as the Letter C."

10. The French *genet* dates to the fourteenth century, the Italian *ginnetto* to the fifteenth.

11. Shakespeare, *Othello*, I.i.112–13.

12. Shakespeare, *Venus and Adonis*, I.i.282; and Philip Massinger, *Renegado* (1624), III.iii.88. See also Massinger, *Fatal Dowry* (1616–19), IV.i.73; idem, *Very Woman* (1634), III.v.55; and John Fletcher, *Thierry and Theodoret* (1607–21), I.i.113.

13. David Nirenberg, "Was There Race Before Modernity? The Example of 'Jewish' Blood in Late Medieval Spain," in *The Origins of Racism in the West*, ed. Ben Isaac, Yossi Ziegler, and Miriam Eliav-Feldon, 232–64, esp. 248–49.

14. Claude Lévi-Strauss, *Totemism*, 89: "We can understand, too, that natural species are chosen [as totems] not because they are 'good to eat' but because they are 'good to think.'"

15. See the *Oxford English Dictionary*, s.v. "jennet"; and Walter Scott, *Ivanhoe,* 23.

16. Generally, see Charles Oman, *The Art of War in the Middle Ages, 378–1515*; Hans Delbrück, *History of the Art of War Within the Framework of Political History*, III: 234; and Joseph R. Strayer, ed., *Dictionary of the Middle Ages*, s.v. "cavalry." For

the specific case of medieval Iberia, see María Jesús Viguera Molins, "La organización militar en Al-Andalus," *Revista de historia militar* Extra 1 (2001): 17–60, esp. 38; idem, "El ejército" in *El reino nazarí de Granada (1232–1492): política, instituciones, espacio y economía*, ed. María Jesús Viguera Molins, 431–73, esp. 441; and Victoria Cirlot, "Techniques guerrières en Catalogne féodale: Le Maniement de la lance," *Cahiers de Civilisation Médiévale* 28, no. 1 (1985): 35–43. Citing contemporary illustrations, James Powers suggests that Christian knights rode *a la jineta* during the central Middle Ages but, under the influence of the French, came to ride *a la brida* after the eleventh century. I have found no evidence to corroborate this claim. See James F. Powers, *A Society Organized for War: The Iberian Municipal Militias in the Central Middle Ages, 1000–1284*, 131–32.

17. On the transformation, see Alvaro Soler del Campo, *La evolución del armamento medieval en el Reino Castellano-Leonés y al-Andalus (siglos XII–XIV)*, esp. 157–72; García Fitz, *Castilla y León frente al Islam*, 386–92, esp. 392; Arié, *L'Espagne musulmane*, 252–53; and Juan Manuel, *Libro de los Estados* in *Obras completas*, ed. José Manuel Blecua, I: 347–56.

18. J. Ferrandis Torré, "Espadas granadinas de la jineta," *Archivo español de arte* 16 (1943): 142–66. For thirteenth-century references to the *jenet* saddle (*silla jineta*), see for instance ACA, R. 65, fol. 97v; and AHM, "Torrella," Arm. 11, Far. 32, as cited in Mariano Gual de Torrella, "Milicias cristianas en Berbería," *Boletín de la sociedad arqueológica Luliana* 89 (1973): 54–63. See the section on shields in the riding manual of Antonio Galvão Andrade, *Arte de cavelleria, de gineta, e estardiota bom primor de ferrar, & alueitiara*, 188–89: "Que trate como serà obrada a Adarga." For thirteenth-century references to the *adarga*, see for instance ACA, R. 65, fol. 97v (1285), and ACA, R. 81, fol. 234r (13 Dec. 1290).

19. García Fitz, *Castilla y León frente al Islam*, 386–87.

20. For instance, Pedro de Aguilar, *Tractado de cavalleria de la gineta* (1572); Eugenio Mançanas, *Libro de enfrenamentos de la gineta* (1583); Bernardo de Vargas Machuca, *Libro de exercicios de la gineta* (1600); Luis de Bañuelos y de la Cerda, *Libro de la jineta y descendencia de los caballos guzmanes* (1605); Gregorio Tapio y Salcedo, *Exercicios de la gineta* (1643); and Galvão Andrade, *Arte de cavelleria* (1678), esp. 451–52.

21. Consuelo López-Morillas, "Los Beréberes Zanāta en la historia y la leyenda," *Al-Andalus* 42, no. 2 (1977): 301–22, esp. 309.

22. Ibn Khaldūn, *Kitāb al-'ibar*, I: 211–14, cit. 212: "wa-ammā alladhī bi'l-karr wa'l-farr fa-huwa qatāl al-'arab wa'l-barbar min ahl al-maghrib." See also *EI*[2], s.v. "furūsiyya." See also *Llibre dels feyts*, chap. 266, which describes Muslim footsoldiers using the same tactic.

23. Ibn Ḥayyān, *al-Muqtabas fī akhbār bilād al-Andalus*, ed. 'Abd al-Raḥmān al-Ḥajjī, VII: 192–93: "He considered their dress (ziyyuhum) good, their lightness in riding noble . . . and he inferred this from their equipment (ālatihim), which was perfectly constructed and suited to their horses"; and *al-Muqtabas*, VII: 190:

"The sides of the saddle were soft and the pommel short, forward and flat(?) (al-muqaddam wa'l-mu'jir)." See Lane, *Lexicon*, s.v. "'ādin," esp. 1981, for the term *'udwiyy*. The *jenet* saddle is mentioned several times in the registers (ACA, R. 58, fol. 23r [15 May 1285], R. 71, fol. 24v [5 Mar. 1286], and R. 71, fol. 110v [1287]).

24. Ibn Khaldūn, *Kitāb al-'ibar*, VII: 212, 214: "wa-qitāl al-zaḥf awthaq wa-'ashadd min qitāl al-karr wa'l-farr. . . . qitāl ahl waṭanihim kullahu bi'l-karr wa'l-farr."

25. Juan de Mariana, "De exercitacione corporis" in *De rege et regis institutione*, II: chap. 5, 130: "Inter se ex equis iaculentur Mauricae pugnae genere, quo alterius agminis pars facto impetum primum procurrit, missisque in adversarios arundinibus iaculorum imagine, pedem referunt ceduntque prementibus adversariis." Cf. Fuchs, *Exotic Nation*, 94.

26. Vargas Machuca, *Libro de exercicios*, fol. 2r: "Aunque es verdad que Berberia dio a España principio della, y España a las Indias, en esta parte se ha perficionado mas que en otra."

27. Covarrubias, *Tesoro*, 640.

28. Fuchs, *Exotic Nation*, 88–102.

29. Ramon Lull, *Liber de fine* in *Ramon Lulls Kreuzzugsideen*, ed. A. Gottron, 83: "illi eorum corpora . . . non muniunt, neque equos. . . . immo quasi nudi sunt hii in bello." See also the description of Las Navas de Tolosa (1212) in Rodrigo Jiménez de Rada, *Roderici Ximenii de Rada Historia de rebus hispanie sive historia gothica* in *Roderici Ximenii De Rada Opera Omnia*, ed. Juan Fernández Valverde, VIII: chaps. 8–9.

30. Juan Manuel, *Libro de los Estados*, in *Obras completas*, ed. José Manuel Blecua, I: 348: "Et en verdad vos digo, señor infante, que tan buenos homes de armas son [los Musulmanes], et tanto saben de guerra, et tan bien lo facen, que si non porque deben haber e han a Dios contra sí . . . et porque non andan armados nin encabalgados en guisa que peuden sofrir feridas como caballeros, nin venir a las manos, que si por estas dos cosas non fuere, que yo diría que en el mundo non ha tan buenos homes de armas, ni tan sabidores de guerra, ni tan aparejados para tantas conquistas." See also the description of the Battle of Moclín (1280), *Crónica del rey don Alfonso X*, in *Crónicas de los reyes de Castilla*, ed. Cayetano Rosell, 58.

31. Reinhart Pieter Anne Dozy and W. H. Engelmann, *Glossaire des mots espagnols et portugais dérivés de l'arabe*, s.v. "jinete"; and Coromines and Pascual, *Diccionario crítico etimológico castellano e hispánico*, s.v. "jinete."

32. Helmut Lüdtke, "Sobre el origen de cat. *genet*, cast. *jinete*, 'caballero armado de lanza i adarga,'" *Estudis Romànics* 8 (1961): 188; and Coromines and Pascual, *Diccionario crítico etimológico castellano e hispánico*, 518.

33. Lüdtke, "Sobre el origen de cat. *genet*, cast. *jinete*," 119. Lütdke cites the example of the Berbers of the Beni-Snus, who pronounce *Zanāta* in a fashion that more closely approximates the *g* of Catalan or the *j* of Castilian.

34. Lüdtke, "Sobre el origen de cat. *genet*, cast. *jinete*," 118. See also Coromines and Pascual, *Diccionario crítico etimológico castellano e hispánico*, 518, which points to the same evidence.

35. Coromines and Pascual, *Diccionario crítico etimológico castellano e hispánico*, 518, argue that the word first appears in Castilian and Catalan in the fourteenth century.

36. Arlette Farge, *The Allure of the Archives*, trans. Thomas Scott-Railton, 75.

37. For a history of the chancery registers of the Crown of Aragon, see the elegant introduction to Robert Ignatius Burns, *Diplomatarium of the Crusader Kingdom of Valencia: The Registered Charters of Its Conqueror James I, 1257–1276*; and Jesús Ernesto Martínez Ferrando, *El Archivo de la Corona de Aragón*, esp. chap. 2.

38. For the career of Jaume I, see the king's "autobiography," the *Llibre dels feyts*, as well as the classic guides: Joaquín Miret y Sans, *Itinerari de Jaume I, "el Conqueridor,"* and Ferran Soldevila, *Vida de Jaume I el Conqueridor*. See also Jaume Aurell, *Authoring the Past: History, Autobiography, and Politics in Medieval Catalonia*.

39. ACA, RP, MR, 627, fol. 137v (1318): ". . . que fassets obrar una casa de volta en aquell loch on solia esser la capeyla sua del palau de Barcelona, en la qual casa fossen posats e conservats les registres els privilegis els altres scrits de la sua cancellaria e dels altres fets de la sua cort." See also Carlos López Rodríguez, "Orígenes del Archivo de la Corona de Aragón (en tiempos, Archivo Real de Barcelona)," *Hispania* 67, no. 226 (2007): 413–54.

40. Gazulla, "Zenetes," 174.

41. For more on the Mongol Khan's invitation, see Denis Sinor, "The Mongols and Western Europe" in *A History of the Crusades*, ed. Kenneth Meyer Setton, 513–44.

42. ACA, R. 18, *passim*. See also a sentence pronounced against Ramon Folc in ACA, R. 47, fol. 14v (s.a.): "Coram vobis Arnaldo Taverner et Bernardo de Prato, iudicibus a domino Rege Aragonum delegatis, proponit idem dominus Rex nomine suo et hominum suorum, contra nobilem Raimundum Fulconis, vicecomitem Cardonen[sium]."

43. On the Valencian crusade, see the many works of Burns, including his *Islam under the Crusaders*; and Ambrosio Huici Miranda, *Historia musulmana de Valencia y su región: novedades y rectificaciones*.

44. Of the numerous works on al-Azraq, the most significant are: Carmen Barceló, "Documentos árabes de al-Azraq (1245–1250)," *Saitabí: revista de la Facultat de Geografia i Història* 32 (1982): 27–41; Robert Ignatius Burns, "La Guerra de Al-Azraq de 1249," *Sharq al-Andalus* 4 (1987): 253–56; idem, "The Crusade Against Al-Azraq"; idem, "A Lost Crusade: Unpublished Bulls of Innocent IV on Al-Azraq's Revolt in Thirteenth-Century Spain," *Catholic Historical Review* (1988): 440–49; and Robert Ignatius Burns and Paul Edward Chevedden, "A

Unique Bilingual Surrender Treaty from Muslim-Crusader Spain," *Historian* 62, no. 3 (2000): 511–34.

45. "Contra Sarracenos semper praevaluit." See Ricardo del Arco y Garay, *Sepulcros de la casa real de Aragón*, 192.

46. Francisco Martínez y Martínez, *Coses de la meua tèrra (La Marina)*, II: 170–73, as cited in Burns, *Islam under the Crusaders*, 332.

47. *Llibre dels feyts* in *Les quatre gran cròniques*, ed. Soldevila, chap. 378: "E havíem oït d'abans que el rei de Castella s'era desavengut ab lo rei de Granada e que el rei de Granada de llong temps havia percaçats los moros d'allèn mar, e que passaven los genets en sa terra, e que allèn porien cobrar tota la terra del rei de Castella." The thirteenth-century chronicle of Alfonso X of Castile also corroborates this information. See *Crónica del rey don Alfonso X* in *Crónicas de los reyes de Castilla*, ed. Cayetano Rosell, 13: "El rey de Granada . . . envió rogar á Aben Yuzaf que lo enviase alguna gente, é envióle mil caballeros." Both documents are also cited by Coromines and Pascual, *Diccionario crítico etimológico castellano e hispánico*, 517.

48. *Crónica del rey Alfonso XI* in *Crónicas de los reyes de Castilla*, ed. Cayetano Rosell, 10: "[D]icen que estos fueron los primeros caballeros jinetes que pasaron aquen la mar."

49. *Llibre dels feyts*, chap. 423: "E nós qui érem en Oriola, que hi érem romases bé per vuit dies, una nuit vengeren-nos dos almogàvers de Lorca, e tocaren a la nostra porta, e podia ésser bé mija nuit. E dixeren-nos que ens feïen saber los de Lorca que vuit-cents genets amb dos míllia atzembles carregadas, e dos míllia hòmens d'armes que les tocaven metien conduit en Múrcia." The *almogàvers* (from Ar. *al-maghāwir*, meaning raiders) were lightly armed Christian footsoldiers and horsemen who engaged in frontier warfare. See also chapter 3.

50. ACA, R. 39, fol. 201v (17 May 1277): "Petrus dei gracia, Rex Aragonum, fidelibus suis vicario et baiulo Gerunde, salutem et graciam. Cum in regno Valencie multitudo creverit janetorum et alcaydus et Sarraceni castri de Montesa fregerint nobis pacta et convenientias quas habebant nobiscum, super restitucione dicti castri [ideo] sumus in g[u]erra cum eis. Mandamus vobis quatenus //visis presentes// non permitatis extrahi de terra nostra nec duci ad aliquas partes equos aut roncinos magnos sub pena amissionis dictorum equorum et roncinorum quos equos et roncinos fideliter reservetis. Datum Xative XVI kalendas Junii, [a]nno domini MCCLXX septimo." Cf. ACA, R. 39, fol. 203v (12 June 1277).

51. Burns, *Islam under the Crusaders*, 282–83.

52. ACA, R. 47, fol. 14v (1284): ". . . fuerat etiam longo tempore pro eo quia Sarraceni in ipso Regno existentes <extexerant> se contra ipsum dominum Regem et terram suam, et rebellarunt cum multis castris et fortaliciis contra eundem dominum Regem adducendo etiam indices Sarracenos ad terram Valencie de partibus Granate et de partibus Barberie in maximum dispendium et desonorem terre sue et tocius Christianitatis in tantum quod ipse Dominum Rex coactus fuit

magnos contra ipsos Sarracenos exercitus congregare. Et cum magnis [..]dibus, laboribus et expensis ipsos Sarracenos devincens divina gracia adiuvante sue dicioni reduxit."

53. ACA, R. 40, fol. 13v (12 Sep. 1277): ". . . Abouyceff, Rex de Marrochs, nec aliqua familia janetorum non transfretaverint ad partes Cismarinas." *Llibre dels feyts*, chap. 556: "E nós estan en Xàtiva haguem ardit d'aquells cavallers genets que eren entrats en la terra."

54. On surrender agreements, see Brian Catlos, "*Secundum suam zunam*: Muslims and the Law in the Aragonese 'Reconquest,'" *Mediterranean Studies* 7 (1999): 13–26.

55. ACA, R. 38, fol. 27r–v (30 Aug. 1276): "Esta es carta de treuga et de pammento que es feta entrel Senyor Enfant Don Pedro fiyo primero et heredero del muy noble Don Jayme Rey d'Arago et qui deus perdone et entrel veillo noble Abrurdriz Hyale Abenayech et el cavero noble Abenzumayr Abenzaquimeran, el alguazir Abulfaratx Asbat, aixi quel dito Senyor Infant attreuga a t[o]dos los castellos et //las que// que son alçadis alas pennas contra ell dito Senyor Infant en todo lo Regno [de] Valentie et de su termino et de Exativa et de Si[. . .]ino. . . . E los dito[s Abrurdr]iz Yhale [*sic*] [Abenayech] et Abenzu[mayr \Ab]ulfaratx/ <treguam> otrossi a toda la terra del regno de [.........] toda la [senyuria] a los logares del dito Senyor Enfant de quiere que sean por ellos [et] por todos lures parentes et los jenetes et otros caveros de moros qui sean aqui en esta terra et en Gran[a]da et //de// \en/ qual que lugar otro que ninguno dellos no fagan dayno ne negun por ellos non fagan dayno en el regna de Valentie ne en [fol. 27v] nenguno otro lugar de Seynuria [de]l Infant. . . ." See also ACA, R. 38, fol. 33v (6 Sep. 1276), in which Pere orders his officers at the port of Algeciras to respect this treaty.

56. *EI*^{2}, s.v. "Moors," citing Polybius; Nevill Barbour, "The Significance of the Word *Maurus*, with Its Derivatives *Moro* and *Moor*, and of Other Terms Used by Medieval Writers in Latin to Describe the Inhabitants of Muslim Spain" in *Actas del IV Congreso de estudios árabes e islámicos*, 253–66, esp. 255, on the Greek; and Ross Brann, "The Moors?" *Medieval Encounters* 15, no. 2 (2009): 307–18.

57. Kenneth Baxter Wolf, ed., *Conquerors and Chroniclers of Early Medieval Spain*, 131, as cited by Brann, "The Moors?" 311. See also Barbour, "The Significance of the Word *Maurus*," 255.

58. For editions of the relevant texts, see Juan Torres Fontes, ed., *Repartimiento de Lorca*, 54: "Venieron Muza Barraham et Zahem et Zahet Azenet con mil caballeros et mataron docientos cristianos et cativaron al tantos." For full text, see Pero Marín, *Miraculos Romanzados* in *Vida y milagros del thaumaturgo español moysées Segundo, redemptor de cautivos, abogado de los felices partos, Sto. Domingo Manso, abad benedictino, reparador del real monasterio de Silos*. For the context, see Juan Torres Fontes, "La actividad bélica granadina en la frontera murciana (ss. XIII–XV)," *Príncipe de Viana Anejo* 2–3 (1986): 721–40, esp. 729; and María

de los Llanos Martínez Carrillo, "Historicidad de los 'Miraculos Romançados' de Pedro Marín (1232–1293): el territorio y la esclavitud granadinos," *Anuario de estudios medievales* 21 (1991): 69–97.

59. ACA, R. 82, fol. 168v (21 Nov. 1290): "Arnaldo de Bastida quod solvat Abenhadalillo, capiti jenetorum, mille centum viginti septem duplas quas ei [d]ebent pro [qui]tacione sua et familie sue, duorum mensum, et ex alia parte, quinque millia solidos pro quitacione quorumdam Sarracenorum Alarabum. Et facta solucione et cetera. Datum Barchinone, XI kalendas Decembris."

60. ACA, R. 252, fol. 189r (10 Mar. 1291) with edition also in Giménez Soler, 351–52n1. I discuss this document in further detail in chapters 4 and 5, below.

61. Antonio Ubieto Arteta, ed., *Crónica Najerense*, 48, 52, and 63, as cited in Barbour, "The Significance of the Word *Maurus*," 257–58.

62. Colin Smith, ed., *Christians and Moors in Spain*, 19, as cited in Brann, "The Moors?" 312.

63. The earliest Arabic work on the Berbers claims to date from the eighth century. Fragments of a work attributed to Wahb b. Munabbih (d. 725–737?) appear in Ibn Qutayba (d. 889), *Kitāb al-ma'ārif*, ed. Tharwat Ukāsha. For other early works that describe the Berbers, see Ibn Khurradādhbih (d. ca. 911), *Kitāb al-masālik wa'l-mamālik*, ed. Khayr al-Dīn Maḥmūd Qiblāwī; Ya'qūbī (d. ca. 897), *Kitāb al-buldān*, ed. Wilhelmus Theodorus Juynboll; Ibn 'Abd al-Ḥakam (d. 871), *Futūḥ Miṣr wa'l-Maghrib*, ed. 'Abd al-Mun'im 'Āmir; and al-Mas'ūdī (d. 956), *Murūj al-dhahab wa-ma'ādin al-jawhar*, ed. Charles Pellat. For an example of ethnic tension, see Ibn Ḥazm, *Jamaharat ansāb al-'arab*, ed. 'Abd al-Salām Muḥammad Hārūn, 496, as cited by López-Morillas, "Los Beréberes Zanāta," 302. Ibn Ḥazm rejected the claim that the Zanāta were descendants of Arabs. See also Ramzi Rouighi, "The Andalusi Origins of the Berbers?" *Journal of Medieval Iberian Studies* 2, no. 1 (2010): 93–108.

64. Ibn Khaldūn incorporates and develops upon other earlier works of importance, such as: Ibn 'Idhārī al-Marrākushī, *al-Bayān al-mughrib fī akhbār al-Andalus wa'l-Maghrib*, ed. G. S. Colin and Évariste Lévi-Provençal; anonymous, *al-Dhakhīra al-saniyya fī ta'rīkh al-dawla al-Marīniyya*, ed. 'Abd al-Wahhāb b. Mansūr; and Ibn Abī Zar', *al-'Anīs al-muṭrib bi-rawḍ al-qirṭās fī akhbār mulūk al-Maghrib wa-ta'rīkh madīnat Fās*, ed. 'Abd al-Wahhāb b. Manṣūr.

65. Muhsin Mahdi, *Ibn Khaldūn's Philosophy of History: A Study in the Philosophic Foundation of the Science of Culture*; Yves Lacoste, *Ibn Khaldoun: Naissance de l'histoire, passé du Tiers-monde*; Aziz al-Azmeh, *Ibn Khaldūn in Modern Scholarship: A Study in Orientalism*; idem, *Ibn Khaldūn: An Essay in Reinterpretation*; Maya Shatzmiller, *L'Historiographie mérinide: Ibn Khaldūn et ses contemporains*; H. T. Norris, *The Berbers in Arabic Literature*, 3–10; Ahmed Abdesselem, *Ibn Khaldūn et ses lecteurs*; Bruce B. Lawrence, ed., *Ibn Khaldun and Islamic Ideology*; and Maya Shatzmiller, *The Berbers and the Islamic State: The Marinid Experience in Pre-Protectorate Morocco*.

66. Bruce B. Lawrence, "Introduction: Ibn Khaldun and Islamic Ideology," in *Ibn Khaldun and Islamic Ideology*, 7–8.

67. Franz Rosenthal, "Ibn Khaldun in His Time (May 27, 1332–March 17, 1406)," in *Ibn Khaldun and Islamic Ideology*, 21.

68. Linda T. Darling, "Social Cohesion ('Aṣabiyya) and Justice in the Late Medieval Middle East," *Comparative Studies in Society and History* 49, no. 2 (2007): 329–57.

69. Gordon D. Newby, "Ibn Khaldun and Frederick Jackson Turner: Islam and the Frontier Experience," in *Ibn Khaldun and Islamic Ideology*, 132.

70. Ibn Khaldūn, *Kitāb al-'ibar*, VII: 3: "The majority of them were in the Central Maghrib, to such a degree that it was associated with them and known for them. Thus, it is called the land of the Zanāta (al-akthar minhum bi'l-maghrib al-awsaṭ ḥattā innahu yunsabu ilayhim wa-yu'rafu bihim fa-yuqālu waṭan al-zanāta)."

71. *EI*², s.v. "Zanāta"; and López-Morillas, "Los Beréberes Zanāta," 304. Ibn Khaldūn, *Kitāb al-'ibar*, VII: 11 and cit. 27: "These Maghrāwa tribes were the largest of the Zanāta groups as well as the most brave and powerful (hā'ulā'i al-qabā'il min maghrāwa kānū awsa'a buṭūn zanāta wa-ahl al-ba's wa'l-ghalab)"; al-Idrīsī (12th c.), *Kitāb nuzhat al-mushtāq fī ikhtirāq al-āfāq*: "The majority of Zanāta are cavalry who ride horses (wa-akthar zanāta fursān yarkabūn al-khayl)"; and Ibn Ḥayyān, *al-Muqtabas*, VII: 192–93, specified that they specialized in light cavalry.

72. *EI*², s.v. "al-Ibāḍiyya."

73. *HEM*, I: 98. Ibn Khaldūn gives two different accounts of the Zanāta's loyalty to the Umayyads leading back to the time of the Caliph 'Uthmān b. 'Affān in Medina. See Ibn Khaldūn, *Kitāb al-'ibar*, VII: 27. On the conflicts with the Fāṭimids, see Ibn Khaldūn, *Kitāb al-'ibar*, VI: 165, 168. See also Ibn 'Idhārī, *al-Bayān al-mughrib*, I: 239–52; and *Mafākhir al-Barbar* [*Fragments historiques sur les Berbères au Moyen Age, extraits inédits d'un receueil anonyme compilé en 712/1312 et intitulé: Kitab Mafakhir al-Barbar*], ed. Évariste Lévi-Provençal, 3–37.

74. Ibn Khaldūn, *Kitāb al-'ibar*, VII: 21: "[Muḥammad b. Abī 'Āmir] relied upon the Zanāta kings to control everything else (mā warā'a dhālika) and obliged them with gifts and honorific robes (khila'). He undertook to honor their arrivals [at court] and enrolled whoever amongst them wished to enroll in the *diwān* of the sultan. Thus, they devoted themselves (jarradū) to the state and the dissemination of its message (bathth al-da'wa)." See *EI*², s.v. "khila'."

75. Ibn Khaldūn, *Kitāb al-'ibar,* VII: 35; Ibn 'Idhārī, *al-Bayān al-mughrib*, I: 252–53.

76. For instance, see Ibn Khaldūn, *Kitāb al-'ibar*, VII: 33, 37–38, and Ibn 'Idhārī, *al-Bayān al-mughrib*, I: 253–54, for the cases of Zīrī b. 'Aṭiyya and al-Mu'izz b. 'Aṭiyya.

77. López-Morillas, "Los Beréberes Zanāta," 305, and *HEM*, I: 98, 206. The first Zanāta transferred to the Umayyad court at Cordoba were fleeing from the Fāṭimids and their Ṣanhāja supporters (Ibn Khaldūn, *Kitāb al-'ibar*, VI: 192–93).

On Berber settlements in al-Andalus, see Pierre Guichard, *Al-Andalus: estructura antropológica de una sociedad islámica en Occidente*; and Helena de Felipe, "Berbers in the Maghreb and al-Andalus: Settlements and Toponymy," *Maghreb Review* 18, no. 1–2 (1993): 57–62. An onomastic study of the *jenets* based on the chancery registers is still called for.

78. M'hammad Benaboud and Ahmad Tahiri. "Berberising Al-Andalus," *Al-Qantara* 11, no. 2 (1990): 475–87.

79. Ibn Khaldūn, *Kitāb al-'ibar*, VII: 61; *Mafākhir al-Barbar*, 43–60. More generally, see *EI*², s.v. "al-Muwaḥḥidun" and "al-Murābiṭūn"; H. T. Norris, "New Evidence on the Life of 'Abdullāh b. Yasīn and the Origins of the Almoravid Movement," *Journal of African History* 12, no. 2 (1971): 255–68; Vincent Lagardère, *Les Almoravides: Jusqu-au règne de Yūsuf b. Tāshfīn*; idem, *Les Almoravides: Le Djihad Andalou (1106–1143)*; Jacinto Bosch Vilá, *Los Almoravides*; Ambrosio Huici Miranda, *Historia política del imperio Almohade*; and Fromherz, *The Almohads*.

80. On the defeat of the Zanāta by the Almoravids, see Ibn Khaldūn, *Kitāb al-'ibar*, VI: 198 and VII: 49.

81. Ibn Khaldūn, *Kitāb al-'ibar*, VII: 52: "lam yazālū 'alā ḥālihim mundhu inqirāḍ zanāta al-awwalīn, wa-hum li-hadhā al-'ahd ahl maghārim wa-'askara ma'a al-duwal."

82. Ibn Khaldūn, *Kitāb al-'ibar*, VII: 63.

83. There is a considerable body of literature debating the concept of the nomad in Ibn Khaldūn: Émile-Félix Gautier, *La Passé de l'Afrique du Nord: Les Siècles obscurs*; Abdallah Laroui, *L'Histoire du Maghreb: Un Essai de synthèse*; Jean Morizot, *L'Aurès ou le myth de la montagne rebelle*; Michael Brett, "Way of the Nomad," *Bulletin of the School of Oriental and African Studies* 58, no. 2 (1995): 251–69; and Maya Shatzmiller, *L'Historiographie mérinide*, 132: "Le *'Ibar* n'est qu'un traitement plus complet du thème du *mafākhir*."

84. *EI*², s.v. "Tilimsān." On the relationship between the Almohads and 'Abd al-Wādids, see Ibn Khaldūn, *Kitāb al-'ibar*, VII: 74, 174.

85. Shatzmiller, *The Berbers and the Islamic State*, 43–54; and Mohammed Kably, *Société, pouvoir et religion au Maroc à la fin de "Moyen-Âge."* More generally, see Ahmed Khaneboubi, *Les Premiers sultans mérinides et l'Islam (1269–1331)*.

86. Ibn Khaldūn, *Kitāb al-'ibar*, VI: 309–11, cit. 310–11: "The Almohads inspired an anxiety in [Abū Zakariyyā, the Ḥafṣid general] regarding the tyranny (istibdād) of Yaghmurāsan and counseled him to create hostility between him and the Zanāta princes of the Central Maghrib, to place obstacles in his plans, and to adorn them [the other Zanāta princes] with the similar tokens of power (albāsahum mā labisa min shārat al-sulṭān wa-ziyyihi)."

87. Robert Brunschvig, *La Berbérie orientale sous les Ḥafṣides des origines à la fin du XV siècle*, I: 50–51; Charles-Emmanuel Dufourcq, *L'Espagne catalane et le Maghreb aux XIIIe et XIVe siècles: De la bataille de Las Navas de Tolosa (1212) à l'avènement du sultan mérinide Abou-l-Hazzan (1331)*, 101–104; and Ramzi

Rouighi, *The Making of a Mediterranean Emirate: Ifrīqiyā and Its Andalusis, 1200–1400*. See also Dominique Valérian, *Bougie, port maghrébin, 1067—1510*.

88. ACA, R. 46, fol. 120r (19 Sep. 1283), records the arrest of certain Christian mercenaries for plotting against the Ḥafṣid sultan. Charles-Emmanuel Dufourcq, "La Couronne d'Aragon et les Hafsides au XIIIe siècle (1229–1301)," *Analecta Sacra Tarraconensia* 25 (1952): 53; and idem, *L'Espagne catalane*, 96, 104, and 262–63. See also Anne-Marie Eddé, Françoise Micheau, and Christophe Picard, *Communautés chrétiennes en pays d'Islam: Du début du VIIe siècle au milieu du XIe siècle*.

89. ACA, R. 47, fols. 81r–82v (June 1285). See also Louis de Mas Latrie, *Traités de paix et de commerce et documents divers concernant les relations des chrétiens avec les arabes de l'Afrique septentrionale au moyen âge*, 286ff; and Brunschvig, *Berbérie orientale*, I: 96.

90. See EI^2, s.v. " 'Abd al-Wādids."

91. Ibn Khaldūn, *Kitāb al-'ibar*, VII: 88–89, 192, on the Battle of Īslī (1271). See also Dufourcq, *L'Espagne catalane*, 314ff.

92. Ibn Khaldūn, *Kitāb al-'ibar*, VII: 223: "Yaghmurāsan appointed his son, 'Uthmān, his successor, and it is said that (za'amū anna) he advised him not to allow himself (lā yuḥddithu nafsahu) to be drawn into battle with the Marīnids or a contest against them (musāmātihim fi'l-ghalab) and not to expose himself on their territory in the desert, but to take refuge (yalūdh) behind walls until they summon him [to battle]."

93. ACA, R. 19, fol. 6r: "Nos ab vos et vos ab nos et puis que romanga aquella pau entrels vestres fills et los nostres en tal manera que vos nos façatz <aiuda> a prendre Cepta et que nos envietz X naus armades et X galees et entre altres lenys et barques que sien a summa de L. . . . Et quens envietz D entre cavallers et homnes de linyatge." See also Dufourcq, *L'Espagne catalane*, 164.

94. Ibn Khaldūn, *Kitāb al-'ibar*, VII: 199 (first expedition); ibid., VII: 203–4 (second expedition); ibid., VII: 213–14 (third expedition); ibid., VII: 215–17 (fourth expedition). For the fourth expedition, see also Muḥammad b. Aḥmad Ibn Marzūq, *al-Musnad al-ṣaḥīḥ al-ḥasan fī ma'āthir wa-maḥāsin mawlānā Abī'l-Ḥasan*, ed. M. J. Viguera, 115, which gives slightly different dates. Lisān al-Dīn Ibn al-Khaṭīb, *al-Lamḥa al-badriyya fi'l-dawla al-Naṣriyya*, ed. Aḥmad 'Āṣī and Muḥibb al-Dīn al-Khaṭīb, 54–55, says only that Abū Yūsuf crossed over three or more times. See also Miguel Ángel Manzano Rodríguez, *La intervención de los Benimerines en la Península Ibérica*, esp. 42–44, 52–54.

95. Anonymous, *al-Dhakhīra al-saniyya*, 143–46, cit. 145–46. Although the translation is my own, the edition of the *Dhakhīra* available to me excludes three lines from the edition employed by L. P. Harvey, *Islamic Spain, 1250 to 1500*, 155–56. See also Ibn Khaldūn, *Kitāb al-'ibar*, VII: 199, which states these troops were salaried (istawfaw 'aṭā'ahum), meaning that they were not volunteers.

96. Ibn Khaldūn, *Kitāb al-'ibar*, VII: 201: "Looking to establish a city along the shore for the purpose of housing his troops, isolated from civilians (ra'iyya) so that

they would be protected from the depredations (ḍarar) of the army. So, he chose a place near Algeciras (al-Jazīra) and ordered the construction of the city known as al-Binya." For more detail on al-Binya, see the extensive research of Antonio Torremocha Silva, including his *Algeciras entre la cristianidad y el islam: estudio sobre el cerco y conquista de Algeciras por el rey Alfonso XI de Castilla, así como de la ciudad y sus términos hasta el final de la Edad Media*; and idem, "Al-Binya: la ciudad palaciega merini en Al-Andalus," in *Ciudad y territorio en Al-Andalus*, ed. Maria del Carmen Barceló Torres, 283–330.

97. Ibn Khaldūn, *Kitāb al-'ibar*, VII: 200–201; anonymous, *al-Dhakhīra al-saniyya*, 146–47, gives more detail on the devastation wrought on the frontier by these troops.

98. ACA, R. 61, fol. 108v (27 Apr. 1283): "Fratri [Raimundo] de Ribelle, castellano Emposte, quia pro certo didicimus janetos et familiam bellatorum Regis Marrochorum et aliorum plurium venturos in brevi pro inferendo dampno in Regno Valencie, vobis dicimus et rogamus ac vos requirimus et monemus quatenus paretis vos et milites vostros, armis, victualibus, et aliis apparatibus ad defendendum Regnum predictum. Ita quod prima die proxime venturi mensis Iunii sitis in dicto Regno ip[so] ab inimicorum incursibus defensuri. Datum Cesarauguste, V kalendas Madii."

99. Ibn Khaldūn, *Kitāb al-'ibar*, VII: 218. These books were packed onto mules and delivered to the sultan. King Jaume, for his part, showed an interest in acquiring any Arabic book. See ACA, R. 50, fol. 132v (Aug. 1281): "[M]osse Ravaya quod libros Sarra<cenicos> navis illius quam cepit Petro de Villario non vendat, scilicet eos dom[ino] Regi reservet." See also Ibn Abī Zar', *Rawḍ al-qirṭās*, 376, and *Crónica del rey don Sancho el Bravo* in *Cronicas de los reyes de Castilla*, ed. Cayetano Rosell, 80.

100. Ibn Khaldūn, *Kitāb al-'ibar*, VII: 219; Ibn Abī Zar', *Rawḍ al-qirṭās*, 376. See also Manzano Rodríguez, *La intervención*, 125–31.

101. De Slane, Arié, Harvey, and others misleading call them "The Volunteers of the Faith." In fact, as Arié herself explains, they were a combination of salaried and unsalaried troops. In Naṣrid sources, such as those of Ibn al-Khaṭīb, they are not called the Ghuzāh but rather the Western Army (al-jund al-gharbī), "western" used here in the sense of "from the Maghrib."

102. See chapter 6 for a full discussion of the Ghuzāh.

103. Generally, see Ibn Khaldūn, *Kitāb al-'ibar*, VII: 379–93. For the revolt, see Ibn Khaldūn, *Kitāb al-'ibar*, VII: 185–86, 383; Ibn al-Khaṭīb, *Iḥāṭa fī akhbār Gharnāṭa*, ed. Muḥammad 'Abd Allāh 'Inān, IV: 77; Ibn Abī Zar', *Rawḍ al-qirṭās*, 303; and anonymous, *al-Dhakhīra al-saniyya*, 98.

104. Implicit here is a rivalry between different strands of the royal family. Abū Yūsuf traced his descent through Umm al-Yumn, the last wife of 'Abd al-Ḥaqq, and mother of Ya'qūb. These three princes traced their line to Ṣawṭ al-Nisā', who Ibn Khaldūn once calls the daughter of 'Abd al-Ḥaqq and on another occasion, his

wife. See Ibn Khaldūn, *Kitāb al-'ibar*, VII: 177, 186, 383, 379–80; and anonymous, *al-Dhakhīra al-saniyya*, 20.

105. Ibn Khaldūn, *Kitāb al-'ibar*, VII: 186.

106. Kably, *Société, pouvoir et religion*, 86–87.

107. Ibn Khaldūn, *Kitāb al-'ibar*, VII: 198. See also anonymous, *al-Dhakhīra al-saniyya*, 98.

108. See also Kably, *Société, pouvoir et religion*, 84.

109. Ibn Khaldūn, *Kitāb al-'ibar*, VII: 191. See also Ibn Abī Zar', *Rawḍ al-qirṭās*, 303; Ibn Marzūq, *al-Musnad*, 101; and anonymous, *Dhakhīra al-saniyya*, 98.

110. Ibn Marzūq, *al-Musnad*, 394, explains that in the time of the Marīnid sultan Abū'l-Ḥasan (r. 1331–1348), among the duties of the Naṣrid sultan was to supply the Marīnid Zanāta troops with money and supplies, including a yearly shipment of five hundred equipped horses. Cf. J. F. P. Hopkins, *Medieval Muslim Government in Barbary until the End of the Sixth Century of the Hijra*, 53–55, 75–78, on the use of Christian militia to collect taxes.

111. Manzano Rodríguez, *La intervención*, 336: "Sí podría resultar que la figure del *šayj al-ghuzā* evolucionara desde una condición de mero título distintivo al principio, para convertirse después en una institución propria del ejército nazarí."

112. See chapter 6 for more detail.

113. Luis del Mármol Carvajal, *Historia del rebellion y castigo de los Moriscos del reyno de Granada*, I: 29–30, as cited in Manzano Rodríguez, *La intervención*, 333.

114. Manzano Rodríguez, *La intervención*, 327; and Kably, *Société, pouvoir et religion*, 86.

115. Ibn Khaldūn, *Kitāb al-'ibar*, VII: 191.

116. Ibn Khaldūn, *Kitāb al-'ibar*, VII: 191; Ibn al-Khaṭīb, *Iḥāṭa*, I: 136; and idem, *al-Lamḥa*, 39. See chapter 6 for more detail.

117. Ibn Khaldūn, *Kitāb al-'ibar*, VII: 117–18. He fell into a rivalry with the Christian renegade and mercenary captain, Hilāl the Catalan.

118. Ibn al-Khaṭīb, *al-Lamḥa*, 39: "junduhum ṣinfān: andalusī wa-barbarī."

119. Ibn al-Khaṭīb, *al-Lamḥa*, 39.

120. Ibn al-Khaṭīb, *al-Lamḥa*, 39: "The majority rarely wears the dress of this country."

121. Ibn al-Khaṭīb, *al-Lamḥa*, 39: "The weapons of the majority are the long rod folded by a short rod with a handle in its middle that is thrown by the fingertips and called the amdās." See also Reinhart Pieter Anne Dozy, *Supplément aux dictionnaires arabes*, s.v. "dassa," which cites the same text.

122. Ibn al-Khaṭīb, *al-Lamḥa*, 39.

123. See Ibn Sa'īd al-Andalusī, as cited in Aḥmad b. Muḥammad al-Maqqarī, *Nafḥ al-ṭīb min ghuṣn al-Andalus al-raṭīb wa-dhikr wazīrihā Lisān al-Dīn al-Khaṭīb*, ed. Muḥammad Muḥyī al-Dīn 'Abd al-Ḥamīd, I: 207–208. Confirmed by Emilio García Gómez, *Ibn Zamrak, el poeta de la Alhambra*, 14–17, esp. 16n1.

Viguera Molins, "La organización militar," 37–38, agreed that the Iberian Muslims abandoned light cavalry and adopted the strategies of their Christian neighbors to the north until the arrival of North African troops in the thirteenth century.

124. Ibn al-Khaṭīb, *al-Lamḥa*, 39: "As for the Andalusi, a close relative (al-qarāba) or man of prominence in the state leads as their captain. Previously, their uniform (ziyyuhum) was like that of their neighbors and Christian counterparts (jīrānihim wa-amthālihim min al-rūm) with regards to wearing long coats of mail (al-durūʿ), suspending their shields (al-tirasa), using unadorned helmets (al-bayḍāt), a preference for metal lances (ittikhād al-ʿirāḍ al-asinna), having misshapen pommels (qarābīs al-surūj) on their saddles, and placing their standard-bearers (ḥamalat al-rāyāt) on horses (istirkāb) behind them. Each one of them had a mark that distinguished his weapons and made him known to others. Now, they have moved away from this uniform, using shorter chain mail (al-jawāshin al-mukhtaṣara), gilded helmets (al-bayḍa al-mudhahhaba), Arab saddles (al-surūj al-ʿarabiyya), lamṭī shields, and light lances." See Dozy, *Supplément aux dictionnaires arabes*, s.v. "lamṭ." The lamṭī shield was a round leather shield used by North African cavalry.

125. See also *Cantigas de Santa Maria*, fols. 68v (Cantiga 46), 240r (Cantiga 181), and 246v (Cantiga 187).

126. Arié, *L'Espagne musulmane*, 250.

127. See, for instance, the cases of Badr al-Dīn b. Mūsā b. Raḥḥū, Jamāl al-Dīn b. Mūsā b. Raḥḥū, and Idrīs b. ʿUthmān b. Abī al-ʿUlā, discussed in chapter 6.

128. See chapters 2, 5, and particularly 6 for more detail about these figures.

129. As Echevarría, *Caballeros en la frontera*, demonstrates, Marīnid princes, some of whom converted to Christianity, also served the Castilian kings in the fifteenth century.

Chapter Two

1. Part of this chapter appeared previously in Hussein Fancy, "Theologies of Violence: The Recruitment of Muslim Soldiers by the Crown of Aragon," *Past & Present* 221, no. 1 (2013): 39–73.

2. On the peace treaty, see Muntaner, *Crònica*, chaps. 41, 47.

3. ACA, R. 52, fol. 66v (28 Oct. 1284): "Bernardo Scribe, mandamus vobis quatenus per Raimundum de Rivosicco faciatis tradi nobili Corrado Lancee, [h]ostiar[io] maiori ac magistro racionali domus nostre, Sarracenos captivos quos ipse tenet, qui s[unt] de terra [Re]gis Granate, et unicuique dictorum Saracenorum faciatis dari predictum Raimundum [t]unicam et ex[p]ensarium usque ad dictum Regem Granate. . . ."

4. ACA, R. 43, fol. 82r (10 Dec. 1284): "Viro nobili et dilecto Conrado Lancee, maiori host[i]ario nostro ac magistro racionali curie nostre, mandamus quatenus

incontenenti cum fuerit Granate, certificens vos si Beregenarius Bovis vel marinarii sui et lignum suum et homines Guillelmi Moliner et lignum suum cives Valencie fuerunt capti et detenti per aliquos de dominacione Regis Granate et ipsos cum eorum [b]onis et quoslibet alios de dominacione nostra quos inveneritis fuisse captos et detentes per aliquos de dominacione dicti Regis Granate sub pace et treuga, recuperetis et dicto Rege Granate secundum quod [iam] super hoc fecistis memoriale."

5. ACA, R. 52, fol. 66v (28 Oct. 1284): ". . . Preterea volumus quod per Abrahim Abençumada, Sar[ra]cenum alaminum nostrum, faciatis dari dicto Corrado Lancee //III// tria millia solidorum regale Valencie de denariis quos ipse recipit et pro nobis colligit de Sarracenis montanarum dicti Regni Valencie pro expensis et necessariis suis quas ipsum facere oportet in viatico quod pro nobis facit ad Regem Granate, et per presentes litteras mandamus dicto Raimundo de Rivosicco quod dicta III millia solidorum in compotum recipiat sibi Abrahim superius nominato. Datum Tirasone, V kalendas Novembris." Cf. Gazulla, "Zenetes," 177n1.

6. ACA, R. 47, fol. 130v (28 Oct. 1284): "Sepan todos que nos don Pedro, por la gracia de Dios de Aragon et de Sicilia Rey, estableçemos procurador nuestro sp[ecia]l vos noble et amado nuestro Corral Lança, Portero Mayor de nuestra casa, et M[a]estro Racional, a faular con los cabos de los genetes et con los otros sobre fecho de lur venida et morada con nos en nuestro servicio, et sobre aquello que ende les auremos de dar, prometemos nos aver por firme qual que cosa por el dicho Corral en aquello sera dicho et fecho o prometido de nuestra parte, et aquello observaremos. E por que aquesta carta sea firme, et non vienga en dubda, mandamos la seellar con nuestra siel pendient. Dato en Taracona, XXVIII dias andados de Octubre, anno domini M CC LXXX, quarto." Cf. Gazulla, "Zenetes," 178. This text also appears at ACA, R. 47, fol. 130r in Castilian.

7. At the same time, a second mission, under the command of Petrus Andosiella, embarked to the ʿAbd al-Wādid court. Andosiella was issued "letter of credence" at the same time as Conrad, and perhaps he had the same goal. There is no evidence of this mission's completion or of its exact purpose. ACA, R. 47, fol. 130v (28 Oct. 1284): "Item fecimus cartam de credencia Eximino Petris Dandossiella apud Regem de Tirimçe. Datum ut supra, vocatur Rex Hatum[an], fijo de Gameraça Benzayen." "Rex Hatuman" refers to Abū Saʿīd ʿUthmān b. Yaghmurāsan (r. 1282–1304). See also ACA, R. 52, fol. 67r (30 Oct. 1284): "Bernardo Scribe, mandamus vobis quatenus per Raimundum de Rivo Sicco faciatis dari incontinenti nobili Corrado Lancee, hostiario maiori domus nostre ac magistro racionali, D solidos regalium qui per eum tradantur Eximino Petri de Andosiella pro legatione nostra apud Regem de Tremiçe si dicto Corrado visum fuerit, quod legatio perfici debeat supradicta, preterea faciatis dari per eundem Riamundum predicto Eximino Petri de Andosiella CC solidos regalium pro vestibus. Datum Tirasone, III kalendas Novembris."

8. Gazulla, "Zenetes," 174: "Jaime I no se sirvió de estas milicias en sus guerras, al menos no hallo indicios que den lugar a sospecharlo."

9. Burns, *Diplomatarium*, esp. introduction; and Martínez-Ferrando, *El archivo de la corona de Aragón*, esp. chap. 2.

10. ACA, R. 17, fol. 57r–v (13 Oct. 1265):

Item pro expensis Janetorum—CCCLXXXVI solidos, VI denarios. . . .
Item pro vestibus Janetorum—DCCCCIII solidos
Item pro vestibus nunciorum Janetorum—LXXXVI solidos
Item pro pannis Janetorum—XXXV solidos
Item CXL solidos, VI denarios pro pannis et aflabays [from Ar. *al-jubba*] et custuris
Item pro sabates Janetorum—XV solidos
Item pro camisis Janetorum—XXXV solidos
Item pro custuris—VIII solidos VIII denarios
Item pro camisis nunciorum Janetorum—V solidos, VIII denarios
Item pro aflabays et custuris—IX solidos, VIII denarios.

11. ACA, R. 17, fol. 57v (13 Oct. 1265): "Item pro q[ui]tacio[ne] alfaquimi domini Infantis."

12. ACA, R. 17, fol. 57r (13 Oct. 1265): "Item Sarraceno domini Infantis pro tunica—XI solidos, VII denarios."

13. María Teresa Ferrer i Mallol, "Évolution du statut de la minorité islamique dans les pays de la Couronne catalano-aragonaise au XIVe siècle," in *Le Partage du monde: Échanges et colonisation dans la Méditerranée medieval*, ed. Michel Balard and Alain Ducellier, 451; idem, *Els sarraïns de la corona catalano-aragonesa en el segle XIV: segregació i discriminació*, 31, 161–62, 167–68; and idem, *La frontera*, 158, 198. For the case of Castile in the fifteenth century, see Echevarría, *Caballeros en la Frontera*.

14. ACA, R. 52, fol. 57r (29 Aug. 1284): "Bernardo Scr[ibe] quod det vel assignet Muçe, genet, LIII solidos IIII denarios iaccenses qui sibi remanent [ad] solvendum de quitacione Albarrasini. Datum Turole, IIII kalendas Septembris."

15. ACA, R. 52, fol. 54v (15 Aug. 1284): "Raimundo de Rivo Sicco quod det expensas Axie, uxorem Abdaluhafet, janeti qui est in servicio Regis, in veniendo [de] Elx usque ad Valenciam. Datum ut supra."

16. ACA, R. 52, fol. 68v (4 Nov. 1284): "Berengario de Conques, baiulo Valencie. Mandamus vobis quatenus solvatis Petro Bertrandi habitatori Valencie sexcentos XXX solidos regalium Valencie, quos Mahomat Abulhaye et Mançor Abenmudaffar et Abrahim Abehalmema, sarraceni janeti [qui] in nostro servicio venerant, sibi debebant cum duobus publicis instrumentis, quorum unum est moriscum et aliud christianite scriptum, que nos recuperavimus ab eodem. Et mandamus per presentes fideli nostro Raimundo de Rivo Sicco, quod de precio baiulie Valencie a vobis ipsos denarios in compotum recipiat. Datum Ces[arau]g[uste], II nonas Novembris." Cf. Gazulla, "Zenetes," 178–79, who mentions another document from 1284.

17. Albert de Circourt, *Histoire des Mores mudejares et des Morisques, ou des Arabes d'Espagne sous la domination des chrétiens*, esp. I: 257; and Luis Querol y Roso, *Las milicias valencianas desde el siglo xiii al xv: contribución al estudio de la organización militar del antiguo reino de Valencia*. For his part, Circourt considered the Mudéjares exempt from the army, the key to their success under the Crown of Aragon. Both Burns, *Islam under the Crusaders*, esp. 289–94, and Boswell, *Royal Treasure*, 185–92, have definitively shown that Mudéjares were expected to service in the Crown's army. A series of relevant documents is presented in Mercédes García-Arenal and Béatrice Leroy, *Moros y judíos en Navarra en la baja Edad Media*, esp. 77–78. See also Ferrer i Mallol, *La frontera*, 31–35; Catlos, *Victors and the Vanquished*, 263; and Echevarría, *Caballeros en la frontera*, 99.

18. AHN, Ordines militares, codex 542, Montesa (28 Apr. 1234): "Contra sarracenos alios aut christianos nisi forte aliqui sarraceni aut christiani facerent aliquod maleffìcium vel forciam vel gravamen casto suo et rebus; et tunc mauri Exiverti una cum fratribus deffenderent se suaque secundum posse suum." Tomás Muñoz y Romero, *Colección de fueros municipales y cartas pueblas de los reinos de Castilla, León, Corona de Aragón y Navarra*, 416: "Et non faciat exire moro in appellito per forza in guerra de moros nec de christianos." Burns, *Islam under the Crusaders*, 119; and Boswell, *Royal Treasure*, 171, 272.

19. For instance, see ACA, R. 10, fol. 77r–v (16 June 1258); ACA, R. 12, fol. 124v (Oct. 1263); ACA, R. 14, fol. 109r (21 Jan. 1271); and ACA, R. 46, fol. 221r (9 July 1284). See Catlos, *The Victors and the Vanquished*, 129–30, on the Mudéjar claims for exemption (*franquitas*).

20. ACA, R. 11, fol. 154r (7 Oct. 1259).

21. ACA, R. 43, fol. 105v (18 Jan. 1285), makes it clear that the Mudéjares of Valencia were under a feudal obligation to appear for service: "Universis aliamis Sarracenorum nostrorum Regni Valencie citra Rivum Xucare ad quos presentes pervenerint, salutem et graciam. Cum racione negociorum in quibus sum[us] arduorum sicut scitis et in estate proxima esse speramus, nos deceat nostros exercitus facere preparari ac etiam congregari ut possimus resistere nostris hostibus qui <cominati> sunt indebite aufferre nobis regna nostra, nostrum nomine regium inmutando, fidelitatem vestram attente requirimus ac vobis dicimus et mandamus quatenus visis hostentibus paretis vestris cum [a]rmis et aliis apparatibus vestras et pane ad quatuor menses. Ita quod in medio mensis Aprilis proximo venturi sitis nobiscum ubicumque vobis [tunc] duxerimus in[iu]ngendum, ut similiter vobiscum possimus dictos hostes nostros offendere d[ivino] auxilio mediante. Scientes quod de dicto exercitu vos excusavissemus liberter si illud bono modo fieri potuisset. Datum in Monte Regali XV kalendas Februarii. Similiter litera missa sint universis aliamis Sarracenorum Regni Valencie ultra Rivum Xucari." See also Echevarría, *Caballeros en la frontera*, 99, for the case of the Mudéjares of Ávila.

22. ACA, R. 57, fol. 203r (13 Sep. 1285), an order to the procurator of Valencia to not compel any Muslim present at the defense of Gerona to contribute to the

war tax. ACA, R 62, fol. 81v (7 Sep. 1284), the Mudéjares of Almonezir were exempted from certain debts they accrued during the period that they served on the Navarrese front: "Guillelmo Else, intelleximus quod racione oblig[acion]is quam asseritis vobis fuisse factam per //no// nobilem Petrum Cornelii de Castro and Villa de Almonezir racione cuiusdam peccunie quantitatis quam dictus nobilis vobis debet ut dicitur pig[n]orastis et etiam pignoratis Sarracen[os] de Almonezir. Unde cum dicti Sarraceni sint in servicio domini Regis et nostro in hunc exercitum quem dominus Rex proponit facere contra regnum Navarre, mandamus vobis ex parte domini Regis et nostra quatenus dictos Sarracenos non pignoretis dum fuerint in dicto servicio. Immo restituatis eisdem [...]qua pignora eis fecistis. Dominus [..] Rex faciet ipsos vobis stare iuri super omnibus querimoniis quas habeatis contra eos." Similarly, see ACA, Perg., Pere II, 117, no. 485 (26 June 1285), as cited in Catlos, *Victors and the Vanquished*, 264.

23. ACA, R. 58, fol. 101v (12 July 1285): ". . . Item ex alia parte salvistis et tradidistis nobis ultra sumam predictam quatuor millia trescentos nonaginta tres solidos et quatuor denarios regalium Valencie in uno sacco quos alyame Sarracenorum Regni Valencie mitebant per vos Sarracenis quos miserant ad servicium nostrum racione dicti exercitus pro eorum salario et expensis [requisitis]."

24. Mudéjar crossbowmen are mentioned several times in this early period: ACA, R. 33, fol. 63v; ACA, R. 34, fol.4v; ACA, R. 34, fol. 26r; ACA, R. 34, fol. 30r; ACA, R. 34, fol. 32v; ACA, R. 37, fol. 48r; ACA, R. 46, fol. 176v; and ACA, R. 65, fol. 20r. They also appear during the war against France and the Aragonese *Unions*, both of which are mentioned below. See also Torró Abad, *El naixement d'una colònia*, 38–42; Derek W. Lomax, *La Orden de Santiago, 1170–1275*, 127; and Soler de Campo, *La evolución del armamento*, 61–75.

25. ACA, R. 46, fol. 44v (8 July 1280): "Fideli suo Raimundo de Alos, baiulo Ilerde, salutem et graciam, mandamus vobis quatenus Mahometo, fabro de Barbastrie, qui veniet coram nobis detis unam fabricam cum omnibus apparamentis ferraiie et ferrum ad sufficientiam qui operabitur cairells et alia opera ferrea ad opus nostri et eidem dum operabitur ad opus nostri provideatis in suis necessariis. Datum in Obsidione Balagerii, VIII idus Iulii." See also García-Arenal and Leroy, *Moros y judíos en Navarra en la baja Edad Media*, 27–28, on making metal weapons.

26. ACA, R. 89, fol. 172r (13 Apr. 1295).

27. *Llibre dels feyts*, chap. 362: "E nos estan en Ualencia uench nos lalcait de Xatiua ab gran companya de sarrains e dels ueyls de la vila ben X, e entra molt alegrament denant nos, e besans la ma, e dix nos con nos anaua? E nos dixem que be, la merce de Deu: e quens pesaua molt lo mal quens hauia feyt Alazrat en nostres castells, e quens maraueylauem con ho soffrien ells. Seyor, si mal uos fa negu sapiats quens pesa molt ens es greu: e nos ueem los molt alegres e pagats, que anch nuyl temps nols hauiem uists tan alegres ne tan pagats. E nos nos cuydam quels pesas lo mal quens hauia feit Alazrat, e quens prefferissen aiuda, anch aiuda negu dels nons profferiren."

28. ACA, R. 33, fols. 104v–105r, records the payments of several Mudéjar communities for the army going to Valencia. ACA, R. 39, fol. 227v (28 July 1277), as cited in Catlos, *Victors and the Vanquished*, 264, gives the Mudéjares of Alagón the choice of serving or paying the king 1000 *solidi*. See also Ferran Soldevila, *Pere el Gran*, II: 1, doc. 83 (25 July 1277), as cited in Burns, *Islam under the Crusaders*, 289.

29. ACA, R. 39, fol. 223r (2 Aug. 1277).

30. See Helene Wieruszowski, "La Corte di Pietro d'Aragona e i precedenti dell'impresa Siciliana," *Archivio storico italiano* 16 (1938): 192–94, esp. 194n3; and Muntaner, *Crònica*, chap. 18.

31. ACA, R. 40, fol. 95r (13 May 1278).

32. Burns, *Islam under the Crusaders*, 323–32; Muntaner, *Crònica*, chap. 31.

33. Muntaner, *Crònica*, chap. 31. ACA, R. 46, fol. 120r–v, instructions for an embassy, recording the deteriorating relationship with Tunis. See also Dufourcq, *L'Espagne catalane*, 238ff.

34. Muntaner, *Crònica*, chap. 30; Dufourcq, *L'Espagne catalane*, 240; and idem, "La Couronne d'Aragon et les Hafsides," 10.

35. ACA, R. 44, fol. 160v (14 Nov. 1279): ". . . damus et concedemus vobis dicto Conrado Lancee et vestris inperpetuum . . . castrum villam villas et alcariis omnes de albayda." ACA, R. 42, fol. 214r (Jan. 1280), the first mention of Lancia as governor. Cf. ARV, Justicia de Valencia, 1, fol. 27r (1280), which refers to him as a "lieutenant procurator"; and ARV, Justicia de Valencia, 1bis, fol. 15v (1280), which refers to him as "procurador en tot lo Regne de Valencia." See also Dufourcq, *L'Espagne catalane*, 201, 244.

36. ACA, R. 52, fol. 67r (1 Nov. 1284): ". . . hostiario maiori domus nostre ac magistro rationali. . . ."

37. For more detail about this figure, see David Romano, "Los hermanos Abenmenassé al servicio de Pedro el Grande de Aragón," *Homenaje a Millás Vallicrosa* 1 (1956): 249; and Hussein Fancy, "The Intimacy of Exception: The Diagnosis of Samuel Abenmenassé," in *Center and Periphery: Studies on Power in the Medieval World in Honor of William Chester Jordan*, ed. Katherine L. Jansen, G. Geltner, and Anne E. Lester, 65–75.

38. ACA, R. 43, fol. 129v (13 Feb. 1279): ". . . fideli nostro Samueli, filio Abrahim Bonnemaiz, in vita vestra alfaquimatum nostrum et scribaniam nostram de arabico. Ita quod vos in vita vestra sitis alfaquimus et fisicus noster et de domo nostra et scriptor noster maior de arabico dum bene et legaliter vos in ipsis officiis habeatis." See also David Romano, "Judíos, escribanos y trujamanes de árabe en la Corona de Aragón (reinados de Jaime I a Jaime II)," *Sefarad* 38 (1978): 73–77; Joaquín Miret y Sans, "Les médecins Juifs de Pierre, roi d'Aragon," *Revue des études juives* 57 (1909): 268–78; and J. Lee Shneidman, "Jews in the Royal Administration of 13th Century Aragón," *Historia Judaica* 21 (1959): 37–52.

39. ACA, R. 56, fol. 93v (4 May 1285): ". . . e lo al que nos en viastes dezir de la salud e del estamiento de dona Agnes e de la otra companyna nuestra que son

aqui, gradeçemos vos lo muyto e pregamos vos que toda via nos lo fagades saber." See also Romano, "Los hermanos Abenmenassé," 292. Doña Agnes was a concubine of King Pere II.

40. ACA, R. 43, fol. 129v (my emphasis): ". . . scriptor noster *maior* de arabico."

41. ACA, R. 48, fol. 6v (28 Apr. 1280): "In Algezira sigillavimus quandam literam Sarracenicam que ut Samuel Alfaquimus dixit erat recognitionis Sarraceorum Xative. . . ."

42. ACA, R. 47, fol. 41r (30 Apr. 1282): ". . . tradidimus Samueli alphaquimo cartam pacis Regis Granate latine et arabice scriptam." Cf. Helene Wieruszowski, "Conjuraciones y alianzas políticas del Rey Pedro de Aragón contra Carlos de Anjou antes de las vísperas Sicilianas," *Boletín de la Real Academia de la Historia* 107 (1935): 583; Dufourcq, *L'Espagne catalane*, 205.

43. Romano, "Los hermanos Abenmenassé," 258–60.

44. ACA, R. 42, fol. 208v (18 Jan. 1279).

45. ACA, R. 46, fol. 100v (8 Aug. 1284): ". . . saber asso trametem nos lo feal alphaquim nostre do Samuel quius dira nostre enteniment sobre asso per queus pregam eus manam que aquels de cascuna de les vostres aliames quel dit alphaquim nostre elegira a asso nos trametats ab companya de balesters et de lancers de cascuna daqueles aliames be aparelats et be adobats et nos darem a aquels bona soldada." Cf. edition in *Colección de documentos inéditos del Archivo de la Corona de Aragón*, ed. Próspero Bofarull y Mascaró, VI: 196.

46. Romano, "Los hermanos Abenmenassé," 265–68.

47. For the relations between Aragon and Sicily, see Wieruszowski, "Conjuraciones y alianzas políticas"; idem, "La Corte di Pietro"; J. Lee Shneidman, "Aragon and the War of the Sicilian Vespers," *Historian* 22, no. 3 (1960): 250–63; and David Abulafia, *The Western Mediterranean Kingdoms, 1200–1500*.

48. On the marriage, see Muntaner, *Crònica*, chap. 1; and Luc d'Achery, ed., *Spicilegium: sive, Collectio veterum aliquot scriptorum qui in Galliae bibliothecis delituerant*, III: 644.

49. Muntaner, *Crònica*, chap. 17.

50. Pere wrote a letter to Louis, disavowing any such intention. See Julián Paz de Espéso, *Documentos relativos a España existentes en los Archivos Nacionales de Paris*, doc. 87, as cited in Shneidman, "Sicilian Vespers," 254. See also Soldevila, *Pere el Gran*, I: 93; and Robert Ignatius Burns, "Warrior Neighbors: Alfonso El Sabio and Crusader Valencia, An Archival Case Study in His International Relations," *Viator* 21, no. 1 (1990): 156–62.

51. The Hohenstaufen pretender to the throne was Conradin, "Little Conrad," son of Conrad IV (1222–54), a brother of Manfred. Wieruszowski, "Conjuraciones," 579; and David Abulafia, "The Kingdom of Sicily Under the Hohenstaufen and Angevins," in *The New Cambridge Medieval History, c. 1198–1300*, ed. David Abulafia, V: 508.

52. Giuseppe La Mantia, *Codice diplomatico dei re Aragonesi di Sicilia: Pietro I, Giacomo, Federico II, Pietro II e Ludovico, Dalla rivoluzione Siciliana del 1282*

sino al 1355, 558; and Wieruszowski, "La Corte di Pietro," 149. For the history for Christian militias in North Africa, see chapter 4.

53. Burns, "Renegades," 350–53; Wieruszowski, "La Corte di Pietro," 192–95; Brunschvig, *La Berbérie orientale*, I: 53; Dufourcq, *L'Espagne catalane*, 200–202, 240–45; Michel Mollat, "Le 'Passage' de Saint Louis à Tunis: Sa place dans l'histoire des croisades," *Revue d'histoire des doctrines économique et sociale* 50, no. 4 (1972): 301; and Gual de Torrella, "Milicias cristianas en Berbería," 58.

54. Shneidman, "Sicilian Vespers," 256–57.

55. Wieruszowski, "La Corte di Pietro," 196.

56. Helene Wieruszowski, *Politics and Culture in Medieval Spain and Italy*; idem, "The Rise of the Catalan Language in the 13th Century," *Modern Language Notes* (1944): 9–20; Hans Schadek, "Die Familiaren der Sizilischen und Aragonischen Könige im 12. und 13. Jahrhundert," *Spanische Forschungen der Görresgesellschaft: Gesammelte Aufsätze zur Kulturgeschichte Spaniens* 26 (1971): 201–348; Marta VanLandingham, *Transforming the State: King, Court and Political Culture in the Realms of Aragon, 1213–1387*; and Fabrizio Titone, "Aragonese Sicily as a Model of Late Medieval State Building," *Viator* 44, no. 1 (2013): 217–50.

57. For instance, ACA, R. 50, fol. 132v (Aug. 1281): "[M]osse Ravaya quod libros Sarra<cenicos> navis illius quam cepit Petro de Villario non vendat, scilicet eos dom[ino] Regi reservet." Cf. Wieruszowski, "Quelques documents," 178, no. 6; Dufourcq, *L'Espagne catalane*, 240; *Documents per l'història de la cultura catalana mig-eval*, ed. Antonio Rubió y Lluch, I: nos. 269, 313, 334.

58. VanLandingham, *Transforming the State*, 118; and Àngels Masiá i de Ros, "El Maestre Racional en la Corona de Aragón," *Hispania* 10 (1950): 25–60; J. Lalinde Abadía, "Contabilidad e intervención en el Reino aragonés," *Estudios de Hacienda Pública* (1976): 39–55; and Tomàs de Montagut i Estragués, *El Mestre Racional a la Corona d'Aragó (1283–1419)*.

59. VanLandingham, *Transforming the State*, 9; and Barry Charles Rosenmann, "The Royal Tombs in the Monastery of Santes Creus."

60. Pietro Edido, *La colonia saracena di Lucera e la sua distruzione*; Julie Anne Taylor, *Muslims in Medieval Italy: The Colony at Lucera*; and Alex Metcalfe, *The Muslims of Medieval Italy*.

61. Wiersuzowski, "Conjuraciones y alianzas," 547: "Desde el año 1279 toda su política exterior tiende forjar la grande alianza para la lucha contra Carlos de Anjou y la reconquista del Sicilia." See also Abulafia, *The Western Mediterranean Kingdoms*, xvi.

62. Wiersuzowski, "Conjuraciones y alianzas," esp. 583–87. For more on these events in Tunis, see chapter 4.

63. Ferrer i Mallol, "La organización militar," 194–98.

64. Ferrer i Mallol, "La organización militar," 196.

65. Occitan and Catalan troubadours sparred back and forth. The court jongleur, Pere Salvatge, penned two poems in Pere's defense. See Martín de Riquer, *Los trovadores: historia literaria y textos*, III: 1590–1600.

66. ACA, R. 47, fol. 130r (28 Oct. 1284): "Item fecimus ei cartas credencie inferius nominatis/Abzultan Hademi, alguazir del Rey de Granada/Muça Abenrrohh/Guillelmo Nehot, consul d'Almeria/Raiz Abuabdille Abenhudeyr, seynnor de Crivelen/ad Iça Abenadriz, catiu del Rey/Raimundo de Santo Literio/Petro Morelle quod traderet Raimundo de Santo Literio super custodie Içe supradicte./ Item dedimus dicto Corrallo litteram de conductu apud officiales Regis Castelle. Datum ut supra./Post[qu]am fecimus ei litteras credencie inferius nominatis et aliam etiam procurat[i]onem super facto jenetorum/Çahit Azanach/Çahim Abebaguen/Tunart."

67. ACA, R. 65, fol. 113r (25 Mar. 1286): "Raimundo de Rivo Sicco, man[damus] vobis quatenus provisionem quam dare debetis Içe Abenadriç et uxori sue de mandato domini Regis tradatis eidem personaliter et non alii sive tradi faciatis. . . ."

68. ACA, R. 64, fol. 176v (Mar. 1286); ACA, R. 78, fol. 30r (6 Feb. 1288); and ACA, R. 80, fol. 108v (14 Dec. 1289). See also Dufourcq, *L'Espagne Catalane*, 217.

69. ACA, R. 90, fol. 18v (28 Aug. 1291). See also Dufourcq, *L'Espagne Catalane*, 219–20.

70. See Pierre Guichard, "Un seigneur musulman dans l'Espagne chrétienne: le 'ra'is' de Crevillente (1243–1318)," *Mélanges de la Casa de Velázquez* 9 (1973): 283–334, esp. 295; and Harvey, *Islamic Spain*, 42–44.

71. Muntaner, *Crònica*, chap. 188 [1296]: "l'arrais de Criveleny se'n venc a ell e es feu son hom e son vassal"; Harvey, *Islamic Spain*, 43–45; and Ferrer i Mallol, *La Frontera*, 33–38.

72. For instance, ACA, CR, Jaume II, caixa 18, no. 11678 (4 June [1303]), a letter from Ibn Hudhayr to Jaume II on the activities of his spies in Granada. See Masià i de Ros, *Jaume II*, 75.

73. ACA, R. 66, fol. 152v (27 July 1286); and ACA, R. 82, fol. 146r (1 Sep. 1290).

74. ACA, R. 130, fol. 77r (Nov. 1303). See also ACA, R. 243, fol. 208v (1316), as cited in Ferrer i Mallol, *La frontera*, 266.

75. ACA, CR, Jaume II, caixa 87, no. 10673 (14 Feb. [1304]); and ACA, CR, Jaume II, caixa 136, no. 476 (29 Apr. 1307). See also Ferrer i Mallol, *La frontera*, 245–46.

76. See, *EI*^{2}, s.v. "al-Mariyya"; José Angel Tapia Garrido, *Almería musulmana*; 'Abd al-'Azīz Sālim, *Ta'rīkh madīnat al-Mariyya al-islāmiyya*; Andrés Giménez-Soler, *El sitio de Almería en 1309*; Ferrer i Mallol, *La frontera*, 103–16; Harvey, *Islamic Spain*, 173–80; and Arié, *L'Espagne musulmane*, 89–93.

77. Francisco Vidal Castro, "Historia política," in *El reino nazarí de Granada (1232–1492): política, instituciones, espacio y economía*, ed. María Jesús Viguera Molíns, 91–96.

78. José Hinojosa Montalvo, "Las relaciones entre Valencia y Granada durante el siglo XV: balance de una investigación," in *Estudios sobre Málaga y el reino de Granada en el V centenario de la conquista*, ed. José E. López de Coca Castañer,

83–111; and idem, "Armamento de naves y comercio con el reino de Granada a principios del siglo XV," in *Andalucía entre Oriente y Occidente (1236–1492)*, 643–57.

79. Mikel de Epalza, "Constitución de rábitas en la costa de Almería: su función espiritual," in *Homenaje al Padre Tapia: Almería en su historia*, ed. José Angel Tapia Garrido, 231–35.

80. Ibn Khaldūn, *Kitāb al-'ibar*, VII: 380–81.

81. ACA, R 235, fols. 1v–2r, *segunda numeración* (22 Dec. 1303). See also Manzano, *Intervención*, 331; and Ferrer i Mallol, *La frontera*, 79–83. See chapter 6 for a full discussion of al-'Abbās b. Raḥḥū.

82. Torres Fontes, *Repartimiento de Lorca*, 47–63.

83. Torres Fontes, *Repartimiento de Lorca*, vii; and Anthony Lappin, *The Medieval Cult of Saint Dominic of Silos*, esp. 275–390.

84. Pero Marín, *Miraculos Romanzados* in *Vida y milagros del thaumaturgo español moysées Segundo, redemptor de cautivos, abogado de los felices partos, Sto. Domingo Manso, abad benedictino, reparador del real monasterio de Silos*. For editions of the relevant texts, see *Repartimiento de Lorca*, ed. Juan Torres Fontes, 52: ". . . veno Zahen, un moro sennor de caballos, con grant companna a correr a Lorca. . . ." Ibid., 54: "Venieron Muza Barraham et Zahem et Zahet Azenet con mil caballeros et mataron docientos cristianos et cativaron al tantos." Ibid., 57: ". . . Zahen, sennor de 300 caballeros. . . ." Ibid., 58: ". . . Zahen, un gener sennor de 200 caballeros." Ibid., 59: ". . . Muza Barrach, sennor de genetes." See also Torres Fontes, "La actividad bélica granadina," 729.

85. ACA, R. 58, fol. 22v (3 May 1285): "Baiulo Exatium quod donet Alaçeno militi Sarraceno nuncio Cahim filio Jahie Abennaquem quinquaginta solidos \regalium/ pro redimendis et quitandis ensibus quos idem Alaçenus et alii qui cum eo venerunt pignori obligaverunt in Exatium."

86. ACA, R. 56, fol. 93v (3 May 1285).

87. ACA, R. 58, fol. 22v (3 May 1285): "Bernardo Martini, baiulo Ville Franche, quod non exigat a nunciis Sarracenis de Cahim, filio Jahie Abebbaquem, illos quindecim solidos quos eisdem accomodavit. Immo si aliquos fideiussores ab eis recepit absolvat, cum dominus Rex mandet per presentes [dict]os quindecim solidi recipi in compotum per Guillelmum de Rocha a dicto Bernardo Martini."

88. ACA, R. 56, fol. 93v (4 May 1285): "Samueli Alfaquimo Regis, sabet que vidiemos vuestras letras, et daquello que nos embiastes dezir sobre feito de Çahim, sus mandaderos vinieron a nos et lu[e]go partieronse daquellas demandas assi que deven venir lu[e]go a nuestro servicio. E non queremos [que] Abrahim Abençumada nin otro se faga faulador desto, ca nos nos aveniemos bien con ellos. Por estis plaze a nos la porferta que vos fiziestes de vuestras mulas al dito Çahim. E si vos se las enviaredes, nos vos pagaremos el precio dellas. De lo que al que nos enviastes dezir de la salud et del estamiento de dona Agnes et de la otra companyna nostra que son aqui, gradeçemos vos lo muyto e pregamos vos que toda via nos lo fagedes

saber. Pero envastes nos dezir algunas cosas que nos non podiemos entender declaradament. E cuydamos que fue por que deziades que deviades venir a nos. E si vos alla non faziades ninguna, plazria a nos vestra venida. Empero o por vestras letras o por vestra venida queremos nos que mas largament et clarament nos lo fagades saber. Datum Figeriis, IIII nonas maii."

89. See also ACA, R. 82, fols. 61v–62r (2 July 1290), in which the Christians and Muslims of Valencia are ordered to pay for the use of *jenets* to protect their kingdom.

90. See chapter 5 for more detail on the interactions between the *jenets* and the Mudéjares.

91. ACA, R. 58, fol. 22v (3 May 1285): "Alfaquino Samueli quod mittat Cahim filio Jahie Abennaquem illas duas mulas suas et dominus Rex satisfaciet sibi de precio ipsarum."

92. ACA, R. 58, fol. 22v (4 May 1285): "Berengario Scribe quod loco Bernardi Scribe donet Alaçeno militi Sarraceno nuncio Cahim filio Jahie Abennaquem ducentos solidos Barchinonenses pro expensis s[u]is et illorum qui sechum venerunt."

93. ACA, R. 58, fol. 22r (4 May 1285): "Raimundo de Rivo Sicco quod cum Cahim filius Jahie Abennaquem debeat venire ad dominum Regem cum genetis et familia Sarracenorum quod tradat eidem unum expensarium per quem faciat provideri sibi et familie sue predicte in expensiis eisdem neccesariis quousque fuerint cum domino Rege. Datum Figeriis, quarto nonas Maii."

94. ACA, R. 58, fol. 22v (4 May 1285): "Bernardo Scribe quod donet //ad// tunicas ad quinque troterios Sarracenos nuncii genetorum."

95. ACA, R. 58, fol. 22r (4 May 1285): "Bernardo Scribe quod donet Alaçeno Sarraceno militi nuncio Cahim filio Jahie Abennaquem, unam aliubam et tunicam panni coloris et calligas presseti vermillii. Et quod donet Hameto Abenobrut aliubam et tunicam exalonis et calligas panni coloris. Et donetis Mahometo de Villena aliubam et tunicam de bifa plana et calligas Narbon[ensis]. . . . Datum Figeriis, IIII nonas May."

96. ACA, R. 58, fol. 23r (4 May 1285): "Bernardo Scribe quod donet Alaçeno geneto militi sellam et frenum bonum et Hammit Abenhobeit, sellam et frenum de minori precio. Datum ut supra."

97. Bernat Desclot, *Llibre del rei en Pere* in *Les quatre gran cròniques*, chap. 153: "Entrels quals ni havia sicents qui eren ballesters serrayns del regne de Valencia, e aportaven tots ballestes de dos peus." See also chaps. 156, 163. See also Joseph Strayer, "The Crusade Against Aragon," *Speculum* 28, no. 1 (1953): 102–13; and Catlos, *Victors and the Vanquished*, 264.

98. Desclot, *Llibre del rei en Pere*, chap. 140: "Mas atendaren se allens prop aquella nit; e lendema mati vench hun avolot en la ost del rey de França, mentre ques dinaven ço es assaber: quel rey d'Arago ab tot son poder e ab deu milia Serrayns ginets, e ab be cent milia homens de peu, que passaven d'amunt per la montanya, e que vienen a entrar en Perpinya, per ço com deyen, quells homens

de la villa de Perpinya li devien lliurar la villa, e puig lo rey d'Arago ques meses alli, e vedaria lo pas als Francesos que no passassen deça, e axi tendria al mig lloch aquells qui passats eren, e quels donat batalla."

99. Desclot, *Llibre del rei en Pere*, chap. 136: "Ans se pres ab Serrayns per destroir lo crestianisme; e ab ells se cuyda defendre a nos, que ab son poder no poria, car nol ha." Translation from Burns, *Islam under the Crusaders*, 291.

Chapter Three

1. Niccolò Machiavelli, *Il Principe*, ed. Lawrence Arthur Burd, chap. 12.

2. Ferrer i Mallol, "La organización militar," 155; idem, *Organització i defensa d'un territori fronterer: la governacío d'Oriola en el segle XIV*; Ludwig Klüpfel, "El règim de la Confederació catalano-aragonesa a finals del segle XIII," *Revista Jurídica de Catalunya* 35 (1929): 195–226, 289–327; and 36 (1930): 298–331, esp. 298–308; and Donald J. Kagay, *War, Government, and Society in the Medieval Crown of Aragon*.

3. See Joan Bastardas, *Usatges de Barcelona,* chap. 64 (usatge 68), 102.

4. García Fitz, *Castilla y León frente al Islam*, traces these transformations.

5. Strayer, "The Laicization of French and English Society."

6. ACA, R. 52, fol. 68v (4 Nov. 1284): ". . . sarraceni janeti [qui] in nostro servicio venerant sibi debebant cum duobus publicis instrumentis, quorum unum est moriscum et aliud christianite scriptum. . . ." Full citation in chapter 2 n16, above.

7. ACA, R. 65, fol. 177v (1286); ACA, R. 65, fol. 186r (1286); ACA, R. 65, fol. 186v (1286); ACA, R. 71, fol. 45r (1287); ACA, R. 71, fol. 49v (1287); ACA, R. 71, fol. 50v (1287); ACA, R. 71, fol. 50v (1287); ACA, R. 71, fol. 51v (1287); ACA, R. 72, fol. 9v (1287); ACA, R. 72, fol. 24v (1288); ACA, R. 72, fol. 32v (1288); ACA, R. 72, fol. 35r (1288); ACA, R. 72, fols. 38v–39r [redacted] (1288); ACA, R. 72, fol. 53v (1288); ACA, R. 78, fol. 34r (1288); ACA, R. 79, fol. 59r (1289); ACA, R. 79, fol. 59v (1289); ACA, R. 79, fol. 61r (1289); ACA, R. 79, fol. 62v (1289); ACA, R. 79, fol. 79v (1289); ACA, R. 82, fol. 61v–r (1290); ACA, R. 82, fol. 64r (1290); ACA, R. 82, fol. 66v (1290); ACA, R. 82, fol. 87r (1290); ACA, R. 82, fol. 146r (1290); ACA, R. 82, fol. 163v (1290); ACA, R. 82, fol. 164v (1290); ACA, R. 82, fol. 168v (1290); ACA, R. 82, fol. 171v (1291); ACA, R. 82, fol. 176r (1291); ACA, R. 82, fol. 183v (1291); ACA, R. 100, fol. 172v (1294); ACA, RP, MR, 620, fol. 134r; ACA, RP, MR, 774, fol. 74v (ca. 1293); and ACA, RP, MR, 774, fol. 77r (ca. 1293).

8. ACA, R. 78, fol. 84r (24 Apr. 1289): "Fuit mandatum Johanni Çapata et Guillelmo Durfortis quod faciant acurrimentum Bucar, jeneto nostro, et aliis jenetis [n]ostris qui [..] [v]enient de partibus Regni Valencie prout aliis de familia nostra cucurristis cum dictus Bucar in servicium nostrum habeat venire in [C]astellam. Et recuperetis presentem litteram et albaranum de eo quod sibi dederint racione predictam. Datum in [Ca]latayube, [V]III kalendas Madii." See also the numerous

entries in ACA, RP, MR, 774. See also Carme Batlle i Gallart, "La casa barcelonina en el segle XIII: l'exemple de la familia Dufort," in *La Ciudad hispánica durante los siglos XIII al XVI: actas del coloquio celebrado en La Rábida y Sevilla del 14 al 19 de septiembre de 1981*, ed. Emilio Sáez, Cristina Segura, and Margarita Cantera Montenegro, II: 1347–60. Similarly, Raimundus Escorne met with the troops of Mahomet Abenadalil, Mahomet al Granadaxi, and Iuceff Abenzubayba when they arrived in Valencia and provided them their salaries and anything else they required. ACA, R. 73, fol. 77v (28 Feb. 1289): ". . . que luego vista la carta vengades a Valencia on nos avemos ordenado que fiel nostre escriviano Raimund Escorna vos de recaudo de venir a nos de quitacio et de lo que ayades menester."

9. See Hugh Kennedy, *Armies of the Caliphs: Military and Society in the Early Islamic State*, esp. 59–65, 71–76; Évariste Lévi-Provençal, *Un recueil de lettres officielles Almohades: Étude diplomatique, analyse et commentaire historique*, esp. 1–19. See also *EI*^{2}, s.v. "dīwān"; and *HEM*, I: 69, 128.

10. Alcover, *Diccionari català-valencià-balear*, s.v. "albaran." In Spanish, it is "albarán." The influence in this case was likely indirect, passing through the Papal Chancery to the Aragonese court.

11. Shatzmiller, *The Berbers and the Islamic State*, 55–68; David Corcos, "The Jews of Morocco under the Marinids," *Jewish Quarterly Review* 54 (1963–64): 271–87; 55 (1964–65), 53–81, 137–50; Norman Stillman, "Muslims and Jews in Morocco," *Jerusalem Quarterly* 5 (1977): 76–83; and idem, "The Moroccan Jewish Experience," *Jerusalem Quarterly* 9 (1978): 111–23.

12. In 1285 King Pere ordered Arnaldus to release several captives from Tunis who had paid for their redemption (ACA, R. 65, fol. 27r [30 Mar. 1285]). He helped administer the slave auctions in Mallorca after the fall of Minorca (ACA, R. 70, fol. 42r [7 Feb. 1287], R. 71, fol. 113v [10 Apr. 1287], R. 72, fol. 41r [27 June 1288]). He also reimbursed Muslim diplomats for their travel expenses (ACA, R. 74, fol. 71r [6 Feb. 1288]).

13. Haste was required in the case of the *jenet* Mahomet Abenabderasmen Ataç. See ACA, R. 67, fol. 77r–v (20 Sep. 1286): "Petro de Podio Rubeo, baiulo Algezire. Mandamus vobis quatenus de illis tribus milibus solidis regalium quos vos <recipere> debetis ab hominibus Algezire, racione redemptionis exercitus, detis et solvatis solutis et cetera Mahome[t] Aben[abderas]men Ataç quadringentos solidos, a Abdorramen filio Abdolmalich Abenfa[y]ina quingentos solidos, item Iuceffo Aveniacob Avenjacol Abenabdulfach CCC LXX solidos, item a Magderva <quadringentos solidos, item a Amoç ducentos solidos, item a Mansor Matino Detzayn Abenmiquel sexaginta solidos, item Abraym Abenhame. . . . [ce]ntum vinginti [solidos], item a Assar centum solidos, item a Ayssa Avenfarrat tribus sociis suis nonag[intos] . . . solidos. [I]t[em a] Alfaig [....] sociis suis centum vinginti solidos, item Machometo> [fol. 77v] Abenfayol quingentos solidos, quos omnes denarios predictis janetis debemus pro quitacionibus eorumdem sine acurri[....] . . . solucionibus et etiam caveatis vobis ne racione predicte solutionis

dicti janeti habeant retardare, alia[s] . . . <salvi> faceremus expensas [qua]s dicti janeti facere haberent. Datum Valencie, XII kalendas Octobris." See also ACA, R. 71, fol. 45r (29 Apr. 1287): "Petro Peregrini quod det Mahometo Abolxahe janeto . . . et recipia[t] ipsi albar[anum] . . . hoc Arnaldum de Bastida." See also ACA, R. 71, fol. 49v; ACA, R. 71, fol. 50v; ACA, R. 71, fol. 51v; and ACA, R. 100, fol. 172v.

14. See, for instance, ACA, R. 65, fol. 186v (2 Mar. 1286), in which Bastida is ordered to pay three *jenets* their salaries for two months with one *albaranum*: "[Arnaldo] de Bastida. Cum Sehit Abdella et Jucefo Aben Jacob et Cassim et Abra[hi]mo Benhamenia [solvat] pro quitacionibus eorum mensium Septembris et Octobris cum albarano Bartholomei de V[illa] Franch[a] . . . solidos Barchinonenses quod albaranum [nos] recuperavimus." The amount that each *jenet* was paid appears in the documentary lacuna.

15. ACA, R. 52, fol. 57r (29 Aug. 1284): "Bernardo Scr[ibe] quod det vel assignet Muçe Genet LIII solidos IIII denarios iaccenses qui sibi remanent [ad] solvendum de quitacione Albarrasini. Datum Turole, IIII kalendas Septembris."

16. For more on the currency of the Crown of Aragon, see James Broadman, *Ransoming Captives in Crusader Spain: The Order of Merced on the Christian-Islamic Frontier*, appendix A. See also Robert Ignatius Burns, *Medieval Colonialism: Postcrusade Exploitation of Islamic Valencia*, 27–33.

17. 1 libra = 20 solidi = 240 denarii.

18. In the year 1300, one *solidus* from Barcelona was equivalent to one *solidus* six *denarii* from Jaca, and one *solidus* three *denarii* from Valencia. The Latin *solidus* gives us the Castilian *sueldo* and Catalan *sou*.

19. For instance, ACA, R. 82, fol. 66v (3 or 4 Sep. 1290): "Eidem fuit scriptum [al]iud albaranum quod solvit nobili [Ma]hometo Abnadalyl pro quitacione sua et familia s[u]e quae cum eo venerunt de Granata pro mense Augusti preterito DXXXVI duplas mirias. Item pro quitacione Sarracenorum peditum pro dicto mense et pro esmend[o] unius equi qui fuit interfectus in rambla Valencie super ludo janethie XXXII duplas et med[ia]m mirias"; and ACA, RP, MR, 620, fol. 69r (1294): "Primerament nos mostra VI albarans den A Eymeric en los quals son deguts an Jahia Abenallu e an Ayça e an Mahomet Bennaçer et an Zahit Almelocaya e an Mahomet Algaçil //per quitacion lur// genets del Seynor Rey Namfos de bonamemoria per quitacion lur. L doblas mirias. E CXX solidos Barchinonenses." For more on Islamic coins in the Crown of Aragon, see Joaquím Botet i Sisó, "Nota sobre la encunyació de monedas arábigues pel Rey Don Jaume," in *Congrés d'històriala Corona d'Agragó, dedicat al rey En Jaume I y la seua época*, II: 944–45.

20. Çayt Abdella, 120 sous or 4 sous per diem (ACA, R. 71, fol. 49v); Maymon de Picaçen, 266 sous of Barcelona or 3 sous per diem (ACA, R. 71, fol. 50v); Mahomet and three brothers, 496 sous of Barcelona or 4 sous per diem (ACA, R. 71, fol. 51v); Mahomet and three brothers, 448 sous of Barcelona or 4 sous per diem (ACA, R. 71, fol. 51v); Zayt and brother, 248 sous of Barcelona or 4 sous

per diem (ACA, R. 71, fol. 51v); Mahomet Abelhaye, 337 sous of Jaca or 11 sous per diem (ACA, R. 72, fol. 32v); Mahomet de Picaçen, 266 sous of Barcelona or 3 sous per diem (ACA, R. 72, fol. 38v); Jucef Aben Jacob and Cassim, 372 sous of Jaca or 6 sous per diem (ACA, R. 72, fol. 53v); and Muça Mufarrax, 510 sous of Barcelona or 4 sous per diem (ACA, RP, MR, 620, fol. 107r). Catlos, "Mahomet Abenadalill," 276, comes to a similar conclusion that the *jenets* were paid between four and six *solidi* per diem. Boswell, *Royal Treasure*, 186, says five *solidi* but calls it "considerably less" than other soldiers were paid.

21. See Ferrer i Mallol, "La organización militar," 170; and Antonio Arribas Palau, *La conquista de Cerdeña por Jaume II de Aragón*, doc. 19. Heavy cavalry were paid more than light cavalry, on average 8 *solidi* per diem. Ferrer i Mallol records that at the end of the fourteenth century, the heavy cavalry received nine *solidi*, and the light received five, citing ACA, R. 1245, fol. 21r–v (30 Sep. 1374).

22. Charles-Emmanuel Dufourcq, "Prix et niveaux de vie dans les pays catalans e maghribins à la fin du XIIIe et au début du XIVe siècles," *Le Moyen Âge* 71 (1965): 506–508, as cited in Catlos, "Mahomet Abenadalill," 276.

23. The expression used in the chancery registers to describe these raids was *vadere ad jenetiam*, going on a *jenet* raid. See ACA, R. 81, fol. 56v: "Mahamot el Viello, janetus noster, ac alii vad[unt] ad jenetiam. . . ." See also ACA, R. 85, fol. 21v: "D[ictus] Moxaref cum aliis tam Christianis quam Sar[racenis qui] vadunt ad jenetiam."

24. *Primera crónica general*, ed. Ramón Menéndez Pidal, fol. 304, for the description of Muslim tactics at the battle of Las Navas de Tolosa (1212), as cited in Soler del Campo, *La evolución del armamento*, 159–60. Cf. *EI*², s.v. "furūsiyya." See also Arié, *L'Espagne musulmane*, 258; Pierre Guichard, *Les musulmans de Valence et la reconquête: XIe-XIIIe siècles*, II: 390; and Ferdinand Lot, *L'Art militaire et les armées au moyen âge en Europe et dans le Proche Orient*, I: 440.

25. Don Juan Manuel, *Libro de los estados*, ed. Robert Brian Tate and Ian Richard Macpherson, 144, as cited in Soler de Campo, *La evolución del armamento*, 163: "Sennor infante, la guerra con los moros no es commo la de los christianos, tanbién en la guerra guerriada commo quando çercan o convaten, o son cercados o convatidos, commo en las cavalgadas et cerreduras, commo en el andar por el camino et el posar de la hueste, commo en las lides; en todo es muy departida la una manera de la otra."

26. Ibn Khaldūn, *Kitāb al-'ibar*, I: 214 (translation is from Rosenthal, trans. *Muqaddimah*, 227): "We have mentioned the strength that a line formation behind the army gives to the fighters who use the technique of *al-karr wa'l-farr*. Therefore the North African rulers have come to employ groups of Franks (ṭā'ifa min al-Ifranj) in their army, and they are the only ones to have done that, because their countrymen only know *al-karr wa'l-farr*."

27. Echevarría Arsuaga, *Caballeros en la frontera*, 101; and García Fitz, *Castilla y León frente al Islam*, 137, 153.

28. ACA, R. 81, fol. 56v (8 Jan. 1289): "Universis hominibus quorumlibet locorum frontariarum terre nostre ad quos et cetera. Cum Mahomet el Viello, janetus noster, ac alii va[dunt] ad jenetiam tam Christiani quam Sarraceni socii predicti Mahomet habeant esse de mandato nostro in partibus frontarie pro tuicione [et] deffensione terre nostre ac etiam pro inferendo dampno inimicis nostris. Dicimus ac mandamus vobis quatenus quandocumque predictum Mahomat al Viello ac socios suos predictos contingerit venire seu accedere ad loca vestra in partibus frontarie tam cum cavalgatis quam sine cavalgatis ipsos in locis vestris predictis cum cavalcatis seu rebus eorum benigne recipiatis et eisd[em] vel rebus suis nullum dampnum vel impedimentum faciatis immo iuvetis et dirigatis eosdem in hiis in quibus poteritis bono modo. Datum ut supra." In 1290, Mahomet Abenadalil also departed for raids along the border of Calatayud alongside Christians. ACA, R. 81, fol. 177r (5 Sep. 1290), which has several lacunae: ". . . et conciliis ac subditis suis Calatayube, Daroce, Tirasone, [....] et omnium et singulorum aliorum locorum qui sint . . . cum Castellanis seu Navarris, sciatis quod nos mitimus nobilem Mahomet Abnadalil vassallum nostrum . . . sua janetorum et Raimundum Sancii de Calatayube et Garciam Sancii de Guorguet de domo nostra, cum aliquibus . . . Christianorum cum eo ad ipsas partes pro defendendis locis predictis et inf<errendum> malum inimicis . . . quare et cetera. Si aliquas treugas habetis vel <tenetis> cum Castellanis vel Navarris ipsis incontinenti easdem . . . . Et si contigerit ipsum Mahometum vel aliquos de familis sua intrare terram inimicorum nostrorum eosdem . . . cum cavalc[at]is vel sine cavalcatis et detis eisdem . . . et vendicionem et non permit[a]tis eis fieri [impediment]um aliquod prebentes ei[sd]em consilium et cetera. Et si contigerit predictum nobilem facere cavalcatam . . . dicta litera present[....] nullum impedimentum et cetera. Datum ut supra." See also Catlos, "Mahomet Abenadalill," 266n30.

29. For Abenadalil, see Catlos, "Mahomet Abenadalill," 278–79, citing ACA, R. 81, fol. 177r and ACA, R. 83, fols. 70v–71r. For the case of al-'Abbās b. Raḥḥū, see chapter 6.

30. ACA, R. 85, fol. 21v (14 May 1290): "Universis hominibus quorumlibet locorum frontariarum dicti domini Regis qui non sint in treuga. Cu[m] Moxarref Abenh[a]lbet, jenetus, qui nunc venit cum familia jenetorum de partibus Castelle ad servicium dicti domini Regis ut sit in frontaria Aragone pro tuicione et deffensione eiusdem frontarie ac pro inferrendo dampno inimicis dicti domini Regis et nostris. Dicimus et mandamus vobis ex parte domini Regis quatenus quandocumque d[ictus] Moxaref cum aliis tam Christianis quam Sar[racenis qui] vadunt ad jenetiam existentibus in frontaria Arag[one] ad servicium dicti Regis contingit venire seu accedere ad loca vestra in partibus frontarie tam cum cavalgatis vel s[ine] cavalgatis ipsos in locis vestris predictis cum cavalgatis et rebus eorum benigne recipiatis et eisdem vel rebus suis nullum dampnum vel impedimentum faciatis aut fieri permitatis immo iuvetis et dirigatis eosdem in hiis in quibus poteritis bono modo, salva semper custodia vestra et rerum vestrarum. Datum Calatayube,

II idus Maii." See also Gazulla, "Zenetes," 194; and Catlos, "Mahomet Abenadalill," 296.

31. ACV, Perg., 738, fol. 8r: "Machamet Almenochoxi qui vocatur Georgius" and "Athame Benbrahi qui vocatur Petro."

32. ACA, R. 81, fol. 237v (13 Dec. 1290): "Universis officialibus civitatum villarum et quorumlibet locorum Aragone. Mandamus vobis quatenus aliquibus [ad]alilis vel almugav[eris] equitum vel peditum vel aliis janetis si intrarent Castellam seu Navarram nullum impedimentum vel contrarium faciatis vel fieri ab aliquibus permitatis immo provideatis eisdem et familie eorum de securo transitu et [con]duct[u] . . . restituentes et re[s]titui faciemus nichilominus eisdem omnes homines bestiarium et alias res quas habunt de terra dictorum inimicorum nostrorum et que nos vel aliquis nostrum ab eisdem cepistis vel etiam extorsistis. Datum u[tsupra]." Muslim raiders from Granada were occasionally called Muslim almogàvers: ACA, R. 100, fol. 102r (14 Nov. 1294); and ACA, CR, Jaume II, caixa 36, no. 4492 (30 Mar. 1312).

33. Desclot, *Crònica*, chap. 7: "Aquestes gents qui han nom Almugavers son gents que no viven sino de fet de armes, ne no stan en viles ne en ciutats, sino en muntanyes e en boschs; e guerreien tots jorns ab Serrayns, e entren dins la terra dels Serrayns huna jornada o dues lladrunyant e prenent dels Serrayns molts, e de llur haver; e de aço viven; e sofferen moltes malenances que als altres homens no porien sostenir; que be passaran a vegades dos jorns sens menjar, si mester los es; e menjaran de les erbes dels camps, que sol no s'en prehen res. E los Adelits que'ls guien, saben les terres e'ls camins. E no aporten mes de huna gonella o huna camisa, sia stiu o ivern; e en les cames porten hunes calses de cuyro, e als peus hunes avarques de cuyro. E porten bon coltell e bona correja, e hun foguer a la cinta. E porta cascú huna llança e dos darts, e hun cerró de cuyro en que aporten llur vianda. E són molt forts e molt laugers per fugir e per encalsar." Cf. Muntaner, *Crònica*, chap. 62: "E aquets anaren cascú ab son çarró acostes: que no creats que menassen adzembla neguna, ans cascú portava lo pa en son çarró, axí com acostumats e nudrits los almugavers; que com van en cavalgada, cascú porta un pa per cascun dia, e no pus: e puix del pa e de l'aygua e de les erbes passen llur temps aytant com llur ops es." See also M. Rojas Gabriel and D. M. Pérez Castañera, "Aproximación a almogávares y almogaverías en la frontera con Granada," in *Estudios de frontera: Alcalá la Real y el Arcipreste de Hita*, ed. Francisco Toro Ceballos and José Rodríguez Molina, 569–82; and Juan Torres Fontes, "El adalid en la frontera de Granada," *Anuario de estudios medievales* 15 (1985): 345–66.

34. See Arié, *L'Espagne musulmane*, 245.

35. Giménez Soler, "Caballeros," 299. See also Alemany, "Milicias cristianas," 133.

36. For instance, Giménez Soler, "Caballeros," 300: "Ésta cubre con su simpática bandera mercancías averiadas, aquélla contribuía en los siglos medios á excitar el entusiasmo popular, pero no era ni el móvil único, ni el principal siquiera."

37. Giménez Soler, "Caballeros," 299: "Eran las relaciones entre los africanos y los cristianos de la peninsula amistosas y hasta cordials"; ". . . posponiéndose los intereses de la religion á los viles y positivos de la utilidad"; and ibid., 300: "La guerra y el comercio, los dos grandes elementos civilizadores, coadyuvaron á esas recíprocas influencias."

38. For instance, Ramón Menéndez Pidal, *La España del Cid*, I: 17–38. Cf. Reinhart Pieter Anne Dozy, *Recherches sur l'histoire et la litterature de l'Espagne*, II: 201–2.

39. Recent and important contributions to this discussion include: Eduardo Manzano Moreno, "Qurtuba: Algunas reflexiones críticas sobre el califato de Córdoba y el mito de la convivencia," *Awraq: Estudios sobre el mundo árabe e islámico contemporáneo* 7 (2013): 225–46; Ryan Szpiech, "The Convivencia Wars: Decoding Historiography's Polemic with Philology," in *A Sea of Languages: Rethinking the Arabic Role in Medieval Literary History*, ed. Suzanne Conklin Akbari and Karla Mallette; Soifer, "Beyond Convivencia"; Novikoff, "Between Tolerance and Intolerance in Medieval Spain"; Tolan, "Using the Middle Ages to Construct Spanish Identity"; Bernabé López García, "Enigmas de al-Andalus: Una polémica," *Revista de Occidente* 224 (2000): 31–50; idem,"30 años de Arabismo Español," *Awraq* 18 (1997): 11–48; idem, "Arabismo y orientalismo en España: Radiografía y diagnóstico de un gremio escaso y apartadizo," *Awraq* 11 (1990): 35–69.

40. David Nirenberg, *Communities of Violence: The Persecution of Minorities in the Middle Ages*, 7. Cf. István Bejczy, "Tolerantia: A Medieval Concept," *Journal of the History of Ideas* 58 (1997): 365–84; and Cary J. Nederman, "Tolerance and Community: A Medieval Communal Functionalist Argument for Religious Toleration," *Journal of Politics* 56, no. 4 (1994): 901–18.

41. ACA, R. 71, fol. 51r (9 May 1287): "Petro Peregrini quod det vestes Maymono, janeto sicut aliis jenetis. Et cum ei dederit et cetera. Datum ut supra"; ACA, R. 71, fol. 51r (9 May 1287): "Eidem quod det vestes Mahometo de Picaçon sicut aliis janetis. Et cum ei dederitis et cetera. Datum ut supra"; ACA, R. 71, fol. 52r (15 Mar. 1287); ACA, R. 82, fol. 164v (my emphasis): "Eidem quod det v[e]stes . . . <ja>neti . . . Regis *prout consuevit* . . ."; ACA, R. 252, fol. 189r (10 Mar. 1291): "X cannos daquel panno que nos les querremos dar para vestir una vegada en el anno."

42. ACA, R. 81, fol. 243v: "Lezdariis Tamariti, Dertuse, Paniscole et omnium aliorum locorum in litore maris constitutorum. Cum nos mitamus apud Valencie sex trosellos pannorum in barcha Guillelmi de Portello pro induenda familia nostra genetorum que est in Valencia. Mandamus vobis quatenus nullam lezdam seu aliquod aliud ius exigatis a dicto barcherio seu deferentibus dictos pannos racione pannorum predictorum." The *lezda* (Rom. *leuda*, Cat. *lleuda*), or occasionally *portaticum*, was a tax levied on all goods entering a port.

43. See chapter 4, below.

44. ACA, R. 82, fol. 168v (21 Nov. 1290): "Eidem [Arnaldo de Bastida]. Mandamus vobis quatenus visis presentibus, detis et solvatis Abenhadalillo, capiti

jenetorum et familie sue v[e]stes competentes vel tresdecim millia solidos Barchinonenses pro eisdem. Et facta solucionem et cetera. Datum ut supra."

45. ACA, R. 82, fol. 146r (4 Sep. 1290); ACA, R. 58, fol. 22r (4 May 1285).

46. For instance, equipment given to the troops of Bucar (ACA, R. 78, fol. 84r [24 Apr. 1289]; see n8 to this chapter). See also ACA, R. 76, fol. 19v (23 Feb. 1288 [1287]): "Geraldo de Fonte, baiulo Valencie. Mandamus nobis quatenus sicut acurrimentum fecistis pro nobis Sayt et Muçe, jenetis nostris. Similiter, volumus quod donetis Çehen, jeneto nostro, qui nobiscum est in servicio nostro vel Açano uxore suo loco sui quinquaginta solidos regalium cum eos racione acurrimenti dari similiter mandemus eidem. Et facta et cetera. Datum ut supra"; ACA, R. 76, fol. 3r (11 Feb. 1287): ". . . Muçe et Sahit, jenetis nostris, . . . pro acurrimento. . . ." For the Ghuzāh, see Ibn Marzūq, *al-Musnad*, 394.

47. ACA, R. 67, fol. 15r (20 May 1286): "Ismaeli de Portella. Mandamus vobis quatenus incontinenti detis Abdeluhayt, janeto, CCL solidos iaccenses quos sibi de gracia pro uno roncino duximus concedendos et facta et cetera. Datum Cesarauguste, XIII kalenas Iunii." ACA, R. 79, fol. 59r (10 June 1289) [a second copy at ACA, R. 79, fol. 59v]: "Arnaldo de Bastida. Mandamus vobis [quatenus] detis Ahemet de Rami, janeto nostro, denarios qui sunt consueti dari pro [racione] quos sibi pro uno roncino de gracia d[u]ximus concedendos. Et facta et cetera. Retineatis ad opus scribanie iuxta precium dicti roncini." ACA, R. 79, fol. 62v (7 Aug. 1289): "Arnaldo de Bastida et cetera. Mandamus vobis, quatenus visis presentibus, detis Cayt, janeto nostro, quad[ri]gentes solidos [pro] uno roncino quos sibi de gracia concessi[mus]. Et facta et cetera. Retineatis scribanie XX solidos. Datum [. . . .] VII idus [A]ugusti." Machomet Abel[h]aye was given 1210 *sous* for ammunitions. ACA, R. 65, fol. 177v (29 Mar. 1285): "Arnaldo de Bastida quod iuxta hordinacionem solvat Machometo Abel[h]aye quatuor millia ducenti et decem solidos barchinonenses quos dominus Rex sibi debebat pro quitacione sua cum II albaranis Bartholomei de Villa Francha que nos recup[er]a[vimus]. Datum Barchinone, IV kalendas Aprilis, anno domini MCCLXXX quinto."

48. ACA, R. 58, fol. 14r (15 Mar. 1284): "Johanni Petri Orticii, mandamus vobis quatenus donetis Muçe janeto nostro unum roncinum precii LXX solidos iaccenses. Datum Osce, idus Marcii." Juçe Beniagub received a mule directly from the royal offical, Petrus de Libiano. ACA, R. 67, fol. 138v (1 Mar. 1287 [1286]): "Petro de Libiano quod det Juçe Beniagub, janeto, unam mulam competentem. Datum Barchinone, kalendas Marcii." ACA, R. 79, fol. 79v (27 Jan. 1289): "Arnaldo de Bastida quod det Massot Canaç, jeneto nostro, unam equitaturam idoneam vel trecentos solidos regalium pro eadem quos sibi de gracia duximus concedendos. Datum Valencia, VI kalendas Februarii." ACA, R. 79, fol. 79v (26 Jan. 1289): "Arnaldo de Bastida. Mandamus vobis quatenus detis Aeça Abenhaçipuet, janeto nostro, unum equum idoneum quem ei de gracia duximus concedendum. Et facta et cetera. Datum Valencia, VI kalendas Februarii." ACA, R. 82, fol. 164v (8 Sep. 1290): "Eidem quod solvat Muçe Almentauri, janeto, quendam roncinum

de precio [C]CC solidis cum quo possit servire domino Regi. Datum Valencie, VI idus Septembris." ACA, CR, Jaume II, caixa 6, no. 919 (8 Dec. 1300): "Jacobus dei gracia Rex Aragonum, fideli scriptori suo Guillelmo de Solanis, salutem et graciam. Dicimus et mandamus vobis quatenus cum ad ciutatem Murcie vos declinare contigerit ematis seu emi faciatis de denariis scribanie ad opus Abdalle, jeneti, quendam roncinum competentem quem sibi providemus de gracia concedendum, ut dictus jenetus nobis melius possit servire. Datum in Alcantarella sub sigillo nostro secreto, VI idus Decembris, anno domini millesimo trescentesimo." Other examples, ACA, R. 82, fol. 164v (8 Sept. 1290); and ACA, RP, MR, 620, fol. 134r (15 Nov. 1296).

49. ACA, R. 58, fol. 39r: "Bernardo Scribe quod emat roncinum fratris Berengarii et ipsum donet Maimon, jeneto." ACA, R. 72, fol. 9v (20 Sep. 1287): "Eidem [Arnaldo de Bastida] quod solvat Bartholomeo de Podio quadringentos solidos iaccenses quod Dominus Rex sibi debet pro precio unius equi quem ab eo emit et dedit Alabeç, janeto, et facta et cetera. Datum in Ortis de Lupa, XII kalendas Octobris." ACA, R. 82, fol. 183v (13 Apr. 1291): "Arnaldo de Bastida et cetera. Cum nos assignavissemus cum carta nostra Berengario de Vilaron DL solidos Barchinonenses habendos, solutis et cetera super denarios quos Episcopus Gerunde tunc nobis dare et solvere debebat quos quidem nos eidem debebamus pro precio unius equi quem ab eo emimus et dedimus Çahen, geneto nostro, et dictus Berengarius nichil habuerit ut asserit de dictis denariis. Mandantes et cetera certifica[...] . . . et de dicta quantitate fuit sibi aliquid persolutum, i[...] quod inveneristis eidem inde deberi de quantitate predicta [supradic]tis eisdem. Et facta et cetera. Datum Gerunde, idus Aprilis."

50. ACA, R. 70, fol. 168r (13 Aug. 1287): "[Fuit] facta litera gui[dat]ico alcayt Abrafim et Abrafimo Muça, Atiça Patrello, Atiça et Muça, et Caçim, Çayt, Abenbey Mahomet et Alaçemi, Hamu, [H]uniç, A[l]ii Acrrayedi, Jacob, Maçet Mahomat Almotihal et Çahat Algorçili, jenetis [....] Barchinone et debebant se re[co]lligere cum aliquibus filiis Miramamonini. Datum ut supra." See also ACA, R. 85, fol. 21v, with full citation in n30, above.

51. ACA, R. 79, fol. 61r (12 July 1289): "Arnaldo de Bastida et cetera. Mandamus et cetera [quod] solvatis Hahen Abenhali, janeto nostro, quingentos solidos Barchinonenses quos sibi damus pro emenda cuiusdam [eq]ui sui quem amisit in servicio nostro. Et facta et cetera. Da[tum] Barchinone, [I]III idus Iulii." ACA, R. 79, fol. 79v (27 Jan. 1289): "Arnaldo de Bastida. Mandamus //vobus// vobis quatenus detis Halfo Abderramen, jeneto nostro, unum equum idoneum in emendam [illius] equi quem amisit in servicio nostro in Borgia et recuperetis et cetera." ACA, R. 82, fol. 87r (7 Dec. 1290): "Fuit mandatum Arnaldo de Bastida quod solvat Mahometo Abenadalilo centum [se]xaginta quatuor dup[las] auri [m]irias quas [domi]nus Rex debet ei pro emenda novem roncinorum quo[s] amisit in servicio domini Regis cum carta sua ut in ea continetur et quod recuperet dictam cartam et presentem cum apocham de soluto. Datum Barchinone, VII idus Decembris, anno

domini MCCXC." See also Catlos, "Mahomet Abenadalill," 264n25, and Gazulla, "Zenetes," 191n1. This particular privilege was also extended to certain Christian soldiers (e.g., ACA, R. 72, fol. 37v).

52. ACA, R. 82, fol. 165r (9 Sep. 1290): "[Ei]dem [Arnaldo de Bastida] quod donet Maymono, geneto nostro, CCCC solidos regalium pro redimendo quemdam roncinum suum quem pro eisdem denariis impignoraverat in Valencia cum de gracia concessimus istud sibi. Et facta et cetera."

53. ACA, CR, Jaume II, caixa 30, no. 3737 (17 Feb. 1310): "<Nos Iacobus dei gracia Rex Aragonum, Valencie, Sardinie, et Corsice, comesque Barchinone, ac Sancte Romane Ecclesie vexillario, amir[an]tus, capitanues generalis. Recognoscimus debere vobis Petro Ramiri de Cascant de familia nobile Arta[ld]i de Luna per emendam cuiusdam açemile vestre quam amisistis in servicio nostro in Ob>sidione <civitatis Almarie quamque geneti secum abduxerunt de orta dicte civitatis facto inde per vos averamento in cancelleria nostra centum octuoginta solidos Barchinone, quos solvemus> vobis vel <cui volueritis loco vestri in cuius testimonium presentam vobis fieri iussimus sigillo nostro sigillatam. Datum [Va]lencie, XII kalendas Marcii, anno domini MCCC nono.>"

54. ACA, R. 71, fol. 155r (30 July 1284): "Bart[ho]lomeo de Villa Francha. Cum Abdul[u]ahet, janetus, sit in servicio domini Regi[s] patris nostri et nostri in Obsidione Albarrazini, mandamus vobis quatenus donetis ei racionem pro duabus bestios et duobus hominibus sicut datis aliis quibus nunc racionem datis. Datum in Obsidione Albarrazini, III kalendas Augusti."

55. ACA, R. 85, fol. 113v (15 Mar. 1290). This document is presented and discussed further in chapter 5 n63.

56. ACA, R. 94, fol. 151r (29 Dec. 1292): "Petro Sancii, iusticie Calatayube, dicimus et mandamus vobis quatenus incontinenti detis et solv[e]tis Paschasio Dominici de Pampilona illos denarios quos per vos eidem dari mandaverimus pro re[d]emptione illius janeti et uxoris sue ac filiorum eorum qui in posse dicti Paschasii Dominici capti detinebantur quosquidem sarracenos ad partes illustris domp[n]i Sancii Regis Castelle a captione predicta per dictum Paschasium absolvi mandaverimus et [....]. Regi Castelle predicto prout iam alias vobis dedimus in mandatis. Datum Calatayube IIII kalendas J[a]nuarii."

57. On affection for the *jenets*, see Catlos, "Mahomet Abenadalill," 302.

58. ACA, R. 73, fol. 77v (24 Feb. 1290): "Don Alfonso por la gracia de dios Rey d'Aragon, de Maylorcha, de Valencia, et comde de Barchinone, a vos don Iuceff Abenzubayba, sal[ut] et buena voluntat. Entendiemos por Adabub Adalil que vos con compayna de genetes queredes venir a nostro servicio la qual cosa a nos plase muyche. E rogamos vos que luego vista la carta vengades a Valencia on nos avemos ordenado que fiel nostre escriviano Raimund Escorna vos de recaudo de venir a nos de quitacio et de lo que ayades menester. E prometemos a vos que quando nos ayamos ganado con la aiuda de dios nostro entendimienta de la guerra que sino os avedez tornar a la [tierra] del Rey de Granada que tanto quanto vos

querades estar en nostra terra que no vos faleçremos de lo que ayades menester fasta que vos ganemos la amor del Rey de Granada como quier que sepamos que tot homne qui a nos serva, sierve al Rey de Granada. Datum Cesarauguste, VI kalendas Marcii./S[e]mblant a don Mahomet al Granadaxi./Semblant a don Mahomet Abnadalil." Adabub Adalil was a *jenet* already in the service of the Crown of Aragon. See ACA, R. 82, fols. 61v–62r (2 July 1290). See also Gazulla, "Zenetes," 188–89; and Catlos, "Mahomet Abenadalill," 259, 261n16.

59. ACA, R. 243, fol. 264v (5 Apr. 1317): "Don Jayme et cetera. Al amado Alabeç Abenrraho, salut e amor. . . ."

60. References to *jenets* who were described as "de domo regis," of the king's household or court, are scattered throughout the registers: ACA, R. 44, fol. 178v (16 Apr. 1280); ACA, R. 55, fol. 49v (1291); ACA, R. 81, fol. 10r (3 Jan. 1290); ACA, R. 82, fol. 146r (4 Sep. 1290); ACA, R. 82, fol. 164v (8 Sep. 1290); ACA, RP, MR, 774, fols. 85v–86r (ca. 1293); ACA, R. 203, fols. 7r–8r (22, 25 Apr. 1305); ACA, R. 203, fol. 13r (14 May 1305); ACA, R. 872, fol. 22r (12 June 1341); and ACA, RP, MR, 2468, fol. 101r (1358).

61. ACA, R. 866, fol. 64r (9 June 1339); ACA, R. 951, fol. 75r–v (14 May 1340); ACA, R. 959, fol. 6r (31 Aug. 1345); ACA, R. 1123, fol. 70r (1344); and ACA, R. 2223, fols. 33v–34r (22 Dec. 1397), as cited in Ferrer i Mallol, *Els sarraïns*, 31, 161–62; and idem, *La frontera*, 158.

62. ACA, R. 90, fol. 22v (2 Sep. 1291): "Universis officialibus et subditis suis ad quos presentes pervenerint et cetera, cum Mahometus Abenadalill et Abrahim Abennamies venerint ad nos ex parte illustris regis granate et inde redeant ad eundem, mandamus et dicimus vobis quatenus ipsis nunciis seu rebus eorum in redeundo apud Granatam nullum impedimentum vel contrarium faciatis, immo provideatis eosdem de securo transitu et ducatu. Datum ut supra." See also ACA, R. 55, fol. 49v (s.a.); ACA, R. 90, fol. 18v (12 May 1291); and ACA, R. 243, fol. 264v (5 Apr. 1317). See also Catlos, "Mahomet Abenadalill," 271n52, 271n54.

63. ACA, R. 82, fol. 164r (4 Sep. 1290): "[Arnaldo de] Bastida. Cum Mahometus Abencinich et Asmet Almergi et Mahometus Abencaremon, de domo nostra, de voluntate nostra [vad]eant apud Granate. Mandamus vobis quatenus donetis predictis Sarracenis expensas idoneas usque ad dictum locum. . . . R[e]cuperetis ab eo et cetera. Datum ut supra."

64. For the context, see Dufourcq, *L'Espagne catalane*, 227ff. See also ACA, R. 100, fol. 400r (18 Mar. 1295, documents trimmed along left margin): ". . . et universis ad quos presentes pervenerint fidelibus amicis et devotis suis. Cum Muca Almentare, sarracenus janetus [noster], lator presentium ad partes Sicilie et Barbarie de nostra licencia accedat ad presens vobis fidelibus mandamus et vos amicos [et d]evotos requirimus et rogamus quatenus predictum Mucam benigne recipientes pariter et tractantes nullum sibi, familie, equitaturis [et] rebus suis in eundo stando et redeundo impedimentum itineris nec iniuirias gravamina seu molestias inferatis . . . permitatis ab aliis irrogari prout nobis cupitis compelare. Immo si

locus afuerit et nos inde requisierit provideatis eidem [nostri] amoris et honoris intuitu de securo transitu et ducatu. Datum Barchinone, XV kalendes Aprilis"; and "... dompno Infant Frederico, cum Muca Almentare, Sarracenus de [officio] nostro ad partes Siculas de nostra licencia [va]dat ad presens fraternitatem vestram rogamus, quatenus predictam Muça benigne recipientes partier et tractantes prout eius ... requirit si nullum impedimentum [..]dium seu gravamen per quoscumque sustineatis fieri vel inferri. Datum Barchinone XV [kalendas] Aprilis." Although he is not referred to as a member of the royal household in these documents, Muça was referred to in this manner elsewhere: ACA, R. 82, fol. 164v (8 Sep. 1290); and ACA, R. 203 (7 May 1305), fols. 7r–8r, 13r.

65. Elena Lourie makes no mention of his role in the king's household.

66. Lourie, "A Jewish Mercenary," 370.

67. Lourie, "A Jewish Mercenary," 369: "The presence of a Jew among the *jenets* would merely emphasize the potentially inter-denominational character of *jenet* bands."

68. I have presented and edited below all the documents related to Abrahim, including a handful not cited by Lourie. All transcriptions are my own. ACA, R. 80, fol. 8r (12 July 1289): "Baiulo et iusticie Xative. In[t]elleximus quod occasione cuiusdam litere a nobis optente per Abrafim el genet, iudeum nostrum, in quam mandabamus vobis quod empararetis mille solidos Regalium quos Abrafim de Dertusia et Coffen, iudeum Xative, tenent in rem[..]dam de Açmeli, Iudeo, qui est in Castella in deservicio nostro et lucrum quod cum eis fecerant et nisi per totum mensem Iunii proxime transactum ille Açmeli venisset hostensurus iustam causam propter quam dicti denarii sibi non debent emparari, compelleretis dictos Abrafim et Co[ffen] [. . .] <bona> eorum ad tradendum vobis loco nostri predictos mille solidos et lucrum quod inde fecerunt cum eis. Unde cum constet nobis quod dictos mille solidos [re]galium quos dicti Abrafim et Coffen tenent et lucrum quod fecerant cum eisdem . . . Mahry joculatorii nostri et non sit intencionis nostre quod aliquid emparetis v[el] accipiatis de bonis dicti Mahry licet [*sic*] sit in Castella. Mandamus vobis quatenus visis presentibus desemparetis ei\s/dem Abrafim et Coffen predictos mille solidos et lucrum predictum et absolvatis eisdem et fideiusso[res] per eos vobis datos pro C morabatinis racione predicta ab ipsis Abrafim et [. . . . . .] restituatis eisdem pignora si qua habuistis ut recepistis [racione] predicta ab ipsis Abrafim et Coffen vel eorum fideiusoribus seu aliquo eorum. . . . IIII idus Iulii anno domini MCCLXXX nono." ACA, R. 80, fol. 70v (18 Oct. 1289), as cited without edition in Lourie, "Jewish Mercenary," 369n10: "Iusticie Xative. Cum nos concessimus Abrahimo el Jenet illos mille solidos quos Abrahim de Tortosa et Coffen, Iudei Xative, tenebant ad usururas [*sic*] pro Mealuchç Alhavi, jucolatore, et intelleximus quod dicti Iudei in frauderi dicti Abrafim et contra mandatum quod nos fecimus in predictis dictos mille solidos dederunt et solverunt cuidam fratri dicti Mealuchç. Vobis dicimus et mandamus vobis quatenus si vobis constiterit ita esse compellatis dictos Iudeos ad solvendum

dictos denarios Abrafimo supradicto cum ipsos concessimus sibi pro uno equo. Datum in Monte Sono, XV kalendas Novembris." ACA, R. 81, fol. 10r (3 Jan. 1290), as cited without edition in Lourie, "Jewish Mercenary," 368n7: ". . . iuratis Valencie. Scire vos credimus quod licet Iudei Barchinone et Valencie habeant privilegium ferendi capas quod illi Iudei Barchinone qui sunt de domo nostra non sunt astricti propter dictum privilegium ad ferendum capam. Quare vobis dicimus et mandamus quatenus . . . Abrafimum Abenamies qui de domo nostra est et Abrafimum el Jenet de dicta domo nostra non compellatis aliquatenus ferendum aliquam capam racione pri[vile]gii supradicti. Datum ut supra." ACA, R. 81, fol. 226r (6 Dec. 1290), as cited without edition in Lourie, "Jewish Mercenary," 369n11: "Iusticie et baiulo Valencie. Quod compellant omnes illos, tam Christianos, Judeos quam Sarracenos, qui debeant aliquid Abrafi[m]o el jenet, tam cum carta quam sine cart[a], ad solvendum illud sibi vel ad faciendum et cetera. Datum Barchinone VIII idus Decembris." ACA, R. 82, fol. 3v (8 Jan. 1290): "[Raimundo Scorne] quod s[olva]t Abrafimo el Jenet illis quod invenerit eidem deberi et factum [et cetera]. Datum ut supra." ACA, R. 82, fol. 164v (8 Sep. 1290), as cited without edition in Lourie, "Jewish Mercenary," 368n8: "Arnaldo de Bastida. Quod cum Raimundus Colrati solvere \de/ suo proprio et Sahit, Jahis, Ju[c]ef[o], et M[.]zoto [..] Jucefo, Mançor, Sahit Abenali, Abrahame el Jenet, Abdella, Asma Alca[r]ax, Mu[ça] Almutayre, Mahometo Alca[....], Daveto, Mahometo Abenjabar, A[.]ç[.] Gua[...], et Sahit et Asmeto Arami, janetis de //domino// domo domini Regis, octo mille cen . . . . . . ginta solidos regalium qui debebantur eisdem janetis pro quitacionibus eorum [..] cautis . . . albaranis dicti Arnaldi et etiam cum albaranis Arnaldi Eymerici, scriptoris portionis. Quod solvat dicto Raimundo dicti VIII mile CLXX[X] solidos Guillelmo facta solucione et cetera. Datum VI idus Septembris." ACA, RP, MR, 774, fols. 62v–63r (ca. 1293): "Abrafim juheu el genet deu queli atorech en d'Almau Sunerii en XXVI cartes del seu compte—XXX solidi, VI denarios Barchinones."

69. The king was willing to accept a substitute saddle if the abovementioned was not available. ACA, R. 71, fol. 24v (5 Mar. 1287): "Dilecto scutifero suo, Petro Eximini de Ayerbe. Mandamus vobis quatenus incontenenti visis presentibus ematis roncinum de pilo bagio qui est de Abutçeyt Asseyt, janeto nostro, et tres frono[s] palafredi cum <pictallos> de pulcroribus quos inveneritis ad emendum et faciatis fieri duo pena vel tria de pulcris calcaribus janetis, ematis etiam quosdam arçons pictos cum leon[i]bus inseritis in eis [q]uos tenet Sarracenus Marchelli Pictoris et [si dicta] sella perfacta fuerit similer ematis eam [...] roncinum cum omnibus supradictis [et] cum ea emerit[is] [n]obis inc[on]tinenti mitatis ubicumque fuerimus et istud non differatis . . . nos [...] faciemus . . . vestram volunt[atem] in precio predictorum. [D]atum [Cui]tad[el]l[a] [. . . no]na[s] . . . ."

70. ACA, R. 90, fol. 79v (5 Oct. 1291): "Matheo de P[....] Dalbet. Que nos concessimus de gracia speciale Sancio de Antilione sellam nostram genetam et frenum jenetum ac etiam quemdam calcaram que vos pro nobis tenetis. Mandamus vobis quatenus sellam, frenum, et calcaram predictam tradatis dicto Sancio

vel cui volerit. Tribus traditis presentem recuperis cum apocha de soluti. Datum ut supra." The Marīnid king also delivered several *jenet* bridles to Jaume II (ACA, CR, Jaume II, caixa 163, extra series, no. 1934). In 1309, the ambassador Pere Boyl also brought several gifts back from the Marīnid sultan, including five Berber horses, five *jenet* saddles, five *jenet* bridles(?), five silver *jenet* swords with fine leather grips, and one large, round tent. ACA, RP, MR, 624, fols. 111r–112r: "V cavalls [B]arbareschs ab V celles genetes e V <feres> genets, e V espaes genetes guarnides dargent ab correges de ceda e I gran tenda redona obrada."

71. ACA, R. 67, fol. 97v (21 Mar. 1286). For more on the context for this document, see Fancy, "The Intimacy of Exception," 74.

72. On the *juegos de caña*, see J. R. Juliá Viñamata, "Jocs de guerra i jocs de lleure a la Barcelona de la baixa edat mitjana," *Revista d'etnologia de Catalunya* 1 (1992): 10–23; idem, "Las manifestaciones lúdico-deportivas de los barceloneses en la Baja Edad Media," in *Espai i temps d'oci a la Història. Actes de les XI jornades d'estudis històrics locals*, ed. Maria Barceló Crespí and Bernat Sureda García, 629–42; and Fuchs, *Exotic Nation*, 89–108. On the festivals, see Marlene Albert-Llorca and José Antonio González Alcantud, *Moros y cristianos: representations del otro en las fiestas del Mediterraneo occidental*; and Teofilo F. Ruiz, "Elite and Popular Culture in Late Fifteenth-Century Castilian Festivals: The Case of Jaén," in *City and Spectacle in Medieval Europe*, eds. Barbara Hanawalt and Kathryn Reyerson, 296–381.

73. ACA, R. 82, fol. 163v (23 Aug. 1290): "Eidem [Arnaldo de Bastida] quod [det] Gayleno, janeto nostro, quinquaginta solidos regalium pro eando vulnere [quod] nuper sibi fecerunt quando ludebat ad genetiam." See also Catlos, "Mahomet Abenadalill," 289. Mahomet Abenadilil was also compensated for a horse lost in a similar match. ACA, R. 82, fol. 66v (6 Sep. 1290): "Eidem fuit scriptum [al]iud albaranum quod solvit nobili [Ma]hometo Abnadalyl pro quitacione sua et familie s[u]e quae cum eo venerunt de Granata pro mense Augusti preterito DXXXVI duplas mirias. Item pro quitacione Sarracenorum peditum pro dicto mense et pro esmend[i] unius equi qui fuit interfectus in rambla Valencie super ludo janethie XXXII duplas et med[ia]m mirias. Datum ut supra."

74. ACA, R. 688, fol. 18v (2 Aug. 1356): ". . . quibusdam militibus sarracenis qui pro prostando nobis servicio in auxilium quod dudum Illustri Regi Francie mitere intendebamus de partibus Granate fecimus procurare. . . ." See also Boswell, *Royal Treasure*, 186–87.

75. Georg Simmel, "Adornment," in *The Sociology of Georg Simmel*, ed. K. H. Wolff, 341, as cited in Webb Keane, "The Hazards of New Clothes: What Signs Make Possible," in *The Art of Clothing: A Pacific Experience*, ed. Susanne Küchler and Graeme Were, 12.

76. ACA, R. 19, fol. 48v; ACA, R. 65, fol. 112r; ACA, R. 252, fol. 34v; and ACA, R. 334, fol. 63r–v.

77. ACA, R. 82, fol. 91r (21 Dec. 1290): "Raimundo de Rivo Sicco quod tradat Mahometo Abenadalillo austurchonem suum et dominus Rex satisfac[iat] sibi in

precio. Datum XII kalendas Ianuarii." ACA, R. 90, fol. 22v (2 Sep. 1291): "Andree Eymerici, falchonario et cetera, mandamus vobis quatenus de falchonibus nostris novis quos tenetis in Valencie, tradatis Mahometo Abenadalill nuncio illustris regis Granate quatuor falchones quos sibi de gracia duximus concedendos. Datum ut supra."

78. ACA, R. 52, fol. 83v (26 Dec. 1284): "Raimundo de Rivo Sicco, quod det Muçe et Çahit, jenetis, mantell[um] et totum de Biffa de Pa[ri]s et cum pennis et tunicam et caligas de panno coloris [quatenu]s solvat dicto Çahit qui sibi restant ad solvendum de quitacione sua usque ad ultimam diem mensis Octobris preteriti anni presentis LXX VII solidos, VI denarios Iaccenses. Item dicto Çahit et Muçe pro quitacione usque ad ultimam diem presentis mensis Decembris CLXXXI solidos, VI denarios. Datum in Turole, VII kalendas Ianuarii."

79. ACA, R. 58, fol. 22r (4 May 1285): ". . . unam aliubam et tunicam panni coloris et calligas presseti vermillii . . . aliubam et tunicam exalonis et calligas panni coloris . . . aliubam et tunicam de bifa plana et calligas Narbon[ensis] . . . ," full citation at chapter 2 n95, above. *Presset* (var. perset, preset, precet) was a colored cloth, imported from the Levant. See also ARV, Protocolos, 11178, fol. 48r (24 Dec. 1295), for details on prices of cloth from Paris, Narbonne, and Jálon; and ARV, Protocolos, 2631, fol. 67v (1295), a Jewish merchant of French cloth; ARV, Protocolos, 11179, fol. 15v (1298), a shop in Valencia that sells "French" cloth.

80. ACA, R. 71, fol. 50r (8 May 1287): "Item eidem Petro quod solutis et cetera, det Çeyt Abdela, jeneto, sex coudes panni coloris et pro tribus suis sociis XVIII coudes de bifa de Sancto Dianisio de colore, quas eis dare debemus cum albarano Iacobi Fivelleri directo Muçe de Portella quod nos recuperavimus. Item uxori sue quatuor coudes de panno coloris quos ei pro vestibus damus prout in albarano Iacobi directo Muçe de Portella quod nos recuperavimus continetur. Et cum eis dederitis et cetera. Datum ut supra." See Alcover, *Diccionari català-valencià-balear*, s.v. "colze." ACA, R. 71, fol. 50v (9 May 1287): "Petro Pelegrini. . . . Item debeantur dicto Çeyt de Picaçen sex cubita de bifa de Paris et tria cubita minus quarta de panno coloris et unam penam et mediam nigram prout hec omnia in litera per nos directa Arnaldo de Bastida quam nos recuperavimus continetur. Dicimus vobis et mandamus quatenus solutis et cetera, solvatis dictis jenetis quantitates predictas et vestes et facta et cetera. Datum apud Castilionem Campi de Burriana, septimo idus Maii." ACA, R. 72, fols. 38v–39r (3 May 1288): "Arnaldo de Bastida. . . . Item debeamus [Ç]ayt de Pitaçen predicto sex cubitos de bifa de Paris et tres cubitos minus quarta de panno coloris et unam [p]enam et mediam nigram cum albarano Iacobi Fivellerii directo Muçe de Portella quod recuperavimus. Mandamus vobis quatenus omnes predictas quantitates et vestes solvatis predictis Maymono et Çayt vel cui voluerint loco sui, et facta et cetera. Datum [Va]lencie V nonas Maii." ACA, RP, MR, 263, fol. 145r (1299): "Item donam per manament del Senyor rey an Muça Almentauri, janet, vestir IIII canes e miga de biffa plana de paris a DXX solidos de XX solidos la cana e monta XC solidos item XVIII solidos per I pena e miga negra. Item VII solidos per calses. E axo monta per tot. CXV solidos

Barchinone." A *cana* was approximately 160 centimeters. ACA, RP, MR, 620, fol. 69r (16 June 1304): ". . . Item mostrans dos albarans de vestir dels dits jenets de VI canas de biffa de paris per dues jubes. . . ." ACA, RP, MR, 620, fol. 107r (15 June 1305): ". . . An Arnau Sabastida de part den Arnau Almerich que dedes a Muça Mufarrax Asxaar tres canas de biffa de paris por una juba. . . ."

81. Marcel Mauss, *Essai sur le don: Forme et raison de l'échange dans les sociétés archaïques*; and Georges Bataille, *La part maudite, precédé de la notion de dépense*.

82. ACA, R 334, fols. 63v–64r (21 May 1302): ". . . el Senyor Rey de Aragon lembia dos falchones grifalles e dos falchones grueros e un falchonero del Rey . . ."; and ACA, R 334, fol. 64v (21 May 1302). For the Islamic context, see *EI*², s.v. "bayzara." See also Louis Mercier, *La Chasse et les sports chez les Arabes*, esp. 81–106, and extensive bibliography. In contrast to medieval Europe, falconry was not solely an elite diversion in the Islamic world. See also Tapia y Salcedo, *Exercicios de la gineta*, 111, who connects falconing and the skill of riding *a la jineta*: "De los exercicios mas generosos de la Gineta es la Cetreria ò Volaterio; para el qual (ademas de tantos preceptos como se necessita) es menester gran diversidad de Pajaros de partes muy remotas"; and Juan Manuel, *El libro de la caza*, ed. G. Baist.

83. Rachel Arié, *El reino Naṣrí de Granada, 1232–1492*, 231, as cited by Catlos, "Mahomet Abenadalill," 288n115. See also José Angel García de Cortázar y Ruiz de Aguirre, "Las necesidades ineludibles: alimentación, vestido, vivienda," in *La época del gótico en la cultura española*, ed. José Angel García de Cortázar y Ruiz de Aguirre, 41.

84. See *EI*², s.v. "marāsim" and "tashrīfāt."

85. An argument made, for instance, in Marc Bloch, *The Royal Touch: Sacred Monarchy and Scrofula in England and France*; and Clifford Geertz, *Negara: The Theatre State in Nineteenth-Century Bali*.

86. Burns, *Islam under the Crusaders*, 298: "Ideology or religion was no absolute obstacle to participation"; idem, *Muslims, Christians, and Jews in the Crusader Kingdom of Valencia: Societies in Symbiosis*, 15: "Military action, quite apart from Muslim-Christian hostilities, provided a friendly contact"; idem, "Renegades, Adventurers and Sharp Businessmen: The Thirteenth-Century Spaniard in the Cause of Islam," *Catholic Historical Review* 58, no. 3 (1972): 341–66, esp. 341–42; Lourie, "A Jewish Mercenary," 368: "If the cultural heterogeneity, the frontier conditions and the combination of geo-political rivalries with religious warfare facilitated the employment of Muslim mercenaries by Christian princes (and vice versa), in spite of that self-conscious confrontation of Christianity with Islam which was one enduring aspect of the Reconquest, then uprooted, outcast, or merely adventurous Jews can scarcely have found the 'ideological' conditions uncongenial to the offering of their swords for sale in medieval Spain"; Barton, "Traitors to the Faith?" 38: "When all was said and done, the search for wealth, status and power, the chief motors of aristocratic behaviour down the ages, was always likely to take precendence over religious or ideological considerations"; Catlos, "Mahomet Abenada-

lill," 286–87: "Indeed, the higher one climbed in noble circles, the rarer the air of confessional identity seems to have become"; ibid., 302: "Neither Abenadalill's culture nor his religion presented a serious impediment for a certain integration in the Aragonese court, and the privileges which he was accorded and the esteem with which he was treated may even indicate a certain affection on the part of the king for his Muslim vassal"; Echevarría Arsuaga, *Caballeros en la frontera*, 86: "El ámbito militar se mostró especialmente receptivo a este tipo de mutaciones, probablemente porque contaba más el valor del enemigo que su religión, y porque el converso era incorporado inmediatamente a filas sin modificar su categoría dentro el ejército, ni en la sociedad, ya que se le consideraba protegido por el monarca"; and García Sanjúan, "Mercenarios cristianos," 443–46.

87. ACA, R. 85, fol. 113v (15 Mar. 1290), as cited above and discussed in detail beginning at chapter 5 n63, below.

88. For instance, ACA, R. 233, fol. 18r (25 Mar. 1304).

89. See chapter 5 for more detail on the interactions between *jenets* and Christian villagers.

90. Cf. Burns, "Royal Pardons in the Realms of Aragon."

91. This privilege evolved over time into a right, which is to say that the *jenets* expected it. See ACA, R. 39, fol. 182v (6 Apr. 1277), and ACA, R. 57, fol. 143r (4 July 1285), where this privilege is granted temporarily. Cf. ACA, R. 81, fol. 84r (19 Apr. 1290), and ACA, R. 252, fol. 189r (1298?), where the privilege is spoken of as an unrestricted right.

92. See ACA, R. 81, fol. 215r (25 Nov. 1290), and ACA, R. 81, fol. 234v (17 Dec. 1290), both discussed in detail in chapter 5.

93. Ibn Khaldūn, *Kitāb al-'ibar*, VII: 191; al-Maqqarī, *Nafḥ al-ṭīb*, VII: 7 and IX: 54; and Arié, *L'Espagne musulmane*, 240.

94. See also Teofilo Ruiz, "Festivés, colours, et symbols du pouvoir en Castille au XVe siècle," *Annales* 3 (1991): 521–46; Diane Owen Hughes, "Sumptuary Law and Social Relations in Renaissance Italy," in *Disputes and Settlements: Law and Human Relations in the West*, ed. John Bossy, 69–99; and Ann Rosalind Jones and Peter Stallybrass, *Renaissance Clothing and the Materials of Money*. See also C. A. Bayly, "The Origins of Swadeshi (Home Industry): Cloth and Indian Society" in *The Social Life of Things*, ed. Arjun Appadurai, 285–322, with thanks to Jane Lynch for bringing these last two references to my attention.

95. Brian A. Catlos, *The Victors and the Vanquished: Christians and Muslims of Catalonia and Aragon, 1050–1300*, 300–302; Ferrer i Mallol, *Els sarraïns*, 41ff; Boswell, *Royal Treasure*, 330ff; Teresa María Vinyoles i Vidal, *La vida quotidiana a Barcelona vers 1400*, 125; and Franciso Roca Traver, "Un siglo de vida Mudéjar en la Valencia medieval (1238–1338)," *Estudios de Edad Media de la Corona de Aragón* V (1952): 115–208, esp. 146, 160.

96. See also Thomas R. Trautmann, *Dravidian Kinship*, 279: ". . . a soteriology, not a sociology of reciprocity"; and Jonathan Parry, "The Gift, the Indian Gift, and the 'Indian Gift,'" *Man* 21, no. 3 (1986): 453–73, esp. 462, 467.

97. See *Libre de les costums generals scrites de la insigne ciutat de Tortosa*, ed. Josep Foguet Marsal, Ramon Foguet, and Joan J. Permanyer i Ayats, 85 (I.ix:4): "Los sarrayns deuen portar los cabells tolts en redon; e deuen portar barba larga. E dels cabells nos deuen tolre a vs ne a costum de crestia. E la sobirana vestedura lur deu esser aljuba o almeixa." Cf. Boswell, *Royal Treasure*, 331–32, who cites two documents from the chancery registers that reiterate the requirements regarding hair. Cf. "Corts de Lleida" (1301) in *Cortes de los antiguos reinos de Aragón y de Valencia y de principado de Cataluña*, I: 190; and "Corts de Zaragoza" (1301) in *Fueros y observancias del Reyno de Aragón*, fols. 10v–11r, as cited in Ferrer i Mallol, *Els sarraïns*, 43n11. See also H. J. Schroeder, *Disciplinary Decrees of the General Councils: Text, Translation and Commentary*, 236–96, canon 68.

98. David Nirenberg, "Conversion, Sex, and Segregation: Jews and Christians in Medieval Spain," *American Historical Review* 107, no. 4 (2002): 1065–93.

99. Alcover, *Diccionari català-valencià-balear*, s.v. "aljuba" and "almeixia." Reinhart Pieter Anne Dozy, *Dictionnaire détaillé de noms de vêtements chez les Arabes*, s.v. "jubba" and "maḥshiya." See also Gonzalo Menéndez-Pidal and Carmen Bernis Madrazo, "Las Cantigas: la vida en el s. XIII según la representación iconográfica. (II) Traje, Aderezo, Afeites," *Cuadernos de la Alhambra* 15–17 (1979–81): 89–154; Rachel Arié, "Quelques remarques sur le costume des Musulmans d'Espagne au temps de Naṣrides," *Arabica* 12, no. 3 (1965): 244–64, esp. 247. *Libre de les costums generals scrites de la insigne ciutat de Tortosa*, I:IX:3: "E no deu esser listada, ne vert, ne vermella."

100. See a letter from King Jaume II forbidding Christians from wearing the *aljuba* in Joaquín Lorenzo Villanueva, *Viage literario a las iglesias de España*, XVI: 231, as cited in Boswell, *Royal Treasure*, 332n10.

101. Boswell, *Royal Treasure*, 45, 331–32. See also ARV, Justicia de Valencia, 1bis, fol. 50r (1280), an arrest for wearing a wool cape of "moltes et diversis" colors.

102. Boswell, *The Royal Treasure*, 37, 45, 51, 331–32; Catlos, *Victors and the Vanquished*, 301.

103. ACA, R. 81, fol. 10r (3 Jan. 1290): ". . . iuratis Valencie. Scire vos credimus quod licet iudei Barchinone et Valencie habeant privilegium ferendi capas quod illi Iudei Barchinone qui sunt de domo nostra non sunt astricti propter dictum privilegium ad ferendum capam. Quare vobis dicimus et mandamus quatenus . . . Abrafimum Abenamies qui de domo nostra est et Abrafimum el Jenet de dicto doma nostra non compellatis aliquatenus ferendum aliquam capam racione pri[vile]gii supradicti. . . ." See also n68, above.

104. John D. Caputo, "Without Sovereignty, Without Being: Unconditionally, the Coming God and Derrida's Democracy to Come," *Journal of Cultural and Religious Theory* 4, no. 3 (2003): 12, commenting on Jacques Derrida, *Voyous*, 155.

105. Echevarría Arsuaga, *Caballeros en la frontera*, esp. chap. 3.

106. On the cultural turn in medieval studies, see Paul Freedman and Gabrielle Spiegel, "Medievalisms Old and New: The Rediscovery of Alterity in North

American Medieval Studies." *American Historical Review* 103, no. 3 (1998): 677–704; Paul Freedman, "The Medieval Other: The Middle Ages as Other," in *Marvels, Monsters, and Miracles: Studies in the Medieval and Early Modern Imaginations,* ed. Timothy S. Jones and David A. Sprunger, 1–26; Caroline Walker Bynum, "Why All the Fuss about the Body? A Medievalist's Perspective," *Critical Inquiry* 22 (1995): 1–33; and Lee Patterson, "On the Margin: Postmodernism, Ironic History, and Medieval Studies," *Speculum* 65, no. 1 (1990): 87–108.

107. Particularly influential is Clifford Geertz, "Religion as a Cultural System" (1966) in *The Interpretation of Cultures*, esp. 90. See the epilogue for a fuller discussion of Geertz.

108. With Iberian studies, see Thomas F. Glick and Oriol Pi-Sunyer, "Acculturation as an Explanatory Concept in Spanish History," *Comparative Studies in Society and History* 11, no. 2 (1969): 136–54; and Thomas F. Glick, *Islamic and Christian Spain in the Early Middle Ages: Comparative Perspectives on Social and Cultural Formation.* Glick and Pi-Sunyer, "Acculturation," 138: "The whole process of national formation has hitherto been discussed in the absence of a scientifically valid theory of cultural relations. This failure to come to grips with the cultural determinants of national identity has landed the historiographic polemic in a morass of confusion and guaranteed that it shall remain there, appeals to philosophers and historical experts notwithstanding." See also Glick, *Islamic and Christian Spain in the Early Middle Ages*, xviii: "In general, viewed from the comparative perspective that motivates this volume, the study of medieval Spain, of the conflict between two opposing and radically different cultural and social blocs, has suffered from an inadequate theory of culture or, from the incomplete conjunction of cultural and social theory."

109. Borrowing a phrase from Peter Brown, *The Cult of the Saints: Its Rise and Function in Latin Christianity*, 13: "Plainly, some solid and seemingly unmovable cultural furniture has piled up somewhere in that capacious lumber room, the back of our mind."

110. Justice, "Did the Middle Ages Believe in Their Miracles?"

111. Michael Taussig's notion of a "public secret" highlights this same tension. See his *Defacement: Public Secrecy and the Labor of the Negative*.

112. Justice, "Did the Middle Ages Believe in Their Miracles?"; Asad, *Genealogies of Religion*; and Gregory, "The Other Confessional History."

113. Lourie, "A Jewish Mercenary," 368; Barton, "Traitors to the Faith?" 38; Catlos, "Muhammad Abenadalill," 279, 302; Echevarría Arsuaga, *Caballeros en la frontera*, 86; García Sanjúan, "Mercenarios cristianos," 443–46; and Burns, "Renegades, Adventurers, and Sharp Businessmen," 341–42.

114. Wieruszowski, "La Corte di Pietro," 196.

115. See chapter 4.

116. Kenneth Pennington, *The Prince and the Law*, 76–118; Jean Bethke Elshtain, *Sovereignty: God, State, and Self*; Walter Ullmann, "The Development of

the Medieval Idea of Sovereignty"; and Gaines Post, "Roman Law and Early Representation in Spain and Italy, 1150–1250."

117. Strayer, "The Laicization of French and English Society," 76. See the epilogue for a fuller discussion of Kantorowicz.

118. Justinian, *Digest* in *Corpus iuris civilis*, 1.2.6: "Quod principi placuit legis habet vigorem"; Justinian, *Digest,* 1.3.31(30): "Princeps legibus solutus est; Augusta autem licet legibus soluta non est, principes tamen eadem illi privilegia tribuunt, quae ipsi habent." Pennington, *The Prince and the Law*, 82; Elshtain, *Sovereignty*, 32; and Ewart Lewis, "King Above Law? 'Quod Principi Placuit' in Bracton," *Speculum* 39, no. 2 (1964): 240–69.

119. Brian Tierney, "'The Prince Is Not Bound by the Laws': Accursius and the Origins of the Modern State," *Comparative Studies in Society and History* 5 (1963): 389–400.

120. On historiography, see Tierney, "'The Prince Is Not Bound by the Laws,'" 379–82. See also Brian Tierney, "Bracton on Government," *Speculum* 38 (1963): 295–317; John Austin, *The Province of Jurisprudence Determined*, ed. Wilfred E. Rumble; Hans Kelsen, *Pure Theory of Law*, trans. M. Knight; and idem, *General Theory of Law and the State*, trans. A. Wedberg.

121. Tierney, "'The Prince Is Not Bound by the Laws,'" 387–94.

122. Justinian, *Code* in *Corpus iuris civilis*, 1.14.4: "Digna vox maiestate regnantis legibus alligatum se principem profiteri"; Justinian, *Digest*, 1.3.2: "Quia omnis lex inventum ac munus deorum est"; Justinian, *Institutes* in *Corpus iuris civilis*, 2.17.18; Accursius's gloss of Justinian, *Institutes* in *Corpus iuris civilis*, 1.2.6.

123. Tierney, "'The Prince Is Not Bound by the Laws,'" 388, 394.

124. See, for instance, Kantorowicz, *The King's Two Bodies*, 207: "The noble concept of the corpus mysticum, after having lost much of its transcendental meaning and having been politicized and, in many respects, secularized by the Church itself, easily fell prey to the world of thought of statesmen, jurists, and scholars who were developing new ideologies for the nascent territorial and secular state."

125. William J. Courtenay, "The Dialectic of Omnipotence in the High and Late Middle Ages," in *Divine Omniscience and Omnipotence in Medieval Philosophy: Islamic, Jewish and Christian Perspectives*, ed. Tamar Rudavsky, esp. 243–56; Pennington, *The Prince and the Law*, 106–11.

126. Jürgen Miethke, "The Concept of Liberty in William of Ockham," *Collection de l'École française de Rome* 147 (1991): 93; Pennington, *The Prince and the Law*, 85, 108; Elshtain, *Sovereignty: God, State, and Self*, 25–27, 36–39; William J. Courtenay, *Capacity and Volition: A History of the Distinction of Absolute and Ordained Power*, 118; and idem, "The Dialectic of Omnipotence," 243: "terrifying potential of arbitrary divine intervention."

127. Kantorowicz, *The King's Two Bodies*, 151ff; Ullmann, "The Development of the Medieval Idea of Sovereignty"; and Lewis, "King Above Law?" 243. On Frederick's self-coronation, see Kantorowicz, *Kaiser Freidrich der Zweite*, 184–86;

and Hans Eberhard Mayer, "Das Pontifikale von Tyrus und die Krönung der lateinischen Könige von Jerusalem: Zugleich ein Beitrag zur Forschung über Herrschaftszeichen und Staatssymbolik," *Dumbarton Oaks Papers* 21 (1967): 141–232. Cf. Albert Brackmann, "Nachwort," *Historische Zeitschrift* 141 (1930): 472–78.

128. Cf. Francis Oakley, "Jacobean Political Theology: The Absolute and Ordinary Powers of the King," *Journal of the History of Ideas* 29 (1968): 323–46.

129. Cf. Carl Schmitt, *Political Theology*, 36: "All significant concepts of the modern theory of the state are secularized theological concepts."

130. Aquilino Iglesia Ferreirós, "La difusión del derecho común en Cataluña," in *El dret comú i Catalunya*, ed. Aquilino Iglesia Ferreirós, 95 ff.

131. José María Font y Rius, "La recepción del derecho romano en la Península Ibérica durante la Edad Media," *Recueil des mémoires et travaux publiés par la Société d'Histoire du Droit et des Institutions des Anciens Pays de Droit Écrit* 6 (1967): 88; Eduardo Hinojosa, "La admisión del derecho romano en Cataluña," *Boletín de la Real Academia de Buenas Letras de Barcelona* 37 (1910): 213; and Joaquín Miret y Sans, "Escolars catalans al estudi de Bolonia en la XIIIe centuria," *Boletín de la Real Academia de Buenas Letras de Barcelona* 8 (1915–16): 137–55.

132. See, for instance, *Costumbres de Lérida*, ed. Pilar Loscertales de Valdeavellano, 169 [compiled 1228], "De legibus romanis"; the *Customs of Perpignan* (1267) in Guillermo María de Brocà, *Historia del derecho de Cataluña, especialmente del civil y exposición de las instituciones del derecho civil del mismo territorio en relación con el Código civil de España y la jurisprudencia*, 196, which replaced customary and Gothic law with Roman law; or usatge 69, "Item statuerunt," in *Usatges de Barcelona*, ed. Joan Bastardas, which includes the principle "quod principi placuit."

133. *CYADC*, II: 1.10.1 and I: 2.4.1.

134. J. Lee Shneidman, "Political Theory and Reality in Thirteenth Century Aragon," *Hispania: Revista española de historia* 22 (1962): 176. Roman law was applied and resisted in other contexts. See, for instance, the struggle between bishops and townsmen in Paul H. Freedman, "An Unsuccessful Attempt at Urban Organization in Twelfth-Century Catalonia," *Speculum* 54, no. 3 (1979): 479–91.

135. Font y Rius, "La recepción del derecho Romano," 97.

136. *CYADC*, II: 2.3.1 (1243): "No sie admes en alguna Cort lo Advocat, que allegara algunas leys, pus las Consuetuts, e Vsatges complescan, e abunden," as cited in Aquilino Iglesia Ferreirós, *La creación del derecho: antología de textos*, 147. I thank Max Turull for his guidance on questions of Roman law.

137. "Corts de Barcelona," in *CYADC*, III: 1.8.1 (1251): "Item statuimus consilio predictorum quod leges Romane vel Gothice, decreta vel decretales, in causis secularibus non recipiantur, admittantur, indicentur, vel allegentur, nec aliquis legista audeat in foro seculari advocare nisi in causa propria; ita quod in dicta causa non allegentur leges vel jura predicta, sed fiant in omni causa seculari allegationes

secundum Usaticos Barchinone, et secundum approbatas constitutiones illius loci ubi causa agitabitur, et in eorum defectu procedatur secundum sensum naturalem. Ne iudices admittant Advocatos legistas. Iudices etiam in causis secularibus non admittant Advocatos legistas, sicut superius dictum est," as cited in Iglesia Ferreirós, *La creación del derecho*, 147–48.

138. Francesc Eiximenis, *Regiment de la cosa publica*, 69, as cited in Nicholas Round, *The Greatest Man Uncrowned: A Study of the Fall of Don Alvaro de Luna*, 121.

139. Burns, "Warrior Neighbors."

140. Jaume Aurell and Marta Serrano-Coll, "The Self-Coronation of Peter the Ceremonious (1336): Historical, Liturgical, and Iconographical Representations," *Speculum* 89, no. 1 (2013): 66–95; Antonio Durán Gudiol, "El rito de la coronación del rey en Aragón," *Argensola: revista de ciencias sociales del Instituto de Estudios Altoaragoneses* 103 (1989): 17–40.

141. Boswell, *The Royal Treasure*; and Yom Tov Assis, *The Golden Age of Aragonese Jewry: Community and Society in the Crown of Aragon, 1213–1327*, esp. 9.

142. David Abulafia, "The Servitude of Jews and Muslims in the Medieval Mediterranean: Origins and Diffusion," *Mélanges de l'école française de Rome. Moyen Âge* 112 (2000): 691.

143. Fancy, "The Intimacy of Exception"; David Romano, *Judíos al servicio de Pedro el Grande de Aragón (1276–1285)*; J. Lee Shneidman, "Jews as Royal Bailiffs in Thirteenth Century Aragon," *Historia Judaica* 19 (1957): 55–66; and idem, "Jews in the Royal Administration."

144. Assis, *The Golden Age of Aragonese Jewry*, 9–10: "The Jews' position during this period was far from that of serfs, even royal serfs."

145. Abulafia, "The Servitude of Jews and Muslims," 693–96.

146. Abulafia, "The Servitude of Jews and Muslims," 704: "To enthusiastic readers of Roman law texts, . . . it was all too easy to assimilate the concept of *servus* to that of slave in Roman law texts, a figure who was indeed possessed by his master"; and idem, "Monarchs and Minorities in the Christian Western Mediterranean Around 1300: Lucera and Its Analogues," in *Christendom and Its Discontents: Exclusion, Persecution, and Rebellion, 1000–1500*, ed. Scott L. Waugh and Peter Diehl, 260.

147. See Mark D. Meyerson, "Slavery and the Social Order: Mudejars and Christians in the Kingdom of Valencia," *Medieval Encounters* 1, no. 1 (1995): 149: "There is perhaps no clearer indication of the Mudejars' status as politically subjugated and socially inferior people than the ease with which they could pass from a state of freedom to one of servitude."

148. Shneidman, "Jews as Royal Bailiffs," 66; David Romano, "Los funcionarios judíos de Pedro el Grande de Aragón," *Boletín de la Real Academia de Buenas Letras de Barcelona* 33 (1969): 8n18; and Meyerson, "Slavery and the Social Order," 146.

149. Luis González Antón, *Las Uniones aragoneses y las Cortes del reino,*

1283–1301; C. Laliena Corbera, "La adhesión de las ciudades a la Unión: poder real y conflictividad social en Aragón a fines del XIII," *Aragón en la Edad Media* 8 (1989): 319–413; and Donald Kagay, "Rebellion on Trial: The Aragonese *Unión* and its Uneasy Connection to Royal Law, 1265–1301," *Journal of Legal History* 18 (1997): 30–43.

150. *Fueros y observancias del Reyno de Aragón*, fols. 7c–9c, as cited in Shneidman, "Political Theory," 184.

151. ACA, R. 47, fol. 52r: "Item demandan los rico homes et todos los otro sobredichos que en los regnos d'Aragon e de Valencia, ni en Ribagorça ni en Teruel, que no aya bayle que jodia sea."

152. ACA, R. 46, fol. 129r: "Item statuimus et ordinamus quod nullus judeus sit baiulus nec teneat baiuliam nec curiam nec sit etiam collector redditum in Valencia nec in alio loco regni, nec officium publicum teneat unde super christianum habeat jurisdictionem." See also *CYADC*, II: 49 (*Recognoverunt proceres*): "Item concedimus capitulum quod aliquis judeus non possit uti jurisdictione vel districtu super christianos."

153. Jaume II also adopted the strategy of naming new noblemen. See F. de Moxó Monotliu, "Jaume II y la nueva concesión de títulos nobiliarios en la España del siglo XIV," *Anales de la Universidad de Alicante: Historia medieval* 9 (1992–1993): 133–43.

154. Romano, "Los funcionarios judíos," 32.

155. ACA, R. 80, fol. 8r (12 July 1289): ". . . Abrafim el genet, iudeum nostrum."

156. ACA, R. 74, fol. 5r (14 Oct. 1287); and ACA, R. 74, fol. 11r (23 Oct. 1287). See also Gazulla, "Zenetes," 187; Catlos, "Mahomet Abenadalill," 295–96; and Bisson, *The Medieval Crown of Aragon*, 90.

157. ACA, R. 98, fol. 110v (15 May 1293): "Cum pro certo didiscerimus quod aliqui nobiles Aragonum noviter ad regem Granate suos nuncios transmiserint pro petendo et habendo auxilio ab eodem. Intellexerimus etiam alios nuncios ad dictum regum Granate misos fuisse per illustrem Alfonse, filium illustris dompni Ferrandi de Castellam, quod intellexerimus etiam quod nobilis Artaldus de Alagone nunc misit ad dictum regum maiordomum suum simul cum quodam Sarraceno janeto pro habenda ab eo aliqua janetorum comitiva pro inferendo nobis dampnum, et nos eorum tractatibus et conatibus intendamus et velimus resistere, sic quod non terre seu subditis nostris dampnum seu nocumentum aliquod inferre non possint." See also ACA, R. 98, fols. 110v–111r (15 May 1293).

158. Henry David Thoreau, "Walden," *The Portable Thoreau*, ed. Carl Bode, 278, with credit to Keane, "The Hazards of New Clothes," 1.

Chapter Four

1. Parts of this chapter appeared in Hussein Fancy, "The Last Almohads: Universal Sovereignty Between North Africa and the Crown of Aragon," *Medieval*

Encounters 19, no. 1–2 (2013): 102–36, and "Monarchs and Minorities: 'Infidel' Soldiers in Mediterranean Courts," in *Globalization of Knowledge in The Post-Antique Mediterranean, 700–1500*, ed. Sonja Brentjes and Jürgen Renn.

2. Brunschvig, *Berbérie orientale*, I: 53–54; Mas Latrie, *Traités de paix*, 158–89; Wieruszowski, "Conjuraciones," 579; and Abulafia, "The Kingdom of Sicily," 508.

3. See Gual de Torrella, "Milicias cristianas en Berbería," 58; and Burns, "Renegades," 350.

4. Brunschvig, *Berbérie orientale*, I: 76–78.

5. ACA, R. 40, fol. 95r (13 May 1278); Muntaner, *Crònica,* chap. 30; Dufourcq, *L'Espagne catalane,* 240; Dufourcq, "Hafside," 10; and Shneidman, "Sicilian Vespers," 256–57.

6. ACA, R. 50, fol. 209v (1 Mar. 1283): Pere receives letters carried by "nunciorum filii Regis Tunicii." See also Dufourcq, *L'Espagne catalane*, 260, 270.

7. Brunschvig, *Berbérie orientale*, I: 96; E. Solal, "Au tournant de l'histoire méditerranéenne du Moyen Âge: L'Expédition de Pierre III d'Aragon à Collo (1282)," *Revue Africaine* 101 (1957): 247–71; and Mikel de Epalza, "Attitudes politiques de Tunis dans le conflit entre Aragonais et Français en Sicile autour de 1282," in *La società mediterranea all'epoca del Vespero*, II: 579–601.

8. Muntaner, *Crònica*, chap. 117; and Brunschvig, *Berbérie orientale*, 93.

9. ACA, R. 48, fol. 27r; ACA, R. 47, fols. 81r–82v (June 1285); Mas Latrie, *Traités de paix*, 286ff; and Brunschvig, *Berbérie orientale*, I: 95–96.

10. ACA, R. 61, fol. 176r–v (22 Dec. 1286); ACA, R. 64, fols. 191r–192r (21 Apr. 1287). Pere de Deo had begun negotiations with Abū Yūsuf before his death in 1286 (ACA, R. 64, fol. 26). See also Ludwig Klüpfel, *Die äussere Politik Alfonsos III von Aragonien (1285–1291)*, 167–71; Gazulla, "Zenetes," 184; and Dufourcq, *L'Espagne catalane*, 282. Cf. ACA, R. 64, fol. 150r (9 Jan. 1286).

11. ACA, R. 64, fol. 191r (21 Apr. 1287): "E con vendra al especificar de la valença que demanem valença de D cavalers janets a aquest estiu a messio et a despesa d'Abenjacob. E sil Senyor Rey navia mes obs que el los li trameta, el Senyor Rey fees lurs obs a aquels mes que mester auria. Item quel Senyor Rey li enviara en sa valença V galees armades ab sa messio. E si mester na mes de X tro en XV galees que les li prestara, et que les pusen fer armar ab la sua mesio de les gens del Senyor Rey. E si altre navili a mester dela terra del Sen[y]or Rey, quel puse[n] aver et armar a messio d'Abenjacob."

12. ACA, R. 64, fol. 191r (21 Apr. 1287): "Item que Abenjacob li vayla contra tots los Christians del mon. El Senyor Rey a el contra tots los Sarrayns del mon"; and ACA, R, fol. 191v (21 Apr. 1289): "Item que Abenjacob ne nuyl hom dels seus no fassen neguna ajuda contral Senyor Rey [ne] nuyl hom [Sarray] ni alter. Nel Senyor Rey nels seus contra Abenjacob a nuyls hom Christian ne altre."

13. Ibn Khaldūn, *Kitāb al-'ibar*, VI: 356: "At the same time, Murghim b. Ṣābir b. 'Askar, admiral of the Banū Dabbāb, was a captive. In the year 82 (1283–84), the Sicilian enemy captured him near Tripoli (Ṭarāblus) and sold him to some

men from Barcelona. Consequently, the tyrant (*al-ṭāghiya*) [i.e., Alfons] purchased him."

14. ACA, R. 64, fol. 191v (21 Apr. 1287): "Item que per rao dela valença quel Rey d'Arago faria o fer faria per lo Rey de Sicilia a Abenjacob en la conquesta de Tuniz, no peresquen enans sien salus a els los tributz, els altres dretz que <au o aver deven> en Tuniz per qualque manera."

15. Although the *jenets* were broadly under the control of the Marīnids, one rarely sees the troops coming from Marīnid North Africa directly. Cf. ACA, Cartas árabes, no. 16 (5 Rabīʿ I, 723/14 Mar. 1323), in which the Marīnids offer the Aragonese Muslim troops.

16. ACA, R. 64, fols. 178r–179r (Apr. 1286). Full edition in Klüpfel, *Die äussere*, 171–73. For the broader context, see Dufourcq, *L'Espagne catalane*, 321–23; and Zurita, *Anales*, II: 281. Christian and Muslim ambassadors from Tlemcen arrived at the Aragonese court in 1288. See ACA, R. 72, fol. 37v (7 Apr. 1288): "Nos Alfonsus et cetera, recognoscimus et confitemur, vobis fideli thesaurario nostro Arnaldo de Bastida quod de mandato nostro dedistis et solvis[tis] nunciis Regis Tirimce tam Christiano quam Sarraceno tam in expensis necesariis eisdem quam in naulio cuiusdam Berna[rdi] armate quam eisdem nauliavisti[s] septingentos triginta solidos Barchinonenses quod quidem denarios volumes vobis recepi in compotum. Datum Barchinone, VII idus Aprilis."

17. Dufourcq, *L'Espagne catalane*, 314–16, 472ff; and Desclot, *Crónica*, chaps. 5, 6, on the "Lord of Constantine." An illegitimate son of Jaume II, Jaume d'Aragó, also rose to prominence in the fourteenth century.

18. ACA, R. 64, fol. 178r: "Primerament que pone su amor con el de seer amigos segunt que fue con su padre el Rey don Pedro et [con] su avuelo el Rey don Jayme."

19. ACA, R. 64, fol. 178v: "Item que todos los Christianos que seran en la terra del Rey de Tirimçe de qualesquier condiciones o senyorias, que sean jutgados por fuero d'Aragon por aquel alcayt que el Rey don Alfonso ala enbiarra."

20. For the last of these stipulations, see ACA, R. 64, fol. 178v: "Item que de por a un clerigo quel dicho alcayt hi levara soldado de cavallero." Generally, on Christianity in North Africa in this period, see Henry Koehler, *L'Église Chrétienne du Maroc et la mission franciscaine (1221–1790)*, and Atanasio López, *Obispos en la Africa septentrional desde el siglo XIII*.

21. Burns, "Renegades," 354.

22. ACA, R. 64, fol. 179r: "Item promete el dicho Rey de Tirimçe de aiudir con su companya al dicho Rey d'Aragon cada que mester oviere su aiuda o por el serva amenestado."

23. ACA, R. 64, fol. 192r–v (Mar. 1286). The document appears directly after the instructions for Pere de Deo, above. See also Dufourcq, *L'Espagne catalane*, 282–84. We know that Conrad Lancia did in fact travel to Tunis on 2 Feb. 1287 (ACA, R 72, fol. 48v).

24. ACA, R. 64, fol. 192r: "Primerament que tots los Christians de sou de qual que lengua sien, sien deius l'alcayt del dit Rey d'Arago et que preguen sou per sa sua man et ques jutgen per ell."

25. ACA, R. 64, fol. 192v: "Item quel alfondech del Rey d'Aragon aia aquellos franquees que avia en temps den Guillem de Moncada. . . . Item quel alfondech de Malorche sia del Rey d'Arago."

26. Ibn Khaldūn, *Kitāb al-'ibar*, VI: 356; anonymous, *al-Dhakhīra al-saniyya*, 134; al-Nuwayrī, *al-Maghrib al-Islāmī fi'l-'aṣr al-wasīṭ*, ed. Muṣṭafā Abū Ḍayf Aḥmad, 451–52; and Ibn Simāk al-'Āmilī, *al-Ḥulal al-mawshiyya fī dhikr al-akhbār al-Marrākushiyya*, ed. 'Abd al-Qādir Būbāyah, 258–59. See also Huici Miranda, *Historia política del imperio almohade*, II: 572–73. According to the *al-Ḥulal al-mawshiyya*, 257, the nickname (*kunya*) came from the fact that "he was never separated from his mace (lā yufāriq al-dabbūs)."

27. See Ibn Khaldūn, *Kitāb al-'ibar*, VII: 179–80. Cf. anonymous, *al-Dhakhīra al-saniyya*, 26–29.

28. Ibn Khaldūn, *Kitāb al-'ibar*, VI: 356. Cf. al-Nuwayrī, *al-Maghrib al-Islāmī*, 451–52. For more on the term *nuzū'*, see Ana Fernández Félix and Maribel Fierro, "Cristianos y conversos al Islam en al-Andalus bajo los Omeyas: Una aproximación al proceso de islamización a través de una fuente legal andalusí del s. III/I," *Anejos de AEspA* 23 (2000): 415–27, esp. 423, which understands the term as "defector." See also Dozy, *Supplément aux dictionnaires arabes*, s.v. "naza'a"; and Felipe Maíllo Salgado, "Contenido, uso e historia de termino 'enaciado,'" *Cahiers de linguistique hispanique medieval* 8 (1983): 157–64. See ACA, Cartas árabes, no. 132 (14 September 1315/13 Jumāda II), for an example of *al-mutanaṣṣir* in the sense of impostor.

29. See Robert Ignatius Burns, "Príncipe almohade y converso mudéjar: nueva documentación sobre Abū Zayd," *Sharq Al-Andalus* 4 (1987): 109–22; and his "Daughter of Abu Zayd, Last Almohad Ruler of Valencia: The Family and Christian Seignory of Alda Ferrandis 1236–1300," *Viator* 24 (1993), 143–87. "Abuceyt," governor of Valencia before its conquest by Jaume I, is decribed in the chancery registers as a "grandson of the Caliph (Aceydo Abuceyt nepoti regis Almomeleni)." See *Colección diplomática de Jaime I, el Conquistador*, ed. Ambrosio Huici Miranda, doc. 279. He was, in other words, one and the same man described by Ibn Khaldūn. After his conversion, he married Maria Ferrandis. Amongst the known Christian and Muslim sons and daughters of Abū Zayd were Alda Ferrandis, Fernándo Pérez, Sancho Ferrandis, Elisenda, Mahomat Abiceit, Ceyt Abohiara, Zeyt Edris, Azanay, Muça, Azmal, Aazón, and Francisco Pérez.

30. Lourie, "A Jewish Mercenary," 370n15. Passing mention in Gazulla, "Las compañías de Zenetes" 180: "Pero como nada tiene que ver con las compañías de zenetes, habremos de dejarlo para otra ocasión"; Robert Ignatius Burns, "Christian-Islamic Confrontation in the West: The Thirteenth-Century Dream of Conversion," *American Historical Review* 76 (1971): 1392; idem, "Príncipe almohade y converso

Mudéjar," 115; Huici Miranda, *Historia musulmana de Valencia y su region*, III: 223; and Catlos, "Mahomet Abenadalill," 291n127.

31. Ibn al-Khaṭīb, *A'māl al-a'lām fī-man būyi'a qabla al-iḥtilām min mulūk al-Islām wa-mā yata'allaqu bi-dhālika min al-kalām*, ed. Sayyid Kasrawī Ḥasan, II: 240; ACA, Perg., Jaume I, nos. 373, 480, and 678; Huici Miranda, *Historia musulmana*, III: 252–64; Roque Chabás, "Çeid Abu Çeid," *El archivo* 5 (1891): 147–51; and Emilio Molina López, *Ceyt Abu Ceyt: novedades y rectificaciones*, 27.

32. AS, A. Est. 1, Leg. 2, Núm. 3, as cited in Chabás, "Çeid Abu Çeid," 160ff. See also León Amorós Paya, "Los santos mártires franciscanos B. Juan de Perusa y B. Pedro de Saxoferrato en la historia de Teruel," *Teruel* 15 (1956): 5–142.

33. Burns, *Islam under the Crusaders*, 249ff.

34. Fierro, "The Last Almohad," 175–76. See also Robert Brunschvig, "Sur la doctrine du mahdī Ibn Tūmart," *Arabica* 2, no. 2 (1955): 137–49; Dominique Urvoy, "La Pensée d'Ibn Tumart," *Bulletin d'études orientales* 27 (1974): 19–44; Vincent J. Cornell, "Understanding is the Mother of Ability: Responsibility and Action in the Doctrine of Ibn Tūmart," *Studia islamica* 66 (1987): 71–103; and Madeleine Fletcher, "The Almohad Tawhid: Theology which Relies on Logic," *Numen* 38, no. 1 (1991): 110–27.

35. Bennison, "Almohad Tawḥīd," 196.

36. Bennison, "Almohad Tawḥīd," esp. 206; and Maribel Fierro, "Conversion, Ancestry and Universal Religion: The Case of the Almohads in the Islamic West (Sixth/Twelfth–Seventh/Thirteenth Centuries)," *Journal of Medieval Iberian Studies* 2, no. 2 (2010): 155–73, esp. 167–68. Cf. Cornell, "Understanding Is the Mother," 89; and Michael Brett, "The Lamp of the Almohads: Illumination as a Political Idea in Twelfth-Century Morocco," in *Ibn Khaldun and the Medieval Maghrib*, ed. Michael Brett, Essay VI, 1–27, esp. 3.

37. Fierro, "The Last Almohad," 193; Fletcher, "Almohad Tawhid"; and García-Arenal, *Messianism and Puritanical Reform*.

38. J. F. P. Hopkins, "The Almohad Hierarchy," *Bulletin of the School of Oriental and African Studies* 16 (1954): 93–112; and Abdellatif Sabbane, *Le gouvernment et l'administration de la dynastie Almohade (XIIe–XIIIe siècles)*.

39. Brett, "Lamp of the Almohads"; Sarah Stroumsa, "Philosophes almohades? Averroès, Maïmonide et l'idéologie almohade," in *Los almohades: problemas y perspectivas*, ed. Patrice Cressier, Maribel Fierro, and Luis Molina, II: 1137–62; *Averroès et l'averroïsme, XIIe–XVe siècle: Un itinéraire historique du Haut Atlas à Paris et à Padoue: Actes du colloque international organisé à Lyon, les 4 et 5 octobre 1999 dans le cadre du temps du Maroc*, ed. Andrés Bazzana, Nicole Bériou, and Pierre Guichard; Ana M. Montero, "A Possible Connection between the Philosophy of the Castilian King Alfonso X and the Risālat Ḥayy ibn Yaqẓān by Ibn Ṭufayl," *Al-Masaq: Islam and the Medieval Mediterranean* 18, no. 1 (2006): 1–26; Allen Fromherz, "North Africa and the Twelfth-Century Renaissance: Christian Europe and the Almohad Islamic Empire," *Islam and Christian-Muslim*

Relations 20, no. 1 (2009): 43–59; and Bennison and Angeles Gallego, "Religious Minorities," 151. See also the extensive work of Jeremy Johns on the influence of the Faṭimids on Norman Sicily, such as his "The Norman Kings of Sicily and the Fatimid Caliphate," *Anglo-Norman Studies* 15 (1993): 133–59.

40. Marie Thérèse d'Alvery and George Vajda, "Marc de Tolede, traducteur d'Ibn Tūmart," *Al-Andalus* 16 (1951): 99–140.

41. ACA, R. 65, fol. 88v (3 Mar. 1286); and Brunschvig, *Berbérie orientale*, I: 2. All the documents related to the four brothers are edited and published in Fancy, "The Last Almohads," appendixes A and B.

42. For instance, ACA, R. 71, fol. 52r (12 May 1287): ". . . conducat aliquam domum idoneam in Valencia uxoribus filiorum Miramoni in qua [. . .] posint esse salve et [se]cure."

43. For instance, ACA, R. 65, fol. 88v (3 Mar. 1286): ". . . Abdeluaheyt et Açmon et Abderamen f[ratrem] janetorum nostrorum, filio ipsi Mi[r]amomulini. . . ."

44. ACA, Cartas árabes, no. 155 (1287, Bilingual): "As long as we both live (ṭūla mā na'īshu naḥnu al-zawj/ab hac die in antea quamdiu ambo insimul vivamus)." See Fancy, "The Last Almohads," appendix B for a full edition. Cf. Dufourcq, *L'Espagne catalane*, 285–86, and Brunschvig, *Berbérie orientale*, I: 98–100, who rely on the Latin transcription in La Mantia, *Codice*, and make no reference to the Arabic text. The Arabic treaty was dated as follows: "This was signed at Jaca with two days remaining in the month of July 1287, the equivalent of 18 Jumādā II, 686 (kutiba fī jāqa yawmayn bāqiyayn min shahr yūliyuh 'ām alf wa-mi'atayn wa-sab'a wa-thamānīn al-muwāfiq li-thāmin 'ashar min shahr jumādā al-ukhrā sanat sitt wa-thamānīn wa-sittimi'a)." Cf. Constable, *Housing the Stranger in the Mediterranean World*, 197–98.

45. ACA, Cartas árabes, no. 155: "On the condition that they satisfy our right (ḥaqqanā/ius nostrum) over these [goods] as was customary before this."

46. ACA, Cartas árabes, no. 155: "And all Christians will settle their disputes (yatakhāṣamū/firment et placitent) under the jurisdiction of your captain."

47. Alemany, "Milicias cristianas," 160–61; Mas Latrie, *Traités de paix*, supplements 32 and 83.

48. ACA, Cartas árabes, no. 155: ". . . as was customary to do in the time of the honorable Don Guillem de Moncada or in the time of the illustrious Don Enrique, son of the king of Castile ('alā mā jarat bihi al-'āda fī zamān mukarrim dūn qilyām damūnqāda aw fī muddat al-mu'aḍḍim dūn anrīq bin al-mu'aḍḍim malik qashtāla/ secundum quod hec consue[verun]t fieri tempore nobilis Guillemi de Montecatheno quondam vel tempore illustris Anrici filii illustris regis Castelle)."

49. The text reads *al-barīl* rather than the more typical *al-barmīl*.

50. ACA, Cartas árabes, no. 155: "wa-yakūn mubāḥan lahum an yaḥmilū jasad jāshū qarīsit bi-'alāmat nāqūs 'alā mā jarat bihi al-'āda/et qui possint portare corpus Cristi cum signo campane sive squille."

51. ACA, Cartas árabes, no. 155: "And moreover, we [Alfons] promise to be a good ally and support you with all of our might to defend or inflict harm on all Muslims with whom you are at war."

52. ACA, Cartas árabes, no. 155: "And we swear by the truth of Muḥammad and the qibla (bi-ḥaqq muḥammad wa-bi'l-qibla/per Mafumeti et per lalquible) and with our hands on the Qur'ān." Ibid.: "And we swear by God with our hands upon the four Gospels (bi'llāh wa-bi'l-arba'i anājīl/per Deum et eius sancta quatuor evangeliam)."

53. ACA, R. 71, fol. 89r (24 Oct. 1287).

54. Muntaner, chaps. 155, 159; *Cafari et continuatorum Annales Januenses*, V: 70 (1285); Ibn Khaldūn, *Kitāb al-'ibar*, VI: 353, Lauria is referred to as "*al-Marākiyā*," the Marquis and lieutenant of Frederick (Fadarīk), son of Alfons (Alrīdākūn), king of Barcelona; and La Mantia, *Codice diplomatico dei Re Aragonesi*, I: 609–12. See also Dufourcq, *L'Espagne catalane*, 266–67.

55. Ibn Khaldūn, *Kitāb al-'ibar*, VI: 356.

56. al-Nuwayrī, *al-Maghrib al-Islāmī*, 452.

57. ACA, R. 73, fol. 90r (1 Dec. 1290), with a full edition in Klüpfel, *Die äussere*, 173–74.

58. Dufourcq, *L'Espagne catalane*, 288, explains that only part of Murghim's ransom was paid. A document that was overlooked by Dufourcq, ACA, R. 83, fol. 82v (17 Sep. 1290) reveals that the remaining 6,000 *duplas* were finally delivered by Murghim in that year, two years after his release, presumably to secure the release of his son, who was held captive in Sicily.

59. Ibn Khaldūn is not clear about when he died. Cf. al-Nuwayrī, *al-Maghrib al-Islāmī*, 452; and Dufourcq, *L'Espagne catalane*, 290, which cites two further documents to which I could not attest.

60. Karl Marx, *Kapital*, vol. 1, chap. 24, sec. 6, commenting sarcastically on Montesquieu: "That is the 'sweet commerce'!"

61. ACA, R. 55, fol. 54r–v (17 Oct. 1291); ACA, R. 64, fols. 191r–192r (21 Apr. 1287); ACA, R 90, fol. 118r (Oct. 1291); ACA, R 252, fol. 121r (18 Nov. 1295); ACA, CR, Jaume II, caixa 91, no. 11093 (24 Mar. 1304); and ACA, Cartas árabes, no. 84bis (14 June 1304).

62. ACV, Perg., 737, fol. 6 (1296); ACV, Perg., 738 (1294), fols. 5–6, for mention of raids to Jerba and Kerkennah; ACV, Perg., 738 (1294), fol. 7, compensation for a *jenet* captured during a battle in North Africa (*in partibus Barbarie*); and ACV, Perg., 738, fol. 8, for mention of three knights from Lucera in the company of *jenets*.

63. ACA, Cartas árabes, 128 (13 May 1313), in which al-Liḥyānī complains of raids by Roger de Lauria; and ACA, Cartas árabes, 133 (11 Oct. 1313), in which al-Liḥyāni sends an ambassador carrying a secret message to Jaume II. See also Michael Lower, "Ibn al-Lihyani: Sultan of Tunis and Would-Be Christian Convert (1311–1318)," *Mediterranean Historical Review* 24, no. 1 (2009): 17–27.

64. ACA, R. 55, fol. 54r–v (17 Oct. 1291): ". . . E aytamben en aiuda dels nostres enamics Christians, nos trametretz al estiu ab lo nostre nauili C cavaller janetz pagats per vos per tres meses"; ACA, R. 64, fol. 176r–v (22 Dec. 1286); ACA, R. 64, fols. 191r–192r (21 Apr. 1287), cited above; ACA, R. 90, fol. 118r (Oct. 1291);

and ACA, R. 252, fol. 121r (18 Nov. 1295). See also ACA, CR, Jaume II, caixa 91, no. 11093 (24 Mar. 1304), which is discussed in chapter 6.

65. ACA, Cartas árabes, 83 (14 Mar. 1323): "wa-amma al-naṣāra al-madhkūrūna alladhīna ṭalabtum fa-lā yumkinu tawajīhuhum li-annahum lam tajari bihi al-'āda." See also ACA, Cartas árabes, 83bis (14 Mar. 1323).

66. *HEM*, III: 66–85; and on the personal guard *HEM*, II: 122–130. See also Mohamed Meouak, "Hiérarchie des fonctions militaire et corps d'armé en al-Andalus Umayyade (IIe/VIIIe–IVe/Xe Siècles): Nomenclature et essai d'interprétation," *Al-Qantara* 14, no. 2 (1993): 371–75; and Viguera Molíns, "La organización militar en al-Andalus." See also Andrew Handler, "The *'abīd* Under the Umayyads of Cordova and the *Mulūk Al-ṭawā'if,*" in *Occident and Orient: A Tribute to the Memory of Alexander Scheiber,* ed. Robert Dán, 229–41.

67. Ibn Sa'īd, *al-Mughrib fī ḥulā al-Maghrib*, ed. Khalīl al-Manṣūr, I: 31: "huwa awwal man istakthara min al-ḥasham wa'l-ḥafad." On the term *ḥasham*, see Meouak, "Hiérarchie," 371–72.

68. *HEM*, III: 71–76. Lévi-Provençal contends that al-Ḥakam's predecessors, 'Abd al-Raḥmān I (756–788) and Hishām I (788–796) also recruited foreign troops. 'Abd al-Raḥmān I had a sizable personal guard of black African soldiers (*'irafat al-sūd*). Cf. *Akhbār al-majmū'a [Ajbar Machmuā. Crónica anoníma del siglo XI*], ed. and trans. E. Lafuente y Alcántara, 109. See also Barton, "Traitors to the Faith?" 26; and François Clement, "Reverter et son fils, deux officiers catalans au service des sultans de Marrakech," *Medieval Encounters* 9, no. 1 (2003): 80.

69. His name appears in several different forms of Ibn Ḥayyān's *Muqtabas* and is conventionally presumed to be Teodulfo.

70. *HEM*, I: 260; III: 73–74.

71. Ibn Ḥayyān, *al-Muqtabas fī ta'rīkh rijāl al-Andalus*, ed. M. Martinez Antuña, III: 94, as cited in Meouak, "Hiérarchie," 374.

72. Ibn Ḥayyān, *al-Muqtabas*, VII: 48, 94, 129, 195, and 196, as cited in Meouak, "Hiérarchie," 374.

73. al-Maqqarī, *Azhār al-riyāḍ fī akhbār 'Iyāḍ*, ed. I. al-Abyārī, II: 287, as cited in Meouak, "Hiérarchie," 375. A large bodyguard of African horsemen and foot soldiers also participated in these investiture ceremonies. See *HEM,* III: 177.

74. Handler, "The *'abid* under the Umayyads," argues that this period had a negative impact on the fate of African slave soldiers.

75. Ibn 'Idhārī, *al-Bayān al-mughrib*, IV: 32: "wa-yarkab fa-yataqaddamuhu al-'abīd." See also Viguera Molins, "Organización," 28.

76. For the Umayyad period see J. M. Ruiz Asencio, "Rebeliones leonesas contra Vermudo II," *Archivos Leoneses* 23 (1969): 215–41. See also Simon Barton, "Traitors to the Faith?" 26.

77. Richard Fletcher, *The Quest for El Cid*; and Simon Barton and Richard Fletcher, eds., *The World of El Cid: Chronicles of the Spanish Reconquest.*

78. Barton, "Traitors to the Faith?" 24; and Burns, "Renegades, Adventurers and Sharp Businessmen," 354.

79. Barton, "Traitors to the Faith?" 28–29.

80. For instance, Sancho the Fat of Navarre, who fought at Las Navas de Tolosa, also allied himself with the Almohads (*Llibre dels feyts*, chap. 138). For more detail, see Burns, "Renegades, Adventurers, and Sharp Businessmen," 351–54.

81. *Llibre dels feyts*, chaps. 75, 90, as cited in Burns, "Renegades, Adventurers, and Sharp Businessmen," 354–55.

82. See chapter 3 n157.

83. María Desamparados Cabanes Pecourt, ed., *Crónica latina de los reyes de Castilla*, 117: "Christiani milites nobiles ducenti qui serviebant ei pro stipendiies suis." See Burns, "Renegades, Adventurers, and Sharp Businessmen," 351.

84. Ibn Khaldūn, *Kitāb al-'ibar*, VI: 311, for the use of Christian militia against the Banū Ashqilūla. Cf. ACA, R. 1389, fol. 31 (ca. 1371–72): "Los barones e richos hombres de nuestro senyorio han de costumbre muy antiga del tiempo aqua que la tierra es de christianos que puedan ir con sus companyas en aiuda de qual Rey se quiera christiano o moro." See also Barton, "Traitors to the Faith?" 32; and Viguera Molins, "Ejercito," 432.

85. Ibn 'Idhārī, *al-Bayān al-mughrib*, IV: 102; Ibn Simāk al-'Āmilī, *al-Ḥulal al-mawshiyya*, 149: "wa huwa awwal man ista'mala al-Rūm bi'l-Maghrib"; Ibn Abī Zar', *Kitāb al-anīs al-muṭrib*, 199; and al-Nuwayrī, *al-Maghrib al-Islāmī*, 391. See also Alemany, "Milicias cristianas," 135–36.

86. A. Maya Sánchez, ed., *Chronica Adefonsi Imperatoris*, in *Chronica Hispana saeculi XII, Corpus Christianorum. Continuatio Medievalis*, 71, ii.§10. Translation adapted from Barton, "Traitors to the Faith?" 27. See also García Sanjuán, "Mercenarios cristianos," 440.

87. García Sanjuán, "Mercenarios cristianos," 440–41; Vincent Lagadre, "Communautés mozarabes et pouvoir almoravides en 519H/1125 en Andalus," *Studia Islamica* 67 (1988): 99–119; and Delfina Serrano, "Dos fetuas sobre la expulsión de mozárabes al Magreb en 1126," *Anaquel de estudios árabes* 2 (1991): 167.

88. Maya Sánchez, *Chronica Adefonsi Imperatoris*, ii.§10, as cited in Barton, "Traitors to the Faith?" 27. For more on Reverter, see texts cited above as well as F. Carreras Candi, "Relaciones de los vizcondes de Barcelona con los árabes," in *Homenaje á D. Francisco Codera en su jubilación del profesorado*, ed. Eduardo Saavedra, 207–15; and Santiago Sobrequés Vidal, *Els barons a Catalunya*, 39–40.

89. Frank, "Reverter," 198, accepts on the authority of the *Chronica Adefonsi Imperatoris* that Reverter was a captive of war. J. E. Ruiz Domènec, "Las cartas de Reverter, vizconde de Barcelona," *Boletin de la Real Academia de Buenas Letras de Barcelona* 39 (1982–85): 96, argues that Reverter came voluntarily.

90. Ibn Khaldūn, *Kitāb al-'ibar*, VI: 245–46; Ibn 'Idhārī, *al-Bayān al-mughrib*, IV: 103; Clement, "Reverter," 94–95; Alemany, "Milicias cristianas," 136; and García Sanjuán, "Mercenarios cristianos," 438.

91. Ibn Khaldūn, *Kitāb al-'ibar*, VI: 205, 259–60, and 264, on 'Alī b. Reverter's role in the conquest of Mallorca by the Almohads.

92. Frank, "Reverter," 201–2; Clement, "Reverter," 95; and Dufourcq, *L'Espagne catalane*, 21.

93. Maya Sánchez, *Chronica Adefonsi Imperatoris*, ii.§110, as cited in Barton, "Traitors to the Faith?" 28. See also Jean-Pierre Molénat, "L'organization militaire des Almohades," in *Los almohades: problemas y perspectivas*, ed. Patrice Cressier, Maribel Fierro, and Luis Molina, 554; and Halima Ferhat, "Lignages et individus dans le système du pouvoir Almohade," in *Los Almohades: problemas y perspectivas*, ed. Patrice Cressier, Maribel Fierro, and Luis Molina, 685–709.

94. On the various interpretations of "Ifarkhān," see Lapiedra, "Christian participation," 238; Victoria Aguilar Sebastian, "Instituciones militares. El ejército," in *El retroceso territorial de al-Andalus. Almorávides y Almohades, siglos XI al XIII*, ed. María Jesús Viguera Molins: 207; and Clement, "Reverter," 81.

95. Salicrú, "Mercenaires castillans," 418.

96. See Ibn Khaldūn, *Kitāb al-'ibar*, VII: 69, on Don Enrique (Dūn Alrīk).

97. David Lopes, "O Cid portugues: Geraldo Sempavor," *Revista Portuguesa de Historia* 1 (1940):93–109; and Eva Lapiedra, "Giraldo Sem Pavor: Alfonso Enríquez y los Almohades," in *Bataliús: el reino taifa de Badajoz: estudios*, ed. Fernando Díaz Esteban, 147–58. The Castilian prince Don Enrique also served the Almohads.

98. Ibn Khaldūn, *Kitāb al-'ibar*, VI: 270. See also Barton, "Traitors to the Faith?" 33; and García Sanjuán, "Mercenarios cristianos," 437. Alemany, "Milicias cristianas," 138–39, connects the rise in the number of these soldiers to al-Ma'mūn's rejection of Ibn Tūmart.

99. P. de Cenival, "L'Église chrétienne de Marrakech au XIIIe siècle," *Hespéris* 7 (1927): 69–84.

100. Alemany, "Milicias cristianas," 138–39; Clement, "Reverter," 81; Barton, "Traitors to the Faith?" 30; and García Sanjuán, "Mercenarios cristianos," 438.

101. Ibn Khaldūn, *Kitāb al-'ibar*, I: 214, translation adapted from Rosenthal, trans. *Muqaddimah*, 227.

102. See Ibn Khaldūn, *Kitāb al-'ibar*, VI: 272–73, for the use of the Christian militia against the rebelling Khulṭ tribe. See also García Sanjuán, "Mercenarios cristianos," 439–40; and Ambrosio Huici Miranda, *Historia política del imperio Almohade*, II: 465. See also 'Umar Mūsā 'Izz al-Dīn, "Al-Tanẓīmāt al-ḥizbiyya 'inda-l-Muwaḥḥidīn fī-l-Maghrib," *Al-Abḥāth* 23 (1970): 52–89; and Fāyiza Kalās, "Al-Jaysh 'inda-l-Muwaḥḥidīn," *Dirāsāt Tārīkhiyya* 31–32 (1989): 197–218.

103. Ibn Khaldūn, *Kitāb al-'ibar*, I: 211–15, suggests that this was generally true for North African rulers when it came to Christian soldiers.

104. Ibn Khaldūn, *Kitāb al-'ibar*, VII: 179.

105. Ibn Khaldūn, *Kitāb al-'ibar*, VII: 182ff and VI: 279; and ACA, R. 15, fol. 130v (3 Feb. 1268). See also García Sanjuán, "Mercenarios cristianos," 439–40; and Alemany, "Milicias cristianas," 130–40.

106. For example, Ibn Khaldūn, *Kitāb al-'ibar*, VII: 180, on the Marīnids.

107. Ibn Khaldūn, *Kitāb al-'ibar*, VII: 83, and cit. 88–89. Upon the capture of Tlemcen, Abū Yaḥyā Yaghmurāsan, the dynasty's founder, incorporated Christian (*al-'asākir min al-rūm*) and Kurdish (*ghuzz*) lanciers and archers (*rāmiḥa wa-nāshiba*). These Christian troops grew so powerful that they conspired against Yaghmurāsan. A failed coup attempt prompted the populace to turn against these troops and massacre them, according to Ibn Khaldūn.

108. ACA, R 55, fol. 49v (1291).

109. See the letters, purported to be translated from Arabic, from Spanish knights seeking employment in North Africa in the Manuel González Jiménez, ed., *Crónica de Alfonso X*, 70–75. On the sons of Ferdinand III, see Alemany, "Milicias cristianas," 161. On Guzmán el Bueno, see Miguel Ángel Ladero Quesada, "Una biografía caballeresca del siglo XV: 'La Cronica del yllustre y muy magnifico cauallero don Alonso Perez de Guzman el Bueno,'" *En la España Medieval* 22 (1999): 247–83; and Luisa Isabel Alvarez de Toledo, "Guzmán el Bueno, entre la leyenda y la historia," *Estudios de historia y de arqueología medievales* 7–9 (1987): 41–58. The primary source for the life of Guzmán el Bueno is the sixteenth-century account in Pedro Barrantes Maldonado, *Ilustraciones de la Casa de Niebla*, ed. Federico Devis Márquez.

110. Ibn Khaldūn, *Kitāb al-'ibar*, VI: 318–19, on the royal guard of the Ḥafṣids; Ibn Khaldūn, *Kitāb al-'ibar*, VII: 109, on the royal guard of the 'Abd al-Wādids; and Ibn Khaldūn, *Kitāb al-'ibar*, VII: 250, on the royal guard of the Marīnids. See also Alemany, "Milicias critianas," 160; and Clement, "Reverter," 82.

111. Ibn Khaldūn, *Kitāb al-'ibar*, I: 214, translation adapted from Rosenthal, trans. *Muqaddimah*, 227–28.

112. Salicrú, "Mercenaires castillans," 419, which calls it an "affair of state."

113. For Tunis, see ACA, R. 13, fol. 216r (Sep. 1264); ACA, R. 21, fol. 140v (s.a.); ACA, R. 46, fol. 120r (Sep. 1283); ACA, R. 47, fols. 81r–82v, cit. 82v (June 1285): "Item que tots los cavallers o homems darmes crestians qui son huy, ne seran daqui avant, en la senyoria del rey de Tunis, que y sien tots per nos, et que nos lus donem cap aquel que nos vulrem"; and ACA, R. 100, fol. 258r. See also Dufourcq, *L'Espagne catalane*, 150–51; Giménez Soler, "Caballeros españoles," 303–4. For Tlemcen, see ACA, R. 14, fol. 141r (1272): "Comendamus et concedimus vobis nobili et dilecto nostro G. Gaucerandi, alcaydiam Tirimicii Christianorum terre nostre militum scilicet mercatorum et quorumlibet aliorum hominum terre et iurisdiccionis nostre qui ibi sunt vel fuerint constituti. . . ." In addition, see ACA, R. 14, fol. 142v (1272); ACA, R. 40, fol. 53v (1277); ACA, R. 73, fols. 104v–105r (May 1291); ACA, R. 93, fol. 281v (Oct. 1292); and ACA, R. 337, fol. 260v (1315). See also Alemany, "Milicias cristianas," 160–61; and Dufourcq, *L'Espagne catalane*, 272.

114. The Castilian and Aragonese troops supported various political factions in the late thirteenth and early fourteenth centuries. For instance, see ACA, CR, Jaume II, caixa 22, no.2863 (1307); and ACA, CR, Jaume II, caixa 118, sin fecha, no. 986 (s.a.), for the involvement of Aragonese troops in a rebellion against Abu

Rabīʻa (r. 1308–1310). See also Giménez Soler, "Caballeros españoles," 308–12; Alemany, "Milicias cristianas," 146–50; Dufourcq, *L'Espagne Catalane*, 456–57; and Clement, "Reverter," 82.

115. For instance, ACA, R. 64, fol. 178v (Apr. 1286), negotiations with Tlemcen: "Item que todos los cristianos que seran en la terra del Rey de Tirimçe de qualesquier condiciones o senyorias, que sean jutgados por fuero d'Aragon por aquel alcayt que el Rey don Alfonso ala enbiarra"; ACA, R. 64, fol. 192r–v (1286), negotiations in Tunis; ACA, R. 64, fols. 191r–192r (Mar. 1286), negotiations with Tunis, which do not mention Christian knights but only navy; ACA, R. 73, fol. 90r–v (Dec. 1290), negotiations with Tunis; ACA, R. 252, fol. 53r–v (May 1293), negotiations with Tlemcen; ACA, R. 252, fol. 99r (July 1294), letter to Tunis; and ACA, R. 337, fols. 195r–196r (July 1313), negotiations with Tunis.

116. Cf. ACB, Perg., 1-6-325, as cited by Batlle, "Noticias," 134, on the use of debased currency to pay soldiers.

117. For example, ACA, R. 47, fols. 81r–82v (1285); ACA, Cartas árabes, no. 155 (1287, bilingual): "ʻalā mā jarat bihi al-ʻāda fī zamān mukarrim dūn qilyām damūnqāda aw fī muddat-al-muʻaḍḍim dūn anrīq bin al-muʻaḍḍim malik qashtāla/ secundum quod hec consue[verun]t fieri tempore nobilis Guillemi de Montecatheno quondam vel tempore illustris Anrici filii illustris regis Castelle"; ACA, R. 73, fol. 90r (1290): "axi con era el temps de Guillelm de Moncada"; and ACA, R. 252, fol. 53r–v (1293). See also Burns, "Renegades," 352; Barton, "Traitors to the Faith?" 33; and Batlle, "Noticias," 128.

118. Although these stipulations are only vaguely referred to in the Almohad period, they were likely similar. See Ibn Khaldūn, *Kitāb al-ʻibar*, VI: 270 [my emphasis]: "wa-istamadda al-ṭāghiya ʻaskaran min al-naṣārā wa-amarahu *ʻalā shurūṭ taqabbalahā minhu al-ma'mūn*."

119. ACA, Cartas árabes, no. 155.

120. ACA, R. 197, fol. 7v (Oct. 1299); ACA, R. 240, fols. 204v–205r (May 1313); and ACA, R. 337, fols. 195r–196r (July 1313). See also Alemany, "Milicias cristianas," 134, 165–68. See Barrantes Maldonado, *Ilustraciones de la casa de Niebla*, 67, for the complaints.

121. See, for example, ACA, R. 14, fol. 141r: ". . . Dantes vobis plenam licenciam et potestatem audiendi et iudicandi causas que ibi inter aliquos christianos predictos terre nostre contigerit ventilari et faciendi ibi iusticie criminales et alias prout faciendum sit et exercendi in omnibus et per omnia officium ipsius alcaydie secundum quod alii alcaydi consuerunt ipsam hactenus exercere. . . ." Among many records naming or confirming captains, see ACA, R. 197, fol. 7v (Tunis); ACA, R. 203, fol. 33v (Tunis); ACA, R. 203, fol. 35r (Tunis); ACA, R. 203, fol. 220r (Tunis); ACA, R. 244, fol. 286v (Tlemcen); ACA, CR, Jaume II, caixa 19, no. 2406 (Tunis); and ACA, CR, Jaume II, caixa 134, Judíos y Musulmanes, no. 178 (Rabat).

122. ACA, R. 244, fol. 286r; ACA, R. 250, fols. 43v–44r (Jaume d'Arago); ACA, R. 250, fol. 50v; ACA, R. 338, fols. 150v–151r; ACA, R. 338, fol. 151v; ACA,

R. 410, fols. 208r–209r; ACA, CR, Jaume II, caixa 6, no. 837; ACA, CR, Jaume II, caixa 37, no. 4604 (1313); ACA, CR, Jaume II, caixa 134, Judíos y Musulmanes, no. 178 (1326); and ACA, CR, Jaume II, caixa 136, Judíos y Musulmanes, no. 471 (1326). Abū Yūsuf sent Garci Martínez de Gallegos to the Iberian Peninsula in 1278 to persuade Christians to lift the siege of Algeciras. See *Crónica de Alfonso X*, 201–2, as cited by Barton, "Traitors to the Faith?" 31.

123. ACA, R. 15, fol. 74r (17 Dec. 1267): "Noverint universi quod nos Iacobus et cetera damus [et] concedimus vobis dilecto nostro Guillelmo Gaucerandi presentem missatgeriam de Tirimice. Ita quod sitis nuncius dicte missatgerie et non aliquis alius. Dantes etiam et concedentes vobis alcaydiam eiusdem loci, ita quod vos sitis alcaydus omnium Christianorum tam militum quam aliorum qui vobiscum apud Tirimice ibunt vel iam \.... / sunt seu de cetero fuerint ibidem. Et quod ipsam alcaydiam habeatis et teneatis eiusdem alcaydie officium exercendo in omnibus. Sicut eam alii alcaydi <hac>tenus habuerunt melius et tenuerunt et percipiatis inde iura que alii alcaydi inde consueverunt percipere et habere. Mandantes universis hominibus tam militibus quam aliis in partibus de Tirimice constitutis vel constituendis tam nostri domini quam alterius, quod vobis tamquam alcaydo nostro obediant in omnibus et <atendant>. Datum Cesarauguste, XVI kalendas Ianuarii anno dominii millisimo CCLX septimo." For the absolution, see ACA, R. 15, fol. 74r: ". . . guerram quam nobiscum habuistis et pro quibuscumque aliis que contra nos feceritis usque in hunc diem. . . ." Cf. ACA, R. 334, fols. 63r–64r, instructions to ambassador to Tunis. See also Dominique Valérian, "Les agents de la diplomatie des souverains maghrébins avec le monde chrétien (XIIe–XVe siècles)," *Anuario de estudios medievales* 38, no. 2 (2008): 885–900.

124. For example, ACA, R. 42, fol. 214v (Feb. 1279), an absolution and protection for a soldier and his army traveling to Tunis; ACA, R. 60, fol. 25r (Feb. 1282), protection for a soldier who had served in North Africa and now serves in the king's army in Sicily; ACA, CR, Jaume II, caixa 136, Judíos y Musulmanes, no. 497 (1312); ACA, R. 201, fols. 46v–47r (1303), absolution for father and son; and ACA, R. 245, fol. 148r.

125. ACA, R. 901, fol. 139r (1357), with thanks to Jaume Riera i Sans for the reference.

126. For instance, Burns, "Renegades, Adventurers, and Sharp Businessmen," 341–42; and García Sanjuán, "Mercenarios cristianos," 443–46.

127. AHN, Codices, 996b, fol. 44r (23 Jan. 1214), as cited in Barton, "Traitors to the Faith?" 24–25. On papal attitudes toward Christian mercenaries, see James Muldoon, *Popes, Lawyers, and Infidels: The Church and the Non-Christian World, 1250–1550*, esp. 45, 52, as well as Mas-Latrie, *Traités de paix*, docs. 10, 15, 17, and 18. For the opinions of Islamic jurists on this issue, see chapter 6, below.

128. BNM, MS. 13,022, fol. 92r–v, as cited in Barton, "Traitors to the Faith?" 25.

129. Barton, "Traitors to the Faith?" and Michael Lower, "The Papacy and Christian Mercenaries of Thirteenth-Century North Africa," *Speculum* 89, no. 3

(2014): 601–31. See also Peter Linehan, *The Spanish Church and the Papacy in the Thirteenth Century*; and Damian J. Smith, *Innocent III and the Crown of Aragon: The Limits of Papal Authority*.

130. Demetrio Mansilla, *La documentación pontificia de Honorio III (1216–1227)*, docs. 243, 439, 562, 579, 588, 590, and 595, as cited in Barton, "Traitors to the Faith?" 37.

131. Barton, "Traitors to the Faith?" 37. See also Muldoon, *Popes, Lawyers, and Infidels*, 41, 52, 54; Alemany, *Milicias cristianas*, esp. 137–42; and Mas Latrie, *Traités de paix*, docs. 10, 15, 17, and 18.

132. Franciscus Balme, ed., *Raymundia seu documenta quae pertinent ad S. Raymundi de Pennaforti vitam et scripta*, 35, as cited in Burns, "Renegades, Adventurers, and Sharp Businessmen," 354.

133. ACA, CR, Jaume II, caixa 25, no. 3189 (1308). These bishops were Dominican and Franciscan legates of the Papacy. See López, *Obispas en el África Septentrional*, 1–10.

134. On Tunis, see Brunschvig, *Berberie orientale*, 447–48. On Tlemcen, see Alemany, "Milicias cristianas," 159.

135. Alemany, "Milicias cristianas," 169.

136. Felipe Maíllo Salgado, "Precisiones para la historia de un grupo étnico-religioso: los farfanes," *Al-Qanṭara* 4 (1983): 265–81; and Salicrú, "Mercenaires castillans," 423–25, who suggests that perhaps a famine or plague prompted the departure of these families.

137. Salicrú, "Mercenaires castillans," 427–31.

138. ACA, R. 1954, fol. 10v; and ACA, R. 2855, fol. 190v, as cited by Alemany, "Milicias cristianas," 68–69.

139. Jacques Heers and Georgette de Groër, eds. and trans., *Itinéraire d'Anselme Adorno en Terre Sainte (1470–1471)*, 106–8.

140. Mas-Latrie, *Traités de paix,* 339–40.

141. Lapiedra, "Christian Participation in Almohad Armies," 237.

142. Lapiedra, "Christian Participation in Almohad Armies," 245.

143. Lapiedra, "Christian Participation in Almohad Armies," 242.

144. Lapiedra, "Christian Participation in Almohad Armies," 236, 247.

145. Cf. Shelomo Dov Goitein, *A Mediterranean Society*, I: 130–31, speaking of the *mamlūk* tradition.

146. On military slaves across history, see a recent collection of essays, Christopher Leslie Brown and Philip D. Morgan, eds., *Arming Slaves: From Classical Times to the Modern Age*. On military slavery in the Islamic context, see David Ayalon, *The Mamluk Military Society*; Patricia Crone, *Slaves on Horses: The Evolution of the Islamic Polity*; Daniel Pipes, *Slave Soldiers and Islam: The Genesis of a Military System*; Christopher I. Beckwith, "Aspects of Early History of the Central Asian Guard Corps in Islam," *Archivum Eurasie Medii Aevi* 4 (1984): 29–43; David Ayalon, "The Mamlūks of the Seljuks: Islam's Military Might at the

Crossroads," *Journal of the Royal Asiatic Society* 6, no. 3 (1996): 305–33; Peter B. Golden, "Some Notes on the *Comitatus* in Medieval Eurasia with Special Reference to the Khazars," *Russian History/Histoire Russe* 28 (2001): 153–170; Matthew Gordon, *The Breaking of a Thousand Swords: A History of the Turkish Military of Samarra, A.H. 200–275/815–889 C.E.*; Peter B. Golden, "The Terminology of Slavery and Servitude in Medieval Turkic," in *Studies on Central Asian History in Honor of Yuri Bregel*, ed. D. DeWeese, 27–56; idem, "Khazar Turkic Ghulams in Caliphal Service," *Journal asiatique* 292, no. 1–2 (2004): 279–309; Reuven Amitai, "The Mamlūk Institution, or One Thousand Years of Military Slavery in the Islamic World," in *Arming Slaves: From Classical Times to the Modern Age*, 40–78; Mohammed Meouak, "Slaves, noirs et affranchise dans les armies Fatimides d'Ifrîqiya: Histoires et trajectoires 'marginales,' " in *D'esclaves à soldats: Miliciens et soldats d'origine servile XIIIe–XXIe siècles*, ed. Carmen Bernand and Alessandro Stella, 15–37; and Yaacov Lev, "David Ayalon (1914–1998) and the History of Black Military Slavery in Medieval Islam," *Der Islam* 90, no. 1 (2013): 21–43.

147. Jacob Lassner, *The Shaping of Abbasid Rule*, 116–36. On the choice of Turkic soldiers, see Helmut Töllner, *Die turkischen Garden am Kalifenhof von Samarra: ihre Entstehung und Machtergreifung bis zum Kalifat Al-Mu'tadids*, 20–21.

148. Crone, *Slaves on Horses*, 78; Étienne de la Vaissière, *Histoire des marchands sogdiens*, 305; David Ayalon, "The Mamluks: The Mainstay of Islam's Military Might," in *Slavery in the Islamic Middle East*, ed. S. Marmon, 90. Whether or not these soldiers were originally slaves or only spoken of as such is a matter of controversy. M. A. Shaban, *Islamic History: A New Interpretation*, 2, 63–64; and Beckwith, "Aspects of Early History of the Central Asian Guard Corps in Islam," argue that the Turks were not originally slaves. Gordon, *Thousand Swords*, 40–41; and Golden, "Khazar Turkic Ghulams in Caliphal Service," 287, argue the opposite.

149. Orlando Patterson, *Slavery and Social Death: A Comparative Study*; and Golden, "Khazar Turkic Ghulams," 293.

150. Golden, "Khazar Turkic Ghulams," 288, 308.

151. A view shared by Golden, "Some Notes on the *Comitatus*"; Beckwith, "Aspects of the Early History of the Central Asian Guard Corps"; Shaban, *Islamic History*, 63–65; Richard Frye, *History of Ancient Iran*, 352–54, and ibid., *The Heritage of Central Asia*, 195–96; and Étienne de la Vaissière, *Samarcande et Samarra: Élites d'Asie centrale dans l'empire abbasside*. Gordon, *Thousand Swords*, 7–8, 156, sees the tradition as fundamentally Middle Eastern.

152. Golden, "Khazar Turkic Ghulams," 288; and Mohsen Zakeri, *Sâsânid Soldiers in Early Muslim Society: The Origins of 'Ayyârân and Futuwwa.*

153. Golden, "The Terminology of Slavery and Servitude," 29.

154. Cf. Crone, *Slaves on Horses*, 79, emphasizes the military function over the political function: "They were designed to be not a military elite, but military automata."

155. Jere L. Bacharach, "African Military Slaves in the Medieval Middle East: The Cases of Iraq (869–955) and Egpyt (868–1171)," *International Journal of Middle East Studies* 13, no. 4 (1981): 481. See also David Ayalon, "On the Eunuch in Islam," *Jerusalem Studies in Arabic and Islam* 1 (1979): 109–22.

156. Lev, "History of Black Military Slavery," 31.

157. Ayalon, "The Mamlūks of the Seljuks," 321; and Meouak, "Slaves, noirs et affranchise."

158. Lev, "History of Black Military Slavery," 30–32; and Zaki Mohamed Hassan, *Les Ṭūlūnides: Étude de l'Egypte musulmane à la fin du IXe siècle, 868–905*, 165–168, on the influence of the 'Abbāsids.

159. Ibn Ṣaghīr, *Akhbār al-a'imma al-rustumiyyīn* in "La chronique d'Ibn Saghir sur les imam rustamides de Tahert," ed. and trans. A. de C. Motylinski, 66, 86, 98, 102, as cited in E. Savage, *A Gateway to Hell, A Gateway to Paradise: The North African Response to the Arabic Conquest*, 101.

160. Golden, "*Comitatus*," 7; idem., "Khazar Turkic Ghulams," 283; Warren Treagold, *Byzantium and Its Army, 284–1081*, 110, 115; Mark Whittow, *The Making of Byzantium, 600–1025*, 169–70; and Alexander P. Kazhdan, ed., *The Oxford Dictionary of Byzantium*, II: 925, s.v. "hetairai."

161. al-Maqdisī, *Kitāb al-bad' wa'l-ta'rīkh*, ed. Cl. Huart, IV: 68, as cited in Golden, "Khazar Turkic Ghulams in Caliphal Service," 284; and Ibn Rusta, *Kitāb al-a'lāq al-nafīsa*, ed. M. J. De Goeje, 120, 124.

162. See also Peter Blanchard, *Under the Flags of Freedom: Slave Soldiers and the Wars of Independence in Spanish South America*.

163. Fernando Rodríguez Mediano, "Delegación de Asuntos Indígenas, S2N2. Gestón racial en el protectorado Español en Marruecos," *Awraq* XX (1999): 173–206; Sebastian Balfour, *Deadly Embrace: Morocco and the Road to the Spanish Civil War*; María Rosa de Madariaga, *Los moros que trajo Franco: la intervención de tropas coloniales en la guerra*; José Antonio González Alcantud, ed., *Marroquíes en la Guerra Civil española: campos equívocos*; and Francisco Sánchez Ruano, *Islam y Guerra Civil Española: moros con Franco y la República*.

164. "Un-Spanish Spaniard: Generalissimo Francisco Franco," *New York Times* (April 2, 1959).

165. "Franco Disbands Moorish Guard as Anti-Moroccan Talk Mounts," *New York Times* (December 28, 1957).

Chapter Five

1. Muça Almentauri's name appears numerous times in the chancery registers, indicating that he was a prominent *jenet*. He was in the king's service for at least fifteen years; the earliest document to mention him dates from 1290 (ACA, R. 82, fol. 164v, a compensation for horses lost in battle) and the last that I encountered

dates from 1305 (ACA, R. 203, fol. 13r, a license to export wheat from the kingdoms of the Crown of Aragon).

2. ACA, R. 93, fol. 226v (2 Aug. 1292); full citation at n20, below.

3. The fact that Muslims bought and drank wine is documented in the Archive of the Crown of Aragon (e.g., ACA, R. 205, fol. 128r). In 1258, for instance, a certain Petrus Arnaldi received permission to build a *funduq* on the island of Minorca in order to sell wine to both Christians and Muslims on the island. See ACA, R. 9, fol. 61v (3 Aug. 1258): "Possitis vinum vendere Christianis et Sarracenis et facere vinum de vindemia [i.e., the grape harvest] illius terre et emere quandocumque volueritis." Muslim communities also managed and tilled their own vineyards (e.g., ACA, R. 11, fols. 182v–183r, in Perpignan; or ACA, R. 12, fol. 40v, in Játiva). Lest one think alcohol provided a well-lubricated means of interaction, in 1283, the Aragonese king ordered that Jews stop selling wine to Christians (ACA, R. 61, fol. 162r).

4. ACA, R. 81, fol. 52r (6 Mar. 1290): "Universis officialibus et cetera. Cum Muça Abenbeyet, Açe Parrello, Yoniç, jeneti habeant mandato nostro venire ad [servi]endo nobis cum uxoribus ac familiis suis. Mandamus vobis quatenus predictis jenetis, uxoribus ac familiis suis [in] veniendo ad nos nullum impedimentum aut contrarium faciatis aut fieri ab aliquo permittatis immo provideatis eisdem [qua]re fuerit de sec[uro] transitu et ducatu presentibus ultra XV dies proximos venturos minime valituris. Datum ut supra." See also Gazulla, "Zenetes," 193.

5. ACA, R. 66, fol. 197r (15 Oct. 1286): "Universis et officialibus ad quos et cetera. Cum Giber et Jahia et Jucefus et Hiahiaten et Dapher, fratres janeti, venerint in servicio nostro et inde redeant cum familia et uxoribus et filiis [sui]s et sint inter omnes quadraginta septem persone. Mandamus vobis quatenus in redeundo nullum impedimentum vel contrariam faciatis immo provideatis eisdem de securo transitu et du[c]atu. Datum ut supra."

6. See Catlos, "Mahomet Abenadalill," 291–92, for his discussion of families. See also Gazulla, "Zenetes," 193, who presents one document related to the wife of Muça Abenbeyt (ACA, R. 81, fol. 52).

7. ACA, R. 71, fol. 50r (8 May 1287): "Item eidem Petro quod solutis et cetera, det Çeyt Abdela, jeneto, sex coudes panni coloris et pro tribus suis sociis, XVIII coudes de bifa de Sancto Dianisio de colore, quas eis dare debemus cum albarano Iacobi Fivelleri directo Muçe de Portella quod nos recuperavimus. Item uxori sue quatuor coudes de panno coloris quos ei pro vestibus damus prout in albarano Iacobi directo Muçe de Portella quod nos recuperavimus continetur. Et cum eis dederitis et cetera. Datum ut supra." Was she perhaps "Garup," who is mentioned in ACA, R. 76, fol. 19r (n15, below)? Cf. ACA, R. 67, fol. 39v (22 June 1286), with full citation in n8, below, in which a wife of a *jenet* appears in Barcelona.

8. ACA, R. 72, fol. 33r (10 Apr. 1288): "Eidem altera, quod cum dominus Rex mandaverit Petro de Libiano quod daret IIII filiis de Miramamonino et uxoribus trium eorum et Issacho Sanagi de familia ipsorum, pannum quem sibi constaret

Muçam de Portella eis debere dare cum albaranis Iacobi Fivellarii. Det eis ipsum pannum pro quem constituerit ipsum Muçam debere dare eisdem. Datum ut supra." ACA, R. 72, fol. 53v (15 Feb. 1288): "Arnaldo de Bastida quod //solvat Jucef Abenjacob// excomputet seu dederit Jucef Aben Jacob et Cassim, janetis, . . . alia summa C viginti solidi Barchinone debitorum eisdem pro LXXX solidos Iaccenses pro vestibus uxorum [e]arum cum duobus albaranis Iacobi Fivellerii. . . ." The wife of one Gibrus Bomandil received grain when she arrived in Barcelona. ACA, R. 67, fol. 39v (22 June 1286): "Petro de Sancto Clemente. Mandamus vobis quatenus de blado nostro quod Berengarius de Conques . . . [pro]videatis uxore Gibri Bomandil et aliorum janetorum de famile sua que sunt in Barchinone in necessarie eorum quoniam nos illud vobis in compotum recipiemus. Datum Barchinone, X kalendas Iulii."

9. ACA, R. 44, fol. 178v (16 Apr. 1280): "Noverint universii quod nos Petrus dei gracia Rex Aragonem, tradimus et concedimus vobis Muça Hivanface jeneto de domo nostra et Axone uxori sue quasdam domos in moraria Valencie que fuerant Xerqui Alhadit . . ."

10. ACA, R. 71, fol. 52r (15 May 1297): "Maymon de Plana, baiulo Valencie, quod conducat aliquam domum idoneam in Valencie uxoribus filiorum Miramoni in qua est posint esse salve et [se]cure."

11. ACA, R. 58, fol. 9r (30 Feb. 1284): "Bernardo scribe quod donet Mahometo Abulhayr pro expensis uxoris et familie sue quam ad partes istas facere venire. Quindecim duplas. Datum ut supra." See also ACA, R. 52, fol. 54v (13 Aug. 1284): "Raimundo de Rivo Sicco quod det expensas Axie uxori Abdaluhafet janeti qui est in servicio Regis in veniendo [de] Elx usque ad Valenciam. Datum ut supra." We know that "Horo" was the wife of Mahomet based on ACA, R. 71, fol. 37$_r$ (n16, below).

12. Cf. Elena Lourie, "Black Women Warriors in the Muslim Army Besieging Valencia and the Cid's Victory: A Problem of Interpretation," *Traditio* 55 (2000): 181–209.

13. See Ibn Khaldūn, *Kitāb al-'ibar*, VII: 188, speaking of a battle between Yaghmurāsan and Abū Yūsuf in 1267: "While the warriors of the two armies prepared for battle, their wives emerged with their faces uncovered (sāfirāt al-wujūh) in order to incite (fī sabīl al-taḥrīḍ) [the men]. They celebrated and shouted encouragement."

14. ACA, R. 58, fol. 29r (6 June 1285): "<Raimundo de Ricco Sicco quod provideat in expensis uxori Maimoni, janeti, prout iam antequam computasset providebat eidem. Datum in Colle de Panissars, II nonas Iunii.>" ACA, R. 58, fol. 49r (3 Sept. 1285): "Dominico de la Fugera, baiulo Calatayube, volumus et placet nobis quod expensas idoneas quas dederitis uxoribus et filiis filiorum de Maramuni qui in servicio nostro existunt, ponatis nobis, a compotu datarum eius contingerit vos reddere compotum nobis, vel aliquis loco nostri. Mandamus etiam vobis quatenus predictis uxoribus et filiis filiorum de Maramuni, detis expensas idoneas pro

tempore futuro dum ipsas uxores et filios in Calatayub, remanere conting[a]t. Datum Barchinone, III nonas Septembris." See also Gazulla, "Zenetes," 180. ACA, R. 65, fol. 38r (Feb. 1286): "Raimundo de Rivo Sicco. Mandamus vobis quatenus detis uxoribus Muçe et Çahit et Maym[u]ni, jane[torum], portiones quas dominus Rex inclite recordationis pater noster eas assignati habendas [c]a[r]ta s[u]a ut in ea videbitis [con]tineri. Datum ut supra." See also Catlos, "Mahomet Abenadalill," 292. ACA, R. 76, fol. 3r (22 Jan. 1288): "Geraldo de Fonte, baiulo Valencie. Mandamus vobis quatenus donetis Muçe et Sahit, jenetis nostris, unicuique eorum centum solidos pro acorrimento \et quitacione/ eorum [e]t uxorum suarum. E[t] facta eis solutione et cetera. Datum ut supra." ACA, R. 82, fol. 69r (5 Sep. 1290): "Fuit scriptum Raimundo Scorne quod quitet uxores Muse et Çayt, jenetorum nostrorum, de eo quod eisdem debentur tam de tempore preterito quam de presenti [die] de[i]nde qualibet die, prout eisdem quitare consuevistis ut in litteris per nos iam super hoc nobis missis plurimus continer. Recuperantes et cetera. Datum ut supra." See also Catlos, "Mahomet Abenadalill," 291. ACA, R. 72, fol. 53v (15 Feb. 1288): "Arnaldo de Bastida quod //solvat Jucef Abenjacob// excomputet seu dederit Jucef Aben Jacob et Cassim, janetis, . . . alia summa C viginti solidi Barchinone debitorum eisdem pro LXXX solidos Iaccenses pro vestibus uxorum [e]arum cum duobus albaranis Iacobi Fivellerii. . . ."

15. Only one document mentions a specific amount, six *denarii*, perhaps per month, dramatically less than the *jenets*' salaries. See ACA, R. 76, fol. 19r (23 Feb. 1287): "Geraldo de Fonte. Mandamus vobis quatenus solutis et cetera quitetis prima die mensis Ianuaris proxime preterita deinde donec aliud mandaremus Aixam, uxorem de Muçe, et Garup, uxorem de [S]ait, et Heç[..], uxorem de M[a]ym[on] vid[elicet] sex denarios regalium pro quolibet ea[r]undem et eisdem uxoribus predictorum janetorum [m]ensis dictarum. Sicut [est] dar[e] [.....]tum. Datum Barchinone, VII kalendas Marcii." See also Catlos, "Mahomet Abenadalill," 292n130.

16. ACA, R. 71, fol. 37r (12 Apr. 1287): "Maymono de Plana, baiulo nostro Valencie. Cum nos mandaverimus per literam nostram quam recuperavimus Petro de Libiano tunc ba[iu]lo [V]alencie quod quitaret Horo uxori Mahometi Abelhaye, janeti, de eo de quo sibi constaret ipsa non fuisse quitatam per Raimundum de Ri[vo] Sicco et dictus Petrus de Libiano ipsam non quitaverit ut intelleximus de aliquot, mandamus vobis· quatenus predictam Horo quitetis de eo de quo vobis constiterit ipsam non fuisse quitatam per Raimundum de Rivo Sicco predictum certificando vos prius si aliquid fuit sibi solutum per Petrum de Libiano predictum de dicta //quantitate// quitacione. Et recipiatis albaranum \de eo/ quod sibi tradideritis et presentem literam recuperetis ab eo. Datum Barchinone, pridie idus Aprilis." Similarly, see the case of the wives of Muse and Çayt (ACA, R. 82, fol. 69r), in n14, above.

17. For more on the role of women in the sphere of credit, see William Chester Jordan, *Women and Credit in Pre-Industrial and Developing Societies*; and

Rebecca Lynn Winer, *Women, Wealth and Community in Perpignan, c. 1250–1300: Christians, Jews, and Enslaved Muslims in a Medieval Mediterranean Town.*

18. The Aragonese kings did occasionally intervene to relieve Mudéjar communities of usurious debts, such as King Pere with respect to the Muslims of Zaragoza (ACA, R. 46, fols. 209r and 215r), only to compel them the following year to pay these, both the debts and the usury (*debetis et usuris*) (ACA, R. 56, fol. 15r–v). Prominent Mudéjares did on occasion receive the same treatment as these *jenets*; see, for instance, ACA, R. 48, fol. 150r (12 Sep. 1280).

19. ACA, R. 95, fol. 93v (23 July 1292): "Bernardo de Claperiis, baiulo Valencie. Cum Muce Elmentauro et Maymono Abenbiahich et Çayedo de Piçaxen et Mahometo de Pataxen, genetis curie nostre de octingentis solidis regalium ordinaverimus provendi, videlicet unicuique ipsorum ducentos solidos regalium in acurrimentum, quitacionem, seu portionum suarum, mandamus et dicimus vobis quatenus uxoribus dictorum janetorum solva[tis] dictos octingentos solidos videlicet unicuique ipsorum ducentos solidos Regalium quibus sibi solutis recuperetis presentem literam cum apocha de soluta. Datum ut supra." As the foregoing indicated, two other *jenets*, the brothers Çayed and Mahomet, mentioned several times in the chancery registers, also had their salaries paid to their wives. As I argue below, *jenets* appear to have entered the Crown in large agnatic groups. If true in this case, all four of these soldiers' wives may have lived together and shared the debt.

20. ACA, R. 93, fol. 226v (2 Aug. 1292): "Fideli suo iusticie Valencie vel eius locum tenenti nec non universis aliis officialibus nostris ad quos presentes pervenerint salutem et cetera. Noveritis nos elongasse de gracia speciali Muçam Almentauri et Maymon Avenborayç, genetos nostros, ac debitores et fideiussores pro eis obligatos a solucione debitorum que debent usque ad sumam nongentorum solidorum regalium a proximo venturo festo beato Marie presentis mensis Augusti in antea usque ad sex menses continue subsequentes dum tamen non fuerint ab ipsis debitis aliter elongati. Et non habeant bona mobilia de quibus possint satisfacere creditoribus suis. Per hanc tam graciam non intendimus elongare debita que debentur prodotibus seu sponsaliciis mulierum nec pro vendicione bonorum in mobilium declarando [..] quod inter bona mobilia non computantur arma seu equi vel equitature proprie et <consuent> boves nec aratori nec vasa vinaria nec utensilia domus nec alia excepta et constitutione pacis et treuge seu aliquas constitutionibus nostras. Quare vobis dicimus et mandamus quatenus predictam graciam elongamenti observetis et observari faciatis predictis Muçe et Maymon ac debitoribus et fideiussoribus pro eis obligatis. Mandamus etiam vobis non compellatis nec compelli permitatis prefatos Muçam Almentaure et Maymon Avenborayç vel eorum bona ad solvendum usorias suis creditoribus nisi ad racionem IIII denarii pro libra prout in tatxacionem quam super dictis usoris fecimus dignocitur contineri. Datum Barchinone, IIII nonas Augustii et cetera."

21. ACA, R. 52, fol. 77_{v}; ACA, R. 71, fol. 49_{v}; ACA, R. 71, fol. 50_{v}; ACA, R. 71, fol. 51_{v}; ACA, R. 72, fol. 33r, ACA, R. 72, fols. 38v–39r [redacted]; and ACA, RP, MR, 774, fol. 75_{r}.

22. I would like to thank Ramón Pujades and Jaume Riera for their assistance in editing this document. Any errors are my own. ACA, CR, Jaume II, caixa 15, no. 1971 (21 Jan. 1304): "Al molt alt e poderos seynor en Jacme per la gracia de deu Rey d'Arago, de Valencia, de Murcia, Comte de Barcelona et de la Santa Ecclesia de Roma seynaler, almirayl, e capitan general. Ab nos en Pere de Montagut procurador vostre del Regne de Murcia e Ferrer des Cortey, batle vostre general del dit Regne, humilment besan vostres mans et vostres peus nos comanam en vostra gracia. Fem nos saber, Seynor, que reebem dues letres vostres en les quals nos envias manar que presessem rahenes d'en Alabes Abarraho, es a saber del dit Alabes son fill et [de] Baratdin Ab[arraho] son fill e de Greneladim Abarraho son fill e de Jahia Abenmudahar son fill e reebudes aquelles que yo dit Ferrer que liuras al dit Alabes lo casteyl de N[orgia] et els locs de Cepti e de Lorqui. Estes que.ns certifficassem plerenament queles dites rahenes fossen fills dels [davant] dits. On seynor vos fem saber que con lo dit Alabes fo vengut d'una cavalcada que tornarem. Comparec denant nos dijous XVI dies de Jener e donavans rahenes en les quals non avia negun daquels que vos Seynor nos trameses a dir salv un, es a saber lo fill de Jahia Abenmudahar, et nos, Seynor, dixem li que ell nons donava les rahenes que nos nos trameses a dir. E ell respos nos que no cuydava aver covinença ab vós, que ell sol del seu linatge agues adonar totes les rahenes. [Et] que cascun cap donas les sues. Et que ells son IIII alcaniellas es a saber IIII linatges e que valia molt mes que cascun linatge donas lo seu per ço con si ell ab son linatge donas tots les dites rahenes los altres tota ora ques vulgessen sen hieren. Et a la perf[...] Seynor con [molt] aguem rahonat en est feyt dixeren que ells darien a[quests] rahenes de cascun linatge primerament lo linatge de [Al]abes Abarraho ques apellen de Benihamema que dara lo fill de son oncle per nom Mahomet Abenboyahie [ho lo seus] fills . . . epres senyor no . . . nengu de la . . . Item lo linatge [ques es appelen] de Ben. . . . qual es cap Aiza Abenayma que dara son neebot fill de son germa per <Thaben> Anbenihiam Abenayma. Item lo linatge ques apellen de Benabdaluet e es cap Jahia Abenmud[ahar] que dara son fill . . . que vós ho manas per vostre letra. Item lo linatge ques apellen de Benihuara et son cap los fills de Taxerfi [que] daran Abrah[im] [A]ben Mahomet lur cosin, germa fill de lur o[ncle]. Et [...] seynor en est feyt no volem res enantar sens liscençia vostra et dixem las quens ho fariem saber et quen fari[em] vostre manament e [tra]metem vós [a dir] aquels rahenes que ells vós an en cor de donar per rahenes. Et creats Seynor per cert que ab que el dit Alabes //ell// e els altres nos vuellen servir quens hic valen mes que no farien atretans [altres tants] cavayls armats que sapiats Seynor que per tota aquesta frontera tremolen et an fort gran pahor d'eyls tots vostres enemics vós Seynor sabets les covinençes que avets ab eyls et sots tan discret Seynor que en aço ordonarets tota ora si a deu plau ço que sera honor et profit vostre et en aço seynor sia vostre mercé que hi manets ço que tendrets per bé et que.ns en fassats trametre en continent vostra resposta per ço Seynor con ja sabets los jenets con son axaquioses [i.e. make excuses] et cuyden-se que.n faç[a] [hoc] . . . et axi es mester seynor que demantinent ajam nostre manament de ço que fer hi denem. Scrita [Murcia]

XXI dia de Jener anno domini MCCC tercio. Et Seynor sia vostra merce que ajam demantinent vostra resposta de ço que.n trendrets per bé que mester hi es segons la manera lur. Nostre Seynor vós den vida longa e victoria sobre vostres enemics."

23. ACA, R. 235, fols. 3v–4r, *segunda numeración* (28 Dec. 1303): "Dilecto suo Petro de Monte Acuto procuratori regni Murcie et fideli suo Fernando de Cortilio bai[u]lo [...]ali eiusdem regni et cetera. Licet per aliam litteram nostram vobis dicte procuratori mandaverimus ut a nobil[..] [Al]abbez et aliis de perencela sua peteretis et reciperetis loco nostri quatuor filios ex ipsis per rahenis recione pacte[..] inter nos et eso inicorum. Et vobis dicto baiulo per aliam litteram mandaverimus ut eum certis certificamus a dicto procuratore que ipse dictos rahenas receperit et traderetis eidem Alabbez castrum de Negra et loca de Cepti et de Lorchi. Nunc tamen significamus vobis quod dicti Alabbez et alii geneti debent vobis dicto Petro tradere pro rahenis videlicet dictus Alabbez, filium suum, et Burrundi Abenrraho, filium suum, et Gemeladin Abenrraho, filium suum, et Jahia Aben Mudahar, filium suum. [....] vobis mandamus ut si dictis [fol. 4r] rahenis vobis dicti procuratori tradderint . . . dictus . . . tradatis dicto Alabbez castrum de Negra et alia loca predicta prout nobis per aliam litteram nostram fecimus ma[n]damientum. Preterea certificetis . . . de eo quod feceri[ti]s in permisis. Datum Valencie IIII, kalendas Ianuarii, anno predicto." Cf. Masià i de Ros, *Jaume II*, 213. The Umayyads similarly secured the loyalty of their Zanāta troops in North Africa by taking hostages. See Ibn 'Idhārī, *al-Bayān*, I: 254.

24. Cf. *Llibre dels feyts*, chaps. 308–9.

25. See chapter 6 for more detail. Badr al-Dīn and Jamāl al-Dīn may also have been named *shaykh al-ghuzāh*. Badr al-Dīn's son, 'Alī, was definitively *shaykh al-ghuzāh* during the reign of Muḥammad V.

26. ACA, Cartas árabes, 84bis (14 Jun 1304), which confirms this taking of captives: "dhakara banū marīn al-wāsilīn ilā hadhā annakum akhadtum minhum arba'a rahā'īn fi'l-ḥusn." See also ACA, R 235, fol. 12r, *segunda numeración* (30 Jan. 1304), a letter from Jaume II, which also confirms that the correct captives were eventually taken.

27. See chapter 6 as well.

28. ACA, R. 94, fol. 151r (29 Dec. 1292): ". . . pro re[d]emptione illius janeti et uxoris sue ac filiorum eorum qui in posse dicti Paschasii Dominici capti detinebantur. . . ."

29. The Crown provided safe passage to Abrahim Abenhamema and his wife to leave the Crown. ACA, R. 66, fol. 152v (27 July 1286): "Universis officialibus et cetera, cum Abrahim Abenhamema, janetus, cum uxore et familia sua prepararint redire ad terram suam, mandamus vobis quatenus in exeundo de terra nostra recto tramite versus Crivileyn . . . [j]ane[to] . . . uxore et familie sue nullum impedimentum vel contrarium faciatis. Datum Figueris." See also Catlos, "Mahomet Abenadalill," 291n126. Similarly, the Crown offered safeguard to Mahomet Abençabot and his wife, but it is not clear whether he was a *jenet* or an ambassador. ACA,

R. 90, fol. 123v (1291): "Universis officialibus et subditis suis et cetera, cum Mahomet Abençabot cum uxore sua et quodam //suo// alio Sarraceno suo proponit exire de terra nostra et redire apud Granatam per mare vel per terram, mandamus et dicimus vobis quatenus eisdem Mahometo, uxori, Sarraceno suo predicto et rebus suis nullum impedimentum vel contrarium faciatis in exeundo de terra nostra, immo provideatis eidem de secure transitu et ducatu [......] ne pretextu Sarraceno suo secum ducat alium Sarracenum."

30. ACA, R. 82, fol. 3v (7 Jan. 1290): "Raimundo Scorne [quod] . . . Daut Alma[..] expensam idoneam de quibus possit ducere vitam suam in civitate Valencie et quod recipiat [a]lbaranum et cetera. Datum in Alcoleya, VI idus Ianuarii."

31. ACA, R. 199, fol. 55r (4 Mar. 1301): "Dilecto consiliario suo Bernardo de Sevriano, procuratori Regni Murcie et cetera. Cum nos Muçe Aventauri, janeto nostro, propter plurima servicia quod cum nobis exhibita gratiose dare concesserimus unum hereditamentum idoneum et suficienter de illis que in regno Murcie nostre curie confiscata sunt seu confiscabuntur de quo sustentare valeat idonee vitam suam et familie sue, idcirco vobis dicimus et mandamus quatenus de hereditamentis predictis que confiscata sunt seu confiscabuntur in dicto regno Murcie, concedatis et assignetis unum idoneum et suficiens, memerato Muçe Aventauri, prout discretioni vestre visum fuerit expedire. Et cum hereditamentum prefatum dicto Muçe assignaveritis //eidere// eidem cartam seu donatione ipsa fieri mandemus et faciamus, inde nos per vestras litteras certas reddere certiores. Datum in Obsidione Montis Falconis, IIII nonas Marcii."

32. ACA, R. 79, fol. 79v (27 Jan. 1289): "Arnaldo de Bastida. Cum Ali Amari emisset de mandato nostro in Iacca equam Abdalla Abenaçiça, quandam janeti nostri, qui in Iacca decessit, precio quinquaginta quinque duplarum quam equam nos eidem Ali dari mandavimus, mandamus vobis quatenus dictas duplas detis dicto Ali qui eas traddet uxori dicti Abdalla quibis sibi solutis et cetera."

33. James Clifford, [Review of *Orientalism*] in *History and Theory*, 19, no. 2 (1980), 211: "It is still an open question, of course, whether an African pastoralist shares the same existential 'bestial floor' with an Irish poet and his readers."

34. In 1287, Alfons ordered his officials to let *jenets* sell any animals they captured during war. ACA, R. 74, fol. 5r (14 Oct. 1287): "Fuit mandatum officialibus quod in locis domini Regis permitant janetos vendere libere bestiare quod ceperunt ab inimicis . . ." Two years later, he wrote again to officials on the frontier, informing them that Mahomet el Viello was arriving for raids in defense of the territory and had the right to sell all goods retained. Royal officials, he explained, should not harm or impeded these soldiers but rather help and guide them. ACA, R. 81, fol. 56v (8 Jan. 1289 [1290]): "Universis hominibus quorumlibet locorum frontariarum terre nostre ad quos et cetera. Cum Mahomet el Viello, janetus noster, ac alii va[dunt] ad jenetiam tam Christiani quam Sarraceni socii predicti Mahomet habeant esse de mandato nostro in partibus frontarie pro tuicione [et] deffensione terre nostre ac etiam pro inferendo dampno inimicis nostris. Dicimus

ac mandamus vobis quatenus quandocumque predictum Mahomat al Viello ac socios suos predictos contingerit venire seu accedere ad loca vestra in partibus frontarie tam cum cavalgatis quam sine cavalgatis ipsos solutis vestris predictis cum cavalcatis seu rebus eorum benigne recipiatis et eisd[em] vel rebus suis nullum dampnum vel impedimentum faciatis immo iuvetis et dirigatis eosdem in hiis in quibus poteritis bono modo. Datum supra."

35. ACA, R. 83, fol. 71r (10 Aug. 1290), is also discussed in detail by Catlos, "Mahomet Abenadalill," 262–63.

36. ACA, R. 81, fol. 215r (25 Nov. 1290). This overlooked document from the chancery registers confirms Catlos' suspicion that Abenadalil was first deployed to the Navarrese front. See Catlos, "Mahomet Abenadalill," 261.

37. See Catlos, "Mahomet Abenadalill," 264–73, with maps.

38. ACA, R. 81, fol. 243r (21 Jan. 1291). See also Catlos, "Mahomet Abenadalill," 269; and Gazulla, "Zenetes," 193n1.

39. ACA, R. 81, fol. 214v (21 Nov. 1290): "Iusticie, iudici, et iuratis Calatayube. Quod cum Mahometus Abenadallil cum f[a]milia sua cepi[sse]t [et] traxisset de partibus Castille quan[d]a[m] predam animalium et aliarum rerum que erant hominum de Soria et aliqui de Calatayube qui composuerunt cum dicto Mahometo racione dicte prede obligaverunt se daturos eidem ce[rt]am peccunie quanti[tatem] certo termino \cum pena/ quam eidem solvere contradicunt, compellant illos et bona eorum et bona eorum ad dandum eidem Mahometo i[p]sam peccunie quantitatem \et penam predictam/ maliciis et diffugiis non admissis. Datum Barchinone, IX kalendas Decembris." Interestingly, mention of the fine was added to the text after an initial draft was written, indicating that it was perhaps an afterthought. The amount of the fine is mentioned in the following document. Cf. Catlos, "Mahomet Abenadalill," 280–81.

40. ACA, R. 81, fol. 234v (13 Dec. 1290), trimmed along right margin: "Petro Sancii, iusticie Calatayube vel eius locum tenenti. Intelleximus quod cum Mahometus Abenadallil <cucurri>[t] in Campo de Soria cepit in dicto campo de Soria aliquos captivos et quod redimerunt se pro quadam quantitate <p>[eccunie] et dederunt [al]iquos homines dicti loci de Calatayube pro fideiussoribus dicto Abenadalillo et promitendo eidem dare et [solver] ad diem certam dictam redemptionem et si forte eam in die prefixa non solvissent quod darent ei [pro pena] duo millia et CC solidos Iaccenses. Unde cum predicto Abenadalillo vel alicui alii loco sui nichil sit satisfactum d[e] [predictis] quantitatibus ut predicitur. Mandamus vobis quatenus si est ita, incontinenti procedatis per modum pigneris vel alium mod[um contra] predictos fideiussores et bona eorum ad solvendum [di]cto Abenadalillo vel cui voluerit dictam quantitatem quam sib[i dare] promiserunt pro redemptione predicta et dictos II millia CC solidos Iaccenses pro pena superius iam expressa et quidquid mis[sionum] iuste fecerit racione predicta. Taliter quod vobiscum inveniat iusticiam breviter de predictis. Datum Barchinone idus De[cembris]." See also Catlos, "Mahomet Abenadalill," 283.

41. ACA, R. 81, fol. 234r (13 Dec. 1290): "Petro Sancii, iusticie Calatayube vel eius locum tenenti. Intelleximus quod cum aliqui jeneti de familia Maho[m]eti Abenadalilli essent in aliquibus aldeis de Calatayube cum magna preda aliqui homines de dictis aldeis rau[b]raverunt dictis jenetis sive furto surripuerunt quosdam roncinos, adargas, et alias res. Quare vobis man[dam]us quatenus visis presentis si est ita, procedatis contra predictos ad restituendum Mahometo Abenadalillo [ve]l cui voluerit omnia supradicta prout de iure et foro fuerint faciendum non expectato a nobis super hoc [a]lio mandamento. Datum Barchinone idus Decembris." See also Catlos, "Mahomet Abenadalill," 281–82; and Gazulla, "Zenetes," 191.

42. ACA, R. 81, fols. 243v–244r (13 Dec. 1290): "Iuratis Calatayube. Intelleximus quod cum Mahometus Abenadalill <cucurrisset in Campo> de Soria, cepit in dicto campo de Soria aliquos captivos et quod redemerunt se pro quadam quantitate peccuncie et dederunt aliquos homines de loc[o] de [Calatayube] pro fideiussoribus dicto Abenadalillo, promitendo eisdem dare et solvere ad certam diem dictam redemptionem. Et si forte eam in die prefixa non solvissent quod darent ei et solvere pro pena, duo millia CC solidos Iaccenses, unde cum predicto Abenadalillo vel alicui alii loco sui nichil sit satisfactus de predictis quantitatibus ut predicitur et mandaverimus per literas nostras Petro Sancii iustice Calatayube vel eius locum tenenti quod si ita est incontinenti procedat per modum pignoris vel alium modum contra predictos fideiussores et bona eorum ad solvendum dicto Abenadalillo vel cui voluerit dictam quantitatem quam sibi dare promiserunt pro redemptione predicta et dictos duos millia CC solidos pro pena superius iam expressa et quicquid missionum iuste fecerit racione predicta et [dictus Abena]dalillus [te]neat sibi quod <dictus iusticia> qui obligatus est cum predictis fideiussoribus ut asserit in redemptione . . . [fol. 244r] . . . noster habeat se maliciose in negocio super observanda iusticie eidem iuxta dictum mandatum nostrum. Mandamus vobis quatenus si forte dictus iusticia maliciose se habuerit evita predicta, compellatis dictum iusticiam et fideiussores alios predictos ad so[lvendum] dicto Abenadalillo vel cui ipse voluerit redemptionem et penam et missiones predictas ut superius est expressum, taliter quod vobiscum inveniat iustica breviter de predictas. Datum Barchinone idus Decembris." See also Catlos, "Mahomet Abenadalill," 281.

43. He wrote letters to the justices of Aragon and Valencia. ACA, R. 81, fol. 234v (13 Dec. 1290): "Super predictis fuit scriptum Johanni Çapata, iusticie Aragone, quod faciat procedi per iusticiam Calatayube per m[odum] pignoris vel alium modum contra predictos fideiussores ad solvendum dicto Abenadalillo quantitatem quam sibi dare promiserunt pro redemptione dictorum captivorum et dictos duos millia solidos pro pena predicta et [quicquid] missionum iuste fecerit racione predicta. Datum ut supra." ACA, R. 81, fol. 243v (21 Dec. 1290): "Iustice Valencie vel eius locum tenenti. Intelleximus quod cum Mahometus Abenadallil cucurrisset in campo [de] Soria cepit in dicto campo de Soria aliquos captivos et quod redemerunt se pro quadam quantitate peccunie et dederunt ali[quos] homines de Calatayube pro fideiussoribus dicto Abenadalillo promitendo eidem dare et

solvere ad diem certam dictam re[demptio]nem et si forte eam in die prefixa non solvissent quod darent et solverent pro pena duo millia et CC solidos ia[ccenses]. Unde cum predicto Abenadalillo vel alicui alii loco sui nichil sit satisfactum de predictis quantitatibus ut dicitur et mandaverimus per literas nostras Petro Sancii, iusticie Calatayube vel eius locum tenenti quod si est ita incontinenti p[roce]dat per modum pignoris vel alium modum contra predictos fideiussores et bona eorum ad solvendum dicto Abena[da]lilli vel cui voluerit dictam quantitatem quam sibi dare promiserunt pro redemptione predicta et dictos II millia CC s[olidos] Iaccenses pro pena superius iam expressa et quicquid missionum inde fecerit, racione predicta. Mandamus vobis quatenus si f[orte] dictus Abenadalillus faticam iure invenerit in iusticiam Calatayube vel eius locum tenentem et vobis inde hostendis publica instrumenta vel alia documenta legitima incontinenti res et bona hominum Calatayube que in civitate Valencie vel a[licubi] poteritis invenire et de eisdem dicto Abenadalillo in redemptione pena et missionibus supradictis prout faciendum fuerit integre satisfacere faciatis. Taliter quod dictus Abenadalillus de predictis vobiscum iusticiam breviter assequat[ur]. Datum Barchinone, XII kalendas Ianuarii." See also Catlos, "Mahomet Abenadalill," 282; and Gazulla, "Zenetes," 192.

44. ACA, R. 81, fol. 237v (13 Dec. 1290): "Universis officialibus civitatum villarum et quorumlibet locorum Aragone. Mandamus vobis quatenus aliquibus [ad]alilis vel almugav[eris] equitum vel peditum vel aliis janetis si intrabunt Castellam seu Navarram nullum impedimentum vel contrarium faciatis vel fieri ab aliquibus permitatis immo provideatis eisdem et familie eorum de securo transitu et ducat[u] . . . restituentes et re[s]titui faciemus nichilominus eisdem omnes homines bestiarium et alias res quas habunt de terra dictorum inimicorum nostrorum et que vos vel aliquis vestrum ab eisdem cepistis vel etiam extorsistis. Datum u[t supra]." Alfons also specified the right of almogàvers to sell goods and captives, suggesting, as argued below, that the *jenets* were not the only ones to face hostility from local villagers. Note also that the king refers to the villagers' actions as "extortion," a phrase often repeated in this context below.

45. A. Friedburg, *Corpus iuris canonici* (Liepzig, 1881), 223 [Lateran III (1179)], as cited in Catlos, "Mahomet Abenadalill," 283n93. The Muslim jurist al-ʿUtbī (d. 869) addressed the opposite problem of Christians buying Muslim slaves. His opinion was cited by Abū al-Walīd Muḥammad b. Aḥmad b. Aḥmad b. Rushd al-Jadd, *al-Bayān wa'l-taḥṣīl wa'l-sharḥ wa'l-tawjīh wa'l-ta'līl fī masā'il al-mustakhrajah*, ed. Aḥmad al-Jabābī, XVI: 387–88, with thanks to Maribel Fierro for bringing this reference to my attention.

46. Catlos, "Mahomet Abenadalill," 280: "Their resistance may have been flavoured by a sense of solidarity with their Sorian neighbours or a spirit of confessional cohesion versus a Muslim foe, but this could have been little more than a convenient rationalization."

47. ACA, R. 81, fol. 234v (13 Dec. 1290): "Petro Sancii, iusticie Calatayube, vel eius locum tenenti. Intelleximus quod Vincentius de Sayona pignori . . . quendam hominem captivum Johanni Petri de Calatayube pro quinquaginta solidos

Iaccenses, et quod dictus Johannes non vulit . . . restituere. . . .” One learns that Vincent was an *adalid* from events described below. See also Catlos, “Mahomet Abenadalill,” 286.

48. ACA, R. 65, fol. 125r (29 Mar. 1286): “Muçe de [P]ortella. Mandamus [v]obis quatenus detis Abdu[a]het, janeto, ducentos solidos Barchinone quos sibi d<ampum et malum> [...] in emenda et restitucione quarumdam rerum quas Conradus Lan[cee] ab eo extorsit in Albayde ut asserit et facta sibi solucione recuperetis ab eo presentem litteram et apocham de soluto. Datum Barchinone, IIII kalendas Aprilis.” See also Catlos, “Mahomet Abenadalill,” 286. Although Catlos sees this as an incident of theft, it may have been more complicated. The case involves Conrad Lancia, who recruited and oversaw *jenets* for the Crown. See chapter 2.

49. ACA, R. 81, fol. 63r (7 Mar. 1290): “. . . quod [ca]pia[t] M[o]sse Maymono, Iudeo Valencie, qui surripuit quibusdam janetis [quadam] albarana sue quitacionis et . . . tam diu quosque reddiderit albarana dictis janetis ut eisdem satisfecerit de ipsis albaranis prout fuerit faciendum.” See also Catlos, “Mahomet Abenadalill,” 285.

50. Catlos, “Mahomet Abenadalill,” 280: “Accustomed as they would have been to cross-border raiding and to all of the misery and opportunity which accompanied it, they also did their best to profit from the situation.”

51. Catlos, “Mahomet Abenadalill,” 283n92: “This type of exchange, which worked to the benefit both of the Castilian and Aragonese townsmen, is one aspect of the regular commercial ties between municipalities on both sides of the frontier.”

52. See Catlos, “Contexto y conveniencia”; and idem, *Muslims in Medieval Latin Christendom, c. 1050–1614*, 515–35.

53. Catlos, *Victors and the Vanquished*, 85: “[T]he ideological counterparts of *jihād* in contemporary Christian society, the ideals of *Reconquista* and Crusade, played an analogous role: justifying actions in certain situations, while answering a need to express a sense of identity and purpose. As such, they can hardly be interpreted as causes or determinants of events, certainly not on any grand scale and normally not when they came into conflict with the ambitions of those individuals who were their purported champions”; and ibid., 294: “If Crusade ideology had emerged in the previous two centuries, in the late thirteenth century it had yet to determine Christian relations to Muslims either abroad or at home.”

54. Catlos, “Contexto y conveniencia,” 263: “La identidad sectaria tendió a no convertirse en una cuestión importante en la interacción cotidiana”; and ibid., 268: “La antipatía asociada a las diferencias sectarias, la confrontación monolítica de Sánchez Albornoz, así como las tendencias hacia la aculturación enfatizadas por Castro no son los determinantes del carácter de la interacción etno-religiosa de la Península Ibérica durante la Edad Media, sino más bien sus consecuencias. En las esferas legal, económica y social fueron los convenios negociados dictados por el mutuo interés—conveniencia—los que determinaron las relaciones entre grupos e individuos a través de las divisiones sectarias etno-religiosas.”

55. Catlos, *Muslims of Medieval Latin Christendom,* 522: "The prohibitions of Canon Lawyers and secular jurists and the fulminations of preachers and missionaries seem to have existed almost within their own sealed world, following their own logic, and with little impact on the social and political practices of princes and their subjects."

56. The justice of Valencia, for instance, was ordered to seize any property that these men held in that kingdom. ACA, R. 81, fol. 243v (full citation in n43, above): ". . . incontinenti res et bona hominum Calatayube que in civitate Valencie vel a[licubi] poteritis invenire et de eisdem dicto Abenadalillo in redemptione pena et missionibus supradictis prout faciendum fuerit integre satisfacere faciatis. . . ." See also Catlos, "Mahomet Abenadalill," 282.

57. Gazulla, "Zenetes," 187; and Catlos, "Mahomet Abenadalill," 295–96.

58. ACA, R. 74, fol. 5r (14 Oct. 1287): "Iusticie et iuratis Cataltayube. Intelle[xim]us quod vos abstulistis janet[i]s nostr[i]s quendam hominem de Cutanda quem ceperunt in presenti guerra. Quare volumus ac vobis mandamus quatenus si vobis constiterit quod dictus homo sit de aliquo inimico nostro, ipsum restituatis dictis janetis [incontin]enti, ipsi vero tenentur nobis dare quintam de eo quod habuerint pro redemptione hominis supradicti. Datum in Epila, II idus Octobris." See also Catlos, "Mahomet Abenadalill," 285n103.

59. Alfamén is approximately thirty miles from Zaragoza toward the Castilian border. ACA, R. 74, fol. 11r (25 Oct. 1287): "Aljamis Sarracenorum Dalmoneçir et de Alfamen et janetis ibidem existentibus et aliis universis ad quos presentes et cetera. Cum locus de Aguaro sit dilecti nostri Alamandi de Gudal, superiunctarii Tirasone, mandamus et dicimus vobis, quatenus, in predicto loco seu hominibus ibidem existentibus au[t] aliquibus bonis seu ganatis eorum nullum malum seu dampnum faciatis nec fieri permitatis. Immo si qua cepistis violenter ab hominibus predicti loci dum modo non sint inimicorum nostrorum ea eisdem visis presentibus restituatis et restitui faciatis. Datum ut supra." See text at n86, below, for a discussion of this document.

60. Specifically, he was ordered to provide them safe conduct all the way to Montseny, north of Barcelona in Catalonia. ACA, R. 80, fol. 66r (11 Oct. 1289): "Scriptum fuit iusticie Calatayube quod absolvat janetos quos homines de Alfama ceperunt et illos traddat seu mutet ad dictum Regem et provideat eis de securo conductu in Monte Sono. V idus Octobris." See also Gazulla, "Zenetes," 187–88.

61. The echo here of James Scott's *Weapons of the Weak: Everyday Forms of Peasant Resistance* is also a critique of it. In this reading, "foot-dragging" is not only resistance to ideology but also the expression of another ideology, a competing form of law and legitimacy.

62. This is precisely what King Alfons himself suspected in his letter to the council of Calatayud. See ACA, R. 81, fols. 243v–244r (13 Dec. 1290), with full citation in n42, above.

63. ACA, R. 85, fol. 113v (15 Mar. 1290): "Iusticie et Iuratis Xative. Cum iam scripserimus vobis quod miteritis ad nos illos j[e]netos quos captos ten[etis], qui venerant de Billena, et istud non feceritis mira[mur] de vobis. Quare irato vobis dicimus et mandamus ex parte Domini Regis et nostra quatenus visis presentibus, mitatis ad nos jenetos predictos [c]um familia sua et omnibus equitaturis et rebus suis, significantes nobis, causam propter quam [retinu]istis eosdem. Et istud nullatenus differatis. Datum ut supra."

64. ACA, R. 81, fol. 215r (25 Nov. 1290): "Fuit scriptum Luppo French de Luna quod predam quam quidam jeneti Abenadalili capitis jenetorum extraherunt [*sic*] de Navarr[a] [q]uam [ean]dem eis ablata fuit per aliquos de familia dicti nobilis faciat eis restitui. Datum Barchinone VII kalendas Decembris [1290]."

65. ACA, R. 81, fol. 237v (13 Dec. 1290), with full citation in n44, above.

66. ACA, R. 81, fol. 224r (7 Dec. 1290, left margin trimmed): "[Petro] Ferrandi recepimus literas vestras et intelleximus ea que in eisdem nobis dici misistis super facto mortis Puçole de qua fuerunt inculpati [Pa]schasius Valentini, Matheus de Galera, Juanyes Bono, et //quidam// alii adalilli nostri cum sociis et familiis eorumdem ad que vobis [re]spondemus quod volumus et placet nobis quod predicti adalilli nostri cum sociis et tota familia sua remaneant et sint in servicio vestro prout esse consueverunt ipsis cum assecurantibus idonee in posse nostro, quod si forte racione dicte mortis proponeretur querimonia contra eos [quod] faciant inde iustitie complementum. Nos enim mandamus per literas nostras universis officialibus nostris quod incontinenti cum ipsi firmaverint . . . restituant et desemperent eis omnia ea que eisdem ceperunt vel emparaverunt racione mortis predicte. Datum Barchinone, VII idus Decembris. . . . [....] scriptum univers[is] officialibus quod cum constiterit eis predictis firmasse in posse dicti Petri Ferrandi desemparent eis et desemparari faciant omnia que eisdem occupaverunt, ac prestent eisdem super inferendo dampno inimicis domini Regis consilium, iuvamen. Datum ut supra." Puçola and his associates received a safeguard and orders to remain on the Navarrese border from King Alfons on November 15, 1289, which is to say their time of service on this front overlapped with Abenadalil's. ACA, R. 80, fol. 104v (two documents): "Iustice, iuratis et concilio d'Albayo. Mandamus vobis quatenus non impediatis nec ab aliquo impediri permitatis Puçola et socios suos \et/ racione alicuius mandati per nos eis in contrarium faci cavalcatam quam nuper adduxerunt de Navarra [nec] alias quas ducturi sunt de locis inimicorum nostrorum, nisi tamen ipsa cavalcata fuerit de hominibus aut locis qui sint sub se[curit]ate [nost]ra et de ipsa securitate a nobis cartam habeant specialem. Man[d]amus etiam vobis quod super cavalcata quam nuper portaverunt de termino de Fustineana nullum impedimentum vel contrarium faciatis prefato Pusola et aliis supradictis nisi ipsa cavalcata vel persone ipsius fuerint aliquorum qui sub predicta securitate nostra sint, et quod de ipsa securitate habeant a nobis cartam ut superius continetur. Datum ut supra"; and "[Fuit scri]ptum dicta Puçola et aliis scutiferis qui sunt in frontaria Navarre quod placet domino Reg[e] quod [....] et remeneant el Bayo et fronteria

Navarre in deffensionem locorum terre domini Regis quosque ab [..] aliud receperint in [..] mandatis. Datum ut supra." See also Catlos, "Mahomet Abenadalill," 284. The wonderful translation of "Puçola" as "Big Flea" is Brian Catlos'.

67. This fact is inferred from the following document, to which I return in n70, below. ACA, R. 81, fol. 237v (13 Dec. 1290): "Petro Sancii, iusticie Calatayube. Mandamus vobis quatenus visis presentibus tradatis et tradi faciatis Paschasio Valentinum et Vincenio de Sayona et aliis sociis eorum <omnia> albarana cartas bestias et alias res quas emparestis sive tenetis emperatis ab eisdem racione mortis Puçole [eo] quem fuer[u]nt ut dicitur inculpati. Datum Barchinone, idus Decembris."

68. ACA, R. 81, fol. 234v (17 Dec. 1290): "Paschasio Valenteni, Juanyes Bono, Raimundo Petri, Galmo Petri et aliis sociis eorum. Intelleximus quod vos abs[tulistis] per violentiam Masseto, Assager et Alabes, jenetis nostris quandum roncinum et quandam equam quare vobis mandamus q[uatenus] [si est] ita incontinenti restituatis dictis jenetis equitaturas predictas al[ias] mandamus per presentes Petro Sancii [de] Calatayube quod vos ad predicta compellant prout fuerint faciendum. Datum Barchinone, XVI kalendas Ianuarii [1290]."

69. ACA, R. 81, fol. 234r (13 Dec. 1290, my emphasis): "[I]usticie Calatayube et Daroce vel eorum locum tenentibus. Intelleximus quod Puçola quod debebat Mahometo [A]benadallil quandam quantitatem peccunie racione quarum dicti rerum quas ipse Puçol[a] recepit de cavalcata [...]erate Castille que erant inter dictum Abendallil et dictum Puçolam. Quare vobis mandamus, quatenus, si [est] ita de bonis dicti Puçole satisfaciatis et satisfieri faciatis dicto Mahometo Abenadallil vel cui [v]oluerit in dicta quantitate peccunie quam ei debebat dictus Puçola racione predicta, *taliter quod dictus [A]benadalillus de vobis pro deffectum iusticie non habeat materiam conquerendi*. Datum ut supra." See also Catlos, "Mahomet Abenadalill," 284.

70. ACA, R. 81, fol. 237v (13 Dec. 1290), with full citation in n67, above. A more detailed letter was issued to Petrus Ferrandi, the procurator of Valencia, who oversaw the operations of the almogàvers during the so-called Guerra Jenetorum, which is discussed later in this chapter, beginning at n101. See ACA, R. 81, fol. 224r (7 Dec. 1290) with full citation in n66, above.

71. ACA, R. 81, fol. 234v (17 Dec. 1290), with full citation in n40, above: ". . . quare vobis mandamus q[uatenus] [si est] ita incontinenti restituatis dictis jenetis equitaturas predictas al[ias] mandamus per presentes Petro Sancii [de] Calatayube quod vos ad predicta compellant prout fuerint faciendum."

72. ACA, R. 81, fol. 215v (20 Nov. 1290): "[Ç]almedine Cesarauguste. Intelleximus quod quidam Sarracenus nomine Mahumet Sugeray, mil[item] dilecti nostri Abendalli[l], capitis jenetorum, diligit mult[u]m quamdam Sarracenam Cesarauguste nomine Fatimam, filiam Abdullasis, quam vult ducere in uxorem. Quare vobis dicimus et mandamus quatenus faciatis et procuretis cum effectu quod d[ictus] Sarracenus dictam Sarracenam habeat in uxorem. Datum ut supra." See also Catlos, "Mahomet Abenadalill," 293n135; and Lourie, "Jewish Mercenary," 371.

73. ACA, Bulas, legajo VI, no. 19 (8 Jan. 1239).

74. Abū al-Ḥasan ʻAlī b. Muḥammad al-Makhzūmī Ibn Ḥarīq of Valencia (d. 1225), who was the teacher of the well-known scholar Ibn al-Abbār, wrote these lines on the eve of the Jaume I's conquest (1238). See A. R. Nykl, *Hispano-Arabic Poetry and Its Relations with the Old Provençal Troubadours*, 331, as cited in Burns, *Islam Under the Crusaders*, 3.

75. On the military strength of the region, see *Llibre dels feyts*, chap. 128; Desclot, *Crònica*, chap. 49.

76. A week after the surrender noted above, Pere issued an order to his officers in Algeciras (a port briefly under Castilian rule in this period) that this treaty should be upheld, providing evidence that some *jenets* did in fact leave after the pacification of Valencia. ACA, R. 38, fol. 33v (7 Sep. 1276): "Infans Petrus et cetera, fidelibus suis baiulo, iusticie, iuratis et universis hominibus Alyazire, salutem et graciam. Sciatis quod nos accipimus et habemus ab hodierna die dominica usque in tres menses continere [*sic*] vent[ur]os et completos treguas cum janetis et omnibus aliis Sarracenis locorum Regni Valencie et castrorum qui s[e] contra nos alciaverunt <exceptis> tamen castris et locis ac que tenet alcaydus Abrahim et excepto castro de Alcalano, Vallis de Alfandec, de Marynenen, et Sarracenis dictorum castrorum et rebus eorumdem. Quare mandamus vobis quatenus dictam treguam per totum dictum tempus observetis et infra dictum tempus non oportet vos similiter vel res vestras cav[e]re a janetis vel aliquibus Saracenis dictorum castrorum et locorum qui sunt in tregua predicta quam quidem treguam precon[i]zant per Alyaziram visis presentibus faciatis. Datum Xative VIII idus Septembris anno domini MCCLXXVI."

77. On the Mudéjares of Valencia, see Burns, *Crusader Kingdom of Valencia*; idem, *Muslims, Christians, and Jews in the Crusader Kingdom of Valencia: Societies in Symbiosis*; Josep Torró Abad, *El naixement d'una colònia*; Ferrer i Mallol, *La frontera amb l'Islam*; and Mark D. Meyerson, *The Muslims of Valencia in the Age of Fernando and Isabel: Between Coexistence and Crusade*.

78. The surrender agreement at Chivert (AHN, Ordines militares, codex 542, Montesa [28 Apr. 1234]) preserved the right to maintain mosques and prayer. Jaume I also conceded to the Muslims of Játiva the right to build a new mosque in 1273 (ACA, R 21, fol. 151v [7 June 1273]). Jaume II protected the right of the Muslims of Alagón (ACA, R 90, fol. 85v [6 Oct. 1291]) and Ricla (ACA, R 94, fols. 144v–145r [27 Dec. 1292]) against Christian encroachments or opposition. In the latter case, Christians blocked Muslims from entering their mosque. For more on the issue, see Ferrer i Mallol, *Els sarraïns*, 85–94; and Ana Echevarría Arsuaga, "De cadí a alcalde mayor. La élite judicial Mudéjar en el siglo XV," *Al-Qanṭara* 1 (2003): 139–68.

79. ACA, R. 19, fol. 83r (16 Dec. 1273).

80. Mudéjares had a variety of community leaders: *alcaydus* (*al-qā'id*), *alamin* (*al-amīn*), *çalmedina* (*ṣāḥib al-madīna*), *almotacen* (*al-muḥtasib*), and *almoixerif* (*al-musharrif*), whose roles seem to have overlapped extensively, particularly in

rural communities. The spelling of these titles varies widely in the chancery registers. See also Jean-Pierre Molénat, "L'élite Mudéjare dans la Péninsule Ibérique médiévale," in *Elites e redes clientelares na Idade Média: problemas metodológicos*, ed. F. T. Barata, 45–53.

81. The early surrender charters of Chivert (1234), Játiva (1245), and Tudela (1115) allowed that Muslims would be judged by a Muslim judge. Complaints abound that royal officials violated Mudéjar legal autonomy (ACA, R. 48, fol. 20v; ACA, R. 89, fol. 41r; ACA, R. 99, fol. 277r; ACA, R. 100, fol. 272v; and ACA, R. 213, fol. 275r, for various examples). See also Burns, *Islam under the Crusaders*, 228; Boswell, *Royal Treasure*, 65–66, 108, 142; Boswell, *Royal Treasure*, 65–66; Catlos, *Victors and the Vanquished*, 177–78; and Echavarría, "De cadí a alcalde mayor."

82. There is evidence in the chancery registers that Arabic continued to be used by Mudéjares throughout the kingdoms of the Crown of Aragon at the end of the thirteenth century: ACA, R. 11, fol. 199 (Játiva); ACA, R. 12, fol. 76v (Lérida); ACA, R. 40, fol. 166 (Zaragoza); and ACA, R. 48, fol. 7v (La Algecira). Cf. Boswell, *Royal Treasure*, 384, claiming that Arabic was used only in Valencia. See also Carmen Barceló, "La lengua àrab al País Valencia (segles VIII al XVI)," *Arguments* 4 (1979): 123–49; and Maria Dolors Bramon Planas, "Una llengua, dues llengües, tres llengües," in *Raons d'identitat del País Valencia*, ed. Pere Sisé, 17–47.

83. Burns, *Islam under the Crusaders*, 188.

84. Burns, *Islam under the Crusaders*, 273.

85. See, for instance, ACA, R. 82, fols. 61v–62r (2 July 1290).

86. ACA, R. 74, fol. 11r (25 Oct. 1287), with full citation in n59, above: "Aljamis Sarracenorum Dalmoneçir et de Alfamen et janetis ibidem existentibus et aliis universis ad quos presentes et cetera. . . ."

87. They moved into houses previously owned by another Muslim. ACA, R. 44, fol. 178v (16 May 1280), with citation in n9, above.

88. ACA, R. 82, fol. 3v (7 Jan. 1290): "Raimundo Scorne [quod] . . . Daut Alma[..] expensam idoneam de quibus possit ducere vitam suam in civitate Valencie et quod recipiat [a]llbaranum et cetera. Datum in Alcoleya, VI idus Ianuarii." See Gazulla, "Zenetes," 194.

89. ACA, R. 199, fol. 55r (4 Mar. 1301): ". . . Cum nos Muçe Aventauri, janeto nostro, propter plurima servicia quod cum nobis exhibita gratiose dare concesserimus unum hereditamentum idoneum et suficienter de illis que in regno Murcie nostre curie confiscata sunt seu confiscabuntur de quo sustentare valeat idonee vitam suam et familie sue . . . ," with full citation in n31, above.

90. See chapter 6 for a fuller discussion.

91. Whereas travelers and traders had to reside in the merchant hostel in the *morería*, the king occasionally granted the privilege of staying inside the city to foreign dignitaries, who may have taken offense at an association with the Mudéjares. For instance, in 1277, two Muslim vistors from Tangia (Ṭanja, modern Tangiers)

arrived at Valencia in order to arrange for the exchange of captives. They traveled with their wives and family and were housed within the walls of Valencia city. They were also given the privilege of trading goods directly from their residence rather than in the market. See ACA, R. 40, fol. 4r (3 Aug. 1277).

92. ACA, R. 70, fol. 31r (18 Dec. 1286): "Baiulo Valencie vel eius locum tenenti quod absolvat Çehit, genetum, quem captum tenet racione vulnerum per ipsum illatorum Alamino Sarracenorum Valencie et filio eiusdem, ex quibus vulneribus nullus est, ut dicitur, mortuus nec sunt talia vulnera quod aliquis eorum ut asseritur, mortem inde assequatur. Quoniam dominus Rex, si ita est, absolvit dictum genetum a captione predicta, et quod [re]sti[t]uat ei ensem quem in dicta ritxa [*sic*] sibi abstulit, ut dicitur. Datum in Portupino, XV kalendas Ianuarii." See also Catlos, "Mahomet Abenadalill," 292–93.

93. See chapter 3 for a more detailed discussion of sumptuary laws in the kingdoms of the Crown of Aragon. See also the case of the Belvis, a prominent Mudéjar family, who were explicitly exempted from these laws. ACA, R. 981, fol. 22r (12 Feb. 1355); and ACA, R. 904, fol. 232r (13 Nov. 1360), as cited in Boswell, *Royal Treasure*, 45.

94. *Libre dels feyts*, chap. 47ff for the conquest of Mallorca; and Ubierto Arteta, ed., *Crónica de San Juan de la Peña*, chap. 37, for the conquest of Minorca. See also David Abulafia, *A Mediterranean Emporium: The Catalan Kingdom of Majorca*; Joan Ramis i Ramis, *Les Illes Balears en temps cristians fins als àrabs*; and Elena Lourie, "Free Moslems in the Balearics under Christian Rule in the Thirteenth Century," *Speculum* 45, no. 4 (1970): 624–49.

95. ACA, R. 70, fol. 60r; ACA, R. 70, fol. 61v; ACA, R. 72, fol. 24v; and ACA, R. 72, fol. 53v. See also Catlos, "Mahomet Abenadalill," 294, which cites an additional document, ACA, R. 70, fol. 49v. ACA, R. 70, fol. 61v (5 Feb. 1286) reads: "Fuit factum albaranum Alabeç, geneto, de uno Sarraceno negro vocato Bilel."

96. The chancery registers contain numerous records of slave sales from the auctions at Mallorca and Barcelona that discriminate carefully between white (*albus*), brown (*laurus*), and black (*niger*) men and women.

97. ACA, R. 57, fol. 189r (29 Aug. 1285, my emphasis): "Universis [offici]alibus quod ubicumque et apud quemcumque reperiantur V Sarraceni et I Sarracena quorum unus est Raimundi [de] Gerunda [et] alius Nicholai de Samares et alius Bernardi de Calle et alius Guillelmi Fratri et alius Bernardi Reig et ipsa Sarracena est A[b]rahim Amiel, civium Barchinone, capiant et occupent et pos[sint] a quolibet detentare et captos cust[o]diare [*sic*] et conservent donec predicti cives dictos Sarracenos probaverint esse suos et tunc tradant eos procuratori dictorum civium cum de eorum dominio fuerit facta fides. *Preterea recipiant idoneam cautionem ab Albohaya et Cassim et Sahat, genetis, quorum opera et insinuatione dicti Sarraceni dicuntur aff[u]gisse* de restituendis dictis Sarracenis ubi probatum f[uerit] contra eos vel de [fac]iendo eis iusticie complemento. Datum Barchinone, IIII kalendas Septembris."

98. ACA, R. 70, fol. 25v (5 and 9 Dec. 1286): "Petro Ferrandi, procuratori Regni Valencie, vel eius locum tenenti. [Cum] intelleximus quod aliqui jeneti et pedites Sarraceni parant se et intendunt intrare hostiliter Regnum nostrum Valencie et ibidem nobis gentibus nostris dampnum inferre, dicimus et mandamus vobis quatenus vocetis //vel// ex parte nostre Magistrum Templi, Magistrum Hospitalis, et Comendatorem de Alcanicio quibus super hoc scribimus et nobiles ac milites in Regno Valencie hereditates habentes ut ad deffensionem Regni Valencie et bonorum suorum, veniant et stent cum equis armis et aliis apparatibus suis ut si forte aliqui hostes nostri intrarent Regnum Valencie possint eis viriliter resistere ac eis dampnum inferre. Datum Maiorice, nonas Decembris.

"Universis nobilibus ac militbus in Regno Valencie hereditates habentibus. Cum intelleximus aliquos Sarraceno[s] se parasse ad expugnandum Regnum nostrum Valencie dilectum vestrum requirimus ac vobis dicimus et mandamus quatenus visis presentibus paretis vos cum equis et armis et aliis apparatibus vestris et stetis ad deffensionem Regni Valencie supradicti et bonorum ac hereditatum vestrarum, ut si forte aliqui hostes nostri intrarent [R]egnum Valencie predictum, possitis eis viriliter resistere ac eis dampnum inferre. Datum ut supra.

"Commendatori de Alcanicio. Cum intelleximus quod jeneti et alii Sarraceni extranei tam equites quam pedites parant et intendunt intrare regnum nostrum Valencie et malum inferre ibidem, requirimus vos ac vobis firmiter dicimus et madamus quatenus incontinenti omni dilatione remota eatis cum militibus et familia ad predictum regnum Valencie et ibi sitis pro resistencia predictis Sarracenis viriliter facienda in defensionem regni predicta et eorum que ibi habetis. Datum Maiorice, V idus Decembris.

"Similiter fratri Bernardo de Miravals.

"Similiter magistro Hospitalis.

"Similiter magistro Templi."

Particular noblemen were also written directly (ACA, R. 70, fol. 92v [11 Apr. 1287]). Almogàvers are mentioned in a letter to Petrus Ferrandi, procurator of Valencia (ACA, R. 71, fol. 49v [5 May 1287]).

99. Letters were issued again to the military orders, ACA, R. 70, fol. 93r (7 Apr. 1287); and ACA, R. 70, fol. 106r (22 Apr. 1287).

100. On the bishoprics, ACA, R. 70, fol. 92v (11 Apr. 1287); and ACA, R. 70, fol. 101r–v (29 Apr. 1287). On revenues, ACA, R. 71, fol. 34r (7 Apr. 1287); and ACA, R. 71, fol. 36r (12 Apr. 1287).

101. ACA, R. 71, fol. 34r (7 Apr. 1287), a series of documents related to financing the war, are the first to refer to it as the Guerra Jenetorum. The war appears to have already ended when in October, Alfons sent the following order, ACA, R. 71, fol. 88r (25 Oct. 1287): "Iacobo Delmars, collectori reddituum Vallis de Meriynen. Volumus ac vobis dicimus et mandamus quatenus soluto eo quod nobilis Petrus Ferrandi, procurator Regni Valencie, vel Petrus Peregrini de domo nostra, assignaverunt aliquibus super redditibus supradictis racione guerre Janetorum,

respondeatis sive responderi faciatis de eisdem redditibus creditoribus nobilis dompni Ferrandi quondam [.....] nostri vel procuratoribus eorum iuxta assignacionem per nos inde ipsis factam cum carta nostra ut in ea continetur. Et hoc aliquatenus non mitetis. Datum in Alagone, VIII kalendas Novembris." I would argue that the war only lasted the summer months.

102. See also Lourie, "Anatomy of Ambivalence," 7–11.

103. ACA, R. 70, fol. 106r (23 Apr. 1287): "Alamino et aliame Sarracenorum de Alhavir, avem entes que per pahor dels moros qui entraren el Regne de Valencie et dels almugavers nosen sots pugats el pug de laucho. En con nos siam venguts en Valencie, deym nos eus manam que tornets tan tost en vestres cases et vestres habetats et pensets de laurar axi con avets acustumat cor nos sem venguts per ço ques tingam sans et segurs. Datum Valencie, IX kalendas Maii."

104. ACA, R. 161, fol. 107r–v (21 Aug. 1316, my emphasis): ". . . In nostri presencia constitutus nuncius aliame Sarracenorum Elchii exposuit humiliter coram nobis quod aliquociens tam de die quam de nocte, cum *insurgit rumor aliquis in dicto loco quod geneti seu Sarraceni de partibus Granate intrant hostiliter terram nostram*, aliqui *homines iuvenes* loci ipsius, temeritate ducti, concitando populum contra Sarracenos loci predicti vociferant et dicunt 'al raval, al raval'. . . ." For a full edition, Ferrer i Mallol, *La frontera*, 265. See a similar incident decades later: ACA, R. 1377, fols. 67v–68r (5 July 1340), as cited in Ferrer i Mallol, *La frontera*, 288–90.

105. A document records the repopulation of the *raval* of Játiva because some Muslims "recently departed with the *jenets*," ACA, R. 75, fol. 7r (3 May 1287): ". . . qui nuper recesserunt cum genetis." There was considerable financial opportunity in the departure and return of such fugitives. See for instance, ARV, Perg. Reials, no. 9 (1347).

106. ACA, R. 78, fol. 57r (22 Apr. 1287): "Item debetis vos dictus nobilis recuperare . . . centum XXX solidos [quo]s dedistis in uno Sarraceno qui erat espia in guerra Janetorum."

107. ACA, R. 100, fol. 202r (14 Nov. 1294, my emphasis): "Petro de Libiano, baiulo generali regni Valencie, salutem et cetera. Noveritis ad nostram audienciam pervenisse quod quadam comitiva Sarracenorum almugaverorum nuper venientium de partibus //Castelle// Regis Granate adgrediebatur intrare in regnum nostrum Valencie pro dampno inferrendo et quod Ferrandus Garcesii de Roda cum quadam comitiva quam secum ducebat obviavit eisdem et deviat eosdem et etiam quosdam ex ipsis captos retinuit et fuerunt invente penes eos *quedam carte seu litere quas dictus Rex Granate mittebat aliamis Regni Valencie quod se insurgerent contra nos et terram nostram* et quod occuparent et subriperent <ruppes> et fortitudines quas occupare possent quoniam ipse Rex Granate erat missum ad ipsos familiam equitum in deffensione et iuvamen eorumdem. Quare vobis dicimus et mandamus quatenus visis presentibus ad frontariam accedatis et recognoscatis loca et castra et fortitu\di/nes ipsius frontarie et si qua defuierit vel necessaria

fuerit ad stabilimenta dictorum castrarum faciatis providere et custodiri diligenter, taliter quod propter malam custodiam seu curam non possit ipsis castris sinistram aliquam evenire. Datum Barchinone, XVIII kalendas Decembrii, anno domini MCCXCIIII."

108. ACA, R. 252, fol. 121r (18 Nov. 1295). See also Dufourcq, *L'Espagne catalane*, 349.

Chapter Six

1. This was the crusade against Almería in 1309. See, *EI*[2], s.v. "al-Mariyya" as well as Tapia Garrido, *Almería musulmana*; Sālim, *Ta'rīkh madīnat al-Mariyya al-islāmiyya*; Giménez-Soler, *El sitio de Almería*; Ferrer i Mallol, *La frontera*, 103–16; Harvey, *Islamic Spain*, 173–80; and Arié, *L'Espagne musulmane*, 89–93.

2. On the Guerra Jenetorum, see chapter 5.

3. Ibn Khaldūn, *Kitāb al-'ibar*, VII: 379.

4. Arié, *L'Espagne musulmane*, 238–43; and Manzano Rodríguez, *La intervención*, 321–71.

5. See chapter 1 for more detail on this first rebellion.

6. Although Ibn Khaldūn makes no mention of Musā b. Raḥḥū's participation in the rebellion, Ibn al-Khaṭīb, *Iḥāṭa*, IV: 78, confirms that he did. See also Manzano Rodríguez, *La intervención*, 343.

7. Ibn Khaldūn, *Kitāb al-'ibar*, VII: 190–91, 383.

8. Ibn Khaldūn, *Kitāb al-'ibar*, VII: 381. The *maḥalla* was a demonstration of force, a regular and punitive mission through his territory by the Almohad caliph to establish his authority. See Jocelyne Dakhlia, "Dans la mouvance du prince: la symbolique du pouvoir itinérant au Maghreb," *Annales* 3 (1988): 735–60; and Maribel Fierro, "Algunas reflexiones sobre el poder itinerante almohade," *e-Spania* 8 (2009), [Online], URL : http://e-spania.revues.org/18653.

9. Ibn Khaldūn, *Kitāb al-'ibar*, VII: 379, 381, cit. 379: "So, they departed for al-Andalus in 661 and had a great impact on the jihād, which brought great honor to their positions. . . . And many of the Zanāta princes (aqyāl) aspired to imitate their deeds. In the central Maghrib, the likes of 'Abd al-Malik b. Yaghmurāsan b. Zayyān, 'Iyād b. Mandīl b. 'Abd al-Raḥmān, and Zayyān b. Muḥammad b. 'Abd al-Qawī gathered and undertook to cross over for the jihād. So, they crossed with whoever surrounded them (khaffa ma'hum) from their tribes in the year 676. So al-Andalus was filled with princes and men of royal stock (a'yāṣ al-malik)." Cf. Ibn al-Khaṭīb, *Iḥāṭa*, I: 136; and idem, *al-Lamḥa*, 39, which mention other tribes.

10. The remnants of a *zāwiyā*, a religious instution, in the Rábita de Albuñol, a fortress from which Ghuzāh raids were launched, hints at the ritual and devotional practices of the ascetic warriors who manned the front lines. See also Arié, *L'Espagne musulmane*, 275–76; Manzano Rodríguez, *La intervención*, 333; and de

Epalza, "Constitución de rábitas en la costa de Almería." For the signifance of the *zāwīya* in the North African context, see *EI*[2], s.v. "zāwīya."

11. Ibn Khaldūn, *Kitāb al-'ibar*, VII: 382: "wa-khāṭabahum al-sultān abū sa'īd [r. 1310–1331] malik al-maghrib fī i'tiqālihi fa-ajābūhu wafr min maḥbasihi wa-laḥaqa bi-dār al-ḥarb."

12. Ibn Khaldūn, *Kitāb al-'ibar*, VII: 382–83.

13. Ibn Khaldūn, *Kitāb al-'ibar*, VII: 213. Abū Yūsuf saw the Ghuzāh as an extension of his own efforts in jihād.

14. See the astute discussion of jihād in the Islamic west in Abigail Krasner Balbale, "*Jihād* as a Means of Political Legitimation," in *The Articulation of Power in Medieval Iberia and the Maghrib*, ed. Amira K. Bennison, 87–105. Cf. Lagardère, *Les Almoravides*.

15. *HEM*, III: 75n2, as cited in Manzano Rodríguez, *La intervención*, 323.

16. Ibn Khaldūn, *Kitāb al-'ibar*, VII: 221.

17. Ibn Khaldūn, *Kitāb al-'ibar*, VII: 383; and Ibn al-Khaṭīb, *Iḥāṭa*, IV: 77–80.

18. Ibn al-Khaṭīb, *Iḥāṭa*, IV: 80.

19. Torremocha Silva, *Algeciras entre la cristianidad y el islam*; and idem, "Al-Binya: la ciudad palaciega merini en Al-Andalus."

20. Ibn Khaldūn, *Kitāb al-'ibar*, VII: 388–89.

21. On the extent of their influence at court, see, for example, Ibn al-Khaṭīb, *al-Lamḥa*, 80, 116–17.

22. For example, see Ibn Khaldūn, *Kitāb al-'ibar*, VII: 383; and Ibn al-Khaṭīb, *A'māl al-a'lām*, II: 255. See also Arié, *L'Espagne musulmane*, 80, 87; and Manzano Rodríguez, *La intervención*, 332.

23. Ibn Khaldūn, *Kitāb al-'ibar*, VII: 191; Manzano Rodríguez, *La intervención*, 333, suggests that these salaries were first conceded during the reign of Muḥammad V.

24. See Manzano Rodríguez, *La intervención*, 370–71, for a list of all the commanders.

25. Ibn Khaldūn, *Kitāb al-'ibar*, VII: 379–81.

26. Ibn Khaldūn, *Kitāb al-'ibar*, VII: 382; and Ibn al-Khaṭīb, *Iḥāṭa*, IV: 78. See text at n123, below, for more detail.

27. Ibn Khaldūn, *Kitāb al-'ibar*, VII: 384.

28. Ibn Khaldūn, *Kitāb al-'ibar*, VII: 386: "ashkhaṣa banī raḥḥū jamī'an ilā ifrīqiya."

29. Ibn Khaldūn, *Kitāb al-'ibar*, VII: 384. Castilian sources share the suspicion. See Manzano Rodríguez, *La intervención*, 349n980.

30. Ibn Khaldūn, *Kitāb al-'ibar*, VII: 384. Yaḥyā b. 'Umar b. Raḥḥū briefly held the post of commander of the Ghuzāh in this period.

31. Ibn Khaldūn, *Kitāb al-'ibar*: VII, 385–86; Ibn al-Khaṭīb, *Iḥāṭa*, IV: 321; and idem, *al-Lamḥa*, 105.

32. Yaḥyā fled to Castile briefly in this period. See Ibn al-Khaṭīb, *Nufādāt al-jirāb fī 'ulālat al-i'tirāb*, ed. Aḥmad Mukhtār al-'Abbadī, 18: "wa-ḥīnamā 'alama

malik qashtāla badrū al-qāsā bi-qudūmihi raḥḥaba bi-maqdamihi." The last commander from this family was 'Alī b. Badr al-Dīn, the grandson of Mūsā b. Raḥḥū. See Ibn Khaldūn, *Kitāb al-'ibar*, VII: 389–91.

33. He was 'Abd al-Raḥmān b. Abī Ifullūsan. See Manzano Rodríguez, 368–69, for questions regarding date when the Ghuzāh were finally disbanded.

34. Ibn Khaldūn, *Kitāb al-'ibar*, VII: 355.

35. Ibn Khaldūn, *Kitāb al-'ibar*, VII: 390. See also Manzano Rodríguez, *La intervención*, 367; Arié, *L'Espagne musulmane*, 118; and Harvey, *Islamic Spain*, 216–17.

36. Ibn Khaldūn, *Kitāb al-'ibar*, VII: 392–93: "wa-aghfala ṣāhib al-andalus hadhihi al-khuṭṭa min dawlatihi wa-maḥā rasmahā min mulkihi wa-ṣāra amr al-ghuzāh al-mujāhidīn ilayhi wa-bāshara aḥwālahum bi-nafsihi wa-'ammahum bi-naẓarihi wa-khassa al-qarāba al-murashshaḥīn minhum bi-mazīd takrimatihi wa-'ināyatihi."

37. Arié, *L'Espagne musulmane*, 117–18; and Harvey, *Islamic Spain*, 215–16.

38. ACA, Cartas árabes, 161 (18 Ṣafar 779/29 May 1377). At this point, as Ibn al-Khaṭīb, *al-Lamḥa*, 39, noted, the Granadan cavalry had also adopted the style of riding *a la jineta*, undercutting the advantage of the Marīnid *jenets*.

39. See also Ibn Khaldūn, *Kitāb al-'ibar*, VII: 389–400, which mentions two other Ghuzāh commanders who fled to the lands of the Crown of Aragon.

40. See also *EI*², s.v. "mārid." The juristic discourse surrounding the moral and legal obligations of those in rebellion against political authority, *aḥkām al-bughāh*, was extensive and fairly normative. See Khaled Abou El Fadl, *Rebellion and Violence in Islamic Law*.

41. See chapter 4.

42. For an excellent survey of this topic, see Michael Bonner, *Jihad in Islamic History*, 11–19, 54–96, which outline the debates from the classical to the early modern periods.

43. Balbale, "*Jihād* as Political Legitimation," 91: "I argue here that in the case of Sharq al-Andalus, these intra-Muslim battles involved important spiritual questions and were not simply a form of *realpolitik*. They were part of the broader Islamic quest to determine what sacred and profane power looked like in the face of a declining caliphate."

44. See Abū Sa'īd Saḥnūn, *al-Mudawwana al-Kubrā*, III: 278, as cited in Khaled Abou El Fadl, "Islamic Law and Muslim Minorities: The Juristic Discourse on Muslim Minorities from the Second/Eighth to the Eleventh/Seventeenth Centuries," *Islamic Law and Society* 1, no. 2 (1994): 146.

45. Aḥmad b. Yaḥyā al-Wansharīsī, *al-Mi'yār al-mu'rib wa'l-jāmi' al-mughrib 'an fatāwā 'ulamā' ahl Ifrīqiya wa'l-Andalus wa'l-Maghrib*, ed. Muḥammad Ḥajjī, II: 121–24, 130–33, and 140–41. For a thorough discussion of the history of and historiography on the "obligation to emigrate," see Jocelyn N. Hendrickson, "The Obligation to Emigrate: Al-Wansharīsī's *Asnā Al-Matājir* Reconsidered," with extensive bibliography.

46. Hendrickson, "The Islamic Obligation to Emigrate," 386–89.

47. For negative opinions of al-Wansharīsī, see, for example, Ḥusayn Mu'nis, "Asnā al-matājir fī bayān aḥkām man ghalaba 'alā waṭanihi al-naṣārā wa-lam yuhājir, wa-mā yatarattabu 'alayhi min al-'uqūbāt wa'l-zawājir," *Revista del Instituto Egipcio de estudios Islamicos en Madrid* 5 (1957): 15–18; and Harvey, *Islamic Spain*, 56. For al-Wansharīsī's sources, see Abū al-Walīd Muḥammad b. Aḥmad b. Aḥmad b. Rushd al-Jadd (d. 520/1126), *al-Muqaddimāt al-mumahhidāt*, ed. Muḥammad Ḥajjī, II: 151–54; and idem, *al-Bayān*, ed. Aḥmad al-Jabābī, IV: 170–71. Muḥammad b. Rabī' was active in Málaga. I am grateful to Peter Sjoerd van Koningsveld, Gerard Wiegers, and Umar Ryad for sharing a draft of this *fatwā* based on a private manuscript. They have also published a paraphrase of the manuscript. See Peter Sjoerd van Koningsveld and Gerard Albert Wiegers, "The Islamic Statute of the Mudejars in the Light of a New Source," *Al-Qanṭara* 17, no. 1 (1996): 19–58.

48. This appears in section 12 of van Koningsveld, Wiegers, and Ryad's transcription; see previous note. See also van Koningsveld and Wiegers, "Islamic Statute," 26–27. This passage is also quoted without citation in al-Wansharīsī's text.

49. Al-Wansharīsī, *Mi'yār*, II: 129–30, translation adapted from Hendrickson, "The Islamic Obligation to Emigrate," 365. Cf. Al-'Utbī as preserved Ibn Rushd al-Jadd, al-*Bayān*, III, 41–42. For more on al-'Utbī, see Ana Fernández Félix, "Al-'Utbī (m. 255/869) y su compilación jurídica al-'Utbiyya. Análisis de su contenido legal y de su aportación al estudio del proceso de formación de la sociedad islámica andalusí." On the *muḥārib*, which may also be translated as bandit, and the question of *ḥirāba*, banditry, see Abou El Fadl, *Rebellion and Violence in Islamic Law*, 51–61.

50. Their opinions overlap with that of the North African jurist Ibn Miqlāsh (ca. mid fourteenth century), who said no thanks would be given to a Mudéjar *jāhid* (one performing jihād) who fraternizes with non-Muslims. BNM, MS. 4,950 fol. 227v, as cited in Miller, *Guardians of Islam*, 35. A partial translation can be found in Hossain Buzineb, "Respuestas de Jurisconsultos Maghrebies en Torno a la Inmigración de Musulmanes Hispánicos," *Hespéris Tamuda* 16–17 (1988–89): 53–67.

51. Al-Wansharīsī, *Mi'yār*, II: 129–30, and V: 34–35.

52. Abou El Fadl, "Muslim Minorities," 141: "The linguistic dichotomy between *dār al-Islām* and *dār al-ḥarb* obscures a much more complex historical reality. The juristic discourse on the issue was not dogmatic and does not lend itself to essentialist positions."

53. For instance, David S. Powers, *Law, Society, and Culture in the Maghrib, 1300–1500*; idem, "Fatwās as Sources for Legal and Social History: A Dispute over Endowment Revenues from Fourteenth-Century Fez," *Al-Qanṭara* 11, no. 2 (1990): 295–341; and Mohammad Fadel, "Rules, Judicial Discretion, and the Rule of Law in Naṣrid Granada: An Analysis of *al-Ḥadīqa al-mustaqilla al-naḍra fī al-fatāwā al-ṣādira 'an 'ulamā' al-ḥaḍra*," in *Islamic Law: Theory and Practice*, ed. R. Gleave and E. Kermeli, 49–86.

54. Abou El Fadl, "Muslim Minorities," 143: "The reaction of different jurists reflected a dynamic process by which doctrinal sources, legal precedents, juristic methodologies and historical reality interacted to produce results." See also Wael Hallaq, *Authority, Continuity, and Change in Islamic Law*.

55. Ibn Rushd al-Jadd, *al-Bayān*, III: 42, translation adapted from Hendrickson, "The Islamic Obligation to Emigrate," 366n105. Cf. Jean-Pierre Molénat, "Le problème de la permanence des musulmans dans les territories conquis par les chrétiens, du point de vue de la loi islamique," *Arabica* 48, no. 3 (2001): 397, 399.

56. Ibn Rushd al-Jadd, *al-Bayān*, III: 10–11. See also Fernández Félix and Fierro, "Cristianos y conversos," 421–22.

57. Ibn Rushd al-Jadd, *al-Bayān*, IV: 86–87, 208–9; cf. IV: 293–94, 375–77; and X: 21–22, as cited in Fernández Félix and Fierro, "Christianos y conversos," 420–21. On Islamic legal opinions concerning the participation of non-Muslims in Muslim armies, see Wadad al-Qadi, "Non-Muslims in the Muslim Army in Early Islam: A Case Study in the Dialogue of the Sources," in *Orientalism: A Dialogue of Cultures*, ed. Sami A. Khasawnih, 109–59, cit. 116: "Suffice it to say, that a reading of the legal, theoretical compendia of the early Muslim jurists leaves no room for doubt that the vast majority of them considered the participation of non-Muslims in the Muslim army as licit, and all of them admitted that it was widely practiced from the earliest time and through the conquests."

58. Al-Wansharīsī, *al-Mi'yār*, III: 133–34. See also Abdel Majid Turki, "Consultation juridique d'al-Imam al-Māzarī sur le cas des musulmans vivant en Sicile sous l'autorité des Normands," *Mélanges de l'Université Saint-Joseph* 50, no. 2 (1984): 703–4; and Abou El Fadl, "Muslim Minorities," 151. Another Mālikī jurist, 'Ubaydallāh al-Maghrāwī al-Wahrānī, issued a fatwa in 909–10/1504 advising Granadans to practice their religion in secrecy. See Harvey, *Islamic Spain*, 55–67.

59. Ḥanafī scholars generally held that the duty to emigrate to Muslim territory was abrogated during the lifetime of Muḥammad. See, for instance, Muḥammad b. al-Ḥasan al-Shaybānī, *The Islamic Law of Nations: Shaybānī's Siyar*, trans. Majid Khadduri, 187, as cited in Abou El Fadl, "Muslim Minorities," 145.

60. Abou El Fadl, "Muslim Minorities," 159–63. The claim was made, for example, by al-Māwardī (d. 450/1058), as cited in Muḥyī al-Dīn al-Nawawī, *al-Majmū' sharḥ al-muhadhdhab*, XIX: 264, as cited in Abou El Fadl, "Muslim Minorities," 150. See also the case of Shams al-Dīn al-Ramlī (d. 1004/1595–96), who defended the right specifically of the Muslims of Aragon to remain in Christian Spain.

61. Abū al-'Abbās Shihāb al-Dīn Ibn Ḥajar al-Haytamī, *Fatḥ al-jawād sharḥ al-irshād*, II: 346, as cited in Abou El Fadl, "Muslim Minorities," 167.

62. van Koningsveld and Wiegers, "Islamic Statute," 35–49.

63. Clifford Geertz, *Local Knowledge: Further Essays in Interpretive Anthropology*, 170: "Between the skeletonization of fact so as to narrow moral issues to the point where determinate rules can be employed to decide them (to my mind, the defining feature of legal process) and the schematization of social action so

that its meaning can be construed in cultural terms (the defining feature, also to my mind, of ethnographic analysis) there is more than a passing family resemblance."

64. Borrowing a turn of phrase from Marshall Sahlins, *How "Natives" Think: About Captain Cook, for Example*, 6.

65. See chapter 4 for a full discussion of these treaties.

66. See Brunschvig, *Berbérie orientale*, I: 63, 66, for instances of jurists witnessing treaties.

67. See ACA, CR, Jaume II, caixa 10, no. 1334 (27 Jan. 1303); ACA, R. 334, fol. 64r (14 Apr. 1302); and ACA, Cartas árabes, 84, 84bis (19 Dhu'l-Qa'da 703/14 June 1304).

68. For instance, Arié, *L'Espagne musulmane*, 85–86; and M. Gaspar Remiro, "Relaciones de la Corona de Aragón con los estados musulmanes de occidente. El negocio de Ceuta entre Jaime II de Aragón y Aburribia Soleiman, sultán de Fez, contra Mohamed III de Granada," *Revista del centro de estudios históricos de Granada* 13. nos. 3–4 (1923): 178–200.

69. *Crónica de Don Fernando Cuarto*, in *Cronicas de los reyes de Castilla*, ed. Cayetano Rosell, 133; and ACA, CR, Jaume II, caixa 120, no. 1172 (8 Aug. 1303): "Conpta lo dit Muça quen Samuel, jueu, tresorer del dit don Ferrando, era en Granada. . . ." See also Gaspar Remiro, "Relaciones," 186–88.

70. ACA, CR, Jaume II, caixa 15, no. 1967 (21 Sep. 1303): "Essos genets que se fueron para vos, qu se fallaron con el en el camino e quell tomaron un cavallo e un aljuba de verde e diex doblas en ella e un par de armellas doro para los brasos e un albornos e otras cosas, que vos dira"; and ACA, CR, Jaume II, caixa 15, no. 1969 (13 Oct. 1303): "Otrosi sabed que de que nos ovimos nuestro amor e nuestra paz puesta con el rey don Ferrando, que esos genetes que se fueron para vos que saltean los caminos e roban e lievan quanto fallan, tan bien de la tierra del rey don Fernando commo de la nuestra. Por que vos rogamos rey, asi commo nos fiamos de la vuestra verdad e asi commo nos vos enbiastes decir por la vuestra carta, que guardariedes muy bien la tregua e la vuestra verdad, quel non querades consentir e que nos fagades tornar todo lo nuestro e si non lo al, non seria tregua." See also Gaspar Remiro, "Relaciones," 192–93, 199–200.

71. ACA, R. 334, fol. 171v (20 Sep. 1303): "Scire vos volumus Regem Granate noviter convenisse et pacis federa fecisse, ut pro certo didiscimus, cum inclito Ferdinando, qui se dicit Regem Castelle, et suspicamur propter ea et pensamus, quod dictus Rex Granate, una cum dicto Ferdinando contra nos guerrificare velit," as cited in Gaspar Remiro, "Relaciones," 202–4; and ACA, Cartas árabes, no. 84 (19 Dhu'l-Qa'da 703/14 June 1304): "wa-matā kāna baynakum wa-bayna ahl qashtāla nifāq fa-yajūzu 'alaykum min hunā min jayshinā alf aw alfān matā iḥtajtum ilayhim."

72. ACA, CR, Jaume II, caixa 120, no. 1172 (8 Aug. 1303): "Encara ma conptat lo dit Muça que alguns rics homens e cavalers del rey de Granada eren molt despegats dels tractamens quel dit rey avia ab los castelans, e an me trames a dir que si vos los aviets mester a vostre serviy, quels puriets aver, a son de CC a CCC jenets."

73. On the imprisonment, see ACA, CR, Jaume II, caixa 87, no. 10673 (14 Feb. [1303?]), a letter from Jaume II to Ibn Hudhayr: "Seynor, de tierra de Granada vos fago saber que estan en paz e bien sessagados, salve que el Rey de Granada fizo \prender/ Alabbes, e esta preso en Almeria por que fue acusado que avia enbiado dezir al Rey de Castiella que non fiziesse avenencia con el Rey de Granada. . . ." Cf. Masià i de Ros, *Jaume II*, 218–19. The other members of the Banū Raḥḥū who joined al-ʻAbbās included his brother ʻĪsā b. Raḥḥū and three sons of Mūsā b. Raḥḥū: Badr al-Dīn, Jamāl al-Dīn, and ʻAlī. See ACA, R. 235, fol. 1r–v, *segunda numeración* (22 Dec. 1303), with full citation in n75, below; and ACA, R. 235, fols. 3v–4r, *segunda numeración* (28 Dec. 1303), with full citation in chapter 5 n23. See also Ibn Khaldūn, *Kitāb al-ʻibar*, VII: 389–400, which mentioned that Badr al-Dīn and Jamāl al-Dīn took refuge in a Christian court before returning to North Africa. The names of other soldiers who came with al-ʻAbbās are less easily identifiable but perhaps also from princely lines.

74. ACA, CR, Jaume II, caixa 15, no. 1971, with full citation in chapter 5 n22.

75. ACA, R. 235, fol. 1r–v, *segunda numeración* (22 Dec. 1303): "Sepan todos quantos esta carta veran como nos Alabez Abenrraho, e sus parientes, e los cabos, e toda la cavalleria, qui metran lures nompnes en esta carta, por toda la cavalleria de los Genetes qui son presentes en Valencia, e aquellos qui son agora en Murcia, prometemos, atorgamos, e juramos a vos Sennor muye alto e poderoso don Jayme, por la gracia de dios Rey de Aragon, que vos serviremos con fe, e con verdat, assi como sierven buenos vassalos lur Sennor, e lur Rey. Encara vos prometemos, e atorgamos, e juramos que guardaremos vos, e todos vuestras cosas, e vuestro cuerpo e vuestros lugares, e vuestra tierra, e vuestros gentes de qualquiere condicion sean. Encara vos prometemos, atorgamos, e juramos, que nos faremos guerra por vos cuentra Rey de Granada, e cuentra Rey de Castiella, et cuentra todos aquellos qui avian guerra con vos, vos con ellos, de qualque condicion sean si quiere Christianos si quiere Moros. Encara vos prometemos, et atorgamos, e juramos, que nos no faremos treuga ni paç, ni amor, ni seguridat, con ninguno, menos de vuestro mandamiento, e vuestra licencia. Encara vos prometemos, e atorgamos, e juramos, que vos daremos rahenes nuestros fillos por el castiello de Negra, e Lorchi, e Cepti los quales vos a nos atorgastes por estatge nuestro, e que nos los tengamos p[or] vos avebos de nuestros estages assi como vassallos tiene castiellos por lur Sennor. Encara vos prom[e]temos, atorgamos, e juramos que cada hora que vos nos demandaredes el dicho castiello de Negra, et los otros lugares sobreditos que nos luego vos rendiemos el dito castiello e los ditos lu[g]ares. Et vos Sennor otrossi quando cobrades los auredes siades tenido de tornar a nos nuestras rahenes. Encara nos prometemos, atorgamos, e juramos que quando nos partiremos de vos, no iremos a tierra de vuestros enemigos, sines de vuestro mandamiento, e vuestro comiado. E si por aventura vos Sennor no erades en la terra e alguno de los cavalleros se querian ir, que lo pueda fazer con albaran del procurador del Regno de Valencia or de Murcia. Encara vos prometemos, atorgamos, e juramos que nos

tangamos e tener fagamos con [fol. 1v] todos aquellos con l[os] [quales] avedes paç or treug[a] [agora] o auredes daqui adelant las ditas paç o treugas a qual[es]quiere luga[re]s o personas las [avedes] dadas \o daredes/ a los faredes dar. Et porque esta carta sea confirmada, e mantenida, metemos en ella nuestros nompnes. Et juramos e[n] presencia de vos Sennor Rey sobredito por el alcoran que todos las cosas, e posturas sobreditas sean tenidas e complidas por nos en buena fe sin mal enganyo. Nomina illorum que subscripserunt sunt hec: Alabeç Abenrraho, Iyca Abenrraho, Bedrebdin Ebemuca Abenrraho, Hiemeledin Ebemuca Abenrraho, Hali Ebemuca Abenrraho, Jaffia Abemutarref, Iyça Avennelima, Auderemel Mafumet Abemutarref, Auderemel Ebbenumar, Cale Abemafumet Abdenalcahue, Jahacob Abenyucef, Hali Abenixa, scrivi//ero// \per ell/ e presencia dell Huahin Zamar Benhabez, escrivieron en presencia dell. Culaymen Benbuchar, escrivieron en presencia dell. Abdelle, escrivieron en presencia dell. Jucef Hali, Mahomet Benmaton, escrivieron en presencia dell. Muça Abemane, escrivieron en presencia del. Jahacob Abemuça, escrivieron en presencia dell. Auderramel Benexiffe, Gazalit Abenibram, escrivieron en presencia dell. Hamo e Beniyucef e Beneyer Abdella, e Benhomar Ayet, e Muça Abenharraquet." Cf. Giménez-Soler, "Caballeros," 357–58; and Masià i de Ros, *Jaume II*, 211–12.

76. ACA, R. 235, fols. 3v–4r, *segunda numeración* (28 Dec. 1303) with full citation in chapter 5 n23; ACA, R. 235, fols. 7v–8r, *segunda numeración* (22 Jan. 1304), a letter from Jaume II to al-'Abbās, concerning terms of service; ACA, R. 235, fol. 8r, *segunda numeración* (21 Jan. 1304), a letter from Jaume II to Ibn Hudhayr, concerning the payment of taxes to al-'Abbās; ACA, R. 235, fol. 12r, *segunda numeración* (30 Jan. 1304), on taking captives; and ACA, R. 235, fol. 70r *segunda numeración* (16 May 1304), another letter from Jaume II to al-'Abbās, concerning payment. See also Giménez-Soler, "Caballeros," 356; and Masià i de Ros, *Jaume II*, 213–15.

77. The case of 'Abd al-Wāḥid b. Abī Dabbūs, the last Almohad, discussed in chapter 4, is the only parallel, but he was not a member of the Ghuzāh and did not offer his alliance as part of his service as a *jenet*.

78. ACA, R. 235, fol. 1v, *segunda numeración*, with full citation in n75, above: "Et juramos e[n] presencia de vos Sennor Rey sobredito por el alcoran que todos las cosas, e posturas sobreditas sean tenidas e complidas por nos en buena fe sin mal enganyo."

79. ACA, R. 235, fols. 1v–2r, *segunda numeración* (22 Dec. 1303): "Sepan todos quantos esta carta veran como nos Don Jayme por la gracia de Dios Rey de Aragon atorgamos a vos Alabeç Abenrraho, e a vuestros parientes, e a los cabos, e a los cavalleros qui son presentes agora en Valencia, e a aquellos qui son en Murcia que vos guardemos, e vos aseguramos mientras seredes en nuestro servicio en nuestra terra. Encara vos atorgamos que vos daremos nuestra carta a todos oficiales e subditos nuestros que vos aguarden e defiendan, e que vos den compra, e venda en todos nuestros lugares, e de nuestra tierra. Encara vos atorgamos que a

vos dito Alabeç liuraremos el castiello de Negra, e Lorchi, e Cepti que los tengades por nos a vuestro estage, e de los sobredito[s] assi como vassallo tiene castiellos por su sennor. Encara vos atorgamos, e queremos que quales quiere de vuestros cavalleros se querran ir que lo puedan fazer exceptado que no vayan a tierra de nuestros enemigos, ni fagan danyo a nos, ni a nuestra tierra. Encara vos atorgamos //que cada hora que vos querades// por gracia, en ayuda de vuestras messiones, toda la quinta o setmo de las cavalgadas que faredes en tierras de nuestros enemigos assi de las vuestras cavalgades como de los cristianos, qui con vos entraran. Encara vos atorgamos que cada hora que vos querades ir, ni partir por mar o por tierra, que seades salvos e seguros de toda nuestra gent en cuerpos e en averes. Encara [fol. 2r] mandamos e queremos que otros cavallero[s] [o] gen[etes] [sine]s nuestra voluntat no [v]engan en nuestra tierra salvo [e]stos que agora son con vos en nuestra tier[ra]. E si algunos [hi] vin[dran] [s]in nuestra voluntat vos [n]o los aculgades en vuestra company[a] menos de nuestra voluntat. Encara que [t]engades e observedes la paz, e las treuguas que nos avemos dadas, o daremos daqui adelant a qualsquiere lugares o personas de quales condiciones que sean. Encara que vos Alabeç rendades a nos o a qui nos mandaremos el dito castiello de Negra, e los otros logares sobreditos toda hora que nos los queremos cobrar de vos assi como vassallo es tenido de render castiello a su sennor. E nos seamos tenidos de render a vos vuestras rahenes. Encara vos atorgamos que qualsquiere castiellos o lugares [t]omaredes del Rey de Granada que sean vuestros. Encara queremos e mandamos que en las cavalgadas \que faredes/ en tierras de nuestros enemigos cristianos no prengades, ni matedes, muller ninguna porque no es costumpne nuestra. E en testimonio destas cosas mandamos poner en est escripto nuestro siello pendient. Feytas estas posturas en Valencia dia lunes XXII dias andadas del mes de Deziembre en el anyo de mille CCC e tres." Cf. Giménez-Soler, "Caballeros," 353–54, which curiously cites Jéronimo Zurita, *Anales de la Corona de Aragón*, V: 61, instead of original text; and Masià i de Ros, *Jaume II*, 212, which has several errors.

80. ACA, R. 235, fols. 7v–8r, *segunda numeración* (22 Jan. 1304): "Al noble e amado Alabeç Abenrraho. . . . E sabet que mandamos por carta nostra muyt expressa a los [fol. 8r] nostros fieles Ferre dez Cortell bayle nostro general del Regno de Murcia e a Pero Escran vezino de Elch que ellos luego vos den dozcentos kaffizes de cenada e cient kaffizes de trigo. . . ." Cf. Masia i de Ros, *Jaume II*, 214–15.

81. The king actually specifies "a fifth or sixth."

82. Jaume II also charged Ibn Hudhayr, the lord of Crevillente, with overseeing al-'Abbās and his soldiers. For instance, he asked Ibn Hudhayr to accompany al-'Abbās on all raids. See ACA, R. 235, fol. 4r, *segunda numeración* (28 Dec. 1303): "Mohomet Abenfundell arrays de Crevillent gratiam suam. Madamus et dicimus vobis quatenus quatenus [*sic*] quicumque Alabbes Abenrraho cum famili[a] sua intrabit in cavalcatis in terris inimicorum nostrorum vos cum familia vestra intretis cum eodem in cavalcatis ipsis. Datum Valencie, v kalendas Ianuarii, anno predicto." Cf. Masià i de Ros, *Jaume II*, 213.

83. ACA, R. 235, fols. 1v–2r, *segunda numeración* (22 Dec. 1303), with full citation in n75, above: "Encara queremos e mandamos que en las cavalgadas \que faredes/ en tierras de nuestros enemigos Christianos no prengades, ni matedes, muller ninguna porque no es costumpne nuestra. . . ."

84. ACA, CR, Jaume II, caixa 16, no. 2026 (27 Jan. 1304): "Sepades que Yuçaf el Aviles, vuestro vassallo, este que esta nuestra carta lieva, se nos querello e dize que en esta tregua que agora a entre nos e vos quel tomaron un cavallo çerca de Guadiex ginetes dessos que biven con el [alabez] viniendo se seguro commo deve ser en la tregua," as cited in Masià i de Ros, *Jaume II*, 215; and ACA, R. 235, fol. 18v, *segunda numeración* (13 Feb. 1304), a letter from Jaume II to Muḥammad III: "Fazemos vos saber Rey que recibiemos vuestra carta, la qual nos enviastes por Jucef el Avilez, vuestro vasallo, en como los genetes qui biven con Alabbez qui est in nuestro servicio, tomaron a el un cavallo cerca de Guadiex durant estra treugua que est entre nos. . . ." Cf. Masià i de Rose, *Jaume II*, 216–17, who cites ACA, R, 235, fol. 184r.

85. ACA, R. 235, fol. 15v, *segunda numeración* (13 Feb. 1304); ACA, R. 235, fol. 19r (16 Feb. 1304); ACA, R. 235, fol. 41r–v, *segunda numeración* (27 Mar. 1304); ACA, R. 235, fol. 45r (22 Mar. 1304); and ACA, R. 235, fol. 53r (21 Apr. 1304). See also Giménez-Soler, "Caballeros," 360–61; and Masià i de Ros, *Jaume II*, 217, 219, 223.

86. ACA, R. 235, fol. 41r–v, *segunda numeración* (27 Mar. 1304): ". . . Avemos entendido que vos sacastes de la tierra del muy noble Don Johan Manuel ganado e hombres." Cf. ACA, CR, Jaume II, caixa 16, no. 2087 (1304).

87. The initial truce lasted until May. A month later, Jaume wrote again to explain that the truce had been extended until August, the month that the peace at Agreda was signed. ACA, R. 235, fol. 48r, *segunda numeración* (9 Mar. 1304); and ACA, R. 235, fol. 53r, *segunda numeración* (21 Apr. 1304). See also Gaspar Remiro, "Relaciones," 241–42.

88. Giménez-Soler, "Caballeros," 363–65, which gives no citation for this document.

89. As confirmed by ACA, R. 235, fol. 45r, *segunda numeración* (22 Mar. 1304), a letter from Jaume II to al-ʿAbbās. See also Gaspar Remiro, "Relaciones," 241–2; and Masià i de Ros, *Jaume II*, 223.

90. ACA, R. 235, fol. 70r, *segunda numeración* (16 May 1304).

91. ACA, CR, Jaume II, caixa 91, no. 11351 (4 Apr. 1304), as cited in Gaspar Remiro, "Relaciones," 242–44.

92. ACA, R. 334, fol. 174v (15 Feb. 1304), a letter from Jaume to his ambassador: "Fem vos saber que nos pensans e veens lo gran servey, quens fa Alabez e sa companya e quens fara, si la guerra es del Rey de Granada, la qual esperam segons que sabets, cercam totes maneres con mils e pus leugerament lo puscam retenir e provehir a ell e a sa gent." See also Gaspar Remiro, "Relaciones," 218–19; and Masià i de Ros, *Jaume II*, 176, 234.

93. ACA, Cartas árabes, 77 (15 Sha'bān 703/24 Mar. 1304): "wa-waṣala ilaynā irsāl banī marīn alladhīna hunālikum fī bilādikum a'azzahum allāh wa-'arafūnā bi-mā ṣadara minkum lahum min al-khayr." Cf. ACA, CR, Jaume II, caixa 17, no. 2265 (24 Mar. 1304): "E plegaren nos misagers de Bene Marin, los quals son la en vostras terra—onrrels Deu—e feeren nos saber ço quels vench de part vostra de be." See also Dufourcq, *L'Espagne catalane*, 374–75.

94. ACA, CR, Jaume II, caixa 111, no. 142 (s.a.): "Jo Hahubeç Abenraho me coman en vostra gracia e besam vostres mans axi com de senyor de qui esper mol de be e de merce. Senyor a vostra alta senyoria vos faç saber que yo reebi la vostra carta en la qual se contenia que vos avietç presa treva ab Castella tro al primer dia de Maig et que manavetç a mi que yo cesas de fer dan a la dita terra de Castella. Et, senyor, yo so pagat de tot ço que vos faretç e ço aparelat de obeir lo vostre manament en totes coses," as cited in Gaspar Remiro, "Relaciones," 240.

95. ACA, CR, Judíos y Musulmanes, no. 521 (18 Mar. 1304): "Al molt honrat et amat en Bernat de Libia de nos en Bertran de Caneles, saluts et bona amor. Fetz vos saber que nos avem trames a la justicia et als juratz de Valent en Domingo Catena sobrel fet daquests genets e creer que Alabeç es molt mal hom, et cada dia es de pigor enteniment e especialment depuys que a[c] la carta dels Seynor Rey de la treva. E reba ses aço matex tot [...] qui devant li pas, e a preses deli terra den Johan Manuel ço es d[al]arcu M ovels e IIII fadrins. E avem lo request moltes vegades quels nos reta e per res nols avem poguts cobrar ans nos en [fiu] fort mal re[s]post. E a li venguts III genets del Rey de Granada oer missatges dels quels el e tota sa companya se son fort alegrats. E nos sabem que tos los Sarrah[ins] de Regno de Valent son venguts a ell e venen cada dia e fan gra[n] noves dell, e son fort alegres, e non volvendre lo bestiar tan car lo te. Per quens es semblant que con mes sie aturara que mes de mal hic pogues tractar. On nos prec que vos daço parlassets ab los prohomens de Valent e que ordonassets els templers que venguessen açi al pus tost que poguessets, que magor mercat aurien açi de tota res que no aqui. E ell no go[sa]ria fer ço que per aventura a encor de fer, que opinio es de tots quants son que ell al exir que sen menara tot ço que puxa, e daquest regne e de la terra Johan Manuel, a qui menaça fort. E els estans açi nou gosaria ferm que exceptats tro a L homens a cavall totz los altres son la pigor gent e la pus avol del mon e la pus arreada. E prec vos que daço siats curos. Scripte en Xativa, XV kalendas Aprilis." See Gaspar Remiro, "Relaciones," 233–34, upon which I relied for the transcription because of the deterioration of the original. Cf. ACA, CR, Judíos y Musulmanes, no. 522 (s.a.), in which Bertran writes to Jaume II. See also Ferrer i Mallol, *La frontera*, 80; and Masià i de Ros, *Jaume II*, 220. As late as May, the issue remained unresolved. See ACA, R. 235, fol. 63v, *segunda numeración* (2 May 1304), a letter from Jaume II to Don Juan Manuel; and ACA, R. 235, fol. 63v, *segunda numeración* (2 May 1304), a letter from Jaume II to al-'Abbās.

96. ACA, CR, *Judíos y Musulmanes*, no. 521, with full citation above: "Cada dia es de pigor enteniment e especialment depuys que a[c] la carta dels Seynor Rey de la treva."

97. ACA, CR, Jaume II, caixa 91, no. 11093 (29 Mar. [1304]): "Al molt alt [e] molt poderos Seynor en Jacme per la gracia de deu Rey d'Arago e de Valent, e de Murcia, com[te] de Barchinona e de la Santa Esglea de [Roma] gamfanoner e almirall e ca[pitan] general. Bernat de Libia, humil servidor e sotsmes vostre besan vostres mans e vostres peus se comana en [la vostr]a gracia. Seÿnor, lestim[ent] del Regne no es en bona condic[io] quant als Sarrayns per ço con [depus] Nalabez vench ab la cavalcada a Xativa he la treva en continent fo cridada, Nalabez no espeega de vendre sa cavalcada. E tots los moros de la terra son se vist ab el e an molt parlat ab ell e parten se del venen lurs heretats e ço que vendre poden, e aperellensen danar poch a poch. Los morad[i]ns ço es aquells qui perhiquen sajusten molt mes que no solen. Per cert, Senyor, que enteniment es m[eu] e de les altres qui conexem los moros que els no estegren axi \sino/ de pus que salsaren latra vegada. Jo, Seynor, fuhi en Xativa e parle molt Abnalabez. Quant en ço que yo pudia entendre en ell, molt se f[a] volenteros de servir vos, mas empero tots los jenets de mes li dixeren yo estan en Xativa, que ells no farien mal al Rey de Granada. Les castells, Seynor, quem menas recognexer del Regne auria obs en cascun malorament e especialment en lo castell de Oenaguilla e de Bayren axi con dob[re] e de guarda si per aventura los alcayts dels castells no volen crexer en les guardes segons que jo los he manat de part vostra, que manats que si faça. En los fets, Seynor, la vostra dis[c]recio sab mils que [sia] a fer que yo nels altres nous purien trametre a dir. E vos Seynor manats hi ço que vos tingats per be. E seria mester que tost vengues lo manament. Escrita en Valent, diluns XX IX dies anats del mes de Març." This document was misfiled amongst the records of 1319. See also Gaspar Remiro, "Relaciones," 237; Masià i de Ros, *Jaume II*, 235; and Ferrer i Mallol, *La frontera*, 80–81.

98. ACA, CR, Jaume II, caixa 91, no. 11093 (24 Mar. [1304]): "Per cert, Senyor, que enteniment es m[eu] e de les altres qui conexem los moros que els no estegren axi \sino/ de pus que salsaren latra vegada."

99. ACA, R. 235, fols. 28v–29r, *segunda numeración,* as cited in Ferrer i Mallol, *La frontera*, 82, 230–31, doc. 10.

100. ACA, R. 235, fols. 42v–43r, *segunda numeración,* as cited in Ferrer i Mallol, *La frontera*, 82.

101. Cf. ACA, R. 235, fol. 57r, *segunda numeración* (22 Apr. 1304), a month earlier when Jaume was ordering the Templars to stop attacks.

102. ACA, CR, Jaume II, caixa 137, Templarios, no. 101 (20 May 1304): "Al molt honrat e molt sani e discret en Bertran de Canelles, frare Berenguer de Cardona, de les cases de la cavaleria del Temple en Aragon e en Catalunya, humil maestre e visitador general en Espanya, salutz e bona amor per tots temps, e aperallada voluntat a tota honor vostra. Fem vos saber que divendres XV dies anatz del mes de Maig, nos ab alcuna companya de Cavall de Regno de Murcia e ab Nalabez e an mille D peons los quals homens a caval erem entre totz CCC homens a caval, e partim de Lorca lot dit divendres e anam lo jorn e la nit, e quant fo tercia nos fam en I loch del Rey de Granada lo qual ha nom Sugena e aqui talam tota lorta

e fem hi gran dan. E apres anauem nosen deues bera e quant haguem passat I coll Nabez qui tenia davanter e corria lalgara trames nos missatge que [la] cavaleria de Bera los quals eren CCCL homens a caval venien deues nos e axi quens apercebessem e quens aparella sem. En aço [...] aperlegam tuyt, e Nalabez aria algareyan an ells e ells [...]aren lo tro sus prop de Bera, e puix vanse mestlan ab Nalabez e matarenh tantost nos haguem misatge den Alabez que pensan se de caytar nos e de acorreli. En aço nos e tota la companya pensam de brocar e de correbe una legua e mes. En aço los debera tantost quens veeren giraren les costs e nos donam en ells e fem los recollir en Bera e matamlos XIII homens a cavall e XXX homens de peu, e fem brocada e nostre ganfano entre dins la raval de Bera, e frares nostres e companya entrarem, e forem tro ales portes de Bera. E si tinguessem los cavals armatz, haguerem barreyada tota la Raval de Bera. En aço avallam nosen a les cres e cremam tot lo blat que havien cullit. En apres talam gran res de lorta debera puix anam nosen a I altre loch prop debera que ha nom les Coves, a aqui talam tota lorta, e atendam nos aqui la nit. En apres lendema ço fo ditmenge dia de Sinquagesima partim de les Coves e anam nos lo Rivamunt de Porxena, talan e creman masses e molins e[..]derrocan. En pres anam nosen a I Castell lo qual ha nom Huercal e aqui nos . . . companya puyam tro sus almur, e aqui apeam totz los frares e laltra companya nostra de caval e pensam de Cobatre lo Castell regeament e f . . . haviem mes foch a les portes del Castell e aportatz los homens del Castell a aço [que] no podien als fer sino que gitaven pedres orbes. En aço que nos combatiem lo dit Castell en Pere de Montagut procur[ador] del Regne de Murcia e Nalabez qui sesperaven davayll en Jacme Pla. Trameterem nos missatges quens deguessem jaquir de combatre e quens navallasem a ells, per ço car veyen venir gran companya domens a caval del Rey de Granada. E axi per aquesta rao jaquim nos de combatre lo Castell e avallam no sen, e guarnim nostres cavalles e replegan los peons e les aczembles en Jacme Toçalet e aqui vengeem nos los genetz de Granada esperonant denant. En Alabez ab CC homens a caval ixquells algareyam e torneyat se ab ells e aqui donaren se los uns abs los altres de grans colps. E axi nos fem manament a alcuns homens a cavals nostres los quals tenien cavals alforratz e alcuns ballesters nostres que feesen una esdemesa deves los genetz e aqui brocarem et ferem los dan. En aço nos ab los cavals armatz pensam de brocar en vos la cavaleria de Granada e havuem feytes III mans e erem mille C homens a cavall ço era saber entre de Bera e [. . . .]deix e aqui ab la merce de nostre senyor metem los en arrancada e pensaren de fugie e axi ençalcam los et matam los C homens a cavall e los altres recolliren se en aquell Castell que nos haviem combatut. E axi sildit Castell nols fos tan prop haguerem pres molt major dan la merce de nostre Senyor nos ni les altres companyes qui ab nos eren noy prenguerem dan, exceptat que nos hi perdem I hom de peu, queli donarem an una treyta e Nalabez quey perde de IIII fins a VI homens a caval. E axi tornam nosem benit ajaure a Nogalt prop de Lorca III legues e len doma ço fa dilluns apres sinquagesma, entram nos en Lorca. E car nos som cextz que a vos plauria tota hara nostra honor e nostre <cueximent> e los profit e la honor del Temple per aquesta raho vos scivim aquestes novelles, altres arditz a la sao dara nous podem fer saher mas si nulles coses a vos plahien que nos fer paguessem per vos. Fetz nos a saber fiançosament, car nos sum aperellat a tota honor vestra. [Verso] Data en Lorca, dimercres XX dies anatz de Maig." Cf. editions in Finke, *Acta Aragonensia*, III: 122–25; Giménez-Soler, "Caballeros," 366–69; and Gaspar Remiro, "Relaciones," 260.

103. It was not unprecedented. In the Chivert Charter (1234), the Muslims of Chivert promised to defend the town alongside the Templars against any Christian or Muslim enemy.

104. Cf. ACA, CR, Jaime II, caixa 16, no. 2026 (27 Jan. 1304), as cited in n84, above, which records a complaint from Granada about al-'Abbās' *jenets* raiding their territory. On this occasion the *jenets* did not directly engage their Granadan counterparts.

105. ACA, R. 235, fol. 78v, *segunda numeración* (20 May 1304): "A la vostra senyoria senyor fem asaber quen Alabez ses molt be e lealment menat en aquesta entrada e veem e conexem queus ha cor e voluntat de servir lealment. . . . Car sert sia a vos senyor que ell vos es obs en aquest regne." Cf. Giménez-Soler, "Caballeros," 368.

106. Finke, *Acta Aragonensia*, I: 146, as cited in Ferrer i Mallol, *La frontera*, 82.

107. ACA, R. 235, fol. 78r, *segunda numeración* (31 May 1304); and ACA, R. 235, fols. 78v, *segunda numeración* (31 May 1304): "Don Jayme et cetera. Al noble, amado, e feel vassallo suyo Alabez Abenrraho et cetera. Sepades que vimos una carta, la qual nos embio el amado nuestro Petro de Muntagut, procurador nuestro en el regno de Murcia, en que nos fi fet daquests genets e creeestros cavalleros e con vuestras companyas, ensemble con el maestro del Temple e con las otras companyas nuestras, que sodes en el regno de Murcia, entrastes correr en [el] regno de Granada, e de como oviestes [fol. 79r] daver façienda con los frontaleros e con las companyas del rey de Granada, [e de c]omo, por la gracia e por la merced de Dios, los venciestes e los esbaratastes. De la qual cosa, faciendo gracias a Dios, loamos la vuestra boneza e la vuestra fieldat, la qual por obra manifesta, con la aiuda de Dios, bien nos avedes demostrada. Rogando a vos, que como ben avedes feyto daqui ad agora, que daqui adelant fagades ben vuestro poder en deffender nuestra tierra e en dar danyo a nuestros enemigos, en manera que por el servicio que feyto nos avedes e cada dia nos feyets e quiriendo a Dios, nos faredes daqui adelant, seamos tenidos de façer vos bien e merced. Otrossi, avemos entendido de conmo en esta bataylla perdiestes companya vuestra e cavallos de que nos pesa. Otrossi, que avedes alguna mingua, por que avriades menester que vos acorrissemos. Ont vos femos saber, que nos en çercha mandaremos provehir sobre aquello en tal manera, que vos seredes ende pagado e que vos avredes que gradesser. Datum ut supra." Cf. Gaspar Remiro, "Relaciones," 266–67; and Masia i de Ros, *Jaume II*, 227.

108. ACA, R. 235, fol. 83r, *segunda numeración* (5 June 1304); Gaspar Remiro, "Relaciones," 278–79; and Ferrer i Mallol, *La frontera*, 83.

109. ACA, R. 235, fols. 80v–81r, *segunda numeración* (1 June 1304): "E aquestes letres los trametem per ço com aviem entes que per raho daquels parlamens que avien hauts ab Alabez avien dupte que hom nols agreujas . . . ," as cited in Ferrer i Mallol, *La frontera*, 231–32, doc. 11. See also ACA, R. 235, fol. 82v, *segunda numeración* (3 June 1304), a letter from Jaume to the Templars on the situation in Valencia.

110. ACA, R. 235, fol. 86v, *segunda numeración* (9 June 1304), a letter from Jaume II to Bertran de Canelles: "A aclo quens trametes adir que fariets daquel Alha que tenits pres a Galinera, vos responem e tenim per be quel soltets"; and ACA, R. 235, fol. 102r–v, *segunda numeración* (28 June 1304): "Quantum vero ad negocium del Alhaig quem captum tenetis, mandamus, licet iam madaverimus [vobis] ut ipsius absolatis et permitatis abire." Cf. Gaspar Remiro, "Relaciones," 273, 286.

111. ACA, R. 235, fol. 87r, *segunda numeración* (10 June 1304): "Intelleximus per dilectum consiliarum nostrum Bernardum de Serriano quod in conflictu, nuper habito inter vos et frontalerios et alios de terra Regis Granate, cepistis quendam sarracenum, qui est de redempcione. Intelleximus etiam quod cum aliqui de familia dicti Regis Granate barrigaverint quandam villam ipsius Bernardi de Serriano, nomine Villam Joyosam, et secum duxerint ducentas viginti personas christianorum et amplius, quod dictus rex Granate seu alii nomine ipsius offerunt se restituturos omnes dictas personas christianorum vel magnam partem ipsarum, vobis restituentibus eidem sarracenum predictum, unde cum istud sit opus misericordie et magne elemosine, et intellexerimus per dictum Bernardum de Serriano quod nobilis Alabbes Abenrah concessit pro [..] redempcione dictorum christianorum disfinire [et] remitere partem suam sarraceni predicti, rogamus vos, quatenus velitis et consenciatis, quod pro deliberacione seu restitucione dicti sarraceni habeantur et recuperentur christiani predicti." See also Gaspar Remiro, "Relaciones," 279–80; and Masìa i de Ros, *Jaume II*, 241–42.

112. I have glossed over some of the complexity of this moment. Muḥammad III agreed in July to join the truce between Castile and the Crown of Aragon. Nevertheless, his agreement provided only a brief reprise before attacks began again. For more detail, see Gaspar Remiro, "Relaciones," 281–82; and Ferrer i Mallol, *La frontera*, 83–85.

113. ACA, CR, Jaume II, caixa 16, no. 2043–2044 (12 July 1304): "Al muyt alto et poderoso senyor don Jayme por la gracia de dios Rey D'Aragon, de Valencia, de Murcia, et compte de Barchinona et de la Santa Romana Eglesia senyaler et almirante et capitanno general. Yo Pere de M[on]tagudo, humil procurador vestro en el dicho Regno de Murcia, beso los vestros piedes et las vestras manas et me encomiendo en la vestra gracia, como a senyor de qui atiendo mucho bien et mucha merçe. Sepa senyor la vestra Real mayestat que recebi las vestras letras et aquella letra que enviavades al Rey de Granada sobre el confirmamiento de la tregua entro a santa mar de agosto et senyor entendi quanto me enviavades a dezir

et a mandar [.] las dichas vestras letras. E yo senyor vistas aquellas envie[....] la dicha vestra carta al Rey de Granada, et quand que aya repuesta della, faç vos lo ho luego a saber. E ahun senyor vos fago saber, que el Rey Abenjacob que envie sus mandaderos et sus cartas al noble d'en Alaabbez Abenrraho et a los otros cavalleros qui eran aqui con ell, en que les enviaria a mandar ques fuessen luego por a ell et por a su serviçio et otrasi el dicho Rey Abenjacob envio a mi una carta en la qual me requeria que yo deviesse reçebir los castiellos que Alabbez tenia vestros et quel deviesse tornar sus rahenes por que ell enviaria por Alabbez et por estos cavalleros, que los avia mester al su serviçio et que se fuessen a recoger a al-jaçira que el les enviaria alli sus vaxiellos por que nos non de huviessemos afan. E senyor Alaabbez vista la carta de Abenjacob et sus mandaderas, vino a mi, et dixo me como Abenjacob que enviaria por ell et por sus sobrinos et por su companya, et demando me de conseio a mi et a otros cavalleros que eramos en semble, que le consellasemos como faria, et nos consellamos le que se fuesse por a vos et a es pedir se de vos asin como la postura era, et dixo ell que lo faria asin que ell se lo avia a coraçon. Otro dia torno a nos, et dixo nos que ell por ren del mundo no poria ir a vos, que los sobrinos et sus fijos et la otra cavalleria se le querian hir se carrera et que por ren del mundo no lo atendrian. E axi dixo me que se es pedria de mi en lugar de [vos] senyor et que me rendria los castielles et yo quel dase su[s] rahenas. E yo senyor huvi mi acuerdo con cavalleros et con el bayle et con otros homnes buenos de Murcia, et dieron me de conseio que yo deviesse reçebir del dicho don Alaabbez su espedimiento, et cobrar los castiellos, et dar le sus rahenas, por que ell non poria aturar asin como asin, que non se fuesse su carrera. E senyor yo viendo que si sende auria a f[aç] lo que Alaabbez quisiesse por tal que el noy pudiesse atayeger, por que ell era tan poderoso de cavalleria. Reçebi los castiellos et die le sus rahenas et espidio se de mi en vestro lugar senyor, et comienda se en la vestra gracia et que todos tiempos sera al vestro serviçio et al nostro mandamiento, et es se ydo su carrera con toda su cavalleria. E senyor va muyt pagado de vos et de quantos somos en el Regno de Murcia. Senyor todo ell estamiento del Regno esta muyt bien gracia a dios. Senyor la tregua que avedes con el Rey de Granada salrra ayna, et si vos mas tregua adelante avedes a aver con ell, antes que esta passe senyor façet me lo a saber, por que seyamos apercibidos en el Regno, que ellos todavia se adelantan algunas neçes affaçer d'anyo, ante que la tregua salga. E comiendo me en la vestra gracia. Scripte en Murcia, dia Domingo, XII dias de Julio, anno domini millesimo CCC quarto." Cf. ACA, CR, Jaume II, caixa 17, no. 2266r–v (22, 23 June 1304); and Giménez-Soler, "Caballeros," 366–68.

114. Cf. ACA, CR, Jaume II, caixa 8, no. 2265 (24 Mar. 1304); and ACA, Cartas árabes, no. 58 (15 Sha'bān 703/24 Mar. 1304).

115. See the handul of documents at ACA, R. 307, fol. 107r (1 Sep. 1304). For instance, as cited in Ferrer i Mallol, *La frontera*, 232–33, doc. 12: "Alabbez et quidam alii de magnatibus regis Granate, cum magna multitudine genetorum et peditum sarracenorum in regnum Valencie hostiliter intraverunt intuleruntque

in eo ac inferre non cessant, pugnando fortitudines et loca comburendo et devastando, dampna et mala que possunt." See also ACA, CR, Jaume II, caixa 104, no. 12999 (13 Oct. 1304): "Encara a trames a dir que Alabeç que era plegat ab mil homens a cavall. . . ." See Masià i de Ros, *Jaume II*, 228–29 for full edition of this last document.

116. ACA, R. 307, fol. 107r (1 Sep. 1304).

117. ACA, R. 235, fol. 142r, *segunda numeración* (27 Sep. 1304), with full edition in Ferrer i Mallol, *La frontera*, 234–35, doc. 14.

118. Sea support failed to arrive in time; see ACA, CR, Jaume II, caixa 18, no. 2282 (10 Sep. 1304), with full edition in Ferrer i Mallol, *La frontera*, 86, 233–34, doc. 13.

119. Almost the entire village of Gandía was abandoned. ACA, R. 307, fol. 120r, as cited in Ferrer i Mallol, *La frontera*, 88, alongside numerous other documents. Some of these Mudéjares later chose to return to Valencia and faced prosecution by the Crown (ACA, R. 203, fol. 94r–v [29 Dec. 1305]).

120. ACA, CR Jaume II, caixa 19, no. 2423 (27 Feb. 1304): ". . . poderos Senyor en Jacme per la gracia de deu Rey d'Aragó et cetera. Jo Gombau d'Entença, <procurador> . . . de Valencia me coman Senyor en la vestra gracia besan vostres peus et vostres mans, com de Senyor de . . . Senyor la vostra magestat que huy que es ditmenge III kalendas Marcii per a manament per vos . . . et de prendre d'aquells moros los quals sen eren anats ab los jenets et eren tornats . . . sens vol[....] vostra [et] en los dit dia presne CCCCL persones enre pochs et grans et masculs et fembres et axi s[.] . . . es mon enteniment que enserch et prenga tots aquells que daqui avant atrobar pore que daquella raho sien. E en . . . mateix pris alcuna partida de bestiar que es fort pocha. E axi Senyor ens en volgut certificar de les dites . . . quants als altres moros qui no sen eren anats de la vostra terra, tenense per assegurats et esta la terra en bon <estar [...] la merça de deu. E axi senyor es enteniment meu que axi mateix faça daquells Sarrahins qui son de Sexona en la . . . enteniment meu quey faça ney enant en res entro que naia manament vostre siu voletz que axiu faça . . . Xativa, VI kalendas Marcii, anno domini MCCCV."

121. See Masià i de Ros, *Jaume II*, for several letters concerning al-ʿAbbās' activities in Granada during this period.

122. Ibn Khaldūn, *Kitāb al-ʿibar*, VII: 259.

123. Ibn Khaldūn, *Kitāb al-ʿibar*, VII: 382; Ibn al-Khaṭīb, *Iḥāṭa*, IV: 78; Ibn al-Khaṭīb, *al-Lamḥa*, 80. See also Andrés Giménez-Soler, "La Corona de Aragón y Granada," *Boletín de la Real Academia de Buenas Letras de Barcelona* 27 (1907): 51–61; Harvey, *Islamic Spain*, 180–81; Arié, *L'Espagne musulmane*, 93–94; and Ferrer i Mallol, *La frontera*, 109–12. Naṣr appealed to the Castilian and Aragonese kings for assistance; see Diego Catalán, ed., *La gran crónica de Alfonso XI*, 297; ACA, R. 243, fol. 264r–v (5 Apr. 1317), as cited in Ferrer i Mallol, *La frontera*, 112.

124. Ibn Khaldūn, *Kitāb al-ʿibar*, VII: 382, refers to him as "Abū al-ʿAbbās."

125. Ibn Khaldūn, *Kitāb al-ʿibar*, VII: 382: "thumma waqaʿat baynahu and bayna abī jayyūsh mughāḍiba laḥaqa li-ajlihā bi'l-ṭāghiya."

126. ACA, CR, Jaume II, caixa 45, no. 5624 (19 Mar. 1317): "A lo que nos enbiastes dezir que el muy noble rey de Aragon, vuestro sennor, que ha veluntad de fazer Guerra contra nuestro enemigo e que vos mando que la fiziesedes vos . . . E lo que nos enbiastes dizir que toviesemos por bien de enbiar al Alabeç Abaraho con cavaleria a esa frontera de Vera e que vos que seriedes con el con la mayor compania que pudiesedes en lugar senalado e a dia çierto . . . a fezer les al maes danno que pudiesedes de vuestra parte e sabria el Alabecc con la nuestra gente que tien en aquel lugar a fezerles danno de la otra parte," as cited in Masià i de Ros, *Jaume II*, 458–59; and ACA, CR, Jaume II, caixa 114, no. 515 (16 Mar. 1317): "Encara faç saber senyor a la vostra molt alta senyoria que algun temp abans del mes de març jo tramis II homes al Rey de Guadix, per fer-li saber que jo avia manament de vos, senyor, que fees guerra al Rey de Granada e quel pregava que ell me des algun endreçament, perque jo senyor pogues servir a vos en pogues dar don a son enemich e specialment quel pregava que trameses Alabeç en un loch que fos convinent, hon nos li poguessem exir e que fossem tuyt ensems, per ço que mils ne poguessem servir a vos e dar don a son enemich, e ell senyor trames me una letra, la qual vos tramet . . . ," as cited in Masià i de Ros, *Jaume II*, 463–65.

127. ACA, R. 243, fol. 264v (5 Apr. 1317): "Don Jayme et cetera. Al amado Alabeç Abenrraho, salut e amor. Fazemos vos saber que recibiemos vuestra carta que nos enviastes con Mahomad fijo de Façan e entendiemos asi lo que se contenia en la dicha vuestra carta como lo que nos dixo de vuestra part el dicho Mahomat. A la qual vos respondemos que ciertos eramos nos e ciertos somos de la buena voluntat que vos havedes al nuestro servicio. E por esto havemos nos voluntat buena a vos de fazer vos toda honrra e toda bien como a aquell que los merescedes. E creet al dicho Mahomat [del] que vos dira de nuestra part sobre aquello que nos enviastes dezir. Dada en Ba[r]celona V dias andados del mes de Abril en el anyo de nuestro senyor de M CCC XVII."

Epilogue

1. Clifford Geertz," 'The Pinch of Destiny': Religion As Experience, Meaning, Identity, Power," *Raritan* 18, no. 3 (1999): 13.

2. I take inspiration from Andrew Cole and D. Vance Smith, eds., *The Legitimacy of the Middle Ages*; and Kathleen Davis, *Periodization and Sovereignty: How Ideas of Feudalism and Secularization Govern the Politics of Time*.

3. For an overview of the *convivencia* debates, see Soifer, "Beyond Convivencia"; Novikoff, "Between Tolerance and Intolerance"; and Tolan, "Using the Middle Ages."

4. Giménez Soler, "Caballeros," 299. He was strongly influenced by Alemany, "Milicias cristianas," 133 [my emphasis]: "Independientes del Califato desde el siglo VIII los musulmanes de Occidente, y separados en intereses de los de Oriente, desde el XI, reinó á partir de esta época un amplio *espíritu de tolerancia* y en

algunos casos de buena armonía entre los soberanos del Almagreb y las naciones cristianas."

5. Giménez Soler, "Caballeros," 299: "En los primeros tiempos el espíritu religioso no era muy fuerte ni en vencedores ni en vencidos; aquéllos iban no á propagar la ley mahometana, sino á buscar botín y riquezas; éstos debieron aceptar casi inmediatamente la religión de sus nuevos amos para obtener beneficios y librarse de gravámenes."

6. Giménez Soler, "Caballeros," 299: "[E]ran las relaciones entre los africanos y los cristianos de la península amistosas y hasta cordiales"; ". . . posponiéndose los intereses de la religión á los viles y positivos de la utilidad"; ibid., 300: "La guerra y el comercio, los dos grandes elementos civilizadores, coadyuvaron á esas recíprocas influencias."

7. Among the other nineteenth- and early twentieth-century liberal positivists, one might mention José Antonio Conde, Pascual de Gayangos, Francisco Codera, and Julián Ribera. See also Tolan, "Using the Middle Ages," 330ff; James T. Monroe, *Islam and Arabs in Spanish Scholarship (Sixteenth Century to the Present)*, 84–85; and López García, "Enigmas de al-Andalus," 45–48. Spanish positivism emerged under the influence of neo-Kantian philosopher Karl Christian Friedrich Krause (1781–1832). For a fuller discussion, see Juan López-Morillas, *The Krausist Movement and Ideological Change in Spain, 1854–1874*, trans. Frances M. López-Morillas. On the neo-Kantian context more broadly, see Michael Freidman, *A Parting of the Ways: Carnap, Cassirer, and Heidegger*, 25–39; and Peter Eli Gordon, *Continental Divide: Heidegger, Cassirer, Davos*.

8. The expression belongs to Leopold von Ranke: "wie es eigentlich gewesen." See also Dorothy Ross, "On the Misunderstanding of Ranke and the Origins of the Historical Profession in America," *Syracuse Scholar* 9 (1988): 31–41.

9. Tolan, "Using the Middle Ages," 330.

10. Manuel Moreno Alonso, *Historiografía romántica española: introducción al estudio de la historia en el siglo XIX*.

11. Menéndez Pidal, *La España del Cid*.

12. Menéndez Pidal, *La España del Cid*, I: 17–38. Dozy, *Recherches sur l'histoire et la littérature de l'Espagne*, II: 201–2: "Lui, l'aventurier . . . qui combattait en vrai soudard, tantôt pour le Christ, tantôt pour Mahomet, uniquement occupé de la solde à gagner et du pillage à faire; lui, . . . qui voilà et détruisit mainte église; lui, cet homme sans foi ni loi . . . qui manquait aux capitulations et aux serments les plus solennels; lui qui brûlait vifs ses prisonniers ou les faisait déchirer par ses dogues." On the rejection of El Cid's historicity, see J. F. de Masdeu, *Historia crítica de España y de la cultura Española*, XX: 354–55.

13. Menéndez Pidal, *La España del Cid*, I: 77: "El Andalus, independizado tan pronto del Oriente, había hispanizado su islamismo. . . . Así, cuando el Norte inició su preponderancia militar, al Andalus se inclinaba fácilmente a la sumisión, falto como se hallaba de un espíritu nacional y religioso; justamente en el siglo XI

el islamismo peninsular se hallaba, como vamos a indicar, diluido más que nunca en ideas racionalistas y antiárabes favorables a la convivencia con los cristianos."

14. "Shallow Enlightenment (*flachen Aufklärung*)" was the Romantic slogan.

15. Johan Gottfried Herder, *Ideen zur Philosophie der Geschichte der Menschheit*, in *Sämmtliche Werke*, ed. Berhard Suphan, XIV: 213 [trans. A. O. Hirschman]: "All the passions of man's breast are wild drives of a force which does not know itself yet, but which, in accordance with its nature, can only conspire toward a better order of things."

16. Thomas Glick, "Darwin y la filología española."

17. M. E. Lacarra, "La utilización del Cid de Menéndez Pidal en la ideología military franquista," *Ideologies and Literature* 3 (1980): 95–127; Pasamar Alzura, *Historiografía, e ideología en la postguerra española*, 311–14; Peter Linehan, *History and the Historians of Medieval Spain*, 206–7; and Tolan, "Using the Middle Ages," 339–40. Menéndez Pidal was not a Francoist sympathizer. See Peter Linehan, "The Court Historiographer of Francoism? La Leyenda oscura of Ramón Menéndez Pidal," *Bulletin of Hispanic Studies* 73 (1996): 437–50; and José Ignacio Pérez Pascual, *Ramón Menéndez Pidal: ciencia y passion*, 285–312. See also Ángel Gómez Moreno, "El Cid y los héroes de antaño en la guerra civil de España," *eHumanista: Journal of Iberian Studies* 14 (2010): 210–38.

18. See chapter 4.

19. Américo Castro, *España en su historia: cristianos, moros y judíos*, 17–45; idem, *The Structure of Spanish History*; idem, *The Spaniards: An Introduction to Their History*; Claudio Sánchez Albornoz, *España: un enigma histórico*. For an overview of the debate, see Glick, *Islamic and Christian Spain*, 6–13; and José Luis Gómez-Martínez, *Américo Castro y el origen de los españoles: historia de una polémica*.

20. Castro, *The Spaniards*, 499–500.

21. Sánchez Albornoz, *España: un enigma histórico*, 297–99.

22. Important exceptions to this trend and influences on the argument below included Szpiech, "The Convivencia Wars"; Tolan, "Using the Middle Ages"; López García, "Enigmas de al-Andalus"; idem, "30 años de Arabismo Español"; and idem, "Arabismo y orientalismo en España."

23. Szpiech, "The Convivencia Wars," 141; Donald L. Shaw, "The Anti-Romantic Reaction in Spain," *Modern Language Review* 63 (1968): 606–11.

24. Most recently, see Rosa María Rodríguez Magda, *Inexistente Al Ándalus: de cómo los intelectuales reinventan el Islam*; Chris Lowney, *A Vanished World: Medieval Spain's Golden Age of Enlightenment*; Serafín Fanjul, *La quimera de Al-Andalus. Madrid: siglo XXI de España*; César Vidal, *España frente al islam: de Mahoma a Ben Laden*; Serafín Fanjul, *Al-Andalus contra España: la forja del mito*; María Rosa Menocal, *The Ornament of the World: How Muslims, Jews, and Christians Created a Culture of Tolerance in Medieval Spain*; and Juan Vernet, *Lo que Europa debe al islam de España*.

25. Georg Simmel, "Die Krisis der Kultur," *Frankfurter Zeitung*, 6, no. 43 (February 13, 1916), drittes Morgenblatt, 1–2 [reprinted in Georg Simmel, *Der Krieg und die geistigen Entscheidungen: Reden und Aufsätze*]. For an overview, see Peter Eli Gordon, *Continental Divide: Heidegger, Cassirer, Davos*, 43–48.

26. Schmitt, *Political Theology*, 36. The expression has a longer history, at least as old as Spinoza's *Tractatus Theologico-Politicus*.

27. Luis Gabriel Ambriose, Victome de Bonald (1754–1840), *Théorie du pouvoir politique et religieux dans la société civile* (1796) and *Législation primitive* (1802). Joseph Marie, Comte de Maistre (1753–1821), *Considérations sur la France* (1796) and *Essai sur le principe générateur des constitutions politiques* (1814 [1809]).

28. Hans Blumenberg, *The Legitimacy of the Modern Age*, trans. by Robert M. Wallace; and Kantorowicz, *The King's Two Bodies.* Kantorowicz was more oblique than Blumenberg about his distaste for Schmitt. Kantorowicz, *The King's Two Bodies*, xviii: "It would go much too far, however, to assume that the author felt tempted to investigate the emergence of some of the idols of modern political religions merely on account of the horrifying experience of our own time in which whole nations, the largest and the smallest, fall prey to the weirdest dogmas and in which political theologies became genuine obsessions defying in many cases the rudiments of human and political reason; in fact, he became the more conscious of certain ideological gossamers the more he expanded and deepened his knowledge of the early development."

29. Kantorowicz, *Kaiser Friedrich der Zweite.*

30. For a fuller discussion, see Martin A. Ruehl, "'In This Time without Emperors': The Politics of Ernst Kantorowicz's *Kaiser Friedrich der Zweite* Reconsidered," *Journal of the Warburg and Courtauld Institutes* 63 (2000): 188–89.

31. Kantorowicz, *The King's Two Bodies*, 19. See also ibid., 207: "The noble concept of the *corpus mysticum*, after having lost much of its transcendental meaning and having been politicized and, in many respects, secularized by the Church itself, easily fell prey to the world of thought of statesmen, jurists, and scholars who were developing new ideologies for the nascent territorial and secular state."

32. Victoria Kahn, "Political Theology and Fiction in *The King's Two Bodies*," *Representations* 106, no. 1 (2009): 77–101, esp. 81.

33. Protestant and Jewish theologians, such as Karl Barth, Jacob Taubes, and Hans Jonas also weighed in on these debates about the relationship of religion and politics. See Benjamin Lazier, *God Interrupted: Heresy and the European Imagination Between the World Wars*, 5–9. The Islamic theologian, Allama Iqbal, has not been but should be considered in this context. See his *The Reconstruction of Religious Thought in Islam*, which heavily influenced modern Islamic movements from Iran to South Asia.

34. Peter Eli Gordon, "Continental Divide: Ernst Cassirer and Martin Heidegger at Davos, 1929—An Allegory of Intellectual History," *Modern Intellectual*

History 1, no. 2 (2004): 222. López García, "30 años de Arabismo Español," makes a similar argument about the *convivencia* debates.

35. Gordon, "Continental Divide," 222–23.

36. Leo Strauss, "Jerusalem and Athens: Some Introductory Reflections," *Commentary*, no. 43 (1967): 45–57.

37. Jonathan Sheehan, "Sacrifice Before the Secular," *Representations* 105, no. 1 (2009): 19: "[W]e only succeed in recycling concepts of theology and the secular in which each (depending on your commitments) becomes an 'intangible core content' hidden as the secret heart of the other." Benjamin Lazier, "On the Origins of 'Political Theology': Judaism and Heresy Between the World Wars," *New German Critique* 105, no. 35 (2008): 164: "On this view, the liberal stance works (unwittingly or not) to produce a fundamentalist-style theocracy as an alternative. It produces theocracy as an enemy against which to marshal its own resources and so, in a weird way, to ensure its own survival. In this vein, political theology represents the embodiment of liberalism's anxieties about itself."

38. Despite writing from different perspectives, Asad, *Genealogies of Religion*, 28; and Taylor, *A Secular Age*, 542–57, agree on this point.

39. Saba Mahmood, *Politics of Piety: The Islamic Revival and the Feminist Subject*, xi: "Within our secular epistemology, we tend to translate religious truth as force, a play of power that can be traced back to the machinations of economic and geopolitical interests." Cf. Geertz, " 'The Pinch of Destiny,' " 4: "Firmer, more determinate, more transpersonal, extravert terms—*meaning*, say, or *identity*, or *power*—must be deployed to catch the tonalities of devotion in our time."

40. Webb Keane, *Christian Moderns: Freedom and Fetish in the Mission Encounter*; and idem, "Secularism As a Moral Narrative of Modernity," *Transit: Europäische Revue* 43 (2013): 159–70.

41. Hent de Vries, introduction to *Religion: Beyond a Concept*, ed. Hent de Vries. Cf. Alister Chapman, John Coffey, and Brad S. Gregory, eds., *Seeing Things Their Way: Intellectual History and the Return of Religion*, 50.

42. Agamben, *Homo Sacer*; idem, *State of Exception*; and Taylor, *A Secular Age*. For critiques, see Peter Eli Gordon, "The Place of the Sacred in the Absence of God: Charles Taylor's A Secular Age," *Journal of the History of Ideas* 69, no. 4 (2008): 647–73; Jonathan Sheehan, "When Was Disenchantment? History and the Secular Age," in Michael Warner, Jonathan VanAntwerpen, and Craig J. Calhoun, eds., *Varieties of Secularism in a Secular Age*, 217–42; and Catherine Malabou, "The King's Two (Biopolitical) Bodies," *Representations* 127, no. 1 (2014): 98–106, esp. 102.

43. See Clifford Geertz, "Religion as a Cultural System" (1966), 90: "[A] religion is (1) a system of symbols which acts to (2) establish powerful, pervasive, and long-lasting moods and motivations in men by (3) formulating conceptions of a general order of existence, and (4) clothing these conceptions with an aura of factuality that (5) the moods and motivations seem uniquely realistic." On the enduring influence of Geertz, see Nancy K. Frankenberry and Hans H. Penner,

"Clifford Geertz's Long-Lasting Moods, Motivations, and Metaphysical Conceptions," *Journal of Religion* 79, no. 4 (1999): esp. 617: "The frequency with which scholars continue to cite Geertz's 1966 essay and endorse its definition of religion uncritically is surprising."

44. Justice, "Did the Middle Ages Believe in Their Miracles?" 9–11.

45. Justice, "Did the Middle Ages Believe in Their Miracles," 11: "[T]hey must speak either in a cynical and nearly sociopathic detachment from the truth-content of their words, or in a nearly delusional bondage to interests they do not even recognize as the source of those words."

46. Mahmood, *Politics of Piety*, 8: "Agency, in this form of analysis, is understood as the capacity to realize one's own interest against the weight of custom, tradition, transcendental will, or other obstacles (whether individual or collective). Thus the humanist desire for autonomy and self-expression constitutes the substrate, the slumbering ember that can spark to flame in the form of an act of resistance when conditions permit." See also Asad, *Genealogies of Religion*, 47.

47. Glenn Olsen, "The Middle Ages in the History of Toleration: A Prolegomena," *Mediterranean Studies* 16, no. 1 (2007): 8, speaking of Robert Moore: "Such a perspective as his, we might conclude, both radically under-describes the unending variety of circumstance and motive actually found in the Middle Ages, and, because it essentially is a moral tale told according to the categories of modern liberalism, is not very interested in the reasons people give for being intolerant, the 'logic' of their thought."

48. Wendy Brown, *Regulating Aversion: Tolerance in the Age of Identity and Empire*; and Asad, *Genealogies of Religion*, 14: "O'Hanlon sympathizes with the Subaltern historians' wish to recover suppressed histories but points to the theoretic danger such an agenda conceals of slipping into 'essentialist humanism.'"

49. Cole and Smith, "Outside Modernity," 46–64; Davis, *Periodization and Sovereignty*, 3, 14, and 98. As Cole and Smith argue, even "New Medievalism," which sought to challenge this periodization, has only reconfigured its relationship to modernity.

50. Hans Blumenberg, "Affinitäten und Dominanzen," in *Ein mögliches Selbstverständnis: Aus dem Nachlaß*, 161–68, as cited in Gordon, *Continental Divide*, 350.

51. Lazier, *God Interrupted*, 3; Sheehan, "Sacrifice Before the Secular," 26.

52. Cf. Justice, "Did the Middle Ages Believe in Their Miracles," 9, who argues differently.

53. Buc, *Dangers of Ritual*, 194.

54. Friedrich Schleiermacher, *On Religion: Speeches to Its Cultured Despisers*, trans. Richard Crouter. See also Thomas Albert Howard, *Protestant Theology and the Making of the Modern German University*, 28; Lazier, *God Interrupted*, 5–6; Sheehan, "Enlightenment, Religion, and the Enigma of Secularization," 1075; and M. B. Pranger, "Religious Indifference: On the Nature of Medieval Christianity," in Hent de Vries, ed., *Religion: Beyond a Concept*, 514.

55. Geertz, "Pinch of Destiny," 3.

56. Asad, *Genealogies of Religion*, 42.

57. Buc, *Dangers of Ritual*, 214–15.

58. Fenella Cannell, "Introduction: The Anthropology of Christianity" in *The Anthropology of Christianity*, ed. Fenella Cannell, 41: "[T]he work belongs to a long tradition of antireligious social science that incorporates Christian models by its refusal of them."

59. Nisbet, *The Sociological Tradition*, 221–63; Milbank, *Theology and Social Theory*, 52–61; and Buc, *Dangers of Ritual*, 194: "The movement from theology to the social sciences proceeded, understandably, on tracks defined in part by theology's progressively greater willingness to see religion as an integrated facet of society."

60. Carlos M. N. Eire, *War against the Idols: The Reformation of Worship from Erasmus to Calvin*; and Sheehan, "Sacred and Profane." See also Anna Sapier Abulafia, *Christians and Jews in Dispute: Disputational Literature and the Rise of Anti-Judaism in the West (c. 1000–1150)*; David Nirenberg, *Anti-Judaism: The Western Tradition*; and Seth Kimmel, " 'In the Choir with the Clerics': Secularism in the Age of Inquisition," *Comparative Literature* 65, no. 3 (2013): 285–305.

61. Buc, *Dangers of Ritual*, 178, 210.

62. For example, Sarah Stroumsa, *Freethinkers of Medieval Islam: Ibn al-Rawandi, Abu Bakr al-Razi, and Their Impact on Islamic Thought.*

63. Derek R. Peterson and Darren R. Walhof, *The Invention of Religion: Rethinking Belief in Politics and History*, 2; Ussama S. Makdisi, *The Culture of Sectarianism: Community, History and Violence in Nineteenth-Century Ottoman Lebanon.*

64. See for instance, Gerard E. Caspary, *Politics and Exegesis: Origen and the Two Swords.*

65. Fenella Cannell, "The Christianity of Anthropology," *Journal of the Royal Anthropology Institute* 11, no. 2 (2005): 335–57; Webb Keane, "Anxious Transcendence," in *The Anthropology of Christianity*, ed. Fenella Cannell, 308–23, cit. 310: "Transcendence, I suggest, haunts modernity in three unrealizable desires: for a self freed of its body, for meanings freed of semiotic mediation, and for agency freed of the press of other people."

66. Asad, *Genealogies of Religion*, esp. 29.

67. See for instance, Caroline Walker Bynum, *Christian Materiality: An Essay on Religion in Late Medieval Europe*; Kellie Robertson, "Medieval Materialism: A Manifesto," *Exemplaria* 22, no. 2 (2010): 99–118; and Steven Justice, "Eucharistic Miracle and Eucharistic Doubt," *Journal of Medieval and Early Modern Studies* 42, no. 2 (2012): 307–32. More broadly, Bruno Latour, "Can We Get Our Materialism Back, Please?" *Isis* 98, no. 1 (2007): 138–42; and Dick Houtman and Birgit Meyer, eds., *Things: Religion and the Question of Materiality.*

68. Hurd, "The Specific Order of Difficulty of Religion," referencing Bruno Latour, *Rejoicing: Or The Torments of Religious Speech*, trans. Julie Rose, 100.

Bibliography

Primary Sources

Achery, Luc d', ed. *Spicilegium: sive, Collectio veterum aliquot scriptorum qui in Galliae bibliothecis delituerant*. 3 vols. Paris: Montalant, 1723.

Aguilar, Pedro de. *Tractado de cavalleria de la gineta* (1572). Málaga: El Guadahorce, 1960.

anonymous, *al-Dhakhīra al-saniyya fī ta'rīkh al-dawla al-Marīniyya*, edited by 'Abd al-Wahhāb b. Mansūr. Rabat: Dār al-Manṣūr, 1972.

Balme, Franciscus, ed. *Raymundia seu documenta quae pertinent ad S. Raymundi de Pennaforti vitam et scripta*. Rome: Domus Generalitia, 1898–1901.

Bañuelos y de la Cerda, Luis de. *Libro de la jineta y descendencia de los caballos guzmanes*, edited by José Antonio de Balenchana. Madrid: Sociedad de Bibliófilos Españoles, 1877.

Barrantes Maldonado, Pedro, *Ilustraciones de la Casa de Niebla*, edited by Federico Devis Márquez. Cádiz: Universidad de Cádiz, Servicio de publicaciones, 1998.

Barton, Simon, and Richard Fletcher, eds. *The World of El Cid: Chronicles of the Spanish Reconquest*. Manchester: Manchester University Press, 2000.

Bastardas, Joan. *Usatges de Barcelona: el codi a mitjan segle XII: establiment del text llatí i edició de la versió catalana del manuscrit del segle XIII de l'Arxiu de la Corona d'Aragó de Barcelona*. Barcelona: Fundació Noguera, 1984.

Beaumanoir, Philippe de. *Coutumes de Beauvaisis*, edited by Amédée Salmon. Paris, 1900.

Bofarull y Mascaró, Prósperode, ed. *Colección de documentos inéditos del Archivo de la Corona de Aragón*. 41 vols. Barcelona: Archivo de la Corona de Aragón, 1847–1919.

Cabanes Pecourt, María Desamparados, ed. *Crónica latina de los reyes de Castilla*. Valencia: J. Nácher, 1964.

Caffarus, de Taschifellone, and Luigi Tommaso Belgrano, eds. *Cafari et continuatorum Annales Januenses*. Genoa, 1890.

Catalán, Diego, ed. *La gran crónica de Alfonso XI*. 2 vols. Madrid: Editorial Gredos, 1977.

Constitucions y altres drets de Catalunya. Barcelona, 1704.

Cortes de los antiguos reinos de Aragón y de Valencia y de principado de Cataluña. Madrid, 1896.

Covarrubias, Sebastián de. *Tesoro de la lengua castellana o española*, edited by Martín de Riquer. Barcelona: Altafulla, 1998.

Crónica del rey don Alfonso X in *Cronicas de los reyes de Castilla, desde Don Alfonso el Sabio hasta los catolicos Don Fernando y Dona Isabel,* edited by Cayetano Rosell, vol. 66 of *Biblioteca de autores españoles*. Madrid: Ediciones Atlas, 1953.

Crónica del rey Alfonso XI in *Cronicas de los reyes de Castilla, desde Don Alfonso el Sabio hasta los catolicos Don Fernando y Dona Isabel,* edited by Cayetano Rosell, vol. 66 of *Biblioteca de autores españoles*. Madrid: Ediciones Atlas, 1953.

Crónica del rey don Fernando IV in *Cronicas de los reyes de Castilla, desde Don Alfonso el Sabio hasta los catolicos Don Fernando y Dona Isabel,* edited by Cayetano Rosell, vol. 66 of *Biblioteca de autores españoles*. Madrid: Ediciones Atlas, 1953.

Crónica del rey don Sancho el Bravo in *Cronicas de los reyes de Castilla, desde Don Alfonso el Sabio hasta los catolicos Don Fernando y Dona Isabel,* edited by Cayetano Rosell, vol. 66 of *Biblioteca de autores españoles*. Madrid: Ediciones Atlas, 1953.

Desclot, Bernat. *Llibre del rei en Pere* in *Les quatre gran cròniques*, edited by Ferran Soldevila. Barcelona: Editorial Selecta, 1971.

Eiximenis, Francesc. *Regiment de la cosa publica*, edited by Daniel de Molins de Rei. Barcelona: Impremta Varias, 1927.

Finke, Heinrich. *Acta Aragonesia: Quellen zur deutschen, italienischen, französischen, spanischen, zur Kirchen- und Kulturgeschichte aus der diplomatischen Korrespondenz Jaymes II. (1291–1327)*. 3 vols. Berlin, 1908–22.

Foguet Marsal, Josep, Ramon Foguet, and Joan J. Permanyer i Ayats, eds. *Libre de les costums generals scrites de la insigne ciutat de Tortosa*. Tortosa: Imp. Querol, 1912.

Fueros y observancias del Reyno de Aragón, Zaragoza: Pedro Cabarte Impressor, 1624.

Galvão Andrade, Antonio. *Arte de cavelleria, de gineta, e estardiota bom primor de ferrar, & alueitiara*. Lisbon: Na Officina de Joam de Costa, 1678.

González Jiménez, Manuel, ed. *Crónica de Alfonso X: según el Ms. II/2777 de la Biblioteca del Palacio Real, Madrid*. Murcia: Real Academia Alfonso X el Sabio, 1998.

Heers, Jacques, and Georgette de Groër, eds. and trans. *Itinéraire d'Anselme Adorno en terre sainte 1470–1471*. Paris: Éditions du Centre national de la recherche scientifique, 1978.

Huici Miranda, Ambrosio, ed. *Colección diplomática de Jaime I, el Conquistador*. 3 vols. in 6. Valencia: Hijos de F. Vives Mora, 1916–1922.

Ibn ʻAbd al-Ḥakam, *Futūḥ Miṣr wa'l-Maghrib*, edited by ʻAbd al-Munʻim ʻĀmir. Cairo: Lajnat al-bayān al-ʻarabī, 1961.

Ibn Abī Zarʻ, ʻAlī. *al-'Anīs al-muṭrib bi-rawḍ al-qirṭās fī akhbār mulūk al-Maghrib wa-ta'rīkh madīnat Fās*, edited by ʻAbd al-Wahhāb b. Manṣūr. Rabat: Dār al-Manṣūr, 1972.

Ibn Ḥajar al-Haytamī, Abū al-ʻAbbās Shihāb al-Dīn. *Fatḥ al-jawād sharḥ al-irshād*. Cairo: Muṣṭafā al-Bābī al-Ḥalabī, 1971.

Ibn Hayyān. *al-Muqtabas fī akhbār bilād al-Andalus*, edited by ʻAbd al-Raḥmān al-Ḥajjī, vol. 7. Beirut: Dār al-thaqāfa, 1965.

———. *al-Muqtabas fī ta'rīkh rijāl al-Andalus*, edited by M. Martinez Antuña, vol. 3. Paris, 1937.

Ibn Ḥazm, ʻAlī b. Aḥmad. *Jamaharat ansāb al-ʻarab*, edited by ʻAbd al-Salām Muḥammad Hārūn. Cairo: Dār al-maʻārif, 1962.

Ibn ʻIdhārī al-Marrākushī, Abū'l-ʻAbbās Aḥmad. *al-Bayān al-mughrib fī akhbār al-Andalus wa'l-Maghrib*, edited by G. S. Colin and Évariste Lévi-Provençal. 4 vols. Beirut: Dār al-thaqāfa, 1998.

Ibn Khaldūn, ʻAbd al-Raḥmān b. Muḥammad. *Kitāb al-ʻibar wa-dīwān al-mubtada' wa'l-khabar fī ayyām al-ʻarab wa'l-ʻajam wa'l-barbar wa-man ʻāṣarahum min dhawī al-sultān al-akbar*, edited by ʻĀdil b. Saʻd. 7 vols. Beirut: Dār al-kutub al-ʻilmiyya, 2010.

Ibn al-Khaṭīb, Lisān al-Dīn. *Aʻmāl al-aʻlām fī-man būyiʻa qabla al-iḥtilām min mulūk al-Islām wa-mā yataʻallaqu bi-dhālika min al-kalām*, edited by Sayyid Kasrawī Haṣan. 2 vols. Beirut: Dār al-kutub al-ʻilmiyya, 2003.

———. *Iḥāṭa fī akhbār Gharnāṭa*, edited by Muḥammad ʻAbd Allāh ʻInān. Cairo: al-Shirka al-Miṣriyya li'l-ṭabāʻa wa'l-nashir, 1975.

———. *al-Lamḥa al-badriyya fī'l-dawla al-Naṣriyya*, edited by Aḥmad ʻĀṣī and Muḥibb al-Dīn al-Khaṭīb. Beirut: Dār al-afāq al-jadīd, 1978.

———. *Nufādāt al-jirāb fī ʻulālat al-iʻtirāb*, edited by Aḥmad Mukhtār al-ʻAbbadī. Cairo: Dār al-kutub, 1968.

Ibn Khurradādhbih, Abū al-Qāsim ʻUbayd Allāh. *Kitāb al-masālik wa'l-mamālik*, edited by Khayr al-Dīn Maḥmūd Qiblāwī. Damascus: Manshūrāt wizārat al-thaqāfah 1999.

Ibn Marzūq, Muḥammad b. Aḥmad. *al-Musnad al-ṣaḥīḥ al-ḥasan fī ma'āthir wa-maḥāsin mawlānā Abī'l-Ḥasan*, edited by M. J. Viguera. Algiers: Bibliothèque Nationale d'Algèrie, 1981.

Ibn Qutayba, ʻAbd Allāh b. Muslim. *Kitāb al-Maʻārif*, edited by Tharwat Ukāsha. Cairo: Dār al-maʻārif, 1960.

Ibn Rushd al-Jadd, Abū al-Walīd Muḥammad b. Aḥmad b. Aḥmad. *al-Bayān wa'l-taḥṣīl wa'l-sharḥ wa'l-tawjīh wa'l-ta'līl fī masā'il al-mustakhrajah*, edited by Aḥmad al-Jabābī. Beirut: Dār al-gharb al-islāmī, 1984.

———. *al-Muqaddimāt al-mumahhidāt*, edited by Muḥammad Ḥajjī. Beirut: Dār al-gharb al-islāmī, 1988.

Ibn Rusta, Aḥmad. *Kitāb al-aʿlāq al-nafīsa*, edited by M. J. De Goeje. Leiden: Brill, 1892.

Ibn Ṣaghīr, *Akhbār al-a'imma al-rustumiyyīn*. "La chronique d'Ibn Saghir sur les imam rustamides de Tahert," edited and translated by A. de C. Motylinski, 3–132. In *Actes du XIVe Congrès International des Orientalistes*. Algiers, 1905.

Ibn Saʿīd, ʿAlī b. Mūsā. *al-Mughrib fī ḥulā al-Maghrib*, edited by Khalīl al-Manṣūr. 2 vols. Beirut: Dar al-kutub al-ʿilmiyya, 1997.

Ibn Simāk al-ʿĀmilī. *al-Ḥulal al-mawshiyya fī dhikr al-akhbār al-Marrākushiyya*, edited by ʿAbd al-Qādir Būbāya. Cairo: Dār al-kutub al-ʿilmiyya, 2010.

al-Idrīsī, Muḥammad b. Muḥammad. *Kitāb nuzhat al-mushtāq fī ikhtirāq al-āfāq*. 9 vols. Rome-Naples: Istituto Universitario Orientale, 1970–84.

Jiménez de Rada, Rodrigo. *Roderici Ximenii de Rada Historia de rebus hispanie sive historia gothica* in *Roderici Ximenii De Rada Opera Omnia*, edited by Juan Fernández Valverde. Turnhout: Brepols, 1987.

Juan Manuel, Infante de Castile. *El libro de la caza*, edited by G. Baist. New York: Georg Olms Verlag, 1984.

———. *Libro de los estados*, edited by Robert Brian Tate and Ian Richard Macpherson. Oxford: Clarendon Press, 1974.

———. *Obras completas*, edited by José Manuel Blecua. Madrid: Gredos, 1982.

Justinian. *Corpus iuris civilis*. Lyons, 1627.

La Mantia, Giuseppe. *Codice diplomatico dei re Aragonesi di Sicilia: Pietro I, Giacomo, Federico II, Pietro II e Ludovico, Dalla rivoluzione Siciliana del 1282 sino al 1355*. 2 vols. Palermo: Società siciliana per la storia patria, 1917.

Lafuente y Alcántara, Emilio, trans. and ed. *Akhbār al-majmūʿa [Ajbar Machmuā. Crónica anoníma del siglo XI]*. Madrid: Rivadeneyra, 1867.

Lévi-Provençal, Évariste. *Mafākhir al-Barbar [Fragments historiques sur les Berbères au Moyen Age, extraits inédits d'un receueil anonyme compilé en 712/1312 et intitulé: Kitab Mafakhir al-Barbar]*. Rabat: F. Moncho, 1934.

Llibre dels feyts in *Les quatre gran cròniques*, edited Ferran Soldevila. Barcelona: Editorial Selecta, 1971.

Loscertales de Valdeavellano, Pilar, ed. *Costumbres de Lérida*. Barcelona: Imp. Escuela Casa Provincial de Caridad, 1946.

Lull, Ramon. *Liber de fine*. In *Ramon Lulls Kreuzzugsideen*, edited by A. Gottron. Berlin: Walther Rothschild, 1912.

Machiavelli, Niccolò, *Il principe*, edited by Arthur Burd. Oxford: Clarendon Press, 1891.

Mançanas, Eugenio. *Libro de enfrenamentos de la gineta*. Toledo: En casa de Juan Rodriquez, mercader de libros, 1583.

Mansilla, Demetrio. *La documentación pontificia de Honorio III (1216–1227)*. Rome: Instituto Español de Estudios Eclesiásticos, 1965.

al-Maqdisī, Muṭahhar b. Taḥrīr. *Kitāb al-bad' wa'l-ta'rīkh*, edited by Cl. Huart. Paris: Ernest Leroux, 1899–1919.

al-Maqqarī, Aḥmad b. Muḥammad. *Azhār al-riyāḍ fī akhbār 'Iyāḍ*, edited by I. al-Abyārī. 3 vols. Cairo: Maṭba'at lajnat al-ta'līf wa'l-tarjama wa'l-nashr, 1939.

———. *Nafḥ al-ṭīb min ghuṣn al-Andalus al-raṭīb wa-dhikr wazīrihā Lisān al-Dīn al-Khaṭīb*, ed. Muḥammad 'Abd al-Ḥamīd. 10 vols. Cairo: al-Maktaba al-tijāriyya al-kubrā, 1949.

Mariana, Juan de. *De rege et regis institutione*. Mainz: Balthazar Lippus, 1605.

Marín, Pero. *Miraculos Romanzados* in *Vida y milagros del thaumaturgo español moysées Segundo, redemptor de cautivos, abogado de los felices partos, Sto. Domingo Manso, abad benedictino, reparador del real monasterio de Silos*, edited by Sebastián Vergara. Madrid, 1726.

Mármol Carvajal, Luis del. *Historia del rebellion y castigo de los Moriscos del reyno de Granada*. Madrid, 1797.

Mas Latrie, Louis de. *Traités de paix et de commerce et documents divers concernant les relations des chrétiens avec les arabes de l'Afrique septentrionale au moyen âge*. Paris, 1866. Supplement, Paris, 1872.

al-Mas'ūdī. *Murūj al-dhahab wa-ma'ādin al-jawhar*, edited by Charles Pellat. Beirut: al-Jāmi'a al-Lubnāniyya, 1965.

Maya Sánchez, Antonio, ed. *Chronica Adefonsi Imperatoris* in *Chronica Hispana saeculi XII,* edited by Emma Falque, Juan Gil, and Antonio Maya Sánchez. Corpus Christianorum Continuatio Medievalis, 71. Turnhout: Typographi Brepols Editores Pontificii, 1990.

Menéndez Pidal, Ramón, ed. *Primera crónica general*. Madrid: Gredos, 1977.

Muñoz y Romero, Tomás. *Colección de fueros municipales y cartas pueblas de los reinos de Castilla, León, Corona de Aragón y Navarra*. Madrid: J. M. Alonso, 1867.

Muntaner, Ramon. *Crònica* in *Les quatre gran cròniques*, edited by Ferran Soldevila. Barcelona: Editorial Selecta, 1971.

al-Nawawī, Muḥyī al-Dīn. *al-Majmū' sharḥ al-muhadhdhab*. Beirut: Dār al-fikr, n.d.

al-Nuwayrī, *al-Maghrib al-Islāmī fi'l-'aṣr al-wasīṭ*, ed. Muṣṭafā Abū Ḍayf Aḥmad. Casablanca: Dār al-nashr al-maghribī, 1985.

Paz de Espéso, Julián. *Documentos relativos a España existentes en los Archivos Nacionales de Paris*. Madrid: Instituto de Valencia de Don Juan, 1934.

Rosenthal, Franz, trans. *The Muqaddimah*. Princeton: Princeton University Press, 1967.

Rubió y Lluch, Antonio, ed. *Documents per l'història de la cultura catalana migeval*. Barcelona: Institut d'Estudis Catalans, 1908–21.

Saḥnūn, Abū Sa'īd. *al-Mudawwana al-Kubrā*. Cairo: Dār al-fikr, n.d.

al-Shaybānī, Muḥammad b. al-Ḥasan. *The Islamic Law of Nations: Shaybānī's Siyar*, translated by Majid Khadduri. Baltimore: John Hopkins University Press, 1966.

Smith, Colin, ed. *Christians and Moors in Spain*. Vol. 1: AD 711–1150. Hispanic Classics. Warminster: Aris and Philips, 1988.

Soldevila, Ferran, ed. *Les quatre gran cròniques*. Barcelona: Editorial Selecta, 1971.

Tapia y Salcedo, Gregorio. *Exercicios de la gineta*. Madrid: Diego Diaz, 1643.

Ubieto Arteta, Antonio, ed. *Crónica de San Juan de la Peña*. Valencia: Anubar, 1961.

———. *Crónica Najerense*. Valencia: Anubar, 1956.

Vargas Machuca, Bernardo de. *Libro de exercicos de la gineta*. Madrid: Pedro Madrigal, 1600.

al-Wansharīsī, Aḥmad b. Yaḥyā. *al-Mi'yār al-mu'rib wa'l-jāmi' al-mughrib 'an fatāwā 'ulamā' ahl Ifrīqiya wa'l-Andalus wa'l-Maghrib*, edited by Muḥammad Ḥajjī, 13 vols. Beirut: Dār al-gharb al-islāmī, 1981.

Wolf, Kenneth Baxter, ed. *Conquerors and Chroniclers of Early Medieval Spain*. Liverpool: Liverpool University Press, 1990.

Ya'qūbī, Aḥmad b. Abī Ya'qūb. *Kitāb al-buldān*, edited by Wilhelmus Theodorus Juynboll. Leiden: Brill, 1860 [1861].

Zurita, Jerónimo. *Anales de la Corona de Aragón*, edited by Ángel Canellas López. Zaragoza: Institución Fernando el Católico, 1967.

Secondary Sources

Abdesselem, Ahmed. *Ibn Khaldūn et ses lecteurs*. Paris: Presses universitaires de France, 1983.

Abou El Fadl, Khaled. *Rebellion and Violence in Islamic Law*. Cambridge: Cambridge University Press, 2001.

———. "Islamic Law and Muslim Minorities: The Juristic Discourse on Muslim Minorities from the Second/Eighth to the Eleventh/Seventeenth Centuries." *Islamic Law and Society* 1, no. 2 (1994): 141–87.

Abulafia, Anna Sapier. *Christians and Jews in Dispute: Disputational Literature and the Rise of Anti-Judaism in the West (c. 1000–1150)*. Brookfield: Variorum, 1998.

Abulafia, David. "The Kingdom of Sicily under the Hohenstaufen and Angevins." In *The New Cambridge Medieval History, c. 1198–1300*, edited by David Abulafia. Cambridge: Cambridge University Press, 1999.

———. *A Mediterranean Emporium: The Catalan Kingdom of Majorca*. Cambridge: Cambridge University Press, 1994.

———. "Monarchs and Minorities in the Christian Western Mediterranean around 1300: Lucera and Its Analogues." In *Christendom and Its Discontents: Exclusion, Persecution, and Rebellion, 1000–1500*, edited by Scott L. Waugh and Peter Diehl, 234–63. Cambridge: Cambridge University Press, 1996.

———. "The Servitude of Jews and Muslims in the Medieval Mediterranean: Origins and Diffusion." *Mélanges de l'école française de Rome. Moyen Âge* 112 (2000): 687–714.

———. *The Western Mediterranean Kingdoms, 1200–1500*. New York: Longman, 1997.

Agamben, Giorgio. *Homo Sacer: Sovereign Power and Bare Life*, translated by Daniel Heller-Roazen. Stanford: Stanford University Press, 1998.

———. *State of Exception*. Chicago: University of Chicago Press, 2005.

Agrama, Hussein Ali. *Questioning Secularism: Islam, Sovereignty, and the Rule of Law in Modern Egypt*. Chicago: University of Chicago Press, 2012.

Aguilar Sebastian, Victoria. "Instituciones militares. El ejército." In *El retroceso territorial de al-Andalus. Almorávides y Almohades, siglos XI al XIII*, edited by María Jesús Viguera Molins, 188–209. Madrid: Espasa Calpe, 1997.

Albert-Llorca, Marlene, and José Antonio González Alcantud. *Moros y cristianos: representations del otro en las fiestas del Mediterraneo occidental*. Toulouse: Presse Universitaire du Mirail, 2003.

Alcover i Sureda, Antoni María, and Francesch de Borja Molls y Casanovas. *Diccionari català-valencià-balear*. Palma de Mallorca: Alcover, 1930–1969.

Alemany, José. "Milicias cristianas al servicio de los sultanes musulmanes del Almagreb." In *Homenaje á D. Francisco Codera en su jubilación del profesorado*, edited by Eduardo Saavedra, 133–69. Zaragoza: M. Escar, tipógrafo 1904.

Alvarez de Toledo, Luisa Isabel. "Guzmán el Bueno, entre la leyenda y la historia." *Estudios de historia y de arqueología medievales* 7–9 (1987): 41–58.

Alverny, Marie-Thérèse d', and George Vajda, "Marc de Tolede, traducteur d'Ibn Tūmart." *Al-Andalus* 16 (1951): 99–140.

Amitai, Reuven. "The Mamlūk Institution, or One Thousand Years of Military Slavery in the Islamic World." In *Arming Slaves: From Classical Times to the Modern Age*, edited by Christopher Leslie Brown and Philip D. Morgan, 40–78. New Haven: Yale University Press, 2006.

Amorós Paya, León. "Los santos mártires franciscanos B. Juan de Perusa y B. Pedro de Saxoferrato en la historia de Teruel." *Teruel* 15 (1956): 5–142.

Arco y Garay, Ricardo del. *Sepulcros de la casa real de Aragón*. Madrid: Diana, artes gráficas, 1945.

Arié, Rachel. *L'Espagne musulmane au temps des Nasrides (1232–1492)*. Paris: E. de Boccard, 1973.

———. "Quelques remarques sur le costume des Musulmans d'Espagne au temps de Naṣrides." *Arabica* 12, no. 3 (1965): 244–64.

———. *El reino Naṣrí de Granada, 1232–1492*. Madrid: Editorial MAPFRE, 1992.

Arribas Palau, Antonio. *La conquista de Cerdeña por Jaume II de Aragón*. Barcelona: Instituto Español de Estudios Mediterráneos, 1952.

Asad, Talal. *Formations of the Secular: Christianity, Islam, and Modernity*. Stanford: Stanford University Press, 2003.

———. *Genealogies of Religion: Discipline and Reasons of Power in Christianity and Islam*. Baltimore: Johns Hopkins University Press, 1993.

———. "Responses." In *Powers of the Secular Modern: Talal Asad and His Interlocutors*, edited by David Scott and Charles Hirschkind, 206–42. Stanford: Stanford University Press, 2006.

Asad, Talal, Wendy Brown, Judith Butler, and Saba Mahmood. *Is Critique Secular? Blasphemy, Injury, and Free Speech*. New York: Fordham University Press, 2013.

Assis, Yom Tov. *The Golden Age of Aragonese Jewry: Community and Society in the Crown of Aragon, 1213–1327*. Oxford: Vallentine Mitchell, 1997.

Aurell, Jaume. *Authoring the Past: History, Autobiography, and Politics in Medieval Catalonia*. Chicago: University of Chicago Press, 2012.

Aurell, Jaume, and Marta Serrano-Coll. "The Self-Coronation of Peter the Ceremonious (1336): Historical, Liturgical, and Iconographical Representations." *Speculum* 89, no. 1 (2013): 66–95.

Austin, John. *The Province of Jurisprudence Determined*, edited by Wilfrid E. Rumble. Cambridge: Cambridge University Press, 1995 [1832].

Ayalon, David. *The Mamluk Military Society*. London: Variorum Reprints, 1979.

———. "The Mamluks: The Mainstay of Islam's Military Might." In *Slavery in the Islamic Middle East*, edited by S. Marmon, 89–117. Princeton: Markus Wiener, 1999.

———. "The Mamlūks of the Seljuks: Islam's Military Might at the Crossroads." *Journal of the Royal Asiatic Society* 6, no. 3 (1996): 305–33.

———. "On the Eunuch in Islam." *Jerusalem Studies in Arabic and Islam* 1 (1979): 109–22.

Al-Azmeh, Aziz. *Ibn Khaldūn: An Essay in Reinterpretation*. London: Cass, 1982.

———. *Ibn Khaldūn in Modern Scholarship: A Study in Orientalism*. London: Third World Centre, 1981.

Bacharach, Jere L. "African Military Slaves in the Medieval Middle East: the Cases of Iraq (869–955) and Egypt (868–1171)." *International Journal of Middle East Studies* 13, no. 4 (1981): 471–95.

Balbale, Abigail Krasner. "*Jihād* as a Means of Political Legitimation." In *The Articulation of Power in Medieval Iberia and the Maghrib*, edited by Amira K. Bennison, 87–105. Oxford: Oxford University Press, 2014.

Balfour, Sebastian. *Deadly Embrace: Morocco and the Road to the Spanish Civil War*. New York: Oxford, 2002.

Barbour, Nevill. "The Significance of the Word *Maurus*, with Its Derivatives *Moro* and *Moor*, and of Other Terms Used by Medieval Writers in Latin to Describe the Inhabitants of Muslim Spain." In *Actas IV del Congreso de estudios árabes e islámicos*, 253–66. Leiden: Brill, 1971.

Barceló, Carmen. "Documentos árabes de al-Azraq (1245–1250)." *Saitabí: revista de la Facultat de Geografia i Història* 32 (1982): 27–41.

———. "La lengua àrab al País Valencia (segles VIII al XVI)." *Arguments* 4 (1979): 123–49.

Barton, Simon. "Traitors to the Faith? Christian Mercenaries in Al-Andalus and the Maghreb, C.1100–1300." In *Medieval Spain: Culture, Conflict, and Coexistence: Studies in Honour of Angus MacKay*, edited by Roger Collins and Anthony Goodman, 23–45. New York: Palgrave Macmillan, 2002.

Bataille, Georges. *La part maudite, precédé de la notion de dépense*. Paris: Éditions de Minuit, 1949.

Batlle i Gallart, Carme. "La casa barcelonina en el segle XIII: l'exemple de la familia Dufort." In *La Ciudad hispánica durante los siglos XIII al XVI: actas del coloquio celebrado en La Rábida y Sevilla del 14 al 19 de septiembre de 1981*, edited by Emilio Sáez, Cristina Segura, and Margarita Cantera Montenegro, 1347–60. 2 vols. Madrid: Universidad Complutense, 1985.

———. "Noticias sobre la milicia cristiana en el Norte de África en la segunda mitad del siglo XIII." In *Homenaje al Profesor Juan Torres Fontes*, 127–37. Murcia: Universidad de Murcia, 1987.

Bayly, C. A. "The Origins of Swadeshi (Home Industry): Cloth and Indian Society." In *The Social Life of Things*, edited by Arjun Appadurai, 285–322. Cambridge: Cambridge University Press, 1986.

Bazzana, Andrés, Nicole Bériou, and Pierre Guichard, ed. *Averroès et l'averroïsme, XIIe-XVe siècle: Un itinéraire historique du Haut Atlas à Paris et à Padoue: Actes du colloque international organisé à Lyon, les 4 et 5 octobre 1999 dans le cadre du temps du Maroc*. Lyon: Presses universitaires de Lyon, 2005.

Bearman, P. J., C. E. Bosworth, E. van Donzel, and W. P. Heinrichs, ed. *Encyclopedia of Islam*. 2nd ed., 12 vols. Leiden: Brill, 1960–2005.

Beckwith, Christopher I. "Aspects of Early History of the Central Asian Guard Corps in Islam." *Archivum Eurasie Medii Aevi* 4 (1984): 29–43.

Bejczy, István. "Tolerantia: A Medieval Concept." *Journal of the History of Ideas* 58 (1997): 365–84.

Benaboud, M'hammad, and Ahmad Tahiri. "Berberising Al-Andalus." *Al-Qantara* 11, no. 2 (1990): 475–87.

Bennison, Amira K., and Maria Ángeles Gallego. "Religious Minorities under the Almohads: an Introduction." *Journal of Medieval Iberian Studies* 2, no. 2 (2010): 143–54.

Bhargava, Rajeev. *Secularism and Its Critics*. New York: Oxford University Press, 1998.

Bisson, Thomas N. *Medieval Crown of Aragon: A Short History*. New York: Oxford University Press, 2000.

Blanchard, Peter. *Under the Flags of Freedom: Slave Soldiers and the Wars of Independence in Spanish South America*. Pittsburgh: University of Pittsburgh Press, 2008.

Bloch, Marc. *The Royal Touch: Sacred Monarchy and Scrofula in England and France*. London: Routledge, 1973.

Blumenberg, Hans. "Affinitäten und Dominanzen." In *Ein mögliches Selbstverständnis: Aus dem Nachlaß*, 161–68. Stuttgart: Philipp Reclam, 1996.

———. *The Legitimacy of the Modern Age*, translated by Robert M. Wallace. Cambridge: MIT Press, 1985 [1966].

Bonner, Michael. *Jihad in Islamic History*. Princeton: Princeton University Press, 2006.

Bosch Vilá, Jacinto. *Los Almoravides*. Granada: Universidad de Granada, 1990.

Boswell, John. *The Royal Treasure: Muslim Communities under the Crown of Aragon in the Fourteenth Century*. New Haven: Yale University Press, 1977.

Botet i Sisó, Joaquím. "Nota sobre la encunyació de monedas arábigues pel Rey Don Jaume." In *Congrés d'històriala Corona d'Aragó, dedicat al rey En Jaume I y la seua época*, vol. 2, 944–45. Barcelona, 1909–13.

Brackmann, Albert. "Nachwort." *Historische Zeitschrift* 141 (1930): 472–78.

Bramon Planas, Maria Dolors. "Una llengua, dues llengües, tres llengües." In *Raons d'identitat del País Valencià*, ed. Pere Sisé, 17–47. Valencia: Editorial Eliscu Climent, 1977.

Brann, Ross. "The Moors?" *Medieval Encounters* 15, no. 2 (2009): 307–18.

Brett, Michael. "The Lamp of the Almohads: Illumination as a Political Idea in Twelfth-Century Morocco." In *Ibn Khaldun and the Medieval Maghrib*, edited by Michael Brett, Essay VI, 1–27. Aldershot: Ashgate, 1999.

———. "Way of the Nomad." *Bulletin of the School of Oriental and African Studies* 58, no. 2 (1995): 251–69.

Broadman, James. *Ransoming Captives in Crusader Spain: The Order of Merced on the Christian-Islamic Frontier*. Philadelphia: University of Pennsylvania, 1986.

Brown, Christopher Leslie, and Philip D. Morgan, eds. *Arming Slaves: From Classical Times to the Modern Age*. New Haven: Yale University Press, 2006.

Brown, Peter. *The Cult of the Saints: Its Rise and Function in Latin Christianity*. Chicago: University of Chicago Press, 1981.

Brown, Wendy. *Regulating Aversion: Tolerance in the Age of Identity and Empire*. Princeton: Princeton University Press, 2008.

Brunschvig, Robert. *La Berbérie orientale sous les Ḥafṣides des origines à la fin du XV siècle*. 2 vols. Paris: Adrien Maisonneuve, 1940.

———. "Sur la doctrine du mahdī Ibn Tūmart." *Arabica* 2, no. 2 (1955): 137–49.

Buc, Philippe. *The Dangers of Ritual: Between Early Medieval Texts and Social Scientific Theory*. Princeton: Princeton University Press, 2001.

Burman, Thomas E. *Reading the Qur'ān in Latin Christendom, 1140–1560*. Philadelphia: University of Pennsylvania Press, 2007.

Burns, Robert Ignatius, ed. *Diplomatarium of the Crusader Kingdom of Valencia: The Registered Charters of its Conqueror James I, 1257–1276*. 3 vols. Princeton: Princeton University Press, 1991.

Burns, Robert Ignatius. "Christian-Islamic Confrontation in the West: The Thirteenth-Century Dream of Conversion." *American Historical Review* 76 (1971): 1386–434.

———. "The Crusade against Al-Azraq: A Thirteenth-Century Mudejar Revolt in International Perspective." *American Historical Review* 93 (1988): 80–106.

———. "Daughter of Abu Zayd, Last Almohad Ruler of Valencia: The Family and Christian Seignory of Alda Ferrandis 1236–1300." *Viator* 24 (1993): 143–87.

———. "La Guerra de Al-Azraq de 1249." *Sharq al-Andalus* 4 (1987): 253–56.

———. *Islam under the Crusaders: Colonial Survival in the Thirteenth-Century Kingdom of Valencia*. Princeton: Princeton University Press, 1973.

———. "A Lost Crusade: Unpublished Bulls of Innocent IV on Al-Azraq's Revolt in Thirteenth-Century Spain." *Catholic Historical Review* (1988): 440–49.

———. *Medieval Colonialism: Postcrusade Exploitation of Islamic Valencia*. Princeton: Princeton University Press, 1975.

———. *Muslims, Christians, and Jews in the Crusader Kingdom of Valencia: Societies in Symbiosis*. Cambridge: Cambridge University Press, 1984.

———. "Príncipe almohade y converso mudéjar: nueva documentación sobre Abū Zayd." *Sharq Al-Andalus* 4 (1987): 109–22.

———. "Renegades, Adventurers and Sharp Businessmen: The Thirteenth-Century Spaniard in the Cause of Islam." *Catholic Historical Review* 58, no. 3 (1972): 341–66.

———. "Royal Pardons in the Realms of Aragon: An Instrument of Social Control." *XV Congreso de historia de la Corona de Aragón. Actas* 1, no. 2 (1993): 36–44.

———. "Warrior Neighbors: Alfonso El Sabio and Crusader Valencia, An Archival Case Study in His International Relations." *Viator* 21, no. 1 (1990): 156–62.

Burns, Robert Ignatius, and Paul Edward Chevedden, "A Unique Bilingual Surrender Treaty from Muslim-Crusader Spain." *Historian* 62, no. 3 (2000): 511–34.

Buzineb, Hossain. "Respuestas de Jurisconsultos Maghrebies en Torno a la Inmigración de Musulmanes Hispánicos." *Hespéris Tamuda* 16–17 (1988–89): 53–67.

Bynum, Caroline Walker. *Christian Materiality: An Essay on Religion in Late Medieval Europe*. New York: Zone Books, 2011.

———. "Why All the Fuss about the Body? A Medievalist's Perspective." *Critical Inquiry* 22 (1995): 1–33.

Calarco, Matthew, and Steven DeCaroli, edited by *Giorgio Agamben: Sovereignty and Life*. Stanford: Stanford University Press, 2007.

Cannell, Fenella, ed. *The Anthropology of Christianity*. Durham: Duke University Press, 2006.

———. "The Christianity of Anthropology." *Journal of the Royal Anthropology Institute* 11, no. 2 (2005): 335–57.

Caputo, John D. "Without Sovereignty, Without Being: Unconditionally, the Coming God and Derrida's Democracy to Come." *Journal of Cultural and Religious Theory* 4, no. 3 (2003): 9–26.

Carreras Candi, F. "Relaciones de los vizcondes de Barcelona con los árabes." In *Homenaje á D. Francisco Codera en su jubilación del profesorado*, edited by Eduardo Saavedra, 201–15. Zaragoza: Mariano Escar, Tipógrafo, 1904.

Caspary, Gerard E. *Politics and Exegesis: Origen and the Two Swords*. Berkeley: University of California Press, 1979.

Castro, Américo. *España en su historia: cristianos, moros y judíos*. Buenos Aires: Editorial Losada, 1948.

———. *The Spaniards: An Introduction to Their History*. Berkeley: University of California Press, 1971.

———. *The Structure of Spanish History*. Princeton: Princeton University Press, 1954.

Catlos, Brian A. "'Mahomet Abenadalill': A Muslim Mercenary in the Service of the Kings of Aragon, 1290–1291." In *Jews, Muslims, and Christians in and around the Medieval Crown of Aragon: Studies in Honour of Prof. Elena Lourie*, edited by Harvey J. Hames, 257–302. Leiden: Brill, 2003.

———. *Muslims of Medieval Christendom, ca. 1050–1614*. Cambridge: Cambridge University Press, 2014.

———. "*Secundum suam zunam*. Muslims and the Law in the Aragonese 'Reconquest.'" *Mediterranean Studies* 7 (1999): 13–26.

———. *The Victors and the Vanquished: Christians and Muslims of Catalonia and Aragon, 1050–1300*. Cambridge: Cambridge University Press, 2004.

Cenival, P. de "L'Église chrétienne de Marrakech au XIIIe siècle." *Hespéris* 7 (1927): 69–84.

Chabás, Roque. "Çeid Abu Çeid." *El archivo* 4 (1890): 215–21; 5 (1891): 143–66, 288–304, and 362–76.

Chakrabarty, Dipesh. *Provincializing Europe: Postcolonial Thought and Historical Difference*. Princeton: Princeton University Press, 2000.

Chapman, Alister, John Coffey, and Brad S. Gregory, eds. *Seeing Things Their Way: Intellectual History and the Return of Religion*. Notre Dame: University of Notre Dame Press, 2009.

Circourt, Albert de. *Histoire des Mores mudejares et des Morisques, ou des Arabes d'Espagne sous la domination des chrétiens*. 3 vols. Paris: G. A. Dentu, 1846.

Cirlot, Victoria. "Techniques guerrières en Catalogne féodale: Le Maniement de la lance," *Cahiers de Civilisation Médiévale*, 28, no. 1 (1985): 35–43.

Clement, François. "Reverter et son fils, deux officiers catalans au service des sultans de Marrakech." *Medieval Encounters* 9, no. 1 (2003): 79–106.

Cole, Andrew, and D. Vance Smith, eds. *The Legitimacy of the Middle Ages: On the Unwritten History of Theory*. Durham: Duke University Press, 2010.

Connolly, William E. *Why I Am Not a Secularist*. Minneapolis: University of Minnesota Press, 1999.

Constable, Olivia Remie. *Housing the Stranger in the Mediterranean World*. New York: Cambridge University Press, 2003.

———. *Trade and Traders in Muslim Spain: The Commercial Realignment of the Iberian Peninsula, 900–1500*. New York: Cambridge University Press, 1994.

Corcos, David. "The Jews of Morocco under the Marinids." *Jewish Quarterly Review* 54 (1963–64): 271–87; 55 (1964–65): 53–81 and 137–50.

Cornell, Vincent J. "Understanding is the Mother of Ability: Responsibility and Action in the Doctrine of Ibn Tūmart." *Studia islamica* 66 (1987): 71–103.

Coromines, Joan, and J. A. Pascual, *Diccionario crítico etimológico castellano e hispánico*. Madrid: Gredos, 1980.

Courtenay, William J. *Capacity and Volition: A History of the Distinction of Absolute and Ordained Power*. Bergamo: Pierluigi Lubrina, 1990.

———. "The Dialectic of Omnipotence in the High and Late Middle Ages." In *Divine Omniscience and Omnipotence in Medieval Philosophy: Islamic, Jewish and Christian Perspectives*, edited by Tamar Rudavsky, 243–69. Dordrecht: D. Reidel Pub. Co., 1985.

Crone, Patricia. *Slaves on Horses: The Evolution of the Islamic Polity*. Cambridge: Cambridge University Press, 1980.

Dakhlia, Jocelyne. "Dans la mouvance du prince: la symbolique du pouvoir itinérant au Maghreb." *Annales* 3 (1988): 735–60.

Darling, Linda T. "Social Cohesion ('Aṣabiyya) and Justice in the Late Medieval Middle East." *Comparative Studies in Society and History* 49, no. 2 (2007): 329–57.

Davis, Kathleen. *Periodization and Sovereignty: How Ideas of Feudalism and Secularization Govern the Politics of Time*. Philadelphia: University of Pennsylvania Press, 2008.

Delbrück, Hans. *History of the Art of War Within the Framework of Political History*. London: Greenwood Press, 1982.

Derrida, Jacques. *Voyous*. Paris: Galilée, 2003.

Devereux, Andrew Yuen-Gen Liang, Camilo Gómez-Rivas, and Abigail Krasner Balbale. "Unity and Disunity across the Strait of Gibraltar." *Medieval Encounters* 19, nos. 1–2 (2013): 1–40.

Downing, Brian M. *The Military Revolution and Political Change: The Origins of Democracy and Autocracy in Early Modern Europe*. Princeton: Princeton University Press, 1992.

Dozy, Reinhart Pieter Anne. *Dictionnaire détaillé de noms de vêtements chez les Arabes*. Amsterdam: Jean Müller, 1845.

———. *Recherches sur l'histoire et la littérature de l'Espagne*. 2 vols. Leiden: Brill, 1881.

———. *Supplément aux dictionnaires arabes*. 2 vols. Leiden: Brill, 1967.

Dozy, Reinhart Pieter Anne, and W. H. Engelmann. *Glossaire des mots espagnols et portugais dérivés de l'arabe*. Amsterdam: Oriental Press, 1965.

Dufourcq, Charles-Emmanuel. "La Couronne d'Aragon et les Hafsides au XIIIe siècle (1229–1301)." *Analecta Sacra Tarraconensia* 25 (1952): 51–99.

———. *L'Espagne catalane et le Maghreb aux XIIIe et XIVe siècles: De la bataille de Las Navas de Tolosa (1212) à l'avènement du sultan mérinide Abou-l-Hazzan (1331)*. Paris: Presses Universitaires de France, 1966.

———. "Prix et niveaux de vie dans les pays catalans e maghribins à la fin du XIIIe et au début du XIVe siècles." *Le Moyen Âge* 71 (1965): 506–8.

Durán Gudiol, Antonio. "El rito de la coronación del rey en Aragón." *Argensola: revista de ciencias sociales del Instituto de Estudios Altoaragoneses* 103 (1989): 17–40.

Echevarría Arsuaga, Ana. *Caballeros en la frontera: la guardia morisca de los reyes de Castilla, 1410–1467*. Madrid: Universidad Nacional de Educacíon a Distancia, 2006.

———. "De cadí a alcalde mayor. La élite judicial Mudéjar en el siglo XV," *Al-Qanṭara* 1 (2003): 139–68.

———. "La conversion des chevaliers musulmans dans la Castille du xve siècle." In *Conversions islamiques. Identités religieuses en Islam méditerranéen*, edited by Mercedes García-Arenal, 119–38. Paris: Maisonneuve et Larose, 2001.

———. *Knights on the Frontier: The Moorish Guard of the Kings of Castile (1410–1467)*, translated by Martin Beagles. Leiden: Brill, 2009.

Eddé, Anne-Marie, Françoise Micheau, and Christophe Picard. *Communautés chrétiennes en pays d'Islam: Du début du VIIe siècle au milieu du XIe siècle*. Paris: SEDES 1997.

Edido, Pietro. *La colonia saracena di Lucera e la sua distruzione*. Napoli: L. Pierro and Son, 1912.

Eire, Carlos M. N. *War against the Idols: The Reformation of Worship from Erasmus to Calvin*. Cambridge: Cambridge University Press, 1986.

Elshtain, Jean Bethke. *Sovereignty: God, State, and Self*. New York: Basic Books, 2008.

Epalza, Mikel de. "Attitudes politiques de Tunis dans le conflit entre Aragonais et Français en Sicile autour de 1282." In *La società mediterranea all'epoca del Vespero*, 579–601. Palermo: Accademia di scienze lettere, 1983.

———. "Constitución de rábitas en la costa de Almería: su función espiritual." In *Homenaje al Padre Tapia: Almería en su historia*, edited by José Angel Tapia Garrido, 231–35. Almería: CajAlmería, 1988.

Fadel, Mohammad. "Rules, Judicial Discretion, and the Rule of Law in Naṣrid Granada: An Analysis of *al-Ḥadīqa al-mustaqilla al-naḍra fī al-fatāwā al-ṣādira 'an 'ulamā' al-ḥaḍra*." In *Islamic Law: Theory and Practice*, edited by R. Gleave and E. Kermeli, 49–86. London: I. B. Tauris, 1997.

Fancy, Hussein. "The Intimacy of Exception: The Diagnosis of Samuel Abenmenassé." In *Center and Periphery: Studies on Power in the Medieval World in Honor of William Chester Jordan*, edited by Katherine L. Jansen, G. Geltner, and Anne E. Lester, 65–75. Leiden: Brill, 2013.

———. "The Last Almohads: Universal Sovereignty between North Africa and the Crown of Aragon." *Medieval Encounters* 19, no. 1–2 (2013): 102–36.

———. "Monarchs and Minorities: 'Infidel' Soldiers in Mediterranean Courts." In *Globalization of Knowledge in The Post-Antique Mediterranean*, edited by Sonja Brentjes and Jürgen Renn. Burlington: Ashgate, forthcoming.

———. "Theologies of Violence: The Recruitment of Muslim Soldiers by the Crown of Aragon." *Past & Present* 221, no. 1 (2013): 39–73.

Fanjul, Serafín. *Al-Andalus contra España: la forja del mito*. Madrid: Siglo XXI de España, 2002.

———. *La quimera de Al-Andalus*. Madrid: Siglo XXI de España, 2004.

Farge, Arlette, *The Allure of the Archives*, translated by Thomas Scott-Railton. New Haven: Yale University Press, 2013.

Felipe, Helena de. "Berbers in the Maghreb and al-Andalus: Settlements and Toponymy." *Maghreb Review* 18, no. 1–2 (1993): 57–62.

Ferhat, Halima. "Lignages et individus dans le système du pouvoir Almohade." In *Los Almohades: problemas y perspectivas*, edited by Patrice Cressier, Maribel Fierro, and Luis Molina, 685–709. Madrid: Consejo Superior de Investigaciones Científicas, 2005.

Fernández Félix, Ana, "Al-'Utbī (m. 255/869) y su compilación jurídica al-'Utbiyya. Análisis de su contenido legal y de su aportación al estudio del proceso de formación de la sociedad islámica andalusí." PhD dissertation, Universidad Autónoma de Madrid, 1999.

Fernández Félix, Ana, and Maribel Fierro. "Cristianos y conversos al Islam en al-Andalus bajo los Omeyas: Una aproximación al proceso de islamización a través de una fuente legal andalusí del s. III/I." *Anejos de AEspA* 23 (2000): 415–27.

Ferrandis Torré, J. "Espadas granadinas de la jineta." *Archivo español de arte* 16 (1943): 142–66.

Ferrer i Mallol, María Teresa. "Évolution du statut de la minorité islamique dans les pays de la Couronne catalano-aragonaise au XIVe siècle." In *Le Partage du monde: Échanges et colonisation dans la Méditerranée medieval*, edited by Michel Balard and Alain Ducellier, 439–52. Paris: Publications de la Sorbonne, 1998.

———. *La frontera amb l'Islam en el segle XIV: christians i sarraïns al País Valencià*. Barcelona: Consell Superior d'Investigacions Científiques, 1988.

———. *Organització i defensa d'un territori fronterer: la governació d'Oriola en el segle XIV*. Barcelona: Consell Superior d'Investigacions Científiques, Institució Milà i Fontanals, 1990.

———. "La organización militar en Cataluña en la Edad Media." *Revista de historia militar* Extra 1 (2001): 119–222.

———. *Els sarraïns de la corona catalano-aragonesa en el segle XIV: segregació i discriminació*. Barcelona: Consell Superior d'Investigacions Científiques, 1987.

Fierro, Maribel. "Alfonso X 'The Wise': The Last Almohad Caliph?" *Medieval Encounters* 15, no. 2 (2009): 175–98.

———. "Algunas reflexiones sobre el poder itinerante almohade." *e-Spania* 8 (2009), http://e-spania.revues.org/18653.

———. *The Almohad Revolution: Politics and Religion in the Islamic West during the Twelfth–Thirteenth Centuries*. Farnham: Ashgate, 2013.

———. "Conversion, Ancestry and Universal Religion: The Case of the Almohads in the Islamic West (Sixth/Twelfth–Seventh/Thirteenth Centuries)." *Journal of Medieval Iberian Studies* 2, no. 2 (2010): 155–73.

Fletcher, Madeleine. "The Almohad Tawhid: Theology which Relies on Logic." *Numen* 38, no. 1 (1991): 110–27.

Fletcher, Richard. *The Quest for El Cid*. New York: Knopf, 1989.

Font y Rius, José María. "La recepción del derecho romano en la Península Ibérica durante la Edad Media." *Recueil des mémoires et travaux publiés par la Société d'Histoire du Droit et des Institutions des Anciens Pays de Droit Écrit* 6 (1967): 85–104.

Frankenberry, Nancy K., and Hans H. Penner. "Clifford Geertz's Long-Lasting Moods, Motivations, and Metaphysical Conceptions." *Journal of Religion* 79, no. 4 (1999): 617–40.

Freedman, Paul. "The Medieval Other: The Middle Ages as Other." In *Marvels, Monsters, and Miracles: Studies in the Medieval and Early Modern Imaginations,* edited by Timothy S. Jones and David A. Sprunger, 1–26. Kalamazoo: Medieval Institute Publications, 2002.

———. "An Unsuccessful Attempt at Urban Organization in Twelfth-Century Catalonia." *Speculum* 54, no. 3 (1979): 479–91.

Freedman, Paul, and Gabrielle Spiegel. "Medievalisms Old and New: The Rediscovery of Alterity in North American Medieval Studies." *American Historical Review* 103, no. 3 (1998): 677–704.

Friedman, Michael. *A Parting of the Ways: Carnap, Cassirer, and Heidegger*. Chicago: Open Court, 2000.

Fromherz, Allen J. *The Almohads: The Rise of an Islamic Empire*. New York: I. B. Tauris, 2010.

———. "North Africa and the Twelfth-Century Renaissance: Christian Europe and the Almohad Islamic Empire." *Islam and Christian-Muslim Relations* 20, no. 1 (2009): 43–59.

Frye, Richard. *The Heritage of Central Asia*. Princeton: Markus Wiener, 1996.

———. *History of Ancient Iran*. Munich: Beck, 1984.

Fuchs, Barbara. *Exotic Nation: Maurophilia and the Construction of Early Modern Spain*. Philadelphia: University of Pennsylvania Press, 2009.

García-Arenal, Mercedes. *Messianism and Puritanical Reform: Mahdīs of the Muslim West*. Leiden: Brill, 2006.

García-Arenal, Mercédes, and Béatrice Leroy. *Moros y judíos en Navarra en la baja Edad Media*. Madrid: Hiperión, 1984.

García de Cortázar y Ruiz de Aguirre, José Angel. "Las necesidades ineludibles: alimentación, vestido, vivienda." In *La época del gótico en la cultura española*, edited by José Angel García de Cortázar y Ruiz de Aguirre, 5–82. Historia de España Menéndez Pidal, edited by Rámon Menéndez Pidal and José María Jover Zamora, vol. 16. Madrid: Espasa Calpe, 1994.

García Gómez, Emilio. *Ibn Zamrak, el poeta de la Alhambra*. Granada: Patronato de la Alhambra, 1975.

García Fitz, Francisco. *Castilla y León frente al Islam: estrategias de expansión y tácticas militares (siglos XI–XIII)*. Sevilla: Universidad de Sevilla, 1998.

García Sanjuán, Alejandro. "Mercenarios cristianos al servicio de los musulmanes en el Norte de África durante el siglo XIII." In *La Península Ibérica entre el Mediterráneo y el Atlántico. Siglos XIII–XV. Cádiz, 1–4 de Abril de 2003*, edited by Manuel González Jiménez and Isabel Montes Romero-Camacho, 435–47. Cádiz: Diputación de Cádiz, Servicio de Publicaciones 2006.

Gaspar Remiro, M. "Relaciones de la Corona de Aragón con los estados musulmanes de occidente. El negocio de Ceuta entre Jaime II de Aragón y Aburribia Soleiman, sultán de Fez, contra Mohamed III de Granada." *Revista del centro de estudios históricos de Granada* 13, nos. 3–4 (1923): 125–292.

Gautier, Émile-Félix. *La Passé de l'Afrique du Nord: Les Siècles obscurs*. Paris: Payot, 1952.

Gazulla, Faustino D. "Las compañías de Zenetes en el reino de Aragón." *Boletín de la Real Academia de la Historia* 90 (1927): 174–96.

Geertz, Clifford. *The Interpretation of Cultures*. New York: Basic Books, 1977.

———. *Local Knowledge: Further Essays in Interpretive Anthropology*. New York: Basic Books, 1983.

———. *Negara: The Theatre State in Nineteenth-Century Bali*. Princeton: Princeton University Press, 1980.

———. "'The Pinch of Destiny': Religion As Experience, Meaning, Identity, Power." *Raritan* 18, no. 3 (1999): 1–19.

Giménez Soler, Andrés. "Caballeros españoles en Africa y africanos en España." *Revue Hispanique* 12 and 16 (1905): 299–372.

———. "La Corona de Aragón y Granada." *Boletín de la Real Academia de Buenas Letras de Barcelona* 27 (1907): 51–61.

———. *El sitio de Almería en 1309*. Barcelona: Tipografía de la Casa Provincial de Caridad, 1904.

Glick, Thomas F. "Darwin y la filología española." *Boletín de la Institución Libre de Enseñanza*, 2nd epoch, no. 12 (October 1991): 35–41.

———. *Islamic and Christian Spain in the Early Middle Ages: Comparative Perspectives on Social and Cultural Formation*. Leiden: Brill, 1979.

Glick, Thomas F., and Oriol Pi-Sunyer, "Acculturation as an Explanatory Concept in Spanish History." *Comparative Studies in Society and History* 11, no. 2 (1969): 136–54.

Goitein, Shelomo Dov. *A Mediterranean Society: The Jewish Communities of the Arab World as Portrayed in the Documents of the Cairo Geniza*. 6 vols. Berkeley: University of California Press, 1967.

Golden, Peter B. "Khazar Turkic Ghulams in Caliphal Service." *Journal asiatique* 292, no. 1–2 (2004): 279–309.

———. "Some Notes on the *Comitatus* in Medieval Eurasia with Special Reference to the Khazars." *Russian History/Histoire Russe* 28 (2001): 153–70.

———. "The Terminology of Slavery and Servitude in Medieval Turkic." In *Studies on Central Asian History in Honor of Yuri Bregel*, edited by D. DeWeese, 27–56. Bloomington: Indiana University, 2001.

Gómez-Martínez, José Luis. *Américo Castro y el origen de los españoles: historia de una polémica*. Madrid: Gredos, 1975.

Gómez Moreno, Ángel. "El Cid y los héroes de antaño en la guerra civil de España," *eHumanista: Journal of Iberian Studies* 14 (2010): 210–38.

González Alcantud, José Antonio, ed. *Marroquíes en la Guerra Civil española: campos equívocos*. Barcelona: Anthropos, 2003.

González Antón, Luis. *Las Uniones aragoneses y las Cortes del reino, 1283–1301*. 2 vols. Zaragoza: Consejo Superior de Investigaciones Científicas, 1975.

Gordon, Matthew. *The Breaking of a Thousand Swords: A History of the Turkish Military of Samarra, A.H. 200–275/815–889 C.E.* Albany: State University of New York Press, 2001.

Gordon, Peter Eli. "Continental Divide: Ernst Cassirer and Martin Heidegger at Davos, 1929—An Allegory of Intellectual History." *Modern Intellectual History* 1, no. 2 (2004): 219–48.

———. *Continental Divide: Heidegger, Cassirer, Davos*. Cambridge: Harvard University Press, 2010.

———. "The Place of the Sacred in the Absence of God: Charles Taylor's *A Secular Age*." *Journal of the History of Ideas* 69, no. 4 (2008): 647–73.

Gregory, Brad. "The Other Confessional History: On Secular Bias in the Study of Religion." *History and Theory* 45, no. 4 (2006): 132–49.

Gual de Torrella, Mariano. "Milicias cristianas en Berbería." *Boletín de la sociedad arqueológica Luliana* 89 (1973): 54–63.

Guichard, Pierre. *Al-Andalus: estructura antropológica de una sociedad islámica en Occidente*. Barcelona: Barral Editores, 1976.

———. *Les musulmans de Valence et la reconquête: XIe–XIIIe siècles*. 2 vols. Damascus: Institut français de Damas, 1990.

———. "Un seigneur musulman dans l'Espagne chrétienne: le 'ra'is' de Crevillente (1243–1318)." *Mélanges de la Casa de Velázquez* 9 (1973): 283–334.

Hallaq, Wael. *Authority, Continuity, and Change in Islamic Law*. Cambridge: Cambridge University Press, 2001.

Handler, Andrew. "The *'abīd* under the Umayyads of Cordova and the *Mulūk Al-ṭawā'if*." In *Occident and Orient: A Tribute to the Memory of Alexander Scheiber*, edited by Robert Dán, 229–41. Budapest: Akadémiai Kiadó, 1988.

Harvey, L. P. *Islamic Spain, 1250 to 1500*. Chicago: University of Chicago Press, 1990.

Hassan, Zaki Mohamed. *Les Ṭūlūnides: Étude de l'Egypte musulmane à la fin du IXe siècle, 868–905*. Paris: Busson, 1933.

Hendrickson, Jocelyn N. "The Obligation to Emigrate: Al-Wansharīsī's *Asnā Al-Matājir* Reconsidered." PhD dissertation, Emory University, 2009.

Herder, Johan Gottfried. *Ideen zur Philosophie der Geschichte der Menschheit*, in *Sämmtliche Werke*, edited by Berhard Suphan. Berlin: Weidmannsche Buchhandlung, 1909.

Hinojosa, Eduardo. "La admisión del derecho romano en Cataluña." *Boletín de la Real Academia de Buenas Letras de Barcelona* 37 (1910): 209–21.

Hinojosa Montalvo, José. "Armamento de naves y comercio con el reino de Granada a principios del siglo XV." In *Andalucía entre Oriente y Occidente (1236–1492)*, edited by Emilio Cabrera, 643–57. Córdoba: Servicio de Publicaciones, Diputación Provincial de Córdoba, 1988.

———. "Las relaciones entre Valencia y Granada durante el siglo XV: balance de una investigación." In *Estudios sobre Málaga y el reino de Granada en el V centenario de la conquista*, edited by José E. López de Coca Castañer, 83–111. Málaga: Servicio de Publicaciones, Diputación Provincial de Málaga, 1988.

Hopkins, J. F. P. "The Almohad Hierarchy." *Bulletin of the School of Oriental and African Studies* 16 (1954): 93–112.

———. *Medieval Muslim Government in Barbary until the End of the Sixth Century of the Hijra*. London: Luzac, 1958.

Houtman, Dick and Birgit Meyer, eds. *Things: Religion and the Question of Materiality*. New York: Fordham University Press, 2012.

Howard, Thomas Albert. *Protestant Theology and the Making of the Modern German University*. New York: Oxford University Press, 2006.

Hughes, Diane Owen. "Sumptuary Law and Social Relations in Renaissance Italy." In *Disputes and Settlements: Law and Human Relations in the West*, edited by John Bossy, 69–99. Cambridge: Cambridge University Press, 1983.

Huici Miranda, Ambrosio. *Historia musulmana de Valencia y su región: novedades y rectificaciones*. 3 vols. Valencia: Ayuntamiento de Valencia, 1969.

———. *Historia política del imperio Almohade*. 2 vols. Granada: Universidad de Granada, 2000.

Hurd, Elizabeth Shakman. *The Politics of Secularism in International Relations*. Princeton: Princeton University Press, 2008.

———. "The Specific Order of Difficulty of Religion." 30 May 2014, *The Immanent Frame*, accessed 30 May 2014. http://blogs.ssrc.org/tif/2014/05/30/the-specific-order-of-difficulty-of-religion.

Iglesia Ferreirós, Aquilino. *La creación del derecho: antología de textos*. 3rd ed. Madrid: Marcial Pons 1996.

———. "La difusión del derecho común en Cataluña." In *El dret comú i Catalunya*, edited by Aquilino Iglesia Ferreirós, 59–279. Barcelona: Fundació Noguera, 1992.

Iqbal, Allama. *The Reconstruction of Religious Thought in Islam*. Lahore: Shaikh Muhammad Ashraf, 1962 [1934].

ʿIzz al-Dīn, ʿUmar Mūsā. "Al-Tanẓīmāt al-ḥizbiyya ʿinda-l-Muwaḥḥidīn fī-l-Maghrib." *Al-Abḥāth* 23 (1970): 52–89.

Johns, Jeremy. "The Norman Kings of Sicily and the Fatimid Caliphate." *Anglo-Norman Studies* 15 (1993): 133–59.

Jones, Ann Rosalind, and Peter Stallybrass. *Renaissance Clothing and the Materials of Money*. Cambridge: Cambridge University Press, 2000.

Jordan, William Chester. *Women and Credit in Pre-Industrial and Developing Societies*. Philadelphia: University of Pennsylvania Press, 1993.

Juliá Viñamata, J. R. "Jocs de guerra i jocs de lleure a la Barcelona de la baixa edat mitjana." *Revista d'etnologia de Catalunya* 1 (1992): 10–23.

———. "Las manifestaciones lúdico-deportivas de los barceloneses en la Baja Edad Media." In *Espai i temps d'oci a la Història. Actes de les XI jornades d'estudis històrics locals*, edited by Maria Barceló Crespí and Bernat Sureda García, 629–42. Palma de Mallorca: Institut d'Estudis Balèarics, 1993.

Justice, Steven. "Did the Middle Ages Believe in Their Miracles?" *Representations* 103 (2008): 1–29.

———. "Eucharistic Miracle and Eucharistic Doubt." *Journal of Medieval and Early Modern Studies* 42, no. 2 (2012): 307–32.

Kably, Mohammed. *Société, pouvoir et religion au Maroc à la fin du "Moyen-Age."* Paris: Maisonneuve et Larose, 1986.

Kagay, Donald J. "Rebellion on Trial: The Aragonese *Unión* and Its Uneasy Connection to Royal Law, 1265–1301." *Journal of Legal History* 18 (1997): 30–43.

———. *War, Government, and Society in the Medieval Crown of Aragon*. Aldershot: Ashgate, 2007.

Kahn, Victoria. "Political Theology and Fiction in *The King's Two Bodies*." *Representations* 106, no. 1 (2009): 77–101.

Kalās, Fāyiza. "Al-Jaysh 'inda-l-Muwaḥḥidīn." *Dirāsāt Tārīkhiyya* 31–32 (1989): 197–218.

Kantorowicz, Ernst H. *Kaiser Friedrich der Zweite*. Berlin: G. Bondi, 1927.

———. *The King's Two Bodies: A Study in Mediaeval Political Theology*. Princeton: Princeton University Press, 1997 [1957].

Kazhdan, Alexander P., ed. *The Oxford Dictionary of Byzantium*. New York: Oxford University Press, 1991.

Keane, Webb. "Anxious Transcendence." In *The Anthropology of Christianity*, edited by Fenella Cannell, 308–23. Durham: Duke University Press, 2006.

———. *Christian Moderns: Freedom and Fetish in the Mission Encounter*. Berkeley: University of California Press, 2007.

———. "The Hazards of New Clothes: What Signs Make Possible." In *The Art of Clothing: A Pacific Experience*, edited by Susanne Küchler and Graeme Were, 1–16. London: University College London Press, 2005.

———. "Secularism as a Moral Narrative of Modernity." *Transit: Europäische Revue* 43 (2013): 159–70.

Kelsen, Hans. *General Theory of Law and State*, translated by A. Wedberg. New York: Russell & Russell, 1961.

———. *Pure Theory of Law*, translated by M. Knight. Berkeley: University of California Press, 1967 [1960].

Kennedy, Hugh. *Armies of the Caliphs: Military and Society in the Early Islamic State*. London: Routledge, 2001.

Khaneboubi, Ahmed. *Les Premiers sultans mérinides et l'Islam (1269–1331)*. Paris: L'Harmattan, 1987.

Kimmel, Seth. "'In the Choir with the Clerics': Secularism in the Age of Inquisition." *Comparative Literature* 65, no. 3 (2013): 285–305.

Klüpfel, Ludwig. *Die äussere Politik Alfonsos III von Aragonien (1285–1291)*. Berlin: W. Rothschild, 1911.

———. "El règim de la Confederació catalano-aragonesa a finals del segle XIII." *Revista Jurídica de Catalunya* 35 (1929): 195–226 and 289–327, and 36 (1930): 298–331.

Koehler, Henry. *L'Église Chrétienne du Maroc et la mission franciscaine (1221–1790)*. Paris: Société d'éditions franciscaines, 1934.

Koningsveld, Peter Sjoerd van, and Gerard Albert Wiegers. "The Islamic Statute of the Mudejars in the Light of a New Source." *Al-Qanṭara* 17, no. 1 (1996): 19–58.

Kosto, Adam J. *Making Agreements in Medieval Catalonia: Power, Order, and the Written Word, 1000–1200*. Cambridge: Cambridge University Press, 2007.

Lacarra, M. E. "La utilización del Cid de Menéndez Pidal en la ideología franquista." *Ideologies and Literature* 3 (1980): 95–127.

Laclau, Ernesto. "Bare Life or Social Indeterminacy?" In *Agamben: Sovereignty and Life*, edited by Matthew Calarco and Steven DeCaroli, 11–22. Stanford: Stanford University Press, 2007.

Lacoste, Yves. *Ibn Khaldoun: Naissance de l'histoire, passé du Tiers-monde*. Paris: F. Maspero, 1966.

Ladero Quesada, Miguel Ángel. "Una biografía caballeresca del siglo XV: 'La Cronica del yllustre y muy magnifico cauallero don Alonso Perez de Guzman el Bueno.'" *En la España Medieval* 22 (1999): 247–83.

Lagardère, Vincent. *Les Almoravides: Le Djihad Andalou (1106–1143)*. Paris: L'Harmattan, 1998.

———. *Les Almoravides: Jusqu-au règne de Yūsuf b. Tāshfīn*. Paris: L'Harmattan, 1989.

———. "Communautés mozarabes et pouvoir almoravides en 519H/1125 en Andalus." *Studia Islamica* 67 (1988): 99–119.

Laliena Corbera, C. "La adhesión de las ciudades a la Unión: poder real y conflictividad social en Aragón a fines del XIII." *Aragón en la Edad Media* 8 (1989): 319–413.

Lalinde Abadía, J. "Contabilidad e intervención en el Reino aragonés." *Estudios de Hacienda Pública* (1976): 39–55.

Lane, Edward William. *Arabic-English Lexicon*. New York: F. Unger, 1955–56.

Lapiedra Gutiérrez, Eva. "Christian Participation in Almohad Armies and Personal Guards." *Journal of Medieval Iberian Studies* 2, no. 2 (2010): 235–50.

———. *Cómo los musulmanes llamaban a los cristianos hispánicos*. Valencia: Generalitat Valenciana, Conselleria de Cultura, Educació i Ciència, 1997.

———. "Giraldo Sem Pavor: Alfonso Enríquez y los Almohades." In *Bataliús: el reino taifa de Badajoz: estudios,* edited by Fernando Díaz Esteban, 147–58. Madrid: Letrúmero, 1996.

Lappin, Anthony. *The Medieval Cult of Saint Dominic of Silos*. Leeds: Maney, 2002.

Laroui, Abdallah. *L'Histoire du Maghreb: Un Essai de synthèse*. Paris: F. Maspero, 1970.

Lassner, Jacob. *The Shaping of Abbasid Rule*. Princeton: Princeton University Press, 1980.

Latour, Bruno. "Can We Get Our Materialism Back, Please?" *Isis* 98, no. 1 (2007): 138–42.

———. *Rejoicing: or The Torments of Religious Speech*, translated by Julie Rose. Cambridge: Polity Press, 2013.

———. *We Have Never Been Modern*. Cambridge: Harvard University Press, 1993.

Lawrence, Bruce B., ed. *Ibn Khaldun and Islamic Ideology*. Leiden: Brill, 1984.

Lazier, Benjamin. *God Interrupted: Heresy and the European Imagination between the World Wars*. Princeton: Princeton University Press, 2008.

———. "On the Origins of 'Political Theology': Judaism and Heresy between the World Wars." *New German Critique* 105, no. 35 (2008): 143–64.

Lev, Yaacov. "David Ayalon (1914–1998) and the History of Black Military Slavery in Medieval Islam." *Der Islam* 90, no. 1 (2013): 21–43.

Levi-Provençal, Évariste. *Histoire de l'Espagne musulmane*. 3 vols. Paris: Maisonneuve et Larose, 1999.

———. *Un Recueil de lettres officielles Almohades: Étude diplomatique, analyse et commentaire historique*. Paris: Librairie Larose, 1942.

Lévi-Strauss, Claude. *Totemism*, translated by Rodney Needham. Boston: Beacon, 1963.

Lewis, Ewart. "King above Law? 'Quod Principi Placuit' in Bracton." *Speculum* 39, no. 2 (1964): 240–69.

Linehan, Peter. "The Court Historiographer of Francoism? La Leyenda oscura of Ramón Menéndez Pidal." *Bulletin of Hispanic Studies* 73 (1996): 437–50.

———. *History and the Historians of Medieval Spain*. New York: Oxford University Press, 1993.

———. *The Spanish Church and the Papacy in the Thirteenth Century*. Cambridge: Cambridge University Press, 1971.

Lomax, Derek W. *La Orden de Santiago, 1170–1275*. Madrid: Consejo Superior de Investigaciones Científicas, 1965.

Lopes, David. "O Cid portugues: Geraldo Sempavor." *Revista Portuguesa de Historia* 1 (1940): 93–109.

López, Atanasio. *Obispos en la Africa septentrional desde el siglo XIII*. 2nd ed. Tánger: Tip. Hispano Arábiga, 1941.

López de Coca y Castañer, José E. "Caballeros moriscos al servicio de Juan II y Enrique IV, reyes de Castilla." *Meridies: revista de historia medieval* 3 (1996): 119–36.

López García, Bernabé. "Arabismo y orientalismo en España: Radiografía y diagnóstico de un gremio escaso y apartadizo." *Awraq* 11 (1990): 35–69.

———. "Enigmas de al-Andalus: Una polémica." *Revista de Occidente* 224 (2000): 31–50.

———. "30 años de Arabismo Español." *Awraq* 18 (1997): 11–48.

López-Morillas, Consuelo. "Los Beréberes Zanāta en la historia y la leyenda." *Al-Andalus* 42, no. 2 (1977): 301–22.

López-Morillas, Juan. *The Krausist Movement and Ideological Change in Spain, 1854–1874*, translated by Frances M. López-Morillas. Cambridge: Cambridge University Press, 1981.

López Rodríguez, Carlos. "Orígenes del Archivo de la Corona de Aragón (en tiempos, Archivo Real de Barcelona)." *Hispania* 67, no. 226 (2007): 413–454.

Lorenzo Villanueva, Joaquín. *Viage literario a las iglesias de España*. 22 vols. in 11. Madrid, 1802–51.

Lot, Ferdinand. *L'Art militaire et les armées au moyen âge en Europe et dans le Proche Orient*. 2 vols. Paris: Payot, 1946.

Lourie, Elena. "Anatomy of Ambivalence: Muslims under the Crown of Aragon in the Late Thirteenth Century." In *Crusade and Colonisation: Muslims, Christians, and Jews in Medieval Aragon*, 1–77. Aldershot: Variorum, 1990.

———. "Free Moslems in the Balearics under Christian Rule in the Thirteenth Century." *Speculum* 45, no. 4 (1970): 624–49.

———. *Crusade and Colonisation: Muslims, Christians and Jews in Medieval Aragon*. Aldershot: Variorum, 1990.

———. "A Jewish Mercenary in the Service of the King of Aragon." *Revue des études juives* 137 (1978): 367–73.

Lower, Michael. "Ibn al-Lihyani: Sultan of Tunis and Would-Be Christian Convert (1311–1318)." *Mediterranean Historical Review* 24, no. 1 (2009): 17–27.

———. "The Papacy and Christian Mercenaries of Thirteenth-Century North Africa." *Speculum* 89, no. 3 (2014): 601–31.

Lowney, Chris. *A Vanished World: Medieval Spain's Golden Age of Enlightenment*. New York: Free Press, 2005.

Lüdtke, Helmut. "Sobre el origen de cat. *genet*, cast. *jinete*, 'caballero armado de lanza i adarga.'" *Estudis Romànics* 8 (1961): 117–19.

Mahdi, Muhsin. *Ibn Khaldūn's Philosophy of History: A Study in the Philosophic Foundation of the Science of Culture*. Chicago: University of Chicago Press, 1971.

Mahmood, Saba. *Politics of Piety: The Islamic Revival and the Feminist Subject*. Princeton: Princeton University Press, 2012.

Maíllo Salgado, Felipe. "Contenido, uso e historia de termino 'enaciado.'" *Cahiers de linguistique hispanique medieval* 8 (1983): 157–64.

———. "Precisiones para la historia de un grupo étnico-religioso: los farfanes." *Al-Qanṭara* 4 (1983): 265–81.

Makdisi, Ussama S. *The Culture of Sectarianism: Community, History and Violence in Nineteenth-Century Ottoman Lebanon*. Berkeley: University of California Press, 2000.

Malabou, Catherine. "The King's Two (Biopolitical) Bodies." *Representations* 127, no. 1 (2014): 98–106.

Manzano Moreno, Eduardo. "Qurtuba: Algunas reflexiones críticas sobre el califato de Córdoba y el mito de la convivencia." *Awraq: Estudios sobre el mundo árabe e islámico contemporáneo* 7 (2013): 225–46.

Manzano Rodríguez, Miguel Ángel. *La intervención de los Benimerines en la Península Ibérica*. Madrid: Consejo Superior de Investigaciones Científicas, 1992.

María de Brocà, Guillermo. *Historia del derecho de Cataluña, especialmente del civil y exposición de las instituciones del derecho civil del mismo territorio en relación con el Código civil de España y la jurisprudencia*. Barcelona: Herederos de Juan Gil, 1918.

Martínez Carrillo, María de los Llanos. "Historicidad de los 'Miraculos Romançados' de Pedro Marín (1232–1293): el territorio y la esclavitud granadinos." *Anuario de estudios medievales* 21 (1991): 69–97.

Martínez Ferrando, Jesús Ernesto. *El Archivo de la Corona de Aragón*. Barcelona: Ediciones Aymá, 1944.

Martínez y Martínez, Francisco. *Còses de la meua tèrra (La Marina)*. 3 vols. Valencia: Impr. Fills de Francés Vives Mòra, 1920.

Masdeu, J. F. de. *Historia crítica de España y de la cultura Española*. 20 vols. Madrid, 1783–1805.

Masià i de Ros, Àngels. *La Corona de Aragón y los estados del Norte de África: política de Jaime II y Alfonso IV en Egipto, Ifriquía y Tremecén*. Barcelona: I.E.E.M. 1951.

———. *Jaume II: Aragó, Granada, i Marroc: apportació documental*. Barcelona: Consell Superior d'Investigacions Científiques, [1951] 1989.

———. "El Maestre Racional en la Corona de Aragón." *Hispania* 10 (1950): 25–60.

Masuzawa, Tomoko. *The Invention of World Religions, Or, How European Universalism Was Preserved in the Language of Pluralism*. Chicago: University of Chicago Press, 2005.

Mauss, Marcel. *Essai sur le don: Forme et raison de l'échange dans les sociétés archaïques*. Paris: Press Universitaires de France, 1950 [1925].

Mayer, Hans Eberhard. "Das Pontifikale von Tyrus und die Krönung der lateinischen Könige von Jerusalem: Zugleich ein Beitrag zur Forschung über Herrschaftszeichen und Staatssymbolik." *Dumbarton Oaks Papers* 21 (1967): 141–232.

Menéndez-Pidal, Gonzalo, and Carmen Bernis Madrazo. "Las Cantigas: la vida en el s. XIII según la representación iconográfica. (II) Traje, Aderezo, Afeites." *Cuadernos de la Alhambra* 15–17 (1979–81): 89–154.

Menéndez Pidal, Ramón. *La España del Cid*. 2 vols. Madrid: Editorial Plutarco, 1929.

Menocal, María Rosa. *The Ornament of the World: How Muslims, Jews, and Christians Created a Culture of Tolerance in Medieval Spain*. Boston: Little, Brown, 2002.

Mercier, Louis. *La Chasse et les sports chez les Arabes*. Paris: M. Rivière, 1927.

Metcalfe, Alex. *The Muslims of Medieval Italy*. Edinburgh: Edinburgh University Press, 2009.

Meouak, Mohamed. "Hiérarchie des fonctions militaire et corps d'armé en al-Andalus Umayyade (IIe/VIIIe–IVe/Xe Siècles): Nomenclature et essai d'interprétation." *Al-Qantara* 14, no. 2 (1993): 361–92.

———. "Slaves, noirs et affranchise dans les armies Fatimides d'Ifrîqiya: Histoires et trajectoires 'marginales.'" In *D'esclaves à soldats: Miliciens et soldats d'origine servile XIIIe–XXIe siècles*, edited by Carmen Bernand and Alessandro Stella, 15–37. Paris: L'Hartmattan, 2006.

Meyerson, Mark D. *The Muslims of Valencia in the Age of Fernando and Isabel: Between Coexistence and Crusade*. Berkeley: University of California Press, 1991.

———. "Slavery and the Social Order: Mudejars and Christians in the Kingdom of Valencia." *Medieval Encounters*, 1, no. 1 (1995): 144–73.

Miethke, Jürgen. "The Concept of Liberty in William of Ockham." *Collection de l'École française de Rome* 147 (1991): 89–100.

Milbank, John. *Theology and Social Theory: Beyond Secular Reason*. Oxford: Wiley-Blackwell, 2006.

Miller, Kathryn A. *Guardians of Islam: Religious Authority and Muslim Communities of Late Medieval Spain*. New York: Columbia University Press, 2008.

Miret y Sans, Joaquín. "Escolars catalans al estudi de Bolonia en la XIIIe centuria." *Boletín de la Real Academia de Buenas Letras de Barcelona* 8 (1915–16): 137–55.

———. *Itinerari de Jaume I, "el Conqueridor."* Barcelona: Institut d'estudis Catalans, 1918.

———. "Les médecins Juifs de Pierre, roi d'Aragon." *Revue des études juives* 57 (1909): 268–78.

Molénat, Jean-Pierre. "L'élite Mudéjare dans la Péninsule Ibérique médiévale." In *Elites e redes clientelares na Idade Média: problemas metodológicos*, edited by F. T. Barata, 45–53. Lisbon, 2001.

———. "L'organization militaire des Almohades." In *Los almohades: problemas y perspectivas*, edited by Patrice Cressier, Maribel Fierro, and Luis Molina, 547–65. Madrid: Consejo Superior de Investigaciones Científicas, 2005.

———. "Le problème de la permanence des musulmans dans les territories conquis par les chrétiens, du point de vue de la loi islamique." *Arabica* 48, no. 3 (2001): 392–400.

Molina López, Emilio. *Ceyt Abu Ceyt: novedades y rectificaciones*. Almería: Universidad de Almería, 1977.

Mollat, Michel. "Le 'Passage' de Saint Louis à Tunis: Sa place dans l'histoire des croisades." *Revue d'histoire des doctrines économique et sociale* 50, no. 4 (1972): 289–303.

Monroe, James T. *Islam and Arabs in Spanish Scholarship (Sixteenth Century to the Present)*. Leiden: E. J. Brill, 1970.

Montagut i Estragués, Tomàs de. *El Mestre Racional a la Corona d'Aragó (1283–1419)*. Barcelona: Fundació Noguera, 1987.

Montero, Ana M. "A Possible Connection between the Philosophy of the Castilian King Alfonso X and the Risālat Ḥayy ibn Yaqẓān by Ibn Ṭufayl." *Al-Masaq: Islam and the Medieval Mediterranean* 18, no. 1 (2006): 1–26.

Moreno Alonso, Manuel. *Historiografía romántica española: introducción al estudio de la historia en el siglo XIX*. Sevilla: Universidad, Servicio de Publicaciones, 1979.

Morizot, Jean. *L'Aurès ou le myth de la montagne rebelle*. Paris: L'Harmattan, 1991.

Moxó Monotliu, F. de. "Jaume II y la nueva concesión de títulos nobiliarios en la España del siglo XIV." *Anales de la Universidad de Alicante: Historia medieval* 9 (1992–1993): 133–43.

Muldoon, James. *Popes, Lawyers, and Infidels: The Church and the Non-Christian World, 1250–1550*. Philadelphia: University of Pennsylvania Press, 1979.

Mu'nis, Ḥusayn. "Asnā al-matājir fī bayān aḥkām man ghalaba 'alā waṭanihi al-Naṣārā wa-lam yuhājir, wa-mā yatarattabu 'alayhi min al-'uqūbāt wa'l-zawājir." *Revista del Instituto Egipcio de estudios Islamicos en Madrid* 5 (1957): 15–18.

Nederman, Cary J. "Tolerance and Community: A Medieval Communal Functionalist Argument for Religious Toleration." *Journal of Politics* 56, no. 4 (1994): 901–18.

Newby, Gordon D. "Ibn Khaldun and Frederick Jackson Turner: Islam and the Frontier Experience." In *Ibn Khaldun and Islamic Ideology*, ed. Bruce B. Lawrence, 122–32. Leiden: Brill, 1984.

Nirenberg, David. "Conversion, Sex, and Segregation: Jews and Christians in Medieval Spain." *American Historical Review* 107, no. 4 (2002): 1065–93.

———. "Was There Race Before Modernity? The Example of 'Jewish' Blood in Late Medieval Spain." In *The Origins of Racism in the West*, edited by Ben Isaac, Yossi Ziegler, and Miriam Eliav-Feldon, 232–64. Cambridge University Press, 2009.

———. *Anti-Judaism: The Western Tradition*. New York: W. W. Norton & Co., 2013.

———. *Communities of Violence: Persecution of Minorities in the Middle Ages*. Princeton: Princeton University Press, 1996.

———. *Neighboring Faiths: Christianity, Judaism, and Islam in the Middle Ages and Today*. Chicago: University of Chicago Press, 2014.

Nisbet, Robert A. *The Sociological Tradition*. New York: Basic Books, 1966.

Norris, H. T. *The Berbers in Arabic Literature*. New York: Longman, 1982.

———. "New Evidence on the Life of 'Abdullāh b. Yasīn and the Origins of the Almoravid Movement." *Journal of African History* 12, no. 2 (1971): 255–68.

Novikoff, Alex. "Between Tolerance and Intolerance in Medieval Spain: An Historiographic Enigma." *Medieval Encounters* 1, no. 2 (2005): 7–36.

Nykl, A. R. *Hispano-Arabic poetry and Its Relations with the Old Provençal Troubadours*. Baltimore: Johns Hopkins University Press, 1946.

Oakley, Francis. "Jacobean Political Theology: The Absolute and Ordinary Powers of the King." *Journal of the History of Ideas* 29 (1968): 323–46.

Olsen, Glenn. "The Middle Ages in the History of Toleration: A Prolegomena." *Mediterranean Studies* 16, no. 1 (2007): 1–20.

Oman, Charles. *The Art of War in the Middle Ages, 378–1515*. Ithaca: Cornell University Press, 1953.

Otero Varela, Alfonso. "Sobre la 'plenitud o potestatis' y los reinos hispánicos." *Anuario de historia del derecho español* 34 (1964): 141–62.

Parry, Jonathan. "The Gift, the Indian Gift and the 'Indian Gift.'" *Man* 21, no. 3 (1986): 453–73.

Pasamar Alzura, Gonzalo. *Historiografía, e ideología en la postguerra Española: la ruptura de la tradición liberal*. Zaragoza: Universidad de Zaragoza, 1991.

Patterson, Lee. "On the Margin: Postmodernism, Ironic History, and Medieval Studies." *Speculum* 65, no. 1 (1990): 87–108.

Patterson, Orlando. *Slavery and Social Death: A Comparative Study*. Cambridge: Harvard University Press, 1985.

Pennington, Kenneth. *The Prince and the Law, 1200–1600: Sovereignty and Rights in the Western Legal Tradition*. Berkeley: University of California Press, 1993.

Pérez Castañera, D. M. "Aproximación a almogávares y almogaverías en la frontera con Granada." In *Estudios de frontera. Alcalá la Real y el Arcipreste de Hita*, edited by Francisco Toro Ceballos and José Rodríguez Molina, 569–82. Jaén: Diputación Provincial de Jaén, 1996.

Pérez Martín, Antonio. "La institución real en el 'ius commune' y en las *Partidas*." *Cahiers de linguistique hispanique médiévale* 23, no. 1 (2000): 305–21.

Pérez Pascual, José Ignacio. *Ramón Menéndez Pidal: ciencia y pasió*, Valladolid, 1998.

Peterson, Derek R. and Darren R. Walhof. *The Invention of Religion: Rethinking Belief in Politics and History*. New Brunswick: Rutgers University Press, 2002.

Pipes, Daniel. *Slave Soldiers and Islam: The Genesis of a Military System*. New Haven: Yale University Press, 1981.

Post, Gaines. "Roman Law and Early Representation in Spain and Italy, 1150–1250." *Speculum* 18, no. 2 (1943): 211–32.

Powers, David S. "Fatwās as Sources for Legal and Social History: A Dispute over Endowment Revenues from Fourteenth-Century Fez." *Al-Qanṭara* 11, no. 2 (1990): 295–341.

———. *Law, Society, and Culture in the Maghrib, 1300–1500*. Cambridge: Cambridge University Press, 2002.

Powers, James F. *A Society Organized for War: The Iberian Municipal Militias in the Central Middle Ages, 1000–1284*. Berkeley: University of California Press, 1988.

Pranger, M. B. "Religious Indifference: On the Nature of Medieval Christianity." In *Religion: Beyond a Concept*, edited by Hent de Vries, 514–23. New York: Fordham University Press, 2008.

al-Qadi, Wadad. "Non-Muslims in the Muslim Army in Early Islam: A Case Study in the Dialogue of the Sources." In *Orientalism: A Dialogue of Cultures*, edited Sami A. Khasawnih, 109–59. Amman: University of Jordan, 2004.

Querol y Roso, Luis. *Las milicias valencianas desde el siglo xiii al xv: contribución al estudio de la organización militar del antiguo reino de Valencia*. Castellón: Sociedad Castellonense de Cultura, 1935.

Ramis i Ramis, Joan. *Les Illes Balears en temps cristians fins als àrabs*. Maó: Institut Menorquí d'Estudis, 1988.

Riquer, Martín de. *Los trovadores: historia literaria y textos*. 3 vols. Barcelona: Editorial Planeta, 1975.

Robertson, Kellie. "Medieval Things: Materiality, Historicism, and the Premodern Object." *Literature Compass* 5, no. 6 (2008): 1060–80.

Roca Traver, Francisco. "Un siglo de vida Mudéjar en la Valencia medieval (1238–1338)." *Estudios de Edad Media de la Corona de Aragón* 5 (1952): 115–208.

Rodríguez Magda, Rosa María. *Inexistente Al Ándalus: de cómo los intelectuales reinventan el Islam*. Barcelona: Nobel, 2008.

Rodríguez Mediano, Fernando. "Delegación de Asuntos Indígenas, S2N2. Gestón racial en el protectorado Español en Marruecos." *Awraq* 20 (1999): 173–206.

Romano, David. "Los funcionarios judíos de Pedro el Grande de Aragón." *Boletín de la Real Academia de Buenas Letras de Barcelona* 33 (1969): 5–41.

———. "Los hermanos Abenmenassé al servicio de Pedro el Grande de Aragón." *Homenaje a Millás Vallicrosa* 1 (1956): 243–92.

———. "Judíos, escribanos y trujamanes de árabe en la Corona de Aragón (reinados de Jaime I a Jaime II)." *Sefarad* 38 (1978): 71–105.

———. *Judíos al servicio de Pedro el Grande de Aragón (1276–1285)*. Barcelona: Universidad de Barcelona, 1983.

Rosa de Madariaga, María. *Los moros que trajo Franco: la intervención de tropas coloniales en la guerra*. Barcelona: Martínez Roca, 2002.

Rosenmann, Barry Charles. "The Royal Tombs in the Monastery of Santes Creus." PhD dissertation, University of Minnesota, 1991.

Rosenthal, Franz. "Ibn Khaldun in His Time (May 27, 1332–March 17, 1406)." In *Ibn Khaldun and Islamic Ideology*, ed. Bruce B. Lawrence, 14–26. Leiden: Brill, 1984.

Ross, Dorothy. "On the Misunderstanding of Ranke and the Origins of the Historical Profession in America." *Syracuse Scholar* 9 (1988): 31–41.

Rouighi, Ramzi. "The Andalusi Origins of the Berbers?" *Journal of Medieval Iberian Studies* 2, no. 1 (2010): 93–108.

———. *The Making of a Mediterranean Emirate: Ifrīqiyā and Its Andalusis, 1200–1400*. Philadelphia: University of Pennsylvania Press, 2011.

Round, Nicholas. *The Greatest Man Uncrowned: A Study of the Fall of Don Alvaro de Luna*. London: Tamesis Books, 1986.

Ruehl, Martin A. "'In This Time without Emperors': The Politics of Ernst Kantorowicz's *Kaiser Friedrich der Zweite* Reconsidered." *Journal of the Warburg and Courtauld Institutes* 63 (2000): 187–242.

Ruiz, Teofilo F. "Elite and Popular Culture in Late Fifteenth-Century Castilian Festivals: The Case of Jaén." In *City and Spectacle in Medieval Europe*, edited by Barbara Hanawalt and Kathryn Reyerson, 296–381. Minneapolis: University of Minnesota, 1994.

———. "Festivés, colours, et symbols du pouvoir en Castille au XVe siècle." *Annales* 3 (1991): 521–46.

Ruiz Asencio, J. M. "Rebeliones leonesas contra Vermudo II." *Archivos Leoneses* 23 (1969): 215–41.

Ruiz Domènec, J. E. "Las cartas de Reverter, vizconde de Barcelona." *Boletin de la Real Academia de Buenas Letras de Barcelona* 39 (1982–85): 93–118.

Sabbane, Abdellatif. *Le gouvernement et l'administration de la dynastie Almohade (XIIe–XIIIe siècles)*. Lille: Atelier national de reproduction des thèses, 2000.

Sahlins, Marshall. *How "Natives" Think: About Captain Cook, for Example*. Chicago: University of Chicago Press, 1995.

Salicrú i Lluch, Roser. "Caballeros granadinos emigrantes y fugitivos en la corona de Aragón durante el reinado de Alfonso el Magnánimo." In *II Estudios de la frontera. Actividad y vida en la frontera. Congreso Internacional en memoria de Don Claudio Sánchez Albornoz*, edited by Francisco Toro Ceballos and José Rodríguez Molina, 727–48. Jaén: Diputación Provincial de Jáen, 1998.

———. "Mercenaires castillans au Maroc au début du XVe siècle." In *Migrations et diasporas Méditerranéennes (Xe–XVIe siècles)*, edited by Michel Balard and Alain Ducellier, 417–34. Paris: Publications de la Sorbonne, 2002.

Sālim, ʻAbd al-ʻAzīz. *Ta'rīkh madīnat al-Mariyya al-islāmiyya*. Beirut, 1969.

Sánchez Albornoz, Claudio. *España: un enigma histórico*. Buenos Aires: Editorial Sudamericana, 1956.

Sánchez Ruano, Francisco. *Islam y Guerra Civil Española: moros con Franco y la República*. Madrid: La Esfera de los Libros, 2004.

Savage, E. *A Gateway to Hell, a Gateway to Paradise: The North African Response to the Arabic Conquest*. Princeton: Princeton University Press, 1997.

Schadek, Hans. "Die Familiaren der Sizilischen und Aragonischen Könige im 12. und 13. Jahrhundert." *Spanische Forschungen der Görres-gesellschaft: Gesammelte Aufsätze zur Kulturgeschichte Spaniens* 26 (1971): 201–348.

Schleiermacher, Friedrich. *On Religion: Speeches to Its Cultured Despisers*, translated by Richard Crouter. Cambridge: Cambridge University Press, 1988.

Schmitt, Carl. *Political Theology: Four Chapters on the Concept of Sovereignty*, translated by George Schwab. Chicago: University of Chicago Press, 2006.

———. *Politische Theologie*, 2nd ed. Berlin: Duncker & Humblot, 1934.

Schroeder, H. J. *Disciplinary Decrees of the General Councils: Text, Translation and Commentary*. St. Louis: B. Herder, 1937.

Scott, David, and Charles Hirschkind, ed. *Powers of the Secular Modern: Talal Asad and His Interlocutors*. Stanford: Stanford University Press, 2006.

Scott, James. *Weapons of the Weak: Everyday Forms of Peasant Resistance*. New Haven: Yale University Press, 1985.

Scott, Walter. *Ivanhoe*. London: Penguin, 2000.

Serrano, Delfina. "Dos fetuas sobre la expulsión de mozárabes al Magreb en 1126." *Anaquel de estudios árabes* 2 (1991): 163–82.

Shaban, M. A. *Islamic History: A New Interpretation*. Cambridge: Cambridge University Press, 1976.

Shatzmiller, Maya. *The Berbers and the Islamic State: The Marinid Experience in Pre-Protectorate Morocco*. Princeton: Markus Wiener, 2000.

———. *L'Historiographie mérinide: Ibn Khaldūn et ses contemporains*. Leiden: Brill 1982.

Shaw, Donald L. "The Anti-Romantic Reaction in Spain." *Modern Language Review* 63 (1968): 606–11.

Sheehan, Jonathan. *The Enlightenment Bible: Translation, Scholarship, Culture*. Princeton: Princeton University Press, 2005.

———. "Sacred and Profane: Idolatry, Antiquarianism and the Polemics of Distinction in the Seventeenth Century." *Past & Present* 192, no. 1 (2006): 35–66.

———. "Sacrifice before the Secular," *Representations* 105, no. 1 (2009): 12–36.

———. "When Was Disenchantment? History and the Secular Age." In *Varieties of Secularism in a Secular Age*, edited by Michael Warner, Jonathan VanAntwerpen, and Craig J. Calhoun, 217–42. Cambridge: Harvard University Press, 2010.

Shneidman, J. Lee. "Aragon and the War of the Sicilian Vespers." *Historian* 22, no. 3 (1960): 250–63.

———. "Jews as Royal Bailiffs in Thirteenth Century Aragon." *Historia Judaica* 19 (1957): 55–66.

———. "Jews in the Royal Administration of 13th Century Aragón." *Historia Judaica* 21 (1959): 37–52.

———. "Political Theory and Reality in Thirteenth Century Aragon." *Hispania: Revista española de historia* 22 (1962): 171–85.

Simmel, Georg. "Adornment." In *The Sociology of Georg Simmel*, ed. K. H. Wolff, 338–44. New York: Free Press, 1950 [1923].

———. *Der Krieg und die geistigen Entscheidungen: Reden und Aufsätze*. München: Dunker & Humblot, 1917.

Sinor, Denis. "The Mongols and Western Europe." In *A History of the Crusades*, edited by Kenneth Meyer Setton. *The Fourteenth and Fifteenth Centuries,* edited by Harry W. Hazard, vol. 3, 513–44. Madison: University of Wisconsin Press, 1969–89.

Smith, Damian J. *Innocent III and the Crown of Aragon: The Limits of Papal Authority*. Burlington: Ashgate, 2004.

Sobrequés Vidal, Santiago. *Els barons a Catalunya*. Barcelona: Vicens-Vives, 1961.

Soifer, Maya. "Beyond Convivencia: Critical Reflections on the Historiography of Interfaith Relations in Christian Spain." *Journal of Medieval Iberian Studies* 1, no. 1 (2009): 19–35.

Solal, E. "Au tournant de l'histoire méditerranéenne du Moyen Âge: L'Expédition de Pierre III d'Aragon à Collo (1282)." *Revue Africaine* 101 (1957): 247–71.

Soldevila, Ferran. *Pere el Gran*. 2 vols. Barcelona: Institut d'estudis catalans, 1950–6.

———. *Vida de Jaume I el Conqueridor*. Barcelona: Aedos, 1958.

Soler del Campo, Alvaro. *La evolución del armamento medieval en el Reino Castellano-Leonés y al-Andalus (siglos XII–XIV)*. Madrid: Servicio de publicaciones del E.M.E., 1993.

Stillman, Norman. "The Moroccan Jewish Experience." *Jerusalem Quarterly* 9 (1978): 111–23.

———. "Muslims and Jews in Morocco." *Jerusalem Quarterly* 5 (1977): 76–83.

Strauss, Leo. "Jerusalem and Athens: Some Introductory Reflections." *Commentary*, no. 43 (1967): 45–57.

Strayer, Joseph R., ed. *Dictionary of the Middle Ages*. 13 vols. New York: Scribner, 1982–89.

Strayer, Joseph R. "The Crusade Against Aragon." *Speculum* 28, no. 1 (1953): 102–13.

———. "The Laicization of French and English Society in the Thirteenth Century." *Speculum* 15, no. 1 (1940): 76–86.

———. *On the Medieval Origins of the Modern State*. Princeton: Princeton University Press, 1970.

Stroumsa, Sarah. *Freethinkers of Medieval Islam: Ibn al-Rawandi, Abu Bakr al-Razi, and Their Impact on Islamic Thought*. Leiden: Brill, 1999.

———. "Philosophes almohades? Averroès, Maïmonide et l'idéologie almohade." In *Los almohades: problemas y perspectivas*, edited by Patrice Cressier, Maribel Fierro, and Luis Molina, vol. 2, 1137–62. Madrid: Consejo Superior de Investigaciones Científicas, 2005.

Szpiech, Ryan. "The Convivencia Wars: Decoding Historiography's Polemic with Philology." In *A Sea of Languages: Rethinking the Arabic Role in Medieval Literary History*, edited by Suzanne Conklin Akbari and Karla Mallette. Toronto: University of Toronto Press, 2013.

Tapia Garrido, José Angel. *Almería musulmana*. 2 vols. Almería, 1976–77.

Taussig, Michael. *Defacement: Public Secrecy and the Labor of the Negative*. Stanford: Stanford University Press, 1999.

Taylor, Charles. *A Secular Age*. Cambridge: Belknap Press of Harvard University Press, 2007.

Taylor, Julie Anne. *Muslims in Medieval Italy: The Colony at Lucera*. Lanham: Lexington Book, 2005.

Thoreau, Henry David. *The Portable Thoreau*, edited by Carl Bode. New York: Penguin, 1982.

Tierney, Brian. "Bracton on Government." *Speculum* 38 (1963): 295–317.

———. "'The Prince Is Not Bound by the Laws': Accursius and the Origins of the Modern State." *Comparative Studies in Society and History* 5 (1963): 389–400.

Tilly, Charles. *Coercion, Capital, and European states, AD 990–1990*. Cambridge: Blackwell, 1990.

Titone, Fabrizio. "Aragonese Sicily as a Model of Late Medieval State Building." *Viator* 44, no. 1 (2013): 217–250.

Tolan, John Victor. "Using the Middle Ages to Construct Spanish Identity: 19th and 20th Century Spanish Historiography of Reconquest." In *Historiographical Approaches to Medieval Colonization of East Central Europe*, edited by Jan Piskorski, 329–47. Boulder: East European Monographs, 2002.

Töllner, Helmut. *Die türkischen Garden am Kalifenhof von Samarra; ihre Entstehung und Machtergreifung bis zum Kalifat Al-Mu'tadids*. Walldorf-Hessen: Verlag für Orientkunde, 1971.

Torremocha Silva, Antonio. "Al-Binya: la ciudad palaciega merini en Al-Andalus." In *Ciudad y territorio en Al-Andalus*, edited by Maria del Carmen Barceló Torres, 283–330. Granada: Universidad de Granada, 2000.

———. *Algeciras entre la cristianidad y el islam: estudio sobre el cerco y conquista de Algeciras por el rey Alfonso XI de Castilla, así como de la ciudad y sus términos hasta el final de la Edad Media*. Algeciras: Instituto de Estudios Campogibraltareños, 1994.

Torres Fontes, Juan, ed. *Repartimiento de Lorca*. Murcia: Ayuntamiento de Lorca, Academia Alfonso X El Sabio, 1994.

Torres Fontes, Juan. "La actividad bélica granadina en la frontera murciana (ss. XIII–XV)." *Príncipe de Viana Anejo* 2–3 (1986): 721–40.

———. "El adalid en la frontera de Granada." *Anuario de estudios medievales* 15 (1985): 345–66.

Torró Abad, Josep. *El naixement d'una colònia: dominació i resistència a la frontera Valenciana, 1238–1276*. Alicante: Institut de Cultura Juan Gil-Albert, Diputació Provincial d'Alacant, 1999.

Trautmann, Thomas R. *Dravidian Kinship*. Cambridge: Cambridge University Press, 1981.

Treagold, Warren. *Byzantium and Its Army, 284–1081*. Stanford: Stanford University Press, 1995.

Turki, Abdel Majid. "Consultation juridique d'al-Imam al-Māzarī sur le cas des musulmans vivant en Sicile sous l'autorité des Normands." *Mélanges de l'Université Saint-Joseph*, 50, no. 2 (1984): 691–704.

Ullmann, Walter. "The Development of the Medieval Idea of Sovereignty." *English Historical Review* 64, no. 250 (1949): 1–33.

Urvoy, Dominique. "La Pensée d'Ibn Tumart." *Bulletin d'études orientales* 27 (1974): 19–44.

Vaissière, Etienne de la. *Histoire des marchands sogdiens*. Paris: Collège de France, Institut des hautes études chinoise, 2002.

———. *Samarcande et Samarra: Élites d'Asie centrale dans l'empire Abbasside*. Paris: Association pour l'avancement des études iraniennes, 2007.

Valérian, Dominique. "Les agents de la diplomatie des souverains maghrébins avec le monde chrétien (XIIe–XVe siècles)." *Anuario de estudios medievales* 38, no. 2 (2008): 885–900.

———. *Bougie, port maghrébin, 1067–1510*. Rome: École française de Rome, 2006.

VanLandingham, Marta. *Transforming the State: King, Court and Political Culture in the Realms of Aragon, 1213–1387*. Leiden: Brill, 2002.

Vernet, Juan. *Lo que Europa debe al islam de España*. Barcelona: El Acantilado, 1999.

Vidal, César. *España frente al islam: de Mahoma a Ben Laden*. Madrid: La Esfera de los Libros, 2004.

Vidal Castro, Francisco. "Historia política." In *El reino nazarí de Granada (1232–1492): política, instituciones, espacio y economía*, edited by María Jesús Viguera Molíns, 47–248. Historia de España Menéndez Pidal, edited by Rámon Menéndez Pidal and José María Jover Zamora, vol. 8/3. Madrid: Espasa Calpe, 2000.

Viguera Molins, María Jesús. "El ejército." In *El reino Nazarí de Granada (1232–1492): política, instituciones, espacio y economía*, edited by María Jesús Viguera Molins, 431–73. Historia de España Menéndez Pidal, edited by Rámon Menéndez Pidal and José María Jover Zamora, vol. 8/3. Madrid: Espasa Calpe, 2000.

———. "La organización militar en Al-Andalus." *Revista de historia militar* Extra 1 (2001): 17–60.

Vinyoles i Vidal, Teresa María. *La vida quotidiana a Barcelona vers 1400*. Barcelona: R. Dalmau, 1985.

Vries, Hent de. *Religion: Beyond a Concept*. New York: Fordham University Press, 2008.

Warner, Michael, Jonathan VanAntwerpen, and Craig J. Calhoun, ed. *Varieties of Secularism in a Secular Age*. Cambridge: Harvard University Press, 2010.

Whittow, Mark. *The Making of Byzantium, 600–1025*. Berkeley: University of California Press, 1996.

Wieruszowski, Helene. "Conjuraciones y alianzas políticas del Rey Pedro de Aragón contra Carlos de Anjou antes de las vísperas Sicilianas." *Boletín de la Real Academia de la Historia* 107 (1935): 547–602.

———. "La Corte di Pietro d'Aragona e i precedenti dell'impresa Siciliana." *Archivio storico italiano* 16–17 (1938): 141–62, 200–17 [reprinted in *Politics and Culture in Medieval Spain and Italy*, 182–222. Roma: Edizioni di storia e letteratura, 1971].

———. *Politics and Culture in Medieval Spain and Italy*. Roma: Edizioni di storia e letteratura, 1971.

———. "The Rise of the Catalan Language in the 13th Century." *Modern Language Notes* (1944): 9–20.

Winer, Rebecca Lynn. *Women, Wealth and Community in Perpignan, c. 1250–1300: Christians, Jews, and Enslaved Muslims in a Medieval Mediterranean Town*. Burlington: Ashgate, 2006.

Zakeri, Mohsen. *Sâsânid Soldiers in Early Muslim Society: The Origins of 'Ayyârân and Futuwwa*. Wiesbaden: Harrassowitz Verlag, 1995.

Index